# SEEK THE FROZEN LANDS

*Frank Nugent*

First published in 2003 by
The Collins Press
West Link Park · Doughcloyne · Wilton · Cork

British Library Cataloguing in Publication Data

Nugent, Frank
    In search of frozen lands : Irish polar explorers 1740–1922
    1. Explorers – Ireland – Biography 2. Polar regions –
    Discovery and exploration – Irish
    I. Title
    919.8'04
    ISBN 1 903464 24 2

Cover design: *Artmark*
Typesetting: *Dominic Carroll, Ardfield, Co. Cork*
Printing: *ColourBooks, Dublin*

This publication has received support from the Heritage Council
under the 2003 Publications Grant Scheme

*Frontispiece*: Etching of HMS *Terror* by Vincent Sheridan

# SEEK THE
# FROZEN LANDS

## Irish Polar Explorers
## 1740–1922

### Frank Nugent

The Collins Press

This book is dedicated to my wife, Carol, and our sons, Ciaran and Eoin,

with much love and thanks for all the help and infinite support given to me during all my adventuring.

It is also written in loving memory of our son, Gavin, who died aged eleven in 1986.

# Contents

# PREFACE

*Seek the Frozen Lands* tells the story of a significant band of Irish explorers, navigators, cartographers, scientists, naval officers and seamen who have contributed to our knowledge of the polar regions of the world. These men made an important contribution to the science, maps and charts of the Arctic and Antarctic from the early nineteenth century until the early twentieth century, when the heroic age of exploration came to an end with the death of its most charismatic figure, Sir Ernest Shackleton.

The names of many of these people are not well known in Ireland; indeed, they and their achievements are not included in history or geography courses in Irish schools. Most undertook these polar journeys in the service of the Crown and were lost in the selective memories of Irish history writers of the twentieth century. The retelling of their adventurous lives provides us with a source of national maritime pride; it is a story of men who dared for duty and glory.

*Quotations and excerpts throughout this book are faithfully transcribed; spelling or grammatical errors within the original passages have not been altered.*

*facing page*
The view from the bridge aboard Shackleton's expedition vessel, *Endurance*; January 1915, a day after she was first beset. The photograph was taken by Frank Hurley.
*Royal Geographical Society*

# ACKNOWLEDGEMENTS

This work is essentially a compilation and extraction from the graft of the many explorers who wrote original expedition accounts, and from others who have written biographies of individual explorers. I have drawn on these sources and on my own primary research in Ireland, at the Public Record Office at Kew, at the Scott Polar Research Institute in Cambridge and at the National Library of Ireland in Dublin. The modern works by Desmond Clarke, M.J. Ross, Ann Savours, Alfred Friendly, James Delgado, Pierre Berton, Roland Huntford, Francis Woodward, Michael Smith and A.G.E. Jones set standards for books in this genre, to which I have tried hard to aspire.

I wish to acknowledge the assistance rendered me by many local historians, librarians, and descendants and relatives of people whose lives are recorded in this book. Help came from many parts of Ireland, Britain and Canada, and I thank the following people for their unselfish assistance: Mervyn Hempenstall, a Carlowman living in Vancouver; Robert Headland and Lucy Martin of the Scott Polar Research Institute, Cambridge; Sheila Bransfield; James Crozier, Peter Kearns and Kieran Murray of Banbridge, Co. Down; May McClintock of Letterkenny, Co. Donegal and John McClintock of Red Hall, Co. Antrim; Dermot Ryan, Terry Connolly, Eugene Gillen and Nora Hickey of Kinsale, Co. Cork; John Hennessy of Cobh, Co. Cork; Niamh Cronin and Tim Cadogan of Cork County Library; Bernard Devanny and other staff of the National Library of Ireland, Dublin; Margaret Carey, librarian, Ian Kenneally, Laurie Flynn and staff at FÁS Head Office Library; Clare Crowther of the Bray Cualann Historical Society; Public Record Office staff at Kew, London; staff of the Public Record Office of Northern Ireland, Belfast; Deirdre Walsh of Bru-Bru, Cashel; Helen O'Carroll, curator of Kerry County Museum in Tralee, and all our friends in Anascaul, Co. Kerry.

The maps were drawn and lettered respectively by Justin May and his father, Garth. Special

*facing page*
HMS *Resolute*, Baffin Bay, 26 June 1858, by G.F. McDougall.
*From* The Eventful Voyage, *G.F. McDougall*

thanks also to artist Vincent Sheridan, whose inspiration and talent not only captures the beauty of the Arctic and the drama of the Franklin mystery, but shows the dignity and suffering experienced by polar pioneers.

Thanks also to my sailing and climbing teammates from 'South Arís' – the Irish Antarctic Adventure of 1997 – who sailed gamely through hurricane and high seas aboard the *James Caird* replica, *Tom Crean*, and with whom I crossed the glaciers of South Georgia in the footsteps of Shackleton and Crean. Thanks also to the crew members of the 50-foot sailing boat, *Northabout*, which navigated in 24 days the Northwest Passage in good style during August 2001. I include all my friends from both these contemporary Irish polar expeditions: Paddy Barry, Mike Barry, John Bourke, Mike Brogan, Jarlath Cunnane, Kevin Cronin, Gearoid O'Riain, Terry Irvine, Jamie Young, Mick O'Rourke, John Murray, Pat Redmond, Brendan Minish, Harry Connolly, Eoin Coyle, Cathal De Barra and Brendan Minish. I wish to thank them all for their fine company and for making many of my own modest polar exploits safe, yet exciting.

I acknowledge the professionalism of those responsible for the editing, design and publication of this book, particularly Dominic Carroll, Maria O'Donovan and Con Collins of The Collins Press. I am also deeply indebted to Joe O'Farrell for casting a critical eye on the final draft and for the index.

This book would not have been possible without the love and support of my wife, Carol, who not only journeyed to Kew and various parts of Ireland in search of Irish polar records but who also read the many drafts. Greater love has no woman.

*facing page*
Dubliner Lieutenant William Browne's watercolour depicting the crews of HMS *Enterprise* and *Investigator* at the site of a bivouac at Cape Seppings, Leopold Island during the first Franklin search expedition.
*From* Ten Coloured Views, *W.H. Brown*

# INTRODUCTION

*They that go down to the sea in ships and occupy their*
*business in the great waters . . . see the works of the Lord,*
*and his wonders in the deepe.*

PSALM 107 (QUOTED BY RICHARD HAKLUYT IN PRINCIPALL
NAVIGATIONS, 1589)[1]

It is not surprising that an island like Ireland, on the western edge of Europe, has continuously produced explorers and navigators, especially since its first inhabitants landed around 8000 BC[2] by boat – probably dug-out or skin-covered boats. These first nomadic settlers – Mesolithic people – were fishermen and blended with later arrivals who brought with them stone axes and cattle – transported by boat – and set up dwellings and farms along the shoreline. In time, Christianity was brought across the seas from Roman settlers in Britain and Gaul. Trade with Brittany, Cadiz and Britain is evidenced in the writings and manuscripts of the time. In the seventh and eighth centuries, Irish scholars were navigating their way to Iona, Iceland and the Faroe Islands. St Brendan's voyage – or voyages – is indicative of their knowledge and competence in navigating and exploring unknown regions.

Their skill and knowledge of navigation was well informed. In 825, Dictuil, a scholar educated at Clonmacnoise – a monastic settlement on the banks of the Shannon – and at the island of Iona off Scotland, wrote *De Mensura Orbis Terrae*, which translates as 'On the Measurement of the Earth'. This geographical treatise is based on a study of the writings of Greeks who had devised the concepts of longitude and latitude. Interestingly, Dictuil also wrote about the midnight sun: 'what ever task a man wished to perform, even picking lice out of his shirt, he can manage it precisely as in broad daylight'.[3] He had apparently been talking to boatmen who had been far enough north to observe the northern lights.

Later still, the Vikings arrived in their long ships, and over the next three centuries established

*facing page*
Tom Crean of Anascaul, Co. Kerry, a participant in three Antarctic expeditions during the early years of the twentieth century. This photograph was taken by Herbert Ponting during the *Terra Nova* expedition.
*Scott Polar Research Institute*

deeper harbours and ports for their larger wooden ships. They exchanged maritime skills with the natives and established towns in Dublin and Limerick that traded Irish wares with Europe. The Normans brought further skills and developed maritime trading links with Seville and Lisbon in Iberia, and with Lubeck and Gdansk in the Baltic. Irish mariners traded with Iceland, Bristol and Chester. In time, the Norman invaders integrated with the native people, so that the blood of the Irish was blended with the blood of those who had arrived on its shores.

It has been estimated that the Irish accounted for an eighth of British navy strength in the late eighteenth and early nineteenth centuries. On Nelson's ship, *Victory*, at Trafalgar, there were 63 Irishmen serving out of a total of 804. It is also recorded that 16,515 Irishmen enlisted for the navy from 1793–96.[4] The contribution made to the development of polar navigation and travel by some of their number has not been fully acknowledged.

There are four streams to the Irish involvement in polar exploration. The first objective was the search for a navigable channel – the Northwest Passage – from the Atlantic to the Pacific Ocean through the Canadian Arctic Islands and the Bering Strait. A second purpose was to discover and prove a viable theory for the calculation of magnetic variation as an aid to navigation and as a possible new method for calculating latitude. The third stream of polar travel in which Irishmen were centrally involved was essentially humanitarian: the search for the lost Franklin expedition of 1845. The fourth stream concerned the quest to be first to reach the South Pole and, later, to be first to cross the last-discovered continent, Antarctica, from the Weddell Sea to the Ross Sea.

It will be seen that the Irish contribution to all four streams was both considerable and heroic. Men such as Francis Crozier, Cornelius Hickey, Dr Henry Mathias, James Hand and Jerome Collins made the ultimate sacrifice, having endured great privation, shipwreck, or having marched across the frozen seas and succumbed to starvation and sickness. Others survived and would benefit from the recognition of their peers, many becoming admirals or key Admiralty advisors, while one became a general. Collectively, they left a legacy of discoveries, charts, maps and knowledge regarding the polar regions. Following recently published accounts of their exploits, some – such as Shackleton and Crean – have become modern household names, not just in Ireland but around the world. But many more, whose exploits were equally heroic and useful, also deserve to have their stories told so that we might take pride in their magnificent contribution to our knowledge of the world. They have left the Irish nation with a rich heritage of heroic exploration, their names dot the charts of the Southern and Arctic Oceans, and for those with an adventurous spirit, their legacy of achievement is inspirational. This book is a summation of their lives and important achievements. Many of them, such as Dobbs, Crozier, Beaufort, McClintock, Shackleton and Crean, have had accounts of their exemplary lives told in previously published biographies. Never before have all of their exciting life stories been presented in a single volume. Doing so will reveal the scope of their activities, and their particular attributes and characteristics. These Irish adventurers were significant players in the quest for polar knowledge and conquest, but their contribution has been, until recently, recorded only in British histories of expeditions and discoveries. It is now time to recognise them as sons of Antrim, Cork, Wexford, Meath, Kildare, Louth, Down, Tyrone, Kerry, Limerick and Dublin.

Within this story, the role of Trinity College as a supportive learning institution also clearly emerges. Professors Lloyd, Ussher and Haughton are seen to provide guidance, scientific advice and skills training to Sabine, Beaufort, Crozier and McClintock, helping them develop as explorers, scientific observers and mariners.

Sir Clements Markham, in his biography of McClintock, delineates three elements to be studied in the lives of all great explorers: their initial training, personal qualities and their motivation for success. This standard for polar-exploration excellence is well met by Bransfield, Sabine, Beaufort, Crozier, McClure, Kellett, McClintock and Shackleton, all of them prime movers in their time. Each met the initial criteria with distinction, each had unique personal skills and leadership qualities, and each possessed strong and individual motivation for achieving success. It is a great pleasure to retell the extraordinary life stories of these great Irish explorers, whose perseverance, endurance, courage and humanity in the polar regions of the earth is worthy of special attention.

1

# EIGHTEENTH-CENTURY EXPLORATION

*Sir, Since these advantages for your people are the perpetual Objects of Your Care, permit me, SIR, to implore Your Royal Patronage . . . with no other View than that of increasing the Commerce and Riches of Your Kingdom . . . and contribute to raise the Power and Fame of Britain . . .*

ARTHUR DOBBS[1]

S ince the fifteenth century, beginning with John Cabot (1576–79) and continuing with Martin Frobisher (1576–78), navigators had searched for a route to the Pacific from the Atlantic by way of Greenland, northern Canada, Alaska and Siberia. A shorter route would eliminate the need to round the treacherous Cape Horn and allow rich merchant ships embarking from and returning to the British Isles to avoid attack from privateers or warring enemies when passing through French, Spanish and Portuguese waters. Subsequent explorers, whose names adorn the maps of North America, also searched

in vain for the elusive passage. Men like John Davis (1585), Henry Hudson (1607–11) and William Baffin (1616) explored the Canadian Arctic but found no route.[2]

### Arthur Dobbs

The first Irishman to make a significant contribution to Arctic exploration was Arthur Dobbs (1689–1765) of Carrickfergus, Co. Antrim, who initiated and supported two expeditions in search of the Northwest Passage in 1741–42 and 1746–47. His *Memorial on the Northwest Passage* in 1731 outlined the rationale for a renewed British search for a shorter route to the great Southern and Western Oceans of America.[3] Then aged 42, Arthur Dobbs – whose ancestors had arrived in Ireland in 1599 – was lord mayor of Carrickfergus, a member of the Irish parliament and surveyor general of Ireland.

Dobbs was born at the seaport town of Girvan, in Ayrshire, Scotland, where his mother,

*facing page*
Governor Arthur Dobbs; portrait by William Hoare, 1755.
*From* Arthur Dobbs Esquire, *D. Clarke*

| 5

Mary – a Stewart from Ballintoy, Co. Antrim – had gone for safety during the war between the Williamite army and the Irish. It is very likely that, up to about seven years of age, Arthur would have attended services conducted by the great Irish wit and satirist, Jonathan Swift, and that Swift may have provided some of his early education. Though little is known of Arthur's education, he very likely attended the local grammar school and, though there are no records of his graduating from university, he clearly was both a classical scholar and scientist.[4]

When he was 22 years of age, Arthur Dobbs purchased a cornetcy in Sir Richard Echlin's dragoons – Echlin was his uncle by marriage. The regiment was first raised to defend Enniskillen during the Jacobite war and was later known as the Inniskilling Dragoons.[5] During two years away with the regiment on a campaign in Scotland, Dobbs' father died; he returned as master to his father's now large estate in Carrickfergus and married the young widow of Captain Norbury, who was left an estate in Timahoe, Co. Kildare by her guardian. Dobbs leased this estate and became engaged in trying to set up a public bank in Ireland, which did not succeed.

He was elected to the Irish parliament as member for Carrickfergus in 1727. He wrote to the Whig prime minister, Walpole, on 4 January 1730 outlining in a long memorandum a call for a more vigorous colonising policy, and suggesting how the colonies might be secured and strengthened in light of French encroachment and exploitation. He suggested that the French expansionist policy could be forestalled if Britain took possession of the string of lakes stretching almost from Quebec to the Ohio, and established forts and settlements therein. He met Walpole to discuss his views but nothing came of it.

Arthur Dobbs was one of the fourteen founding members of the Dublin Society for the Improvement of Husbandry, Manufacturers and other Useful Arts and Sciences (later the Dublin Society, now the Royal Dublin Society). The society was founded at the rooms of the Philosophical Society in Trinity College on 25 June 1731 with a view to providing work for the jobless and food for the hungry. Dobbs supported legislation against Catholics on political grounds, but advocated a relaxation of some of the Penal Laws to permit Catholics lease land on the same terms as Protestants. He fought both in the Irish parliament and later as governor of North Carolina for the repeal of the Navigation Acts, which forbade direct trade between Ireland and the rest of the Empire, as he was convinced that many ties bound Ireland and England. He was an ardent unionist and an imperialist whose economic thinking is entirely aligned with that of Adam Smith.

About this time, Dobbs became interested in finding the Northwest Passage through the Hudson Bay to the great Southern and Western Oceans of America, the existence of which had occupied the attention of explorers for many years.[6] He wrote another memorandum in 1731, again urging a voyage of discovery so as to open up the Western Ocean to British trade and to forestall any French discovery of a passage to the Pacific. He appealed to both national pride and commercial interest, detailing the benefits that would arise from a shorter route to the abounding riches of the South Seas. He compared the discovery zeal of Elizabeth's mariners with the indolence of contemporary explorers. Dobbs also attacked the lack of enterprise and willingness to explore by the Hudson's Bay Company (an argument John Barrow would use to good effect in the following century), which was still mindful of the tragic and expensive consequences of the 1719 company-sponsored expedition led by Captain James Knight. That expedition departed the Thames in June 1719 and was never seen again; the crew, it is thought, died of hunger and starvation at Marble Island. Indian stories told of the five men who survived longest; the last of them died while trying to bury his comrade. The Knight expedition cost a reputed £6,000, which cooled the company's interest in any further risky ventures.

Dobbs had studied journals and papers dealing with the elusive passage and, believing that such a passage existed, promoted the need for expeditions of discovery. The historian George Bryce wrote about Dobbs:

> At this period a man of great personal energy appears on the scene of English commercial life, who became a bitter opponent of the Company, and possessed such influence with the government that the Company was compelled to make a strenuous defence. This man was Arthur Dobbs, an Irishman of undoubted ability and courage. He conducted his campaign against the Company along a most ingenious and dangerous line of attack.[7]

Dobbs then had a strange piece of luck: a new lord lieutenant, the Duke of Dorset, was appointed to Ireland and, while sailing back to England after a stay in Dublin, the ship encountered heavy seas and was forced ashore at Banbury, a rocky inlet near Carrickfergus. Dobbs and his household helped the party, which included Lady Dorset, and put them up in Castle Dobbs for three days, during which he had their ear regarding his plans for the Northwest Passage.

Dobbs, with his new and highly influential friends, crossed the Irish Sea with the vice-regal party. He was introduced to Colonel Bladen of the Board of Trade who put the Irishman's memorandum before the first lord of the Admiralty, Sir Charles Wager. Wager, in turn, provided Dobbs with a letter of introduction to Sir Bibye Lake, governor of the Hudson's Bay Company. Lake promised Dobbs that he would influence the company when conditions and circumstances permitted. The Hudson's Bay Company had, in 1670, been granted by royal charter sole trade and commerce rights for the vast territories that then comprised more than a third of today's Canada. He met Prime Minister Walpole again during that visit, and he clearly impressed him. In 1773, on the death of Sir Edward Lovet Pearce, Walpole gave Dobbs the position of engineer and surveyor general of Ireland at a salary of £300 per annum.

Meanwhile, preparations for a Northwest Passage expedition were at last under way at the Admiralty. Two vessels were deployed, the *Furnace* – a bomb-type vessel, strongly built to take the recoil of heavy mortars – under the command of Christopher Middleton, a former Hudson's Bay Company captain, and the *Discovery*, a smaller vessel under the command of William Moor, an experienced seaman who had also been in the service of the Hudson's Bay Company. The Admiralty supplied both ships, though Dobbs and his partners, mostly merchants from London, provisioned and fitted out the vessels for the voyage. Following many irritating delays, the expedition departed from the Nore, off the Kent coast, on 8 June 1741. In August, it reached Prince of Wales Fort at Hudson Bay where, it seems, Middleton was cordially received by Robert Pilgrim of the company, who was temporarily in charge. Anchored in the Churchill River, the expedition overwintered.

It was June 1742 before the ice broke sufficiently to permit the expedition sail again. Middleton's journal is a meticulous record, containing detailed observations on the weather and tides, with descriptive notes on the coastline and particulars of soundings of bays and rivers. He mapped his course with great accuracy; every point and inlet charted and named by him stands out on our maps today as a memorial to his painstaking care. He named a large bay – which was thought to be the sought-after passage – Wager Bay after Sir Charles Wager, who supported Dobbs within the Admiralty. Middleton called a headland further north Cape Dobbs 'after my worthy friend'. Forced to delay a while, he resumed his journey northward on 3 August through Welcome Bay. A majestic headland, he called it Cape Hope; in rounding it, however, he found his way blocked by land and an ice-strewn sea, which he named Repulse Bay as he could see no sign of a passage. There was no other way but to return the way he had come. Middleton

proved that no passage existed on the western coast of Hudson Bay as far as Southampton Island and the entrance to Frozen Strait.

To Dobbs must go some of the credit for such success as the expedition achieved, for it was his initiative, drive and energy that made it possible, and his efforts are acknowledged by the northern cape that now bears his name. But Dobbs was not pleased with Middleton's achievement; he refused to believe a route farther north was impossible and chose instead to believe some of Middleton's crewmen who claimed that the route lay through Wager Bay. Dobbs accused Middleton of conspiring with his former employers and acting treacherously toward the government, and even of having taken a bribe of £5,000 from his old employers not to make discoveries. Several of Middleton's officers took part against him, claiming he had misrepresented facts and tampered with them to conceal the truth.[8] Parliament passed an Act that offered a reward of £20,000 to any of His Majesty's subjects who should sail between Hudson Bay and the Western and Southern Oceans of America.

Dobbs refused to cut his losses; he organised a private expedition with the support of merchants, forming the North West Committee for the purpose. He gave command to William Moor, who sailed in the *Dobbs Galley*, and Francis Smith, who sailed in the *California*. The expedition operated in difficult conditions (seven men died during the first cold winter at York Fort), and was harassed by disagreement, incompetence and controversy. Nevertheless, it made some useful additional charting, having largely followed Middleton's previous course. He entered what appeared to be a north-west trending channel at Chesterfield Inlet and, having pushed further up Wager Bay than Middleton, came to an abrupt end at an unnavigable river. With many men suffering from scurvy, Moor returned home in August 1747.

Thus ended Dobbs' investment in his private passion, but he continued to be a critic of the lack of exploratory vigour displayed by the Hudson's Bay Company. He now embarked on a new project: the settling of Protestant families from Ireland in North Carolina, a mission reflecting his ideas regarding the extension and strengthening of Britain's colonies. Having purchased 400,000 acres of land in the present counties of Mecklenburg and Cambanus in North Carolina, Dobbs managed to settle a number of families from his estates in Antrim and Kildare, assisting many of them with the passage by organising two emigrant ships in April 1751 and May 1753.[9]

It became clear to Dobbs that the government needed to implement a policy of vigorous settlement in America in order to counteract French designs. He offered himself as a potential governor on the continent of America, and when the sitting governor of North Carolina died in 1752, he pressed his case again which, when approved, also included the provision that his salary be paid in Britain. He sailed in June 1755 on the man-of-war, *Garland*, accompanied by his son, Edward. He brought with him government funding and arms for the defence of North Carolina. He was sworn in as governor of North Carolina on 31 October 1755, just as the battle for supremacy between the French and British was about to commence.

Dobbs spent the first year organising and meeting the representatives of the settlers and establishing his priorities. He spent two months on a personal survey of his lands, while seeking a place to locate the seat of government. Anxious to provide for a defence of the coast, he established a North Carolina army and militia, and set about building forts in preparation for a war against the Catholic French, whom he hated as much as the pope. In 1757, Pitt was restored to government. On 8 May, a force of more than 8,000 men, supported by a strong fleet, was assembling in Ireland. Most of the soldiers were drawn from Irish stations and drafted to Cork to await transport. The fleet of warships, under the command of Admiral Holbourne, appeared off the Old Head of Kinsale and, on the following day, was anchored in Cork Harbour. Over a hundred ships sailed for America and assisted the colonists in their defence of North Carolina from the French.

In 1762, Dobbs – then aged 73 – married the fifteen-year-old heiress, Justina Davis, at St Philip's Church, New Brunswick. This provoked much lampooning from the colonists whose loyalty to English landowners, including Dobbs, had become strained. He died on 27 March 1765 while preparing to come home to Ireland with his young bride. He is buried in the grounds of St Philip's Church; the grave, however, can no longer be found.

*Molesworth Phillips*
On 17 January 1773, Captain James Cook and the crews of *Resolution* and *Adventure* become the

first men to cross the Antarctic Circle. In January 1775, Cook – on his second Antarctic cruise – discovered the island of South Georgia; two weeks later, he discovered the South Sandwich Islands (though they were initially called Sandwich Land). After three years of sailing in the Southern Ocean, circumnavigating and charting the edge of the pack ice, he writes, 'yet I believe firmly that there is a tract of land near to the pole, which is the source of all the ice spread over this vast Southern Ocean'. On his next voyage, Cook would join the quest for the Northwest Passage. Leaving Plymouth aboard *Resolution* in July 1776, he sailed to Cape Town. Accompanying Cook on this voyage was Molesworth Phillips. Born in Swords, Co. Dublin in 1755, he was the son of a surgeon, John Phillips, himself the illegitimate son of Robert Molesworth, the first Viscount Molesworth of Swords. Phillips was a second lieutenant in the marines and was selected to accompany Captain Cook on what turned out to be his final voyage. *Resolution* was found to be leaky during its passage to Cape Town. There, she was joined by her consort, *Discovery*, and the two ships sailed to the Iles Kerguelen, which they charted, before sailing on to New Zealand.

On 18 January 1778, Cook discovered the Hawaiian Islands. The following month, the two ships sailed up the west coast of America to attempt a Northwest Passage from the west. Cook visited the coasts of Canada and Alaska in an attempt to find a passage; he sailed through the Bering Strait, crossing the Arctic Circle en route. He then headed south, back to Hawaii. Here, on 14 February 1779, Cook – regarded by many as the greatest navigator of his time – was attacked and killed by natives of Hawaii after having gone ashore to recover a stolen boat. Phillips was in command of Cook's shore party and was wounded. He escaped, with just one other marine, by swimming to a boat. In an official account published in 1784, he is credited with having killed Cook's murderer. With an heroic reputation following this escapade, Molesworth Phillips later married Susannah Burney, the sister of Fanny Burney, the novelist. They lived in Ireland on the Belcotton estate in the townland of Termonfeckin, Co. Louth, which he inherited in 1795 from his uncle, William Eccleson. He married again – to Ann Maturin – when his first wife died in 1800, adding two more children to his three by Susannah. He also had a number of illegitimate children.[10] In 1798, he had been promoted to the rank of brevet lieutenant colonel. However, having squandered his estate, he served time in jail in 1817 for a debt of £27. Molesworth Phillips died of cholera at his home in Lambeth, London on 11 September 1832.[11] He was buried in the grave of Susannah's brother, James (who was an old comrade from Cook's last voyage) in St Margaret's, Westminster.

*Polar Exploration after the Napoleonic Wars*
Engagement in European wars interrupted polar exploration by the Admiralty until the end of the Napoleonic Wars in 1815. Then, the Admiralty, in an attempt to secure further naval superiority and to seek commercial advantage, began what became a half-century of tireless endeavour to discover the Northwest Passage through the

Canadian Arctic islands and along the coast of Alaska through the Bering Strait into the Pacific. Royal Navy manpower was reduced at this point from its peak of 130,000 men. By 1846, of 1,151 officers on the books, only 172 were in full employment. The navy decided that its officers could be usefully employed in completing the details of geographical and hydrographical surveys 'on which', John Barrow, the second secretary of the Admiralty wrote, 'grand outlines had been boldly sketched by Cook, Vancouver and Flinders.'

Another motivating force for polar exploration in particular (apart from the prospect of finding and charting new territories or discovering new routes to the Orient) was the opportunity to test and improve new navigational techniques and instruments. Captain Cook had taken with him Larcum Kendall's first timepiece, K1, on *Resolution* from 1772–75 and from 1776–79. The instrument, originally designed by John Harrison, was built by Kendall and purchased by the Admiralty for £450. This accurate machine, tested and proved on the seas by Cook, helped solve one of the most difficult problems facing navigators: the need to accurately fix their position at sea. The timepiece allowed mariners to ascertain latitude by establishing accurately the difference in local time with the time at a fixed position, such as the Royal Observatory at Greenwich.[12]

Another phenomenon about which a better understanding was required were variations observed in the earth's magnetism and its effects on magnetic compasses. The Admiralty sought a solution to the calculation of its elements and deviations from any spot on the earth's surface at any time. In 1819, the Norwegian physicist, Hansteen, produced his study, *Magnetism of the Earth*.[13] Hansteen's work was based on a worldwide survey and observations of magnetic behaviour on the earth's surface, with a view to predicting its magnetic elements. The making of further magnetic observations, particularly in the polar regions, and the charting of the earth's magnetism led to lifelong collaboration between a group of naval officers interested in matters of science and improved navigation. This group included John Ross from Stranraer, Scotland and his nephew, James Clark Ross, William Edward Parry of Bath, Francis Rawdon Crozier of Banbridge, Co. Down, Edward Sabine of Dublin and a man who was to become a legend, John Franklin from Spilsby in Lincolnshire. For Sabine, James Clark Ross and Francis Crozier, the surveying, data collection and charting of the earth's magnetism was to become a crusade. In this pursuit, Trinity College, Dublin – in particular, Professor Humphrey Lloyd – provided academic support to Sabine, Crozier and, later, to Leopold McClintock[14] of Dundalk, who was to play a major role in developing the naval polar sledge. Francis Beaufort of Collon, Co. Louth, who has become renowned as perhaps the greatest of the Admiralty's hydrographers and who was a very influential member of the Arctic Council and adviser to the Admiralty, provided the moral and institutional support of his office to these explorers.

## 2

# BRANSFIELD SIGHTS THE ANTARCTIC PENINSULA

*If any one should have the resolution and perseverance to clear up this point by proceeding farther than I have done, I shall not envy him the honour of the discovery; but I will be bold to say, that the world will not be benefited by it.*

CAPTAIN JAMES COOK[1]

The South Shetland Islands are separated from the northern flank of the Antarctic Peninsula by the Bransfield Strait, named after the Corkman who, in February 1819, was charged with responsibility by his naval superiors for charting new lands found in the vicinity of latitude 62° south, longitude 62° west. The Southern Ocean current, which encircles Antarctica, affects the strait, flowing as it does westward along the southern side of Joinville Island. The islands are inhabited by penguins – Adelie, gentoo, chinstrap and macaroni – and by fur seals which abounded before the island's discovery but were hunted practically to extinction within a few years by American and British sealers.

It was William Smith, of Blythe in Northumberland – a pilot who had learned his ice navigation in the Greenland whale fisheries – who accidentally discovered the South Shetland Islands. While carrying a cargo of heavy equipment in his brig, *Williams*, from Valparaíso to the River Plate off Cape Horn, Smith was forced in heavy seas to sail south and, on 18 February 1819, thought he saw land. He was forced to haul off during the night because of snowfall and a gale. The next day was clear and, in the sunshine, he had no doubt about his discoveries which he marked on his charts at latitude 62° 40' south, longitude 60° west. The *Williams* was built and operated by a consortium of four owners, one of whom was William Smith. Two of the other owners also bore the Christian name William – hence the ship's name.[2] Smith sailed again from Valparaíso in October 1819, determined to revisit his discoveries. This time, he sent his first mate ashore, the Union Jack was

*facing page*
Captain Donat Henchy O'Brien, Captain of HMS *Slaney*. Edward Bransfield named O'Brien Island, South Shetland Islands, in honour of the 'great escapist' of the Napoleonic War.
*From* The Escapes of Captain O'Brien, *D.H. O'Brien*

planted and the new lands claimed for the Crown. He named them New South Britain.[3] A chart was drawn up by William H. Goddard, showing twelve islands and innumerable rocks. Though a desolate place, its shores were swarming with seals. Smith was persuaded by John Miers, the merchant who had chartered his vessel, to rename his discoveries New South Shetland. Miers and other British merchants resolved to charter the *Williams* for a further voyage of discovery.

Meanwhile, HMS *Andromache* arrived in Valparaíso and its commander, Captain Shireff, having heard of Smith's discovery, persuaded Miers to relinquish the brig to himself, stating that he would act directly in the interest of His Majesty's government. The vessel was refitted and loaded with everything necessary for the voyage, and, in one week, put to sea. Shireff placed his master, Edward Bransfield, in command, with William Smith as his master and pilot.

The South Shetland Islands were breeding grounds for an immense number of fur seals. News of the discovery spread so rapidly that, in 1821, between 30 and 50 sealers – many of them American – arrived and commenced a ruthless slaughter, killing, in two years, 320,000 fur seals, while sealing the fate of 100,000 pups through the loss of their mothers. The absence of any authority to control the sealers resulted in the practical extermination of the seal colonies in three years. William Smith benefited from this unfettered exploitation, bringing back to England in September 1821, 30,000 skins. His reward for his exploits, however, was for his ship and cargo to be seized, as his partners had become bank-

rupt while he was away. Nevertheless, the naming of Smith Island and Cape Smith provided recognition of his South Shetland discoveries.

*South American Background*

Shireff's main mission at Valparaíso was to assert and maintain a British naval presence in South American waters, and to offer protection and support for British merchants and subjects who had business interests and investments there. This was against the background of emerging, autonomous South American states such as Chile, Paraguay and Peru, which had succeeded in breaking free of Spanish control following the defeat of Napoleon at Trafalgar and Waterloo. Napoleon had placed Joseph Bonaparte on the Spanish throne in 1808. A Chilean independence movement, led by José de San Martin and Bernardo O'Higgins,[4] raised a Chilean patriotic army and, having crossed the Andes, defeated the Spanish forces at the battle of Chacabuco in February 1817 and occupied the capital Santiago. The father of Bernardo O'Higgins, Ambrose O'Higgins, was born near Dangan Castle, Co. Meath, and had been a former captain general of Chile and the viceroy to Peru. A year later, Bernardo – whose mother was Chilean – became supreme director of Chile, which then declared itself independent. The Spanish defeated the patriot army at Rancagua in March 1818. But O'Higgins – despite a broken arm caused by a gunshot wound – regrouped his troops; with reinforcements under the command of San Martin, he defeated the Spanish who took to their ships and sailed to Peru, leaving the

Chilean patriots in control. The Spanish efforts to regain control with reinforcements from Spain were thwarted by storms off Cape Horn and by the establishment of the Chilean navy which, with the aid of British naval officers, captured Spanish strongholds in Chile and several Spanish ships, one of which was renamed *O'Higgins*. On 14 July 1821, the Spanish authority in Lima, Peru was overthrown.

The newly independent South American states had no intention of exchanging Spanish control for British. Shireff's role was to protect British interests; the discovery of new lands in the region offered the prospect of an independent British base and possible safe harbours in the region. American influence and the activities of its whalers and sealers in the Southern Ocean were also of concern to competing British merchants.

### Edward Bransfield

Edward Bransfield was born in Ballinacurra, Midleton, Co. Cork in 1785. This date is calculated from his age and date of death as recorded on his death certificate.[5] A gravestone in Ballinacurra burial ground records the death of Richard Bransfield, who died in January 1818 aged thirteen months, and the erectors of the stone, William and Norry Bransfield and their family.[6] The Cork Historical and Archaeological Society records that the most notable Bransfield of Midleton and district was Edward, who is thought 'to have been pressed in the Royal Navy at Ballinacurra in June 1803 when 20 years of age'.[7] Bransfield was born in Ballinacurra in 1785, the son of a sea captain.[8] It appears he was educated and from a Protestant family of English origin. In 1803, he was pressed by a press gang and transported by the tender, *Dryad*, into the navy at either Ballinacurra or Youghal, Co. Cork. He and a number of other Corkmen were embarked on one of the ships which maintained the close inshore blockade of the French base at Brest for the following three years.

Cork had a long tradition of providing officers and men to the navy, and the county derived much of its prosperity from supplying it with butter and beef. As well as ships of war, the port of Cork was busy with merchant ships: as many as 600 merchant ships were at anchor at one time, alongside many small, coastal craft.[9] The press gang was the popular name for the impressment service, whose purpose was to force men, particularly those with ship experience, to join the navy at a time of war. A story is told of a press gang operating in Cove (Cobh),[10] Co. Cork at that time. The officer in charge raided a public house where he expected to find a number of able seamen. A wake was discovered to be in progress, but the officer became doubtful about the sincerity of the mourners due to their high spirits. His suspicions aroused, he ordered the coffin to be opened, whereupon the 'corpse' raised his head and leaped out of the coffin with fits of laughter. The 'recently deceased', we are told, willingly accompanied the press gang and turned out to be an excellent seaman.[11]

Navy pay was 30 per cent lower than that of a merchant seaman at that time and, when the war with France broke out in 1803, the demand for men was so great that the government resorted to impressment. William Brown (1777–1857) of the Argentine navy – later Admiral Brown – who was born in Foxford, Co. Mayo, was in 1796 pressed and sent aboard an English man-of-war. He served several years in the navy, and afterwards obtained the command of an English merchant ship. He settled in Buenos Aires, where he was given a command in the new Argentine republic, winning many battles against the Spanish.[12]

The log of HMS *Dryad* engaged at Cork Harbour from 10 March to 12 June 1803 for the purpose of raising men yields facts regarding the enlistment of many local seamen, which very likely included Edward Bransfield. The log, signed by William Donnett, covers the period 19 February to 15 June 1803.[13] The extract from this document outlines its mission and progress. The tender was moored at Spithead on Saturday 19 February, recorded off the Old Head of Kinsale on Thursday 17 March and at anchor in Cove, Cork Harbour on Friday 18 March.

> Monday 21st March: Prest 2 men.
> Tuesday 22nd: Sent boat up the river and prest 6 men.
> Wednesday 13th April: Punished in *Antonio* with 3 doz lashes for theft
> Sunday May 1st Sent party of marines on board the *Maria* tender with 47 new raised men.
> Friday 6th of May: Received new raised men from Waterford and Irish Beef.
> Friday 13th May: Punished J. McCampbell (S) with 4 doz lashes for theft.[14]

The press operation was carried out with great determination in Cork city and harbour. About 300 men are reported to have been seized in the city on 14 March and another 100 taken at Cove.[15] The *Amphion*, *La Loire* and *Princess Charlotte* were also engaged in the operation. Merchant vessels arriving in the harbour were raided and members of the crew seized for naval service. The recruitment operation in Cork was under the authority of Captain John Chilcott and Lieutenant Edward Townsend. What was known as a 'hot press' took place in Cork on 26 March when a large number of citizens were seized. It took the intervention of the city magistrates to free those who where not seamen from navy impressment. Impressment and volunteer enlistment continued during April from every ship arriving at Cove, and was augmented on 24 April with the arrival from Youghal of the naval cutter, *Diligence*, with 50 impressed men. By February 1804, it is reported that:

> Upwards of 1500 seamen have been put into service since Captain Chilcott's command of this duty took place; and what is singular of this number, the zeal and activity of Lieut. Townsend, collected about 400 at Cove during the short space of three months – a number which has been often not exceeded in the course of a war.[16]

In 1782, bounties were offered to men enlisting in the marine service; the Irish parliament offered 5 guineas to each recruit and, from the English, a bounty of 3 guineas and a crown was available. Volunteers over twenty years of age had to be at least 5 feet 4 inches tall. The bounty was not available to men over 40 years of age. The pay for recruits was 8.5 pence per day, paid from date of entry.[17]

The muster book for the 110-gun HMS *Ville de Paris*, under the command of Captain T.R. Ricketts, contains the marine-enlistment record of Edward Bransfield and seven others pressed in Cork Harbour and transferred to *Ville de Paris*. The record, dated 3 June 1803, shows that no bounty was paid to Bransfield, presumably because he was underage; listed as aged nineteen[18] and classified 'Ord.' (ordinary seaman), the record shows his full wages were calculated at £10, 4 shillings and 9 pence (per annum). In the column for payments to dependants, he requested that £4, 9 shillings and 7 pence be paid from 1 July 1803, presumably to his parents. On 1 July, he requested a two-month wage advance of £1, 11 shillings; the record also includes deductions for clothing issued to him aboard *Louisa*. This, perhaps, had been the ship on which recruits were conveyed from Cork to Brest. The other Corkmen whose enlistment is recorded on the same day were Patrick Reardon, aged 21, Patrick Callaghan, aged 22, Cornelius Hearthy, William Rowlin, John Scanlan, Edward White and Cornelius Collins.[19] It was not unusual at that time for men to be recruited into the navy in this manner, as Manwaring and Dobrée tell us in *The Floating Republic*, the story of a navy mutiny at the Nore and Spithead in 1797:

> There was no escape; they were prisoners. Many of them had been kidnapped, torn forcibly, sometimes with knocking on the head, not only from seamen's taverns or wharfside brothels, but from their wives and families amid riots and tumults of impotent would-be rescuers. Worse still perhaps, they had been seized as they entered home waters after a voyage abroad of two or three years [an instance of nine is recorded], pounced on when in sight of their homes – often without the pay due to them – and shipped on to warships for an indefinite period, without prospect of release until the end of the war, whenever that might be, and without hope of a holiday – since men allowed on shore seldom came back . . . Huddled with the dregs of the gaols, or men who had been shipped as boys, probably for some trivial offence . . . pestered with thieves with whom their small belongings were not safe; never free from fiendish bullying of officers high and petty, they lived a life without hope. There was no leisure, no leave, and no books, to qualify their miserable existence: there was nothing to make a man feel himself a human being. The life was brutalising, cruel, and horrible; and with it apart from the dangers of the sea, the men who lived in these disgusting conditions, and fed on the most outrageous food, were expected to show spirit in fight, in which ghastly wounds were hastily botched up in dim light by inexperienced surgeons and during which badly maimed men were simply thrown overboard.[20]

From such awful conditions, Bransfield would rise to the position of commander. Aboard the *Ville de Paris* in August 1805, he was made an AB (able-bodied seaman). The majority of the crew came from Cork; they were mostly volunteers, with a number of pressed men. Regardless of the recruitment route, they were often punished for drunkenness, fighting and insubordination. The crew was transferred to the 100-gun *Royal Sovereign* in November 1806 when the *Ville de Paris* was put out of commission.

During this period, Bransfield served with a midshipman named William E. Parry, who was to become a household name for his voyages in search of the Northwest Passage. Bransfield, though forcibly recruited to the navy, worked his way up to quartermaster, then midshipman in 1808, clerk in 1809 and midshipman again in 1811–13. Succeeding captains spoke highly of him as a diligent, sober man who paid attention to duty and was always obedient to command. He was commended to the notice of the Admiralty as a good seaman, who could take a distance by moon, sun and stars. In April 1813, he became second master under Captain E. Waller aboard HMS *Goldfinch*, which operated in the Mediterranean, and off Portugal and Brest. His rise through the ranks was undoubtedly helped by his existing skills as a mariner and his interest in navigation. He was examined and received his master's certificate from Trinity House – the Admiralty's training school – at the end of April 1814, making his first appearance in the Navy List. While operating in the blockade squadron, the *Goldfinch* managed to spend three days in Cork, from 6–8 September 1814, giving Bransfield the first opportunity in eleven years to visit his family. He served on *Phoebe* as acting master and later as master, escorting convoys returning to Cork and Portsmouth. He was assigned to *Elects* in October 1815, followed by *Patchoulis* for a short time.

He was now recognised for his excellence as a navigator, for his skills in stowing and harbour duties, and for his qualities as a leader of men. In 1816, Bransfield joined the frigate *Cydnus*, captained by F.W. Aylmer; Captain Aylmer's family had settled in Ireland in the seventeenth century and its forebears included Admiral Matthew Aylmer of Balrath, Co. Meath. In taking up this post, Bransfield relieved none other than James Weddell who would later make very significant Antarctic discoveries of his own, reaching 74° 15' south in 1823 – the highest latitude achieved at that time. In August 1816, Bransfield served as master aboard HMS *Severn*, again under Aylmer; he took part in the bombardment of Algiers and won commendations and a medal, inscribed: 'Algiers bombarded its fleet destroyed & Christian slavery extinguished'. His 'remark book' records that, during this voyage, he observed the latitude of various places using both artificial and sea horizons. He observed for latitude from the top of Genoa lighthouse, measuring values with instruments of that time, which speaks very highly of his ability as an observer.

In September 1817, Bransfield was appointed master of the large, 44-gun frigate, *Andromache*, over the heads of many others more senior to him in the Navy List. He sailed to South America, then in the process of rejecting European rule. This opportunity led to Bransfield's Antarctic discovery, which would bring him fame and which, to this day, makes a strong case for Britain's claim to have made the first Antarctic mainland sighting.[21] On arrival at Valparaíso, Shireff ordered Bransfield, with three midshipmen of the *Andromache* – Mr Poynter, Patrick Blake, the master's mate,[22] and Mr Bone – to survey the coasts and harbours of New South Shetland, and to observe, collect and preserve every object of natural science. Dr Adam Young of HMS *Slaney* was added to the crew of the *Williams*, which was provisioned for twelve months in case she was trapped in ice.[23] Included in her stores were four bullocks and other livestock, which were driven aboard. She left Valparaíso on 20 December 1819.[24] On Christmas Day, the journal of Midshipman Poynter tells us the crew

were indulged with Two gallons of Liquor extra and in the evening we managed to muster a Fiddler among the crew who proved himself a very tolerable scraper – for the first and probably the last time in my life I witnessed the refusal of Grog by our crew en masse – In the course of the afternoon their Jorum as a Nightcap – When offered they all to a man refused it, said the Officers wished to make them drunk and they would 'be damned if they would be so' – Soon however they changed their minds and the result wound up the pleasures of the day.[25]

Bransfield and his team of surveyors arrived off the South Shetlands on 16 January 1820. During the following days, despite bad visibility, they tracked the northern coast of the islands, charting its outline as best they could in such

conditions. On 22 January 1820, they entered a bay of a long island, sounding it carefully and finding a safe anchorage. They named the islands, New South Britain, and the bay, George's Bay (now King George Bay). The journal of Midshipman Poynter tells us:

After breakfast Mr. Bransfield proceeded in her [the whaleboat] to affect a landing where he might plant the British Union, taking possession of this Land in the Name and on behalf of H M George the 3rd his Heirs and Successors and Naming it 'New South Britain' – At half past 8 we observed the Boat land on a shingle beach bearing NNW of us and perceiving soon after with the aid of our Glasses the Jack planted – we hoisted on board the Ensign and Pendant, Fired a Gun and concluded the ceremony by serving to each Man a Glass of Grog to drink His Majesty's Health.

The season was late, but Bransfield surveyed each of the islands discovered by Smith, getting as far as 63° south in weather which produced a mixture of foggy and hazy days. On 30 January, they found themselves among a group of small islands and sighted a high range running in a north-easterly and south-westerly direction. This was the first reported sighting of the Antarctic Peninsula and mainland, which Bransfield named Trinity Land. He was unsure if it was a single coastline or a further series of islands, but with changing visibility and wind direction, and without the cover of another vessel, he chose to sail northward while still able to do so. They found Hope Island the next day and passed north of O'Brien Island – named after Dr Young's captain aboard HMS *Slaney* – sketching and charting each island as they went by. They landed on the southern extremity of Clarence Island where Bransfield again planted a Union Jack, claiming it for King George. The weather continued to make their work difficult and perilous. They were unsure if Elephant Island was an island or connected to the mainland, but named one of its extremities Cape Valentine. Attempting to ascertain if the new lands were connected to Cook's Sandwich Land by sailing south, they were stopped when ice was encountered; they counted 38 large icebergs, just short of 65° south and deep into what was soon to become known as the Weddell Sea. They discovered Ridley Island to the northeast of George Island, and were then driven east in a storm. On 19 March, as the season closed, they came upon Greenwich Island. Stopping off on the way home at Cumberland Bay, Isla Robinson Crusoe and Archipelago de Juan Fernández, they delighted in the fruits and vegetables of the island and, with handlines, caught a plentiful supply of fresh fish from their anchorage.

Bransfield reached Valparaíso on 14 April 1820 where he handed over the *Williams'* log, along with his charts and his officers' journals, to Captain Searle of HMS *Hyperion*, which was lying in the bay. His original logs and charts are since lost. However, some of his officers made their own copies of the ship's log, and these are now in the possession of the Scott Polar Museum and other museums. The crew were committed to secrecy regarding their discovery of new territories.[26] Bransfield resumed command of the *Andromache*, which embarked Lord Cochrane – who had assisted the Chilean navy to defeat the Spanish – and the vice-queen of Peru. Both they and their families took passage to England, arriving at Spithead on 31 August 1821. Bransfield was paid off on 18 September. Though never employed by the navy again, he was retained in reserve at half pay.

The *Literary Gazette* published a full account of the voyage of the *Williams* on 3 November 1821, based on information received from Midshipman Thomas Main Bone. The article stated that on 30 January 1820, as they rounded Tower Island, a bigger mass of land was sighted beyond it:

> They very unexpectedly saw land to the SW; and at four o'clock were encompassed by islands, spreading from NE to E. The whole of these formed a prospect most gloomy that can be imagined, and the only cheer the sight afforded was in the idea that this might be the long sought southern continent, as land was undoubtedly seen in latitude 64°.[27]

Bransfield was not long idle. Within a couple of months, he returned to sea as a captain in the merchant navy, working as master of the *Swiftsure*, trading between London and Gibraltar for four years. This was followed by service on *Bolivar*, trading with Lima. When eventually he retired from the sea (he was last reported off Brighton in the *Calcutta* in 1839), he settled in Brighton where he died aged 67 on 31 October 1852. His death certificate states he died of

'Organic Disease of Stomach nearly 1 year certified'. In his will, Bransfield left his Algiers Medal to his former first lieutenant on *Andromache*, Captain Thomas Porter, who had been a friend in later life. To his widow, Ann, he gave a life interest in the remainder of his property which, on her death, was to pass to the children of his brother, William, at Midleton, Co. Cork. Ann Bransfield lived at their home at 61 London Road, Brighton on a widows' pension of £50 per annum until her death at the age of 73 on 9 December 1863.[28] The grave of Edward Bransfield and his wife at the Extra Mural Cemetery, Brighton was renovated in 1999. An inscription added at that time recognises his achievement as the first man to sight part of mainland Antarctica.[29]

Edward Bransfield's life is a wonderful example of how ability and dedication to duty can be stepping stones to success and achievement, regardless of an individual's starting point. Bransfield was the living embodiment of a competent mariner; he rose from life as an ordinary seaman to AB, quartermaster, clerk, midshipman and ship's officer. Ultimately, he became a qualified master and an experienced ship's captain. He was obviously a 'doer' who, regardless of his origins or the adversity he encountered during his life, was motivated to do things right. Despite the risks inherent in sailing very close to the pack ice under sail alone and in conditions of fog and gale, he proved capable of charting the islands – of managing that risk. His stature steadily grew in the navy, as did his degree of skill and competence. Self-disciplined and conscientious, he completed any given task to his own, self-set high standards, and his memory will forever be preserved on the charts of Antarctica: Bransfield Strait, Mount Bransfield on Trinity Peninsula, Bransfield Rocks and Bransfield Island off Joinville Island.

*Rival Claims to Antarctic Discovery*

The Russian government was also interested in the southern continent. In 1819, it dispatched Captain Thaddeus Bellingshausen with two vessels – the *Vostok* and the *Mirni* – on a circuitous clockwise voyage of discovery in the high latitudes, similar to that undertaken by Cook. On 27 January 1820, Bellingshausen reached latitude 69° 21' south, longitude 2° 14' west, his 'furthest south'. He sighted an ice field, which seemed to be covered with small hillocks, but he was unaware that he had made an historic first sighting of mainland Antarctica three days before Bransfield.

He overwintered in Sydney and a year later – on 11 January 1821 – he discovered west of the South Shetland Islands an island 9 miles long and with a very high altitude. He named it Peter I Island. Bellingshausen next sailed east towards the South Shetland Islands, sighting high mountains across a field of impenetrable ice at latitude 68° 43' south, longitude 73° 10' west. He did not land, but from a distance of 40 miles, he sighted what he called Alexander Land, or Antarctica.

The importance of Bransfield's charts and records were further underlined when, a week later, Bellingshausen sailed his vessels among the South Shetland Islands and came across eight British and American sealing vessels. He invited on board the captain of the *Hero*, who was none other than the American, Nathanial Brown

THE SOUTH SHETLAND ISLANDS
FIRST CHARTED by BRANSFIELD

Cornwallis Is
ELEPHANT IS.
Clarence Is
O'BRIEN IS.
KING GEORGE ISLAND
Robert Is.
Greenwich Is.
Livingstone Is.
Nelson Is.
Snow Is.
BRANSFIELD STRAIT
Smith Is.
Deception Is.
Hope Is.
D'URVILLE IS.
ANTARCTICA PENINSULA
JOINVILLE IS.
TRINITY LAND

Palmer. Palmer claimed many years later that he told Bellingshausen of his discovery of the Antarctic continent during the course of his sealing activities in January 1821. He also stated that Bellingshausen suggested the land be known as Palmer Land. Palmer's log for 17 November 1820 certainly shows that he sighted the coast of the Antarctic Peninsula. Americans still call it Palmer's Land and dispute Bransfield's claim.

Bellingshausen's charts and reports clearly indicate that he sighted the Antarctic mainland first, but for some reason his discoveries were not published or reported by the Russians for ten years, making the question of who first sighted and landed on Antarctica still a matter of debate. However, Smith's discoveries and Bransfield's accurate chart and published written accounts add greatly to the British claim to these early Antarctic discoveries and go some way to countering the claims of both the US and Russia.

*Discovery of South Orkneys*

The South Orkneys were discovered in 1821 and claimed in the name of the king by George Powell, an English sealing captain. He had travelled there with an American sealer, Nathanial Brown Palmer, and both men kept records; Powell published a chart of both the South Shetlands and South Orkneys soon afterwards. It was from here, in 1823, that a very significant voyage was made by a former naval officer turned merchant sealer, James Weddell, in his 160-ton sailing brig, *Jane*, accompanied by the 65-ton cutter, *Beaufoy*. The vessels sailed to 74° 15' south, 34° 16' west in a clear open sea later named in Weddell's honour. It would be 1911 before another ship would visit, and it was in the same Weddell Sea that Shackleton's *Endurance* would be crushed and lost in 1916.

*Captain Donat Henchy O'Brien*

O'Brien Island in the South Shetlands was named by Bransfield in honour of Captain Donat Henchy O'Brien of HMS *Slaney*, a ship of Shireff's South American fleet. Donat Henchy O'Brien was born in Co. Clare in March 1785; his first name was derived from Donogh O'Brien, king of Thomond (1208–44), and Donat described himself as a descendant of one of the ancient kings of Ireland. His second name was his mother's surname. She was a sister of Councillor FitzGibbon Henchy, a reputable Dublin lawyer of the time. Donat entered the navy on 16 December 1796 when only eleven years old, and was made midshipman aboard HMS *Overyssel*, a Dutch battle ship which had been seized in Cork Harbour in 1795. His patron was Captain – later, Rear Admiral – Edward Walpole Brown. O'Brien saw action with *Overyssel* at the Helder where, as master's mate, he was in command of a flat-bottomed boat which assisted in the landing of the army.

In 1800, he joined HMS *Atlante* as acting lieutenant before returning to his former ship. He served in a number of different vessels in the following years, including the *Beschermer* and *Amphion*, and was captured by the French at Brest when the frigate, HMS *Hussar*, on which he served, was wrecked on the rocks off the Illes des Saintes in February 1804. He was held prisoner in Givet before being transferred to Verdun. He was held here until August 1807, when he made a dash for freedom with three others. Recaptured at Étapes on the coast of Picardy, in sight of English cruisers in the channel, O'Brien was sent to a mountain fort at Bitche in the Vosges, a secure prison reserved for undesirable prisoners

of war. He escaped alone while under escort, and made his way to the Austrian border. Again, he was arrested, at Lindau on Lake Constance, and was conveyed to a subterranean casement at Bitche. After a year, he and three others managed to manufacture a rope and let themselves down 200 feet of walls to freedom. Pretending to be Americans, they crossed the Austrian frontier close to Salzburg, and from there made their way to Trieste, where they were picked up by a boat from *Amphion*, one of O'Brien's old ships.

O'Brien's narrative, *The Escapes of Captain O'Brien*,[30] which also recounts his five years of suffering when a prisoner of war in France during the Napoleonic Wars, was originally published by the *Naval Chronicle* at the time in the form of sixteen 'naval bulletins' addressed to Emperor Napoleon. O'Brien rewrote the story in 1839 and published it in book form. Its promoters declared it to be as interesting and captivating as Defoe's *Robinson Crusoe*. O'Brien resumed service in the Mediterranean, with distinction, and was promoted to commander in 1813. This, he stated, was accomplished 'entirely by his own exertions and unassisted by interest'.[31] His next appointment was to HMS *Slaney*, and he was promoted to the rank of post captain on 5 March 1820. On 28 June 1825, O'Brien married Hannah Walmsley of Castle Mere, Lancashire. He was later promoted to rear admiral on the reserve half-pay list – on 8 March 1852 – and died on 13 May 1857 at Yew House, Hoddlesdon, aged 73.

# 3

# SABINE AND CROZIER ENTER THE ARCTIC

*On the shores of bleak Boothia winter darkness was over*

*Brave Crozier led his men in search of fresh food*

*22nd of April, their ships they deserted*

*Terror his home was beset towards its doom.*

FROM 'LAMENT FOR FRANCIS CROZIER'[1]

Early Irish involvement in Arctic exploration was linked to the study of terrestrial magnetism, the search for a navigable Northwest Passage through the Canadian Arctic regions and its accurate mapping, and the search for Franklin's Northwest Passage expedition of 1845.

## Sir Edward Sabine

The study of terrestrial magnetism centres on Sir Edward Sabine. Born in Great Britain Street (now Parnell Street), Dublin on 14 October 1788, he was the fifth son and ninth child of Joseph Sabine of Tewin, Hertfordshire.[2] His mother, Sarah, died within a month of his birth. Edward was educated at Marlow and at the Royal Military Academy at Woolwich, which he entered on 25 January 1803. He received a commission as a second lieutenant in the Royal Artillery and was stationed at Woolwich. He was promoted to first lieutenant on 20 July 1804 and, on 11 November, sailed to Gibraltar where he was stationed until August 1806. On his return, he was posted to the Royal Horse Artillery in which he served at many home stations until the end of 1812.

Sabine was promoted to second captain on 24 January 1813 and, on 9 May, sailed to Canada in the packet, *Manchester*. When eight days out, she was attacked by the *Yorktown*, an American privateer, but the *Manchester* was carrying light guns and cannonades, and was able to maintain a running fight for twenty hours, after which an hour's close engagement compelled her to strike her colours. Sabine and his soldier servant had been of great service in working the guns.

On 18 July, the *Manchester* was recaptured by

*facing page*
Sir Edward Sabine, soldier and scientist. Born in Dublin, he devoted much of his life to the organisation of worldwide magnetic observation, data collection and analysis. Portrait (oil) by Stephen Pearce.
*National Portrait Gallery*

the frigate, *Maidstone*, and Sabine was landed at Halifax, Nova Scotia from where he proceeded to Quebec. In the winter of 1813–14, there was an advance of American militia on Quebec, and Sabine was directed to garrison a small outpost. He was engaged during August and September in the Niagara frontier campaign, under Lieutenant General Gordon Drummond, and was present at the siege of Fort Erie. He took part in the assault on that fort on 15 August, when the British lost twenty officers and 326 men. Sabine was also involved in another action, on 17 September, against a sortie; the British loss here was twenty officers and 270 men. He was twice favourably mentioned in dispatches and was privileged to bear the word 'Niagara' on his dress and appointments.

He returned home in August 1816 to devote himself to scientific studies in terrestrial magnetism, astronomy and ornithology under the supervision of his brother-in-law, Henry Browne, a Fellow of the Royal Society and at whose home in London he met other like-minded people. His first link with the Arctic occurred shortly after his own election as a Fellow of the Royal Society, in 1818, when he was appointed astronomer to the Arctic expedition of John Ross in search of a navigable route to the Pacific from the Atlantic via a Northwest Passage. It was on this expedition that Sabine undertook his first pendulum and magnetic experiments in the Arctic. The problem of longitude had been solved by John Harrison's marine chronometer in 1764. An unresolved problem was the need for a general theory for correlating magnetic variation with geographic locations, with a view to possibly establishing another method of determining longitude. The expedition was provided with two ships. One, the *Isabella*, was commanded by John Ross, a 40-year-old, red-headed Scot. An extrovert, he was genial and quite outspoken. Jane Griffin, who was to become John Franklin's second wife, sketched this profile of John Ross in 1819:

> He is short, stout . . . not very gentlemanly in his person, but his manners and his language are perfectly so; his features are coarse and thick, his eyes grey, his complexion ruddy and his hair of a reddish sandy hue . . . Yet not withstanding his lack of beauty, he has a great deal of intelligence, benevolence and good humour in his countenance.[3]

Lieutenant William Edward Parry commanded the second expedition ship, *Alexander*. Aged 27, he was the well-educated son of a doctor from fashionable Bath. In regard to his study of science, and particularly the observation of terrestrial magnetism, Sabine established a lifelong association with both William Parry and James Clark Ross – John Ross' nephew, then only seventeen years of age and midshipman to his uncle aboard *Isabella*.

The expedition returned prematurely when John Ross mistakenly observed that Lancaster Sound was a bay with land and mountains in the background. He was so convinced he had sighted land that he named the mountains Croker Mountains, after the first secretary of the Admiralty, John Wilson Croker. Croker, who was the son of the surveyor general of customs and excise in Ireland, was born in Galway on 20 December 1780. He was educated at Portarlington and Trinity College, Dublin where, in 1800, he received a BA; later, in 1809, he received a degree and doctorate in law. He was an MP for many constituencies in Ireland, England and the Isle of Wight, including Downpatrick (1807–12), Athlone (1812–18) and University of Dublin (1827–30). He was a Fellow of the Royal Society and, in 1809, a founder of the *Quarterly Review* in which he wrote over 260 articles until 1864. He served as secretary of the Admiralty from October 1809 to November 1830. Croker also edited Boswell's *Life of Dr. Johnson* and other books. He died on 10 August 1857.[4]

Many of the officers, including Parry and Sabine, were not so sure of Ross' assertion or his decision to return to England. This was a great disappointment to John Barrow, the second secretary of the Admiralty, and the primary advocate within the Admiralty for further Arctic exploration. Sabine produced a report on the expedition's biological observations and research, which appeared in the *Transactions of the Linnean Society*.[5] Twenty-four species of bird from Greenland were listed, of which four were previously unlisted, and one, the *Larus Sabini*, was a new discovery.[6] He also contributed an account of the 'Esquimaux' of the west coast of Greenland to the *Quarterly Journal of Science* in 1819.[7] Controversially, Sabine published a pamphlet which criticised John Ross' handling of some of the scientific observations and which also questioned Ross' assertion that no passage was possible from Lancaster Sound.[8] This created a bitter enmity between Barrow and John Ross.

In 1819, Parry was sent with *Hecla* and *Griper*, and sailed through Lancaster Sound to complete the longest Arctic passage ever made under sail alone, passing westward through the 'Croker Mountains' and through a passage he named Barrow Strait. The 'mountains', named and charted by John Ross, were found by Parry to be non-existent. On 4 September 1819, he was stopped by a solid wall of ice from shore to shore at 110° west from Greenwich, in latitude 74° 44' 20" north, barring the way to the Bering Strait. However, the achievement of the officers and men entitled them to a prize of £5,000 from parliament for reaching that meridian. But already the pack ice was forming about them and they were forced to cut a channel to gain entry to Winter Harbour on Melville Island, where they overwintered.

Sabine was again the scientific officer, and James Clark Ross, now Parry's midshipman on *Hecla*, was involved with Sabine in making magnetic measurements and taking lunar observations.[9] Parry's organisation of his young team – he himself was the oldest at 29 years of age – his maintenance of the winter routine, his insistence on cleanliness, his care for men's health and the measures he took to prevent boredom set standards for future expeditions. During the tedious stay for the winter months in Winter Harbour, when the sun was 96 days below the horizon, they roofed the ships with thick cloth to insulate them from the weather. There were classes on navigation and routines for making scientific observations. William Beechey, the first lieutenant on *Hecla*, organised theatrical and musical

The crews of *Hecla* and *Griper* cutting into Winter Harbour, September 1819.
*From* Journal of a Voyage, 1819-20, William E. Parry

productions in the 'North Georgia Theatre', and Sabine edited a weekly journal for the amusement of the party, entitled the *North Georgia Gazette and Winter Chronicle*. In all, they produced 21 editions. The quality and variety of food ensured the health and well-being of all on board. Provisions included high-quality tinned meats and soups, lemon juice, pickles, vinegar and kiln-dried flour, all of which was well packed to keep it dry. These stores, brought from home, were supplemented with plenty of fresh game, ptarmigan, musk-oxen and caribou.

When the ships were able to depart on 1 August 1820, they attempted to voyage further west to the Bering Strait and on to the Pacific. They were stopped by solid, 40–50-foot thick, multi-year ice. Their furthest point west was 113° 46' 43.5" west, from where they sighted land to the south of Melville Island. Parry named it Banks Land. Finding no route west or south, Parry went home. *Hecla* and *Griper* were away from May 1819 until November 1820.

Sabine tabulated the observations and arranged virtually all the appendices of Parry's journal, and Parry warmly acknowledged his valuable assistance on the expedition. In 1821, Sabine received the Copley Medal of the Royal Society for the various communications relating to his researches during the Arctic expeditions.

Parry's success generated great enthusiasm for further expeditions, and Sabine was selected to conduct a series of experiments for determining variation, in different latitudes, of magnetic inclination and force, a subject that had engaged his attention in the first Arctic voyage. He sailed aboard the *Pheasant* on 12 November 1821 on a voyage that would take him to Guinea, Maran-ham, Ascension, Sierra Leone, Trinidad, Bahía and Jamaica for the purpose of scientific observations. Later, he sailed from London aboard *Griper* on a voyage that took in New York, Trondhjem, Hammerfest, Greenland and Spitzbergen. On 13 August, he landed on an island off the east coast of Greenland at 74° north, and it was subsequently named after him: Sabine Island. Another small island, where he had carried out pendulum observations, was named Pendulum Island.[10]

*Franklin's Overland Expedition 1819–22*

In 1819, while Parry was searching for a searoute to the Canadian Arctic coast, the Admiralty supported a land expedition led by Lieutenant John Franklin. With a small party consisting of five navy personnel, he was to survey and map the Canadian Northern Territories coastline eastward from the Coppermine River.

It is worth looking at the extraordinary early naval career of John Franklin. Born in the town of Spilsby, Lincolnshire on 16 April 1786, the youngest of a family of twelve, he was five weeks short of his fourteenth birthday when he joined the navy on 9 March 1800. No writer of fiction or for the screen could have conceived such an action-filled life as that led by Franklin. At fifteen years of age, he was at Nelson's Battle of Copenhagen aboard the warship *Polyphemus*. He later joined his cousin, Captain Flinders – one of the leading cartographers of his day – in what must have been for Franklin a floating classroom. He served aboard the *Investigator* on a three-year

voyage of discovery and exploration with a ship's complement that included the naturalist, Robert Brown, an astronomer, and a number of artists and surveyors. It was on this expedition that the first complete circumnavigation of Australia took place. During his three years in Australia, Franklin survived being shipwrecked on a reef and was marooned on a sandbank for weeks while awaiting rescue.

He was back in England in time to join Nelson's fleet at Trafalgar as midshipman/signalman aboard *Bellerophon* in yet another bloody battle. His captain, a Captain Cooke, fell dead at his feet on the poop deck during the action that was to ensure British naval superiority in Europe. With two successful engagements under Nelson's command on his record, his military education was completed with the humility of his first defeat in the last great battle of the American War of Independence at New Orleans. On 8 January 1815, Franklin was serving with HMS *Bedford* when the highly trained British forces attacked the American fortifications. They suffered 2,000 casualties in that famous battle, compared to the thirteen men counted dead among the greatly outnumbered American frontiersmen from Tennessee and Kentucky, whose strength was an ability to shoot straight and whose simple strategy was to pick off the officers.

The outbreak of peace in Europe and America led to three years of inaction on half pay for Franklin, in stark contrast to the whirlwind commencement of his naval career. His polar career began when he was appointed lieutenant in command of the *Trent* as part of a two-ship expedition led by Captain Buchan, who commanded

Sir John Franklin, shortly after he had completed his two Canadian overland expeditions. Watercolour by W. Derby, c. 1820.
*From* Life of Admiral Sir Leopold McClintock, *Sir Clements Markham*

a change of wind direction freed them from danger.

This was the background of the man the Admiralty chose to travel overland in 1819 to the shores of the Arctic Ocean. For the epic journey, undertaken with the aid of snowshoes and canoe, they were supported by two rival trading companies – the North West Company and Hudson's Bay Company – who helped them find voyageurs,[11] Indian guides and hunters. Having charted 350 miles of the Canadian Arctic coast, which had been painstakingly mapped east of the Coppermine River, including Bathurst Inlet and Kent Peninsula, and having recorded the latitude and longitude of key landmarks, they began the return journey. Without the help of the Indian guides, who had left them when they reached the Arctic Ocean, they had a rough time and only nine of the party managed to come back alive. They survived starvation on occasions by eating lichens and their own moccasin boots. One of the voyageurs, Michel, an Iroquis, was suspected of cannibalising three of his fellow voyageurs who were missing; when he shot Midshipman Hood in the back of the head and claimed that Hood had accidentally shot himself, Dr Richardson, the expedition's surgeon and naturalist, ambushed and summarily shot Michel dead. Richardson did not risk further investigation or a trial as he feared he or Hepburn, a Scotsman, would be next. The other midshipman, George Back, in the meantime managed to find help from the local Indian chief, who dispatched members of his tribe with food. The Indians nourished them, warmed them with a blazing fire and looked after them until they

the *Dorothea*. Their mission was to sail to the North Pole and to attempt a return via the Bering Strait or through Baffin Bay. There was a belief at the time that an open sea existed to the North Pole. They got as far as Spitzbergen at 80° north before experiencing the pressure of the pack ice. The vessels barely survived a gale in which crashing breakers filled with chunks of icebergs and floes pounded them. The *Dorothea* was close to foundering and the damage to the ships was such that Buchan decided to go home as soon as recovered, saving only nine out of the original twenty-strong team.

Franklin returned to England in October 1822. His *Narrative of a Journey to the Shores of the Polar Sea*, illustrated with sketches and drawings by Hood and Back, both of whom were very accomplished artists, was a best-seller. One of Hood's paintings depicts Green Stockings, the beautiful, fifteen-year-old daughter of a Copper Indian family who travelled with the party as guides and hunters. It transpired that Back and Hood had argued bitterly and were prepared to fight a duel at daybreak for her sexual favours. Franklin averted a tragedy by sending Back to Fort Chipewyan on a 1,100-mile midwinter journey for supplies and ammunition. It is believed Hood fathered Green Stockings' child. None of this came to light until 30 years later when Hepburn, one of the party, told the full story.

*Commander Francis Crozier*

The voyages to the Arctic by Parry in 1821–23 and 1824–25 introduced another Irishman to polar exploration: Francis Rawdon Moira Crozier. It was to be his life's work until his tragic death a quarter of a century later. He was also actively engaged in scientific observation, and was to become a great friend and colleague to James Clark Ross, with whom he shared many polar adventures.

Francis was born in Banbridge, Co. Down in September 1796, son of attorney-at-law George Crozier of Banbridge and Dublin whose ancestors came to Ireland in the seventeenth century from Liddlesdale in the Scottish border country

of Cumberland and Roxburghshire. The family originally settled near Newtownbutler, Co. Fermanagh. Francis' mother, Jane Elliot Graham, came from Ballymoney Lodge, Banbridge, Co. Down. He was one of thirteen children. Francis Rawdon Moira Crozier had a brilliant career as a naval officer. A painstaking scientist, he explored both the Arctic and Antarctic, and was involved in some of the most important expeditions of his time.

He joined the navy on 10 June 1810 at Cork, when he was thirteen years of age, and was made a first-class volunteer on board the 34-gun *Hamadryad*, formerly a Spanish vessel that had been captured in 1804. In 1812, Crozier progressed to the rank of midshipman aboard the *Briton* – 44 guns and 300 men – which was ordered to Valparaíso to arrest the US frigate, *Essex*, which was interfering with British whale fisheries. On its return trip, the *Briton* visited Pitcairn Island where, at that time, the last of the *Bounty* mutineers, John Adams, was still alive. On return to England, Crozier spent two years on the Thames guard ship, *Meander*, and on the Portsmouth flagship, *Queen Charlotte*. In 1818, he was appointed mate of the *Dottrel* and served at the Cape of Good Hope, having passed his mate's exams in February 1817.[12]

*Parry's Second Voyage 1821–23*

He returned to England in 1821 in time to accompany Parry on two successive expeditions in search of the Northwest Passage, a search with which his name will be forever associated. Francis Crozier and James Clark Ross were assigned as midshipmen aboard *Fury* under Parry, who held overall expedition command. Aboard the accompanying ship, *Hecla*, was Midshipman Edward Bird, and a lifetime partnership was initiated between these three talented, young officers now under the command of the highly respected, energetic, pragmatic and innovative Parry.

W.E. Parry and G.F. Lyon commanded *Fury* and *Hecla*, respectively. Both ships were well prepared for Arctic duty. *Fury* was made identical to *Hecla* – which was completely overhauled – to facilitate the interchangeability of both ships' parts. The effects of condensation were addressed by the installation in the living and sleeping quarters of a coal-burning stove and warm-air ducting by a Mr Sylvester. A lining of cork insulation was also fitted to the ships' sides and to the underside of deck floors to address the problem of the ship icing up during overwintering. The planning of the ships' diet to avoid the debilitating effects of scurvy was based on the experience of Parry. The diet included a large amount of tinned meats and soups, together with bread baked from the large quantities of dried flour brought in preference to storing biscuits. Lemon juice, laced with rum to hinder freezing, was stored in kegs rather than glass jars. Vast quantities of carrots in tin casings, crystallised lemon acid, cranberries, lemon marmalade, concentrated malt and hops, along with seeds of mustard and cress to be grown aboard as required were also intended as antiscorbutics. Potatoes and beetroot were brought for the outward leg, and salted beef was left in favour of corned beef and salted pork. A transport ship,

the *Nautilus*, accompanied them to the edge of the ice, carrying coal and 25 bullocks.

Parry's second expedition concentrated on trying to find a parallel route, south of Lancaster Sound, which they approached from the Hudson Strait. They spent two winters on this expedition, exploring all possible routes west from Hudson Bay. By sailing north of Southampton Island to the Frozen Strait, they eliminated the possibility of the existence of a viable westward passage from Repulse Bay. By the time Parry's detailed exploration of 600 miles of coastline was complete in that corner of the American continent, October had arrived and they were in urgent need of winter quarters. They once again cut a channel into the young ice to an island they named Winter Island.

The improvements to the ships' heating systems made their quarters warmer, drier and more comfortable. Captain Lyon managed the fortnightly theatrical entertainment aboard *Fury*. In one successful production of Richard Brinsley Sheridan's, *The Rivals*, Crozier played Sir Lucius O'Trigger. Reading and writing classes were conducted for the seamen, and were attended by over twenty of the seamen on each ship. Evidence of the effectiveness of the classes can be gauged by Parry's pride in his assertion that every pupil could read his Bible at the end of the expedition. Musical evenings for officers were held in the cabins of Parry and Lyon, which substituted for their exclusion from the social circles at home.

In February, they became aware of the presence of a village of snow huts and went out to meet the Eskimos. They were astonished to find over 60 men, women and children living in these well-constructed huts, which featured low passages leading to apartments, each with a perfectly constructed dome. They remarked how well organised the women were for cooking, with either a fireplace or a lamp beside the bed where they were seated. One woman – Iligliuk – made maps, which proved useful to Parry.

The quality and warmth of the clothing worn by Parry's men was improving with experience, including the use of layers of wool after experiments with waterproof canvas, or mackintosh. Snowboots were made from strong cloth and thick, cork soles. The boots were fitted loose to allow for better circulation and comfort. During the voyage, the young officers and midshipmen were engaged in surveying expeditions using boats and snowshoes, and also became experienced in working with Eskimo dog-pulled sledges.

Crozier observed substantial local magnetic attraction which caused serious errors in the ship's compass. He also went ashore for four days with a shore party to observe and record tidal movements. On their return to England, James Clark Ross was promoted to lieutenant and his ability as a naturalist was recognised with his election to Fellow of the Linnean Society.

## Parry's Third Expedition 1824–25

The third Parry voyage set out to prove if Fury and Hecla Strait was connected to Prince Regent Inlet. They chose to approach the inlet through Lancaster Sound, but 1824 was a bad ice year, unsuitable for exploration, with ice extended to Baffin Bay. As a result, they did not reach Lancaster Sound until 10 September. On this

voyage, Parry sailed in *Hecla*, with Crozier as one of his midshipmen. Ross was appointed second lieutenant of *Fury*, in which Bird served as midshipman. They overwintered at Port Bowen on the eastside of Prince Regent Inlet. An observatory was set up on shore to measure magnetic intensity. The ships were released from the ice on 20 July 1825. On 31 July, disaster struck during a northern gale, when *Fury* ran aground. The damage sustained eventually caused her to be abandoned. She was taking water quicker than could be kept up with by four pumps and all hands. A makeshift harbour was found between grounded floes, and they set about repairs. Further gales hampered the work and they feared that *Hecla* might also be damaged. *Fury* was abandoned on 21 August; *Hecla* sailed home to England with both crews and little to add to their knowledge of the route. It was Parry's last attempt to find the elusive Northwest Passage. His experiences demonstrated the variance in ice conditions from year to year, and the three expeditions had improved the skills and resourcefulness of the navy for polar exploration. In addition, the expeditions had exposed Francis Crozier and James Clark Ross to the demands of polar command.

## Franklin's Second Overland Expedition 1825–27

John Franklin married Eleanor Porden in August 1823. She was a poet and an independent-minded heiress, the daughter of a wealthy London architect. She was 28 years of age when she married Franklin and, in June 1824, gave birth to a daughter, also named Eleanor. But the birth seemed to rapidly promote the consumption she had contracted around the time of her marriage and she was unwell while he was making his very detailed plans for a second overland expedition, which he himself had proposed to the Admiralty.

Franklin left England in February 1825. Brave Eleanor died from tuberculosis six days after he departed. He was not to know of her death until he reached Penetanguishene, the naval depot on Lake Huron.[13] Dr Richardson and Lieutenant Back again joined him; their plans and preparations were informed by their previous experience. An advance party, which included carpenters, was sent ahead to build winter quarters, this time at the Great Bear Lake. They were helped by the now unified and expanded Hudson's Bay Company, which controlled the northern lands of what was then British North America. They built and brought specially designed lightweight boats for river navigation and a 'walnut shell' for crossing rivers – a special, 9-foot-long, portable boat with a skin made from Mr Mackintosh's prepared canvas. Mr Mackintosh of Glasgow also provided two waterproof canvas suits for each person and covers for their food and kit. During this voyage, Franklin and his men mapped and explored westward from the Mackenzie River along 400 miles of coast, and between the Coppermine and the Mackenzie Rivers.

Franklin returned to England in 1827 and was knighted by the king. He was now a national hero, under whose command the mapping of most of the roof of Canada had been overseen. On 5 November 1828, he married Jane Griffin, a friend of Eleanor's and in whose circle he had socialised before his departure. He brought her back a gift of three pairs of moccasins from the Arctic. He was 42, she 36 years old and another independent-minded woman. She was widely travelled, had her own fortune and enjoyed a wide social circle. Her travelling companion on many of her journeys was John Franklin's niece, Sophy Cracroft. Jane and Sophy were both attracted by the adventure and glamour of the polar explorers and naval officers.[14]

In 1836, after a period of duty in the Mediterranean, Franklin accepted the post of lieutenant governor of Van Diemen's Land – now Tasmania – one of Britain's Australian colonies. He sailed there with Lady Jane to represent His Majesty's government in a penal colony where, since 1788, many Irish prisoners had been sent for crimes ranging from murder and robbery to failure to pay rent arrears or stealing food to feed their starving children.

*Parry's North Pole Expedition*

In March 1826, Crozier was promoted to the rank of lieutenant and, in May 1827, was elected a Fellow of the Royal Astronomical Society. He was to spend some time on half pay waiting for a posting. His waiting ended when he was asked to join Parry in an attempt to reach the North Pole from Spitzbergen. The ship chosen was the *Hecla*, and James Clark Ross was appointed second-in-command to Parry. Innovative as ever, Parry brought two specially made boats fitted with sledge runners so that the boats could be hauled over the ice between leads of open water. In practise, the boats proved too heavy and the southward drift of ice made progress northward difficult. Crozier remained in charge of *Hecla*, while Parry and Ross led the polar parties in a struggle to their 'furthest north' of 82° 43' 32" north, where they were forced to abandon the journey. Crozier was, in the meantime, engaged in making a series of astronomical and magnetic observations.

A letter to Ross during this expedition reveals Francis Crozier's true nature. It shows his thoughtfulness, his thoroughness and attention to detail, and it clearly shows his warm affection for Ross and his messmates:

Therefore I hope with the blessing of God you will find us right here on your arrival in due season – We think of you sometimes, always at dinner-time – Although the prayers of the wicket availeth not, I am induced sometimes to remember you in mine . . . I start tomorrow morning with two boats and 12 men to leave the surveying one at Walden Isle for you – when that is done I hope everything for you will be done – how much we would give just to know whereabouts you are, whether sailing or hauling God send the former – I hope you had fine weather as fine as we have here – but fear you cannot – I could fill this sheet with conjectures made here everyday as to where you are and what you are doing – I cannot explain the mingled sensations I experienced the day I parted with you at Walden Isle. I did not think I was so soft (amiable weakness you must say). But I assure you my heart (as Paddy says) was in my mouth till I got on board . . . old Crawford desires his love to you all – God bless you my boy and send you all back safe and sound by the appointed time is the constant prayer of your old messmate, F. Crozier.

Following this expedition, a further period on half pay was spent in Banbridge until, in April 1831, he was appointed to the new, 46-gun frigate, *Stag*. He remained with her until December 1835, serving as first lieutenant in the latter half of the commission. The vessel served mainly in Portuguese waters, with brief intervals serving the home station, and also undertook a short visit to West Africa.

Meanwhile, in May 1829, James Clark Ross had sailed with his uncle, John Ross (who had been out of favour with the Admiralty since his 'Croker Mountain voyage'), on a privately sponsored Northwest Passage expedition aboard a paddlesteamer, the *Victory*. They were forced to abandon the ship in May 1832 and survived the winter after a long march to Fury Beach where they found the stores left by Parry in 1825. The expedition had its successes, including a number of sledge journeys made by James Clark Ross with the support of Eskimos and their dog teams. He established that no westward channel existed south of Boothia Peninsula, named by John Ross in honour of the expedition's sponsor, Felix Booth, a gin manufacturer. More significantly, the younger Ross reached the magnetic North Pole, the location of which he confirmed with his dip-needle instruments.

They returned home in October 1833 aboard the *Isabella*, which they had sighted and chased

in their boats. John Ross was knighted for his achievements, and though James Clark Ross declined the offer of a knighthood, he accepted his promotion to the rank of post captain and the granting of full pay for the four years. The apprenticeship of James Clark Ross was over. The narrative of this extraordinary expedition is in itself a massive testimony to the all-round skills of the two Rosses of Stranraer: hardy expeditionists, reluctant steam pioneers, Arctic survivors, magnetic observers, navigators and anthropologists. The appendices are filled with colour pictures and descriptions of lively Eskimo people – their language and lifestyle – depicting them as a happy, caring and capable people. John Ross also included short biographies of his own men, zoological information and the surgeon's review of the diet of the native 'Boothians'.

Crozier resumed his polar career in January 1836 when he volunteered to sail with James Clark Ross on a rescue mission in search of eleven British whalers beset for the winter in Davis Strait. Appeals and petitions to the Admiralty from shipowners and families of the sailors had brought about an agreement whereby the owners and underwriters provided and fitted out the ship, while the Admiralty would pay the crew and supply stores and provisions. The ship chosen by Ross was the *Cove*, but her Atlantic crossing to Greenland was a stormy one. The bowsprit was carried away and the *Cove*, which was for a short time thrown over on her broadside before righting herself, was badly damaged during a five-day storm of force 10–11 off Iceland. When the hurricane subsided, they were forced to return to port at Stromness in the Orkney Islands to carry out repairs. By the time they reached the stricken whalers, one ship, the *Middleton*, was sunk, with her survivors transferred to other ships. A message arrived that another of the missing ships, the *Abram*, had arrived in Hull with crew members from three other ships. However, one of the ships – the *William Torr* – had vanished. After a sustained search in June and July, they left the Arctic for home. The only report regarding the whereabouts of the *William Torr* was the finding of an oil cask with her name on it by a ship en route from Venice to Hull.[15]

For his services on *Cove*, Crozier was promoted to the rank of commander in January 1837. He returned once more to Banbridge, just before his family left the town following his mother's death in November 1838. As the bachelor brother, he assisted his older sister's move to Dublin where they found a house close to where his brother resided; he was a clergyman in Dublin. While in Dublin, he visited Professor Lloyd of Trinity College to discuss developments in magnetic instrumentation.

As a result of the work of John Ross, Edward Parry and John Franklin, the coastline of North America in 1828 was further outlined and it appeared that it only remained to complete the detail. John Barrow of the Admiralty, however, was still seeking the elusive route, which he felt was within England's grasp. Francis Crozier's polar destiny was about to unfold as the ever-reliable second-in-command to his friend, James Clark Ross, and later, in the same role, to the man who would become a legend, Sir John Franklin.

# 4

## SABINE, LLOYD AND BEAUFORT LEAD THE WAY

*There is nothing worth living for but to have one's name on an Admiralty chart.*

ALFRED, LORD TENNYSON

Pendulum observations were seen as an important component of the scientific work of nineteenth-century Arctic expeditions. Two Dubliners, Humphrey Lloyd and Edward Sabine, collaborated in this regard. They successfully developed a range of instruments, constructed under Lloyd's direction in Dublin, and collated the data necessary to enable Sabine construct a magnetic profile of the globe. The accurate mapping and charting of the oceans and coastlines, its currents and tides, along with the recording of weather in the interests of both merchant shipping and the navy, became the life-work of another Irishman, Francis Beaufort of Navan, Co. Meath. He served for 26 years as hydrographer to the navy, a post to which he brought great dis-

tinction and credit. All three men had one thing in common: they were dedicated, painstaking and hard working in pursuit of scientific excellence for the benefit of all.

Sabine had made the first observations of magnetic inclination and force at St Thomas in 1822. His data, used as a base for comparison with later observations of the Portuguese, were important in showing the remarkable secular change that had been in progress during the interval. The account of Sabine's pendulum experiments, published by the Board of Longitude in 1825, is an enduring monument to his indefatigable industry, his spirit of inquiry and his wide range of observation. In 1826, he was honoured with the award of the Lalande Gold Medal of the Institute of France. Prior to this, he was appointed joint commissioner with Sir John Herschel to work with an Anglo-French-government commission to determine the precise difference of longitude between the observatories of Paris and Greenwich by means of rocket signals. The difference was found

*facing page*
**Professor Humphrey Lloyd; an outstanding scientist and teacher. Lloyd invented an instrument for the simultaneous measurement of magnetic dip and intensity.**
From *Some People and Places in Irish Science and Technology,* C. Mollan et al

to be nine minutes 21.6 seconds. This compares with the currently accepted difference of nine minutes 21 seconds.

Edward Sabine's scientific capacity was combined with an attractive personality. His grace, manners and cheerfulness made him universally popular. He married Elizabeth Juliana Leeves of Torrington, Sussex in 1826. An accomplished scientific translator, she aided her husband for more than half a century. Among the works she translated was Humbold's *Cosmos*, published in four volumes from 1849–58, and *The Aspects of Nature* (1849, two vols.). She also translated Arago's meteorological essays and Admiral Ferdinand Von Wrangel's *Narrative of an Expedition to the Polar Sea* (1840), under the direction of her husband.[1]

In 1827, Sabine was promoted to first captain and obtained from the Duke of Wellington[2] general leave of absence to carry out scientific studies, so long as he was not required by the Royal Artillery. Sabine acted until 1829 as one of the secretaries of the Royal Society. He was recalled to the navy in 1830 due to unrest in Ireland,[3] where he served for seven years. There, he met and collaborated with Humphrey Lloyd, professor of natural history and experimental science at Trinity College, Dublin.

*Professor Humphrey Lloyd*
Lloyd was born in Dublin on 16 April 1800, the eldest son of Rev Bartholomew Lloyd and Eleanor McLaughlin. He received his early education at Mr White's School in Dublin. He entered Trinity College, gaining first prize in a field of 63 competitors for the entrance exam, which at that time was classical.[4] His college career was distinguished; he obtained a scholarship in 1818 and graduated in first place with a degree in 1819, taking the Gold Medal for science. He subsequently gained an MA, in 1827, and for theological studies, a BD (Bachelor of Divinity) and DD (Doctor of Divinity) in 1840. He became a junior fellow in 1824 and a senior fellow in 1843. He devoted himself to scientific study and experimental philosophy and, in 1831, succeeded his father as Erasmus Smith professor of natural and experimental philosophy. His work on physical optics and terrestrial magnetism brought him international fame and recognition. He married Dorothea Maria Redford in 1840;[5] they had no children. He was president of the Royal Irish Academy from 1846–51, president of the British Association in 1857 and was awarded the German order, Pour le Mérite, in 1874. He went on to become vice-provost of Trinity in 1862 and provost in 1867. He lived for many years at Kilcroney Abbey, Enniskerry, Co. Wicklow and, from 1867, at Provost's House in Trinity College.[6]

When the government in 1838 supported the British Association and the Royal Society in their efforts to improve knowledge of terrestrial magnetism, it was proposed to establish observing stations at various points in Great Britain and India. Lloyd was a member of the magnetic committee of the British Association, which was chaired by the astronomer, Sir John Herschel, regarded by many as the foremost astronomer of the nineteenth century. Lloyd, as a result of this activity, devised the instruments and wrote the instructions for the conduct of the observatories.

The magnetic observatory at Trinity College, Dublin, which was originally established by Lloyd's father, was placed in his charge. One of the first to be built, it was constructed in the grounds of Provost's House simultaneously with the observatory at Greenwich. Officers appointed to take charge of magnetic observatories were trained in Dublin by Lloyd in both the practical use and care of the instruments. Many of the instruments used in the Dublin observatory were devised by Lloyd in collaboration with Sabine and manufactured in the Dublin suburb of Rathmines at the optical engineering works of Howard Grubb.[7] These instruments were copied and installed in observatories in the British colonies and at many Continental observatories. Lloyd and Sabine's instruments were based on the principles of the German mathematician, Karl Friedrich Gauss. These instruments achieved great accuracy in measuring both magnetic dip and intensity.

Lloyd was an outstanding university teacher and made an important contribution to the founding of the School of Engineering in Trinity College. Francis Crozier was one of those who took advice from Lloyd; his letters recount that he had to pay the entire cost of his new equipment. His scientific studies were important to him; he learned about the measuring of ocean depth, air and sea temperatures, and about the collection and recording of biological and zoological specimens. The naval commander already competent in navigation, surveying, ship craft and management was also becoming a competent astronomer and scientist.

### Magnetic Crusade

In 1834, Sabine and Lloyd – in conjunction with James Clark Ross – conducted the first systematic magnetic survey ever made of the British Isles. Sabine extended it single-handedly to Scotland

Sir James Clarke Ross, the leading polar explorer of the nineteenth century. Portrait by Stephen Pearce.
*Courtesy of National Portrait Gallery*

in 1836 and, in the following year, in conjunction with Lloyd, Ross and additional observers, it was extended to England. With the exception of the mathematical section of the Irish report, which was completed by Professor Lloyd, Sabine completed the remainder of the reports; these were published by the British Association. He was promoted to brevet major on 10 January 1837, and tasked with superintending a number of fixed observatories in both hemispheres.

At an 1835 meeting in Dublin of the British Association for the Advancement of Science, Sabine – in presenting his translation of the Norwegian Hansteen's *Magnetism of the Earth* – referred to the blanks still to be filled in order to complete a magnetic chart of the globe. An appeal was made to the British government to send an expedition to the southern continent with the aim of verifying the exact location of the magnetic South Pole. A number of theories existed regarding the number and location of the poles. Sabine favoured Hansteen's theory that there were four poles.[8]

A formal resolution was carried at another British Association meeting in Newcastle-upon-Tyne in 1838, calling on the British government to send an expedition to make magnetic observations between Australia and Cape Horn. Captain Washington of the Royal Geographical Society (RGS) endorsed the resolution. Support for a Southern Ocean expedition also came from another important Irish man of science – a man who first came to public prominence when he was appointed by the Admiralty in 1829 to the post of hydrographer of the navy. He was the largely self-educated Captain Francis Beaufort,

born in the Church of Ireland rectory, Navan, Co. Meath. His influence at that time from within the Admiralty, and as a member of the Royal Society,[9] was significant in the granting by the chancellor of the exchequer of sufficient funds for the proposed Expedition of Discovery and Research in the Southern and Antarctic Regions, planned for 1839–43.

*Sir Francis Beaufort*

Francis Beaufort was the son of Rev Daniel Augustus Beaufort,[10] Church of Ireland rector of Navan, Co. Meath and a descendent of Huguenots who had settled in Dublin in 1774. Francis was very close to his father and was greatly influenced by him throughout his life. His father, though diminutive in size, was ebullient and a very active character with interests in architecture, geography, topography, travelling and – as might be expected – religion. A topographer of distinction, he had produced what was considered the best map of Ireland before the Ordnance Survey's official map appeared. Published in London in 1792, it sold over 2,000 copies in eighteen months.[11] Geographically exact and beautifully produced – with an accompanying memoir – an interesting feature of the map was that, while it listed features such as rivers, towns, bays and mountains, it also claimed to list every religious establishment in Ireland.[12] Studying this map, one might think that there were no Roman Catholic churches in Ireland at the time. Dr Beaufort's map was otherwise an accomplishment that demonstrated his skills as a surveyor, an astronomer and as a draughtsman.

His work as an architect involved him in building and renovating seventeen churches in his lifetime. His wife, Mary Waller of Allentown, Co. Meath, was an intelligent and cultivated woman who spoke fluent French and Italian, and who was much loved by all her children. She was married at 28 years of age; all her children were born before the family moved to Collon, a small town in Co. Louth. John Foster, later Baron Oriel and MP for Co. Louth, was the speaker of the Irish House of Commons in 1789 when he presented Dr Beaufort with the vicarage at Collon. As chancellor of the exchequer in Ireland in 1784, Foster had secured the passage of the Corn Law which, by granting large bounties for the export of corn and by imposing heavy duties on its import, encouraged a substantial change in farming from pasture to tillage. It is interesting to note that Foster's daughter, Patience, married John McClintock, also an MP in the Irish House of Commons (1766) and whose grandson, Leopold, was to become one of the most accomplished Arctic explorers of the nineteenth century.

All seven Beaufort children were born in the rector's house in Navan, situated above the junction of the Blackwater and Boyne Rivers; the first child died shortly after birth; the second, Frances Ann (Fanny), had a natural talent for painting and drawing. She illustrated one of the novelist Maria Edgeworth's early educational books and would later become the fourth wife of Maria's father, Richard Lovell Edgeworth, and thereby become Maria's stepmother. Fanny lived to the age of 94 and was acknowledged as a steady and tactful matriarch of his very large family. William Lewis, the eldest son, was born in

1771; he fulfilled his father's wishes by becoming a clergyman. He married the daughter of the bishop of Cork and Ross, and became the rector of Glanmire, Co. Cork. Three younger sisters followed Francis, who was born in 1774: one died

Sir Francis Beaufort. He devised a wind scale which equated wind speeds with a simple description. From a painting by Stephen Pearce.
*Courtesy of National Portrait Gallery*

Dr Henry Ussher, the first Andrews' professor of astronomy at Trinity College, Dublin. He provided five months of formal education to the fourteen-year-old Francis Beaufort at the Dunsink Observatory.
From *Dunsink Observatory 1785-1985*, Patrick A. Wayman

theorems in plane geometry and logarithms. Francis took an early interest in astronomy. Among his papers is a sheet dated 12 December 1788 and labelled 'Observations of Francis Beaufort'. It contains his observations of three different colours on the moon's surface – purple, red and greenish yellow. His grasp of celestial matters suggests his father's encouragement and tutoring.

In 1788, when he was just fourteen years of age, his father sent him to his friend, Dr Henry Ussher, who had become, in 1783, the first Andrews' professor of astronomy at Dublin's Trinity College. In taking up his new position, which was established by a bequest from Trinity's former provost, Dr Francis Andrews, Ussher took on the major role in deciding the site, the form and the general provisions of the Dunsink Observatory, which was completed in 1785. Francis Beaufort undertook a five-month period of study at the college's newly founded observatory near Finglas village, on the northern outskirts of Dublin.[13] His initials can be clearly read on the first page of Ussher's transit book – a list of longitudes and latitudes determined in Ireland – which was started on 1 January 1788. The fourteen-year-old recorded the longitude and latitude of the midland town of Athlone, where the River Shannon divides Co. Westmeath from Co. Roscommon. He also recorded the latitude of Galway. Beaufort was very proud of his time spent with the great man and he obviously benefited significantly from this study, as later became apparent. This one piece of formal education in science which the future 'Beaufort of the Admiralty' received from the Dublin professor was,

in her teens, while Henrietta (Harriet) and Louise both remained unmarried throughout their lives. Harriet wrote children's books anonymously, while Louise wrote travel journals and a book on entomology. She also read to the Royal Irish Academy an essay she had composed on Irish art and architecture. They were a close family who found intellectual stimulus from within, and which contributed much to their education.

We know little of the early life of Francis. We know he was short in stature and survived smallpox as a child without ill effects. We also know that he was sent to Master David Bates' Military and Marine Academy in Dublin when he was aged ten or eleven years – a course which obviously prepared him for a life at sea. A hard-covered school notebook has survived. It is neatly scripted with a fine pen and contains perhaps, Henry Ussher's most valuable educational transaction. His biographer, Friendly, wrote in admiration:

> For a boy who went to sea at the age of fourteen, and whose only formal introduction to exact science was five months at Dunsink observatory, to become the professional associate of the foremost British scientists of the age was a triumph in self education . . . the great men with whom he worked, from the astronomer Airy to the chemist Wollaston, were university taught; Beaufort's schoolroom were the cramped and turbulent cockpits and gunrooms of frigates.[14]

He was also fourteen years old when first he met Alicia Wilson, the girl he would eventually marry twenty years later. She thought he was bashful but brusque in manner, well informed and a well-behaved boy. It also appears she fell for him at first sight.

Dr Beaufort moved to London in 1789 to publish his map and to pursue a legal matter. Young Francis was now waiting for the opportunity to get his career started in either the navy or with a merchant trader. At a cost of 100 guineas, his father arranged for the fourteen-year-old to sail with the ship's company on the merchant ship, *Vansittart*, bound on a long trading and surveying voyage to the East Indies. His father bade him farewell at Gravesend, two months short of his fifteenth birthday. Francis was sick early in the passage and, later, the ship struck rocks and had to be abandoned by her crew.

They took to the boats and were five days on the open sea before being rescued. This early lesson in the education of the Admiralty's greatest chart-maker taught him about the need to improve the accuracy and reliability of sea charts for both merchant shipping and the navy, so as to enable navigators to find safer routes along the coasts and across the seas of the world.

He joined the Royal Navy and was a midshipman on the frigate, *Latona*, under Captain Albemarle Bertie, during the Spanish Armada of 1790.[15] In 1794, he served aboard the 32-gun *Aquilor*, under Robert Stopford, and followed him to the 88-gun *Phaeton*, on which he saw much service. He won praise and promotion for his conduct in the French wars, and in campaigns in the North and South Atlantic, the English Channel and the eastern Mediterranean. On 10 May 1796, he was made a lieutenant at the age of 22, and was first lieutenant of the *Phaeton*, under Captain James Nicol Morris, when he commanded a daring raid using three of his ship's boats to surprise the enemy. They boarded and took the Spanish *San Josef*, with 26 guns, from under the guns of Fuengirola Castle, near Malaga. Beaufort's description of the action was scrawled almost illegibly in a letter to his father from aboard *Phaeton* on 28 October 1800:

> I have never dissembled or deceived my dearest parents in anything respecting my health, I therefore expect implicit belief. A Spanish King's polacre of 14 guns from 24 pounds to 4 lay in a tempting situation although under Fangerolle castle near Melino. Your son had the honour of

leading the boats upon the night of the 27th to the attack, but suffice it at present to say that after a short conflict my brave fellows carried her. I saw us complete masters of the deck and then I sank wounded in more places than one but none are now dangerous. The captain's behaviour to me on this occasion is beyond everything I could have expected. He has written in the most handsome manner to Lord Keith and spoken to him too and is now writing Ld. Spencer [first lord of the Admiralty]. Some time ago I happened to tell him that I was related to Lady Spencer. He asked me if I had objection to his mentioning that in his letter. I said no and he has done it. Was that wrong? The particulars of this business you may expect in my next. Till then be assured I am fast recovering – God bless you all.

F. Beaufort.[16]

Beaufort had, in fact, nineteen wounds: three sabre cuts – received in an encounter with Spanish marines while leading his men aboard – and sixteen slugs fired into him at point-blank range from a blunderbuss. This action won him his much-prized and long-awaited promotion to the rank of commander, on 13 November 1800, when he was also awarded a wound pension of £45. The letter is indicative of his own awareness of the need to use the support of those with power and influence to progress his career. It took him nine months to recover from his wounds, first in a hospital in Gibraltar and then in the English naval hospital at Almade, near Lisbon. He arrived back in London on 1 September 1801.

For the next five years, Beaufort was unemployed at sea, so he came back to Collon and visited his sister, Fanny, now living at Edgeworthstown. He worked during this time with his brother-in-law, Richard Lovell Edgeworth, in establishing the world's first line of telegraph signals, from Dublin to Galway. The purpose of this project was to create a warning system that would alert Dublin in eight minutes in the event of a French landing on the west coast. The 'ingenious Mr Edgeworth's' concept proved difficult to operate, particularly in poor weather or visibility, and the system failed its pilot runs miserably, much to the disgust of Beaufort and at a financial loss to Edgeworth. With the defeat of Napoleon, it fell into disuse and was abandoned.

Beaufort was an integral part of the Edgeworth family and owed a great part of his early development and informal education to contacts with that learned and progressive household. Hubert Butler tells us that they were warm and intelligent people who were far from provincial in their outlook, were more European than many of their British contemporaries, and who operated within a philosophy of rational conduct.[17] The Edgeworth home was a bastion of independent thinking. Robert Lovell Edgeworth was an inventor and educationalist who believed in learning from experience, and who encouraged people to think for themselves. He and his daughter, Maria, were the progenitors of the progressive school with its educational toys and uninhibited ethic.[18] Edgeworth's estate was well run, his tenants content and his children happily living in their plain, large house in the Irish Midlands, a habitation as famous as Madame de Staël's at Coppet or Tolstoy's at Yasnaya Polyana. Mr and Mrs Hall, who visited Edgeworthstown, wrote of it:

> From the mansion has issued so much practical good to Ireland but to the whole world. It has been long the residence of high intellect, well-directed genius, industry and virtue. It is a place that perhaps possesses larger moral interest than any other in the Kingdom.[19]

Beaufort, though largely self-educated – ably supported by an inventive and creative father – clearly benefited from the intellectual stimulation and progressive environment he found in Edgeworthstown. When his first wife, Alicia, died, he married Edgeworth's daughter, Honora.

In June 1805, Beaufort was appointed to the command of the *Woolwich*, an armed store ship aboard which he made an accurate survey of the entrance to the River Plate during the presence of the fleet off Buenos Aires in 1807. This survey was well received and its output marked out Beaufort as a cartographer of great talent. In May 1809, he was appointed to the *Blossom*, employed in convoy duty on the coast of Spain. On 30 May 1810, he was advanced to post rank and appointed to the frigate, *Frederiksteen*. For the next two years, he was employed in the surveying of the coast of Karamania and, incidentally, in suppressing some of the most barbarous of the Mainote pirates. His work was brought to an untimely end following an attack by Turks on his boat's crew on 20 June 1812. Beaufort was badly wounded in the hip, and after months in danger and suffering in Malta, was obliged to return to England; the crew of the *Frederiksteen* was paid off.

The account of this survey and exploration he published in a volume entitled *Karamania or a brief description of the South Coast of Asia Minor, and of the Remains of Antiquity* (1817, 8 vols.). He refused to accept any payment for the manuscript on the grounds that the material for the work was acquired on His Majesty's service and in the execution of his public duty. For many years after his return to England, he was engaged in drawing the charts of his survey with his own hand. The charts were so technically and tastefully well drawn that they were engraved directly from his own drawings, as sent to the hydrographer's office.

In 1829, Beaufort was appointed hydrographer to the navy and, during the next 26 years, his name became a synonym in the navy for hydrography and nautical science.

*The Beaufort Scale*

One of the first initiatives Beaufort as hydrographer introduced to the navy was to order the commander of the *Beagle*, Robert Fitzroy, to keep a record of the weather using a wind scale and notation which Beaufort himself had perfected in his personal weather logs since 1806. The crew of the *Beagle*, on its departure from Plymouth in December 1831 to survey the shores of Patagonia and the South Seas, included the naturalist Charles Darwin, on board for this most famous voyage of scientific discovery. Beaufort recommended the young Darwin to Captain Fitzroy;

Hereafter I shall estimate the force of the wind according to the following scale, as nothing can convey a more uncertain idea of wind and weather than the old expressions of moderate and cloudy &c &c.

| | | | |
|---|---|---|---|
| 0 | Calm | 7 | Gentle steady gale |
| 1 | Faint air just not Calm. | 8 | Moderate gale |
| 2 | Light airs | 9 | Brisk gale |
| 3 | Light breeze | 10 | Fresh gale |
| 4 | Gentle breeze | 11 | Hard gale |
| 5 | Moderate breeze | 12 | Hard gale with heavy gusts |
| 6 | Fresh breeze | 13 | Storm |

And the weather as follows &c

| | | | |
|---|---|---|---|
| b | Blue sky | h | Hazy |
| f | Fair weather | dp | Damp air |
| d | Dry warm atmosphere | fg | Foggy |
| s | Sultry | r | rain |
| p | Passing clouds. | sr. | Small rain |
| c | clear, i.e. that is clear hard horizon but not blue sky. | dr | Drizzling rain |
| | | hr. | Hard rain |
| cl | Cloudy | sh | Showers |
| w | Watery sky | hsh | Hard Showers |
| wd | Wild, forked, confused threatening clouds. | s.d | Settled weather |
| | | sy | Steady breeze |
| dk | Dark heavy atmosphere | sq. | Squally. |
| l | Lightning | hsq | Hard Squalls |
| t. | Thunder. | bk. | Black horizon & clouds |
| g | Gloomy dark Weather | thr. | Threatening appearance |
| gr | Greasy threatening appearance | | |

the *Beagle*'s captain had requested the companionship of a naturalist to study the flora and fauna while he charted the coastline. Before the departure of *Beagle*, he discussed the voyage with both young men. Alfred Friendly, his biographer, claims that there is evidence that Dalrymple, the previous hydrographer, had suggested to Beaufort the adoption of an earlier wind scale which equated wind speeds in miles per hour with a simple description – i.e. 50 mph equals storm or tempest. By the time he was appointed hydrographer, Beaufort had perfected the scale to twelve gradations in the force of the wind, and to seventeen letters to describe the state of the weather. In 1838, the Admiralty ordered the Beaufort Scale to be put into use throughout the fleet and, in 1854, it was adopted for international use.[20]

*facing page*
The Beaufort Wind Scale as first written in the journal of Francis Beaufort in 1806; he later correlated the gradations of wind to the amount of sail a fully rigged ship would carry in various wind intensities.
From *Beaufort of the Admiralty*, Alfred Friendly

# CROZIER, CAPTAIN OF *TERROR*

*Beholding with Silent Surprise the great and wonderful*

*works of nature in this position we had an opportunity to*

*discern the barrier in its splendid position. Then I wished I*

*was an artist or a draughtsman instead of a blacksmith and*

*armourer.*

C.J. SULLIVAN, BLACKSMITH ABOARD HMS *EREBUS*[1]

The Antarctic voyages of *Erebus* and *Terror*, from 1839–43, were the most important voyages of discovery in the nineteenth century. James Clark Ross was appointed to command this prestigious voyage to the Southern Ocean and into the unknown continent, which was to be resourced by two bomb ships. Ross chose Crozier to command the *Terror*, with himself in charge of the *Erebus*, assisted by Commander Bird as his first lieutenant. All had served with Parry during his Arctic exploits; they had now come of age and were ready to make their own mark in Terra Incognito Australis, where the American Wilkes and a French expedition under D'Urville had made recent voyages and discoveries. The expedition's brief from the men of science was as wide-ranging as it was specific. The Admiralty's orders were probably drafted by Beaufort who, as a former naval commander, had the good sense to leave a lot of discretion to the commander. Ross and Crozier's passion for science and discovery did not need any external motivation. On a visit home to his sisters in July, Crozier availed of the opportunity to receive instruction in the use of nautical instruments from Lloyd in Dublin. He purchased and shipped a number of instruments to London's Chatham Docks on 21 July for use on the Antarctic expedition to which he had just been appointed.[2]

James Clark Ross and Francis Crozier together were a great team. Ross was now clearly the navy's most accomplished polar explorer and commander, and was an expert scientist on the subject of terrestrial magnetism. He was a handsome and distinguished-looking fellow who,

*facing page*
Francis Rawdon Moira Crozier, sailor and scientist. He commanded HMS *Terror*, and was second-in-command to James Clarke Ross on his Antarctic voyages of 1839–43 and to Sir John Franklin on his last Antarctic voyage, in 1845.
*Courtesy of Mr James Crozier, Banbridge*

following his reaching of the magnetic North Pole, enjoyed the confidence and support of the Admiralty, the men of science and the public. It was hoped that Britain would take the lead in following up on Captain Cook's and Bransfield's Southern Hemisphere discoveries. Crozier was to Ross a close and affectionate friend; he was also an experienced and accomplished polar commander, and well regarded as a scientist. His loyalty, genial nature and understated competence made him a very supportive second-in-command, a role that suited his shy and whimsical character and also suited Ross' more autocratic style. Crozier, descended from Scottish Protestant forebears, shared with Ross a belief that God would see them through each new challenge.

Each ship had a crew of 64, made up of twelve officers, eighteen petty officers, 26 able-bodied seamen and eight marines. Aboard *Erebus*, Edward Bird – another Parry veteran – was first lieutenant. The surgeon[3] was Robert McCormick, a naturalist whose naval record included the voyage aboard HMS *Beagle* on its second survey voyage to South America. His assistant surgeon on that occasion was the genius, Charles Darwin, whose observations over five years aboard the *Beagle* led to the development of his theory of natural evolution. *Erebus* had for its assistant surgeon – and naturalist – another who was to achieve fame, Joseph Dalton Hooker; his father was professor of botany at Glasgow University. Hooker was to become one of the most famous scientists of the nineteenth century and would be appointed director of Kew Gardens in 1865. Crozier's first lieutenant was

Archibald McMurdo, who had been on *Terror* with Sir George Back in 1836–37 during his unsuccessful attempt to reach Repulse Bay. *Terror* had on that occasion arrived back to Lough Swilly, Co. Donegal in a sinking condition, having been crushed first and then battered in storms and gales. McMurdo was to become immortalised when Ross named a bay in his honour, the place that would later serve as the point of embarkation for Scott and Shackleton in pursuit of the South Pole. *Terror* had the substantial damages caused to her during that voyage repaired before being handed over to Crozier to commission her for the Antarctic. Back's expedition had also introduced to the Arctic a young Irish officer, Robert McClure, from Wexford.

Crozier took charge of the fitting out of both ships, including the fitting of Mr Sylvester's heating stoves and flue systems to both vessels.[4] Twenty-six tons of tinned food made up of meats, vegetables, soups and gravy were supplied, along with cranberries, mixed pickles, mustard and peppers. 'Warm clothing of the best quality was also furnished to both ships, to be issued gratuitously to the crews whilst employed amongst the ice to protect them from the severity of the climate.'[5] Both commanders knew the value of a warm and healthy crew on such a long voyage and it was probably one of the best-resourced expeditions ever to have set out from Britain. The sergeant of marines was William Cunningham of Belfast, whose journal[6] gives a fascinating insight to the expedition from a below-decks perspective when read in conjunction with Ross' own two-volume narrative[7] of the expedition.

The voyage was planned in three distinct stages: the journey south to Hobart in Van Diemen's Land where a permanent magnetic-observation station would be established, setting up en route at St Helena and at the Cape of Good Hope two other stations. These stations were to be in place so that simultaneous observations could be made at all stations on May 29–30. At moorings off Gillingham, readings were taken to determine the effects caused to compasses by the ships' iron. They set out on 5 October 1839, crossed the Bay of Biscay and proceeded to Madeira, where at Funchal they checked the rates of the ship chronometers and involved themselves in checking the height of Pico Ruivo by barometer. They proceeded to Cape Verde Islands, where they made magnetic observations, and on to St Paul Rocks where Mr Dayman made a sketch survey of the rocks and McCormick collected some geographic specimens.

The next leg brought them to Trinidad. They crossed the equator and spent some time making observations of 'the line of no dip', which both ships observed simultaneously. Here, Ross reflected on the occasion when he had observed the dip instrument in the vertical position at the magnetic North Pole, and speculated on his prospects of being first to record the dip needle in a vertical position at the magnetic South Pole. They headed from Trinidad to St Helena where a permanent magnetic station was to be set up to facilitate simultaneous observations in 'all the foreign and British observatories that constitute the great magnetic co-operation'.[8] When Lieutenant Lefroy and his party set up the observation station, however, they quickly discovered that, because of its volcanic rock, it was unsuitable for magnetic measurement.

In the three weeks spent at St Helena, they found time – like any visitors – to make an excursion to the tomb of Napoleon, which was already a tourist destination. The expedition left the island on 9 February, crossing the line of least intensity again to reach the African coast before rounding the Cape of Good Hope. Here, they stopped at Simons Bay, leaving Lieutenant Wilmot to set up and operate a permanent observatory. Three weeks were spent here and, on departure, they loaded three bullocks to provide fresh meat for the next leg. Sergeant Cunningham had to deal with two deserters, caught by the civil police, and with drunken crewmen on their return to the ship.

The next leg, which began on 6 April, brought them to Kerguelen Islands for further magnetic observations and also brought them into a colder climate where warm clothing was the order of the day. They were in the regions frequented by the great albatross and the Cape pigeon, which could now be observed following their vessels. During their 68-day stay at Kerguelen, Crozier supervised the magnetic observations day and night. There was only three days without rain, and gales blew on 45 days. Some of the observations were carried out at pre-arranged dates so data could be collected simultaneously with other magnetic observatories.

On reaching Hobart in Van Diemen's Land – after a stormy passage during which *Erebus* lost overboard its boatswain – Ross learned details of two rival Antarctic explorations for the discovery of the magnetic South Pole: a French expedition,

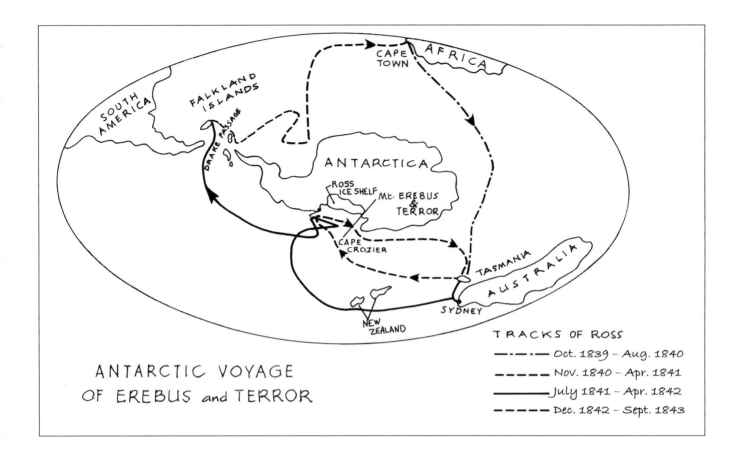

ANTARCTIC VOYAGE
OF EREBUS and TERROR

TRACKS OF ROSS
—·—·— Oct. 1839 – Aug. 1840
— — — Nov. 1840 – Apr. 1841
————— July 1841 – Apr. 1842
- - - - - Dec. 1842 – Sept. 1843

under the command of Dumont d'Urville, and a US expedition, commanded by Lieutenant Charles Wilkes. D'Urville, who had left Hobart on 1 January 1840, entered the pack at the point appropriate to Gauss' theory and, after nineteen days' sailing, some of his officers landed upon a small islet lying some distance from the mainland and procured specimens of its granite.[9] D'Urville, in a seven-week round trip with his two ships, *Astrolabe* and *Zelee*, sailed alongside the coast, which is in and around the latitude of the Antarctic Circle, for 150 miles between longitudes 136° east and 142° east. Not daring to enter the solid pack, which they skirted in ships unprepared for the full rigours of Antarctic exploration, D'Urville charted his discoveries. The Frenchman showed his true romantic nature

when he named the coast, Terre Adelie, after the woman whose companionship he declared he missed during his three years away from home.

A letter to Ross from Wilkes, complete with a tracing of his voyage map, outlined the American's 'discoveries', which were, for the most part, lands that had already been discovered by whalers. In a state of indignation at the secrecy of the Americans and at the attempt by both the French and the Americans to reach the magnetic South Pole ahead of the much-publicised British expedition, Ross resolved not to be seen to follow either nation. He did not dispute the right of the French or Americans to attempt to penetrate from the point of Gauss' prediction, and chose instead a more easterly meridian to make his attack on the pack. It was an inspired choice.

Sir John Franklin was lieutenant governor of Van Diemen's Land, where it was agreed to position a permanent magnetic-observation station. The site was chosen by Ross and was later named the Rossbank Observatory. Franklin personally supervised the building operation while Crozier, who had chief responsibility for the hourly magnetic observations, kept a hammock there. Franklin wrote to John Barrow regarding the observatory on 20 August 1841:

I have been made very happy by the selection of this place for the Magnetic Observatory and that Ross has in consequence made it his Head Quarters; we have therefore had the pleasure of seeing much of him and Crozier – and it is truly interesting to see them together. The same spirit animates each. Ross directs with all his forethought, knowledge and judgement – the other joins him most cordially in every operation – and the execution of their orders is promptly and cheerfully carried out by the officers and men. Such are the persons who must succeed – if human effort and skill can attain success.[10]

Lieutenant Kay – Franklin's nephew – remained permanently at the station that had been erected under the direct supervision of John Franklin. The colonial observatories were issued with magnetometers which, though clearly derived from those recommended by Gauss, had been modified by Humphrey Lloyd of the Dublin Magnetic Observatory.[11]

Ross and Crozier were entertained royally by the Franklin entourage, which included Franklin's niece, Sophia Cracroft. Crozier, though a lot older than 'Sophy', was very taken with her, but her eyes at that time were for Ross. Lady Jane recorded in her journal: 'Sophy Cracroft was sorry when it [the expedition] sailed: Crozier had fallen in love with her, but she had been flirting with Ross.'[12] The handsome James Clark Ross, who was impervious to Sophia's overtures, infatuated her in turn; Ross was engaged to Anne Coulman in England. Crozier later entertained ideas of marriage to Sophia, and he continued his courtship of her on his return from the first Antarctic voyage.

*Erebus* and *Terror* left Hobart on 12 November 1840 and met the pack at 64° south, 10° east on 30 December. They sat out snow, fog and a heavy swell until favourable winds arose on the morning of 5 January. Then the two ships, in full sail, attacked the pack ice – now visible in all directions – with their specially prepared and strengthened bomb vessels protected by copper sheeting. The ships shuddered occasionally as they collided with thicker floes. For days, they made slow but steady progress. The pack appeared to thicken, as did the clouds, but at last they were through to open water. It was a most remarkable feat of sailing without the aid of steam; a triumph for all concerned – for Ross and Crozier and for the shipyard. It was a just reward resulting from the collective experience gained in their Arctic voyages with Parry, which had prepared them and their vessels. All the time, the magnetic needles indicated an increasing dip as they approached their main objective. Then, the horizon was filled a hundred miles away with high mountains and they 'had the most enchanted view of the magnificent range of mountains, whose lofty peaks, perfectly covered with eternal snow, rose to elevations varying from seven to ten thousand feet above the level of the ocean.'[13] They named prominent features as they came into view after notables of their time, their promoters and colleagues. Significantly, Ross remembered Sabine first:

The highest mountain of this range, I named after Lieutenant-Colonel Sabine, of the Royal Artillery, Foreign Secretary of the Royal Society, one of the best and earliest of friends of my youth, and to whom this compliment was more especially due, as having been the first proposer and one of the more active and zealous promoters of the expedition.[14]

A cape was named after John Barrow, second secretary of the Admiralty and president of the Royal Geographical Society, for his lifetime championing of the Northwest Passage. At Crozier's request, a cape was named after his kind and lamented friend, the late Marquis of Downshire. The next range of mountains they called the Admiralty Range, and they proceeded to name

HMS *Erebus* and *Terror* in sight of Mount Sabine on 11 January 1841. Named by James Clarke Ross in honour of Edward Sabine, the Dublin-born scientist. Watercolour by J.E. Davis.
From A Voyage of Discovery 1839–43, *J.C. Ross*

the mountain peaks after each of the lords of the Admiralty. They found the shores of the mainland completely covered with ice, which projected into the sea, and the heavy surf along its edge forbade any attempt to land upon it. A strong tide that ran between the ice-bound coast and some islands caused their situation to be critical. At 71° 56' south, 171° 7' east, in clear weather, they decided to land on some small islands, the largest of which they ceremonially took possession of in the name of the recently crowned Queen Victoria – 'The whitest if not brightest jewel in her crown', declared Hooker. Possession Island, they observed, was made up of igneous rock, was swarming with 'inconceivable myriads of penguins', bore no vegetation and was only accessible from its western end. They loaded geological specimens and penguins, and gladly escaped the stench of guano built up over ages.

On 15 January, they came close to another range of snow-covered mountains, and these they named after the eminent philosophers of the Royal Society: the most conspicuous peak was named after Sir John Herschel who Ross called 'the greatest philosopher of our time'; another was named Mount Lloyd after Rev Dr Humphrey Lloyd of Trinity College, Dublin; another he named after the Rev Dr Robinson of Armagh. Ross rewarded them all for their zealous and active promotion of magnetic research in the Antarctic regions. They observed 30 sightings of right and sperm whales during that day's sailing. Ross named another island Coulman Island, after the father of his fiancée. He sighted it on her birthday, and its southernmost point he christened

Cape Anne in her honour.[15]

Their magnetic readings indicated that the magnetic South Pole lay about 500 miles to the southwest, and that the coastline they were following led south. Ross decided to follow the coastline and hoped for a turn west in the coast or perhaps a channel leading toward their main objective. On 22 January, they reckoned they were at 74° 20' south at noon and, by 7 p.m., calculated they were further south than Weddell and therefore further south than all their predecessors. An extra allowance of grog was advanced to the crew to toast 'sweethearts and wives' in the rejoicing of the event. On 26 January, they calculated the magnetic Pole was only 174 miles west of their position. At noon the following day, they were at latitude 75° 48' south, longitude 168° 33' east. Ross left *Erebus* and Crozier left *Terror*, each accompanied by officers, to land on another island, 12-miles long and 6-miles broad, which they named Franklin Island after their recent host. Soaked in the process of making a tricky landing, they collected rock specimens and returned 'painfully cold' to their ships. They noted a total absence of vegetation on the island, and observed the nesting places of the white petrel and the rapacious skua gull. On 28 January 1841, the discovery of an active volcano was 'esteemed a circumstance of high geological importance and interest' by Ross. The mountain, at 12,400 feet, was accompanied by an extinct twin which stood 10,900-feet high; they named them Mount Erebus and Mount Terror, respectively. A small, round island, which had been in sight all morning, was named Beaufort Island as a compliment to

Captain Francis Beaufort, of the Royal Navy, Hydrographer to the Admiralty, who was not only mainly instrumental in promoting the sending forth of our expedition, but afforded me much assistance, during its equipment, by his opinion and advice: and it is very gratifying to me to pay this tribute of respect and gratitude to him for the many acts of kindness and personal friendship I have received at his hands.[16]

The next day, as they sailed further south beneath Mount Erebus and Mount Terror, they observed a perpendicular cliff of ice; it had no fissures or promontories and it varied in height from between 150–200 feet above the level of the sea, which was perfectly flat and level on top. The range of lofty mountains completed the scene and provided an extraordinary sight as they sailed south – away from their main objective, the magnetic South Pole – with no access west through what Ross likened to the cliffs of Dover. Ross named the eastern cape beneath Mount Terror after Crozier. He wrote:

My friend and colleague Commander Francis Rawdon Crozier, of the *Terror*, to whose zeal and cordial co-operation is mainly to be ascribed, under God's blessing, the happiness as well as success of the expedition; under the circumstances we were placed in, it is impossible for others fully to understand the value of having so tried a friend, of now more than twenty years standing, as commander of

the second ship, upon which the harmony and right feeling between the two vessels so greatly depends.[17]

Cape Crozier is renowned as one of only two dozen colonies of emperor penguins. Ross went on to name the western promontory at the foot of Mount Erebus, Cape Bird – after his first lieutenant on *Erebus* – and the mountain range that now blocked their passage to the magnetic South Pole, he named Parry Mountains, in honour of their great mentor. Ross, in remembering Parry, was returning a compliment; Parry had honoured him greatly in naming the northernmost known land after him.

As they sailed a hundred miles along the coast, they took soundings – noting depths of 400 fathoms – and charted their findings. In the afternoon, Ross went aboard *Terror* to consult with Crozier and to compare chronometers and barometers. They found that, after three months, the chronometers differed by only 4 seconds, equivalent at that latitude to a distance of a quarter mile; their barometers were in perfect agreement. These two men of science were thorough in every respect and were rewarded on 31 January when they made the first sighting of an emperor penguin, thinking at first it was merely a larger bird of the king species. On 1 February, they reached their 'furthest south' for the season, at latitude 78° 4' south. By then, they had sailed 250 miles from Cape Crozier.

They sailed off the barrier – now known as the Ross Ice Shelf – and retraced their route north, heading back to Hobart. They observed icebergs with flat tops grounded on a bank 60 miles away

from the barrier, indicating the barrier's nature as a moving glacier calving icebergs into the sea. They also observed the brown coating on the pack, indicating perhaps volcanic ash deposits and which later proved to be micro-organic and the basic source of Antarctica's food chain. Passing Mount Erebus in good visibility, the crews of *Terror* and *Erebus* were treated to a spectacular volcanic display when it erupted. In clear view of the coastline, a bay was noted – perhaps a place to find a winter harbour from where they could explore in the following spring. Ross named this bay in honour of *Terror*'s first lieutenant, but heavy ice prevented their boats landing at the now-named McMurdo Bay. This ice-filled bay was to become one of the most famous places in the Antarctic. In the quest for

the South Pole during the early twentieth century, it became a place familiar to Ernest Shackleton, Tom Crean and other Irishmen who were to serve with Scott and Shackleton in the age of heroic exploration.

On 6 April 1841, they sailed back to the Derwent River, fully intact and with all crew fit. Ross, Crozier and their men were celebrities to the inhabitants and people of Van Diemen's Land. There were dinners and receptions, a new nautical theatre production and a grand ball on *Erebus* and *Terror*, which were lashed together for the occasion – *Erebus* became the ballroom while supper was served on the *Terror*. Three hundred and fifty guests attended, with music provided by the band of the 51st Regiment and the Hobart Town Quadrille Band. The ship was decked in

*Terror* and *Erebus* discover Beaufort Island (foreground) and Mount Erebus on 28 January 1841. James Clarke Ross named the island in honour of Francis Beaufort who, in his role as hydrographer to the navy, was considered by Ross as instrumental in both promoting the expedition with the government and in providing its equipment. Watercolour by J.E. Davis.
*From* A Voyage of Discovery 1839–43, *J.C. Ross*

flags and flowers on what was known afterwards as the 'glorious first of June'. Lady Franklin missed the great occasion as she was away on one of her own expeditions. It is unclear if Sophia Cracroft was with Jane or was present for the grand ball.

After the ball, the ships were refitted before they set sail on their second Antarctic voyage. They first visited Sydney and then New Zealand to set up further observatories and to take readings at appointed days, while the botanists surveyed the environments. This time, *Erebus* and *Terror* entered the pack along the 146°-west meridian, aiming at the eastern extremity of the Ross Ice Shelf to carry on their explorations, but this was a different season with thick fog making safe progress difficult. They entered the pack in December – keeping within hailing distance of one another – following open leads in a south-west course for 40 days. Occasionally, whales burst through the surface of the water, breaking the monotony for the sailors. For New Year's Day, they moored each side of a floe and set up a magical and surreal scene: a grand fancy ball was staged in the 'Antarctic Hotel', and snow statues of Bacchus and Britannia were built for this Victorian polar pageant. Captain Crozier opened the ball with Miss Ross, dancing a quadrille, followed with reels and country dances, the participants clad in heavy boots.

This mood was not to last long, as the wind and seas rose up in gusts and swells. They were driven into the heavy pack, which was broken up around them and hurled against the ships

hard as rolling granite, which were dashed

against them with so much violence that their masts quivered as if they would fall at each successive blow; and the destruction of the ships seemed inevitable from the tremendous shocks they received.[18]

Crozier and his crew were without their rudder, which had been ripped away from the sternpost by crashing blocks of ice in the boiling sea. *Erebus* also had rudder problems and both ships went with the tumbling floes, each man wondering if the ship would survive. Ross was full of admiration for his men's coolness, steady obedience and untiring exertions. He also tells how close the two ships were sailing to each other:

> [*Terror*] rose to the top of one wave, the *Erebus* was on the top of the next one to the leeward of her, the deep chasm between them filled with heavy rolling masses; and as the ships descended into the hollow between the waves, the main topsail yard of each could be seen just level with the crest of the intervening wave, from the top of the deck of the other; from this some idea may be formed of the height of the waves, as well as the perilous situations of our ships.[19]

The storm subsided after 28 hours. They then drove their ships into the thick of the pack and moored each side of a floe so as to carry out repairs to the steering. After three days of efforts by the artificers from both ships, Ross reported that 'at last by much perseverance and the patient ingenuity of her commander [Crozier] and senior lieutenant [McMurdo]' the rudder repairs were completed. We pick up the story on March 20; Sergeant Cunningham gives another flavour of polar sailing:

> . . . blowing a gale, shipping heavy seas and freezing very keen. One and half inch rope at least a foot in circumference with ice. At 7 p.m. furled mainsail and close reefed topsails which was the most difficult job. The ice about the decks thicker than I ever saw before – no walking or standing and the sea washing over you and forming icicles instantly. The *Erebus* presented a most dreary appearance everything appearing ice except her chopper (cheerful side note – 'Spliced the main brace') came on to blow uncommon in the night – turned up two watches and they were employed most part of the night seas washing over them – lower deck very wet and exceedingly uncomfortable, people's clothes all wet.[20]

The gale abated on the evening of 21 March, the wind veered northward and a course was again set for the south. Just before midnight on 23 March, the Great Ice Barrier was seen from the masthead. After 800 miles, they had reached the barrier again. What had taken five days the year before had now taken 47, and already the early signs of winter signalled it was time to leave. After a short survey, they reached a point where the barrier was only 107 feet above the sea, and they were 6 miles further south than the previous year, at latitude 78° 9' 30" south. In

reaching this point, Ross, Bird and Abernethy all recorded the feat of having been nearest to both of the earth's poles.

When further progress south into the Weddell Sea was blocked by thick ice, Ross decided to sail northward along the pack toward the Falkland Islands. They had some uneasy nights mixing among chains of icebergs. On 9 March, at latitude 60° 20' south, Ross ordered a course due east to make the next planned magnetic observation position – 'the supposed position of the second focus of greatest magnetic intensity' – and thence toward Cape Horn.[21] Within a few days, the wind increased and heavy snow fell as darkness descended; in the presence of many large icebergs, they close reefed the mainsails till daylight. In the early morning light, the watch became aware of a huge iceberg – 200-feet high – on their port bow. The ships were sailing on parallel courses and *Terror* was on the port side of *Erebus* when suddenly, both had to tack to avoid the lurking berg whose foam was breaking over their decks. There was no room and, inevitably, they tacked into one another's course and collided. *Terror*'s flying boom and lower studding boom came away in the first engagement. In the rolling sea, they passed in crashing movements which brought booms and boom irons down onto the deck, now manned by all hands, many in their nightclothes. Crozier shouted orders as quarter boat and ice plank were splintered when *Erebus* eventually passed. The helm responded to his 'hard to port' order as he steered *Terror* into the black hole – the gap between two icebergs. *Terror*, under topsail and foresail, responded well as she was directed into a gap no bigger than

three times the width of her beam. Later, in a letter home, John Davis, the second master of *Terror*, wrote:

All this time we had been bodily drifting on the bergs, so that when we cleared *Erebus* we found an enormous iceberg under our lee. A dreadful shipwreck and death appeared inevitable; there was no alternative but to run for the dark place we had seen before, which might be an opening, or be smashed in the face of the cliff. The helm was immediately put to starboard and with the assistance of the sails she answered very well; we were immediately rushing past an enormous berg, the ship being perfectly covered with the foam caused by the sea breaking against it. Every moment we were expecting the ship to strike ice right ahead. 'Hard a port' was screamed from forward (then indeed hope died within us); 'Hard a port; brace round the head-yards.' 'Shiver the main topsail,' cried the captain as if he was steering into a harbour. The men flew to the ropes, although I should think at that moment that there was not one on board but thought all hope was fled. She came round, and passed through an opening between two bergs not twice the breadth of the ship, the foam and spray dashing over us on each side as we passed. Several other alarms were given owing to the brash [small stuff washed from bergs] looking like more bergs in the darkness, but we were safe but did not know it. The next cry was 'Where is the *Erebus*?' – our own danger had made us entirely forget her for the time.[22]

Ross, meanwhile, was demonstrating his great seamanship and leadership qualities as captain of the very experienced crew of *Erebus*, her lower sails and booms in tatters. He wrote:

Amidst the roar of the wind and sea, it was difficult both to hear and to execute the orders that were given, so that it was three quarters of an hour before we could get the yards braced bye, and the main-tack hauled on board sharp aback – an expedient that perhaps had never before been resorted to by seamen in such weather: but it had the desired effect; the ship gathered stern-way washing away the gig and quarter boats, and with her lower yard-arms scraping the rugged face of the berg, we in a few minutes reached its western termination; the 'undertow' as it is called, or the reaction of the water from its vertical cliffs, alone prevented us from being driven to atoms against it. No sooner had we cleared it, than another was seen directly astern of us, against which we were running; and the difficulty now was to get the head of the ship turned around and pointed fairly through between the bergs, the breadth of the intervening space not exceeding three times her own breadth, this however we happily accomplished;

and in a few minutes after getting before the wind, she dashed through the narrow channel, between two perpendicular walls of ice, and the foaming breakers which stretched across it, and the next moment we were in smooth water under its lee.[23]

Davis pondered on his own performance in this crisis:

I wonder I did not lose my self-possession; but no, perhaps it was from the example that I did not, but I repeated the orders and got what was necessary done more coolly in appearance than I felt. The Captain himself when it was over, said that he had not the slightest idea what he did during the time or how we got through. The men on the whole behaved very well throughout; only one was running around out of his senses, but two or three were crying. It was truly a time when 'shrieked the timid and stood the brave'.[24]

They escaped without loss of life and bore away under light sail in a westerly gale. The whole day was spent repairing the damage; the best bower anchor of *Erebus* was found driven 7 or 8 inches into her solid timbers about 3 feet under the waterline. It could not be removed but broke away in heavy seas 500 miles later, leaving metal stuck into the bow. In a rolling sea, the course was resumed so as to continue the programme of magnetic observations at latitude 60° south, longitude 125° west.

En route for Cape Horn, further violent

storms were encountered and, while reefing the sails of *Erebus*, James Angelly fell overboard. Despite frantic rescue efforts, the seaman drowned – the third death aboard *Erebus* since leaving home. Sergeant Cunningham noted 'how unfortunate *Erebus* was and thanked God that *Terror* had met no accident.'[25] More observations and experiments were conducted in the vicinity of Cape Horn and, in April 1842, Port Louis in the Falkland Islands was reached. It is thought that Ross chose the Falklands for his last winter stopover to prevent his crew jumping ship. At the Falklands, there was no escape except on the ship you arrived on.

For five months, they were busy repairing the damaged hull of *Erebus*. The holds of each ship were emptied in turn to ventilate and to restock with stores provided by HMS *Carysfort*, which also brought a new bowsprit for *Terror*. To complete this operation, the ships' companies constructed a pier and, alongside it, a storehouse into which each ship's stores were unloaded and sorted before being loaded.

Astronomical and meteorological observatories were established near a fort built in 1764, and a magnetic observatory was set up at about 30 feet above sea level. A turf house was built nearby to accommodate the observers. Meanwhile, Ross and Crozier assisted the governor of the island, Lieutenant Clement Moody, in surveying and selecting the most appropriate port and capital for the recently retaken British colony.[26] Port William was recommended over Port Louis, based on Ross' assertion that the future of the colony depended on its maritime affairs and that Port Louis was a very limited port

compared with Port William. Their findings and recommendations were accepted by Beaufort and the Admiralty, and the new capital was subsequently renamed Stanley in honour of the colonial secretary.

A good excuse for onshore celebrations in the small colony arose when the Navy List showed that Crozier and Bird were promoted, as were a number of others, based on Ross' report of the first Antarctic voyage. McMurdo was invalided home and Lieutenant Sibbald was left on the Falklands to continue with the observations.

The ships tracked back to Cape Horn to make simultaneous readings on the agreed date of 21 September. While at anchor in St Martin's Cove on Hermite Island, a magnetic station was established. Fuegian Indians were encountered ashore – completely naked despite a recorded temperature of 41°F (5°C). It was noted that the women did all the work; also noted was the ability of the men for mimicry, singing and dancing. Readings at the magnetic station were taken from 29 September until 6 November, while all other observations continued until early December. On return to the Falkland Islands, they carried timber and 800 young beech trees, no doubt to the benefit of the colony.

*Erebus* and *Terror* sailed on their third and last Antarctic voyages on 17 December 1842. Ross planned this time to penetrate the Weddell Sea and to add to the discoveries made in 1822 by that great whaler. They first travelled to the South Shetland Islands where they spent Christmas Day feasting on a fat ox presented to each ship by the governor of the Falkland Islands. They made many important discoveries in North Graham Land during a season when, according to Hooker, officers and men slept with their ears open, listening for the look-out's cry of 'Berg ahead', followed by 'All hands on deck.' The officers of the *Terror* told him

that their commander never slept a night in his cot throughout that season in the ice, and that he passed it either on deck or in a chair at night. There were nights of grog and hot coffee, for the orders to splice the mainbrace were many and imperative if the crew were to be kept up to the strain on their nerves and muscles.[27]

Crossing Weddell's tracks on 14 February, they found only impenetrable pack ice and not the open sea Weddell had described. On 5 March, having crossed the Antarctic Circle for the third time, they had reached 71° 30' south, 14° 51' west. It was time to go home. When they arrived off Folkestone on 2 September 1843, they had been away four years and five months.

The expedition collected a mass of magnetic observations, charted many exciting new geographic discoveries and collected many new species of flora and fauna. During the four-and-a-half years spent in the Southern Hemisphere, the expedition had opened up Antarctica for

HMS *Erebus* and *Terror* colliding while tacking to avoid a huge iceberg on their port sides on 13 March 1842. It was truly a time when 'shrieked the timid and stood the brave' wrote John Davis, second master of *Terror*. Crozier steered *Terror* through the black hole that was the gap between two icebergs. Watercolour by J.E. Davis.
*From* A Voyage of Discovery 1839–43, *J.C. Ross*

HMS *Erebus* passes through a chain of icebergs. Ross displayed his seamanship when he steered *Erebus* through a space not exceeding three times her own breadth between two perpendicular walls of ice. Watercolour by J.E. Davis.
*From* A Voyage of Discovery *1839–43, J.C. Ross*

future explorers, located the magnetic South Pole and mapped many islands and great chunks of the coastline on the last discovered continent. Such was the amount of magnetic data brought back by Ross and Crozier that it took until 1868 – 25 years after the return of the expedition – for Sabine and the Royal Society to publish a final summary of compiled results and computations. Sabine also produced a 'magnetic map' of the Southern Hemisphere, the sum of a lifetime's achievements by Sabine, Ross, Crozier and Lloyd. Beaufort's role in support of all this activity was understated, but it was nevertheless very significant. Extracts from the journal of the

Hobart Observatory in March 1843 recorded the observation of a comet which was communicated on Lieutenant Kay's behalf by Sabine to the Royal Astronomical Society of London. The comet's tail was also observed and recorded in the ships' logs of *Erebus* and *Terror* as they recrossed the Antarctic Circle on 10 March 1843.[28]

The Scots-Irish team of Ross and Crozier, powered only by sail, pointed the way via the Ross Ice Shelf to the South Pole taken a half-century later by Scott, Shackleton and Amundsen. Their combined achievement as mariners, navigators, cartographers and scientists were very poorly acknowledged by the Admiralty and were poorly communicated to the public. This was partly due to the length of time the expedition was out of the public eye and also to Ross' delay in completing and publishing his narrative which, when published, was a little terse and failed to capture the public's imagination. It was soon overshadowed by John Barrow's quest for success in the Arctic and the subsequent search for Franklin. Collectively, these various factors seem to have obscured the real significance and boldness of the expedition's significant discoveries. However, those Antarctic voyages – considered retrospectively – must rate with those of Captain Cook as among the greatest voyages of discovery.

When Ross finally published his narrative of the voyages, he generously acknowledged the excellence of Crozier in his supporting role, which he characterised as both zealous and cordial:

> I cannot conclude the narrative of the voyage of the *Erebus* and *Terror* without expressing the high sense I entertain of the cordial and zealous support, I invariably received from my excellent colleague Captain Crozier, and the officers and crews of both ships, by whose unanimity, exertions and skill, uninterrupted observations were made during the course of the expedition, which will elucidate several points of importance and interest in science, while they present others for examination, and afford a basis of comparison, should that sound mode of prosecuting inquiry be adopted. The geographical researches, moreover, will, I trust, be deemed to have contributed their share to the extension of our knowledge of the more remote southern regions of the earth.[29]

The skill of Ross and Crozier as hands-on commanders of sailing vessels is obvious, and their ability to maintain a healthy, disciplined and very productive crew over four-and-a-half years was exemplary. Quite simply, Ross and Crozier were individually very skilled mariners and scientists who understood and appreciated each other's role and character. Both led by example and expected the same behaviour from their subordinates. They were hard working and zealous in all their endeavours, and were role models for their junior officers.

# 6

# THE FRANKLIN EXPEDITION

*The Northwest Passage to the Indies! – that Golden Dream,
as fatal to the English valour as the Guiana one to the
Spanish – and yet, hardly, hardly, to be regretted, when we
remember the seamanship, the science, the chivalry, the
heroism, unequalled in the history of the English nation,
which it has called forth among those our later Arctic
voyagers, who have combined the knight-errantry of the
middle age with the practical prudence of the modern, and
dared for duty more than Cortes or Pizarro dared for gold.*

CHARLES KINGSLEY[1]

Following his final Antarctic voyage, James Clark Ross was knighted and married his fiancée, Anne Coulman, who secured a promise from him never again to go exploring. Crozier, best man at Ross' wedding, had his promotion to captain and his election as a Fellow of the Royal Society to celebrate; he was nominated by some of the most famous scientists of his day. In matters of love, however, it seems he fared poorly; he received a message from Lady Franklin through Ross that appears to indicate rejection of his advances – perhaps, even, a proposal of marriage – to Sophia Cracroft, niece of John Franklin. Crozier, in a bid to get over his rejection, travelled overland to Paris and Italy, and moved about Florence, apparently in an unsettled state of mind.

In the period since Back's last unsuccessful voyage to Repulse Bay, in 1836, Peter Dease and Thomas Simpson of the Hudson's Bay Company, during three successive summers from 1837–39, succeeded in linking the previous discoveries of Franklin, Back, Richardson and Beechey along the North American coastline. They connected and correlated their own discoveries with the maps of the aforementioned naval explorers between the Bering Strait and the estuary of the Great Fish River.

While Ross and Crozier were cruising in the Antarctic, Sir John Barrow was planning a resumption of his quest to discover a Northwest Passage

*facing page
Franklin's Dream;
etching by Irish artist
Vincent Sheridan.
By kind permission of the
artist*

which, in his view, ought to precede any attempt to reach the North Pole. In December 1844, Barrow – then nearing the end of his long career as second secretary of the Admiralty – submitted a document to the first lord of the Admiralty, Lord Haddington, entitled 'Proposal for an attempt to complete the discovery of a Northwest Passage'. The document is a classic; its arguments are logical and well made, justifying further public investment in exploration and science. By invoking past successes and inferring that the enlightened support of Queen Elizabeth for William Baffin had subsequently led to the current English power base on the continent of America, Barrow suggested that the discovery of the Northwest Passage was on the point of completion; indeed, success was now practically assured as the navy had the ships and officers capable, willing and ready to embark on one final voyage. The paper had the full approval of highly respected men of exploration and science, including Parry, Beaufort and Sabine, and even suggested that the expedition might only take one season and would cost only one-third of the amount spent on the recent successful Antarctic voyage. Barrow also stressed the advantages Arctic training had brought to the navy in producing a 'finer set of officers and seamen'. Finally, he pointed out that for England not to be the first nation to link the Atlantic to the Pacific would be neglectful, bearing in mind the possibility of the route being discovered by the young, progressive and adventurous American fleet or the active and ambitious Russian fleet.

The prime minister, Sir Robert Peel, asked for further information regarding the scientific dis-coveries that the attempt might yield and for confirmation by experts of the viability of Barrow's plan. The council of the Royal Society considered the scientific matter on 16 January 1845 and, in a resolution, agreed that important scientific discoveries were likely to accrue from the proposed expedition.[2] It concurred with John Barrow's minute regarding the accession to geographical knowledge and supported the extension of information with regard to magnetic phenomena in the North Polar region. Lord Haddington also sent John Barrow's proposal to John Franklin, James Clark Ross and Edward Parry for their views. All three of these distinguished and knighted polar commanders agreed with Barrow that the direction the attempt should take should be southward and westward, between Point Walker and Banks Land. Parry, who was comptroller of steam machinery, recommended the provision to each ship of a movable screw propeller powered by a 50-horse-power steam locomotive. He was convinced that the use of steam-powered propellers would revolutionise polar exploration. Ross agreed with Barrow's choice of route, but suggested that, should progress south and southwest prove impractical, an attempt north through the Wellington Channel should then be made. Lastly, Sabine provided the Admiralty with a report outlining the important additions the expedition could contribute to the science of terrestrial magnetism. All of these letters of support were submitted to Sir Robert Peel, who gave his consent to the proposed undertaking. It was decided to re-equip *Erebus* and *Terror*, and to send the expedition in the spring to seek a Northwest Passage.

To the great pleasure of Sir John Barrow, this decision was made just before he retired from the Admiralty.

The first step was to select a commander for the expedition. Sir James Clark Ross was approached by the Admiralty, but had promised his new wife on his return from Antarctica that he would not participate in the proposed Northwest Passage expedition. Ross, in a letter from Sabine in January 1843 informing him of John Barrow's moves to renew the quest for the Northwest Passage, was told that 'No one will go to the North Pole until you return; but it is waiting for you and Crozier.' Ross, in a letter to Beaufort, said:

> I have lately heard confidentially that there is to be another Northern Expedition and as you were so good as to mention this subject to me some time ago and asked if I had any wish to command it, I should not be acting with due openness and candour to two of my best friends [Beaufort and Sabine] if I delayed any longer giving an unequivocal reply to that question – especially as it is high time the commander of such an enterprise should be engaged making the necessary preparations. If the expedition is to sail next spring, I have no hesitation in saying (after the most mature reflection) that I have no wish, but on the contrary great and well founded objections to return so soon to the severe and arduous service to which I have already devoted considerable pecuniary sacrifice and without the smallest equivalent advan-

tage, and as Sir John Franklin wishes for the opportunity of completing a work which he so well began, on which he was so long engaged and being so pre-eminently qualified for the command of such

Sir John Franklin before he sailed in May 1845 in what he hoped would be the first successful navigation of the Northwest Passage.
*National Maritime Museum*

an Expedition, I feel the less reluctance in declining an honour which a few years ago was the highest object of my ambition.

I understand also that the ships are to be fitted as steamers, a measure to which I could not consent if the command were placed in my hands and which alone would be a sufficient reason for not wishing to undertake the service as it is proposed at present to carry it forward.[3]

A follow-up letter four days later to Beaufort clarified his position further and indicated that they should proceed 'while those in power are willing to promote it . . . and with Franklin as its commander and Crozier or Bird as his second.'[4]

Beaufort was, by then, in a very influential position, being the go between for the Admiralty and the scientific community. Instrumental in the development of *A Manual of Scientific Inquiry*, for the use of naval officers, he believed that a huge amount of useful data from around the world relating to many branches of science could be observed, recorded and collected by ships' officers – particularly the medical officers – for analysis by scientists in the various scientific institutions. There were thirteen sections in the manual, each written by a luminary in a particular branch of science, including the great astronomer, Sir John Herschel, who wrote the section on meteorology, Charles Darwin, who contributed the section on geology, and Sir Edward Sabine, author of the piece on terrestrial magnetism.

After 21 years of married life, Beaufort's devoted wife, Alicia, died in August 1834 after an unsuccessful fight against cancer lasting two painful years. Following Alicia's death, his unmarried sisters, Harriet and Louise, came from Ireland to look after his children. His relationship with Harriet was always very close; she idolised him and it was with her he most corresponded while at sea. His biographer, Alfred Friendly, produced evidence to show that during this period, Beaufort's relationship with Harriet was for a time sexual; this aspect of their relationship ended before his second marriage four years later.[5] He was long an admirer of Honora Edgeworth and was greatly attracted to her scholarly family circle. Having set his sights on marrying her, they were duly wed at Edgeworthstown on 8 November 1838. He was 64 and Honora 46. She was tall, thin and elegant, a dependable confidante with a great capacity for conciliation. She made an excellent companion for Beaufort and a capable guardian to his children. The two older boys were secure at school and four girls, whose ages ranged from eight to fifteen, found Honora's interest in balls and social events more to their liking than had their paternal aunts from Collon.

John Barrow supported Commander James Fitzjames' appointment, but the Admiralty thought him too young for the responsibility of leadership. Sir John Franklin, who had been unexpectedly recalled to England in June 1844 from his position as governor of Van Diemen's Land by the colonial secretary, Lord Stanley – following a dispute between Franklin and his administrative secretary, whom he had dismissed – now sought after the command in a bid to clear his name and to re-establish the glory of his earlier Arctic exploits. His wife, Jane, who was very active in seeking the post for her 58-year-old husband, sought support from the other polar knights, Ross and Parry. She wrote to Ross that if he himself, 'the only perfectly right person', did not wish to take the command, 'she hoped it would be offered to her husband'.[6] The matter was finally resolved when the first lord sought Parry's view regarding Franklin's age and fitness, about which Parry was unequivocal: 'He is a fitter man to go than any I know, and if you don't let him go, the man will die of disappointment.'[7]

Lord Haddington, the first lord, wanted Crozier as leader, but Crozier – knowing the importance to Franklin of the position – declined. He made it known through Ross that his preference was to serve as second-in-command to Ross; in the event of Ross declining, he would be prepared to go as second-in-command to Parry or Franklin. Crozier would not have wished to fall foul of Franklin or Jane, as he still entertained thoughts of continuing his courtship – indeed, of marrying – Sophia, Franklin's niece.

On 3 March 1845, Franklin was appointed to *Erebus* and given the command of the expedition. Captain Crozier was appointed second-in-command of the expedition, and again given command of *Terror*. Barrow's nominee, Commander James Fitzjames, was appointed second-in-command aboard *Erebus*. There was one critical voice regarding the expedition plan: Dr King, who had accompanied Back down the Great Fish River, believed that without the support of an overland party, a safe passage could not be discovered without the ships being seriously exposed to besetment from ice. He told Barrow that he was sending Franklin to 'form the nucleus of an iceberg'.

Crozier had returned from France in February 1845, staying at the home of the now Sir James and Lady Ross at Blackheath while the fitting out and strengthening of the ships was under way at Woolwich. He was very fond of Anne Ross, whom he nicknamed, 'Thot'. Elsewhere, Franklin was suffering an attack of influenza just days before departure. He fell asleep on a sofa in their lodgings and Jane threw a Union Jack over his feet. When he awoke, he rebuked her with the

Jane Franklin, wife of Sir John Franklin. She was to play a leading role in the subsequent search for him and his expedition.
*Vancouver Maritime Museum*

Francis Rawdon Crozier (left), commander of *Terror*, and James Fitzjames, second-in-command aboard *Erebus*.
*National Maritime Museum*

words, 'Don't you know they lay the Union Jack over a corpse.'

Jane's diary records Franklin's thoughts on his team in comparison to Ross': 'Those Ross had taken south, Hooker excepted, compared poorly with his.' Franklin, she wrote, knew how to handle men better than Ross, who 'is evidently ambitious and wishes to do everything himself . . . Franklin had a way with sailors that no man could imitate' and '*Terror* was envious of *Erebus*'.

Jane also observed that '*Terror* was less merry, or perhaps it was just that Captain Crozier, missing his old leader and not recovered from Miss Cracroft's rejection of his hand, felt irrationally despondent.' This observation is interesting when one notes that it was Fitzjames – who had no Arctic experience – with assistance from his close friend, John Barrow jnr., with whom he had sailed on HMS *Excellent*, who had made the crew appointments, many of whom were his friends.[8] Apart from Crozier and Graham Gore, first lieutenant of the *Erebus*, very few had polar experience. Franklin's last Arctic voyage had taken place in 1818, under Captain Buchan; his other expeditions were overland. It is quite extraordinary that none from either Ross or Crozier's recent Antarctic crew were chosen. It was considered good practice to have a balance of experience with an influx of new blood.

Included in the crew on HMS *Terror* was Cornelius Hickey from Limerick, a 24-year-old caulker's mate on his first naval voyage. How this young Limerick man with no previous naval record came to be selected is interesting. Had he merchant sailing experience or perhaps some ship-building experience? All we know from *Terror*'s muster list is his name and place of birth. Baptismal records exist for two Cornelius Hickeys, both at St Mary's Church. If, as is likely, he was the son of Thomas Hickey and Margaret Boyle of St Mary's parish in Limerick city, his baptism was recorded on 18 May 1821.[9]

What has come to be known as the Franklin expedition was on paper one of the best-planned, best-organised and best-equipped expeditions ever mounted by the navy. The public viewed the departure with pride and expectation. The fitting out in Woolwich included covering the bows with sheet iron. The cabins were installed with a new hot-water heating system. The now-famous sailing mortar-bomb ships were for the first time powered with auxiliary railway engines adapted for marine use. The engine for the *Erebus* had a previous life on the Greenwich railway and *Terror*'s came from the Dover line, complete with its original funnel, as Crozier

bemoaned (see his last letter to Ross, below). The shipwrights of the navy's Woolwich shipyard were particularly proud of their new invention whereby the screw propellers could be raised so as to avoid engagement with ice. The expedition was stocked and fully provisioned for at least three years, despite John Barrow's assertion in his proposal that one navigable season of eight weeks could finally deliver the elusive geographical enigma, the north-west sea route to the Orient. Surprisingly, apart from a large supply of warm underclothing and wolf-skin blankets, the crew was dressed in standard navy-issue clothing.

On Sunday 18 May, Sir John Franklin conducted divine service for the first time since he was appointed. Lady Jane, his daughter, Eleanor, and Sophia Cracroft were present. One wonders did she and Crozier have parting words or a glance? Franklin had laid on Sophia 'an earnest charge' to remain with Lady Jane until he came back. From that day for 30 years they were scarcely ever separated.[10] The expedition departed the Thames on 19 May with 133 officers and men, accompanied by a couple of supply vessels as far as Whalefish Islands, Baffin Bay.

Franklin, in a letter to his wife written en route to Greenland, speculated on the need to pass at least one winter in the polar region:

> it is very possible, that our prospects of success and the health of our officers and men might justify our passing a second winter in these regions. If we do not succeed in our attempt, we shall try in other places, and through God's blessing

we hope to set the questions at rest . . . To the Almighty care I commit you and dear Eleanor. I trust He will shield you under His wings and grant the continual aid of His Holy Spirit. Again, that God may bless and support you both is and will be the constant prayer of your most affectionate husband . . .

Crozier was also writing; in what turned out to be his last letter to his friend, Ross – and to Anne, Ross' wife – he expressed his serious misgivings as he embarked on his last Arctic adventure:

All things going well and quietly but we are, I fear, sadly late. From what we can learn, the winter here has been very severe with much easterly wind; there was, however, an early break-up of the ice and the last account of whalers is that fish were plenty and ships as high as Women Isles (73°). What I fear is that, from our being so late, we shall have no time to look round and judge for ourselves, but blunder into the ice and make a second 1824 of it. James, I wish you were here, I would then have no doubt as to our pursuing the proper course. I must be done with this croaking. I am not growling, mind. Indeed I never was less disposed to do so . . . All goes smoothly but, James dear, I am sadly alone, not a soul have I in either ship that I can go and talk to. 'No congenial spirit as it were.' I am generally busy but it is after all a very hermitlike life. Except to kick up a row with the helmsman or abuse Jobson at times I would scarcely ever hear the sound of my voice. The Transport is nearly clear and my sugar and tea have not made an appearance. The sugar is a real loss to me but the tea I care not for. I cannot at all events say much for Fortnum and Mason's punctuality. They directed things to Captain Fitzjames, Terror, but by some strange accident they discovered my name sufficiently accurate to send me the bill and I was fool enough to pay it from their declaring that the things were absolutely delivered on board . . . how I do wish the engine was again on the Dover Line and the Engineer sitting on top of it; he is dead and alive wretch full of difficulties and is now quite dissatisfied because he has not the leading stoker to assist him in doing nothing . . . Well my dear friends I know not what else I can say to you – I feel lonely and when I look back to the last voyage I can see the cause and therefore no prospect of having a more joyous feeling. The bustle of the season will however be life to me and come what may I will endeavour to sit down at the end of it content. I find by the instructions that Fitzjames is appointed to superintend the Mag. Observations. I will therefore take just so much bother as may amuse, without considering myself as one of the Staff.[11]

Crozier's misgivings were soon borne out when he sent home an armourer and a sail-maker, both of whom he considered 'perfectly useless either at their trade or anything else'. He also invalided home two other men, reducing the ship's complement to 62 from the rated 64.

The Admiralty instruction to Franklin was very simply outlined: to enter Lancaster Sound from Baffin Bay; from there to proceed west for about 350 miles to Cape Walker (which was mapped by Parry); from there to seek a route south to the North American coastline; and from there to follow the navigable passage identified by Dease and Simpson to Point Barrow. Dease and Simpson had also outlined the south shores of a number of islands lying to the north of the American mainland. In the event of no success to the south or southwest, they were instructed to go north of the Parry Islands, passing through Wellington Channel, and to seek a route west from there to the Bering Strait.

The fateful ships were seen on 19 July leaving Upernavik off the coast of Greenland, and the last recorded sighting of *Erebus* and *Terror* was on 26 July in latitude 74° 48' north, longitude 66° 13' west by the crew of the whaling ship, *Prince of Wales*. While Franklin and Crozier were waiting for an opportunity to cross Baffin Bay to Lancaster Sound, the whaler was visited by the second-in-command of one of the ships. Captain Dannet declined an invitation to dinner from Franklin, preferring to take advantage of favourable winds. He remarked on the high spirits of Franklin's men. None of those who sailed from there into the Arctic ever returned, and their fate is still shrouded in mystery.

7 _____

# McCLURE, McCLINTOCK AND KELLETT
# SEARCH FOR FRANKLIN

*In Baffin Bay where the whale fish blow*

*The fate of Franklin no man can know*

*The fate of Franklin no one can tell*

*Lord Franklin, his men as well*

FROM 'LADY FRANKLIN'S LAMENT' (TRADITIONAL BALLAD)

The response to the absence of news from the Franklin expedition and the initial organisation of the search is an object lesson in how responsibility and leadership shared or divided in an emergency is inappropriate. The search saga also brings into question the advice and decisions of some of the distinguished experts, including Sabine and Beaufort. A total of 39 expeditions searched for Franklin and his men over eleven years until their fate was known. It was a period of the most heroic and romantic exploits in polar and maritime-exploration history.

The lack of word from *Erebus* and *Terror* eventually raised concern. Dr King, who accompa-nied Sir George Back down the Great Fish River in 1833, urged the Admiralty in 1847 to send a relief party down that river. He also suggested – correctly, it transpired – where the party was likely to have become beset. Had a party been sent to where he suggested at that stage, there is no doubt that some survivors would have been rescued. However, Sir James Clark Ross, whose opinion was sought by the Admiralty, rebutted the persistent Dr King's concern, declaring it premature, and he further expressed strongly his view that there were no circumstances in which the crews would make for the Great Fish River.

When, in 1848, there was still no news of the expedition, Sir John Richardson of the Hudson's Bay Company – whose second-in-command was an Orkney Islander named Dr John Rae – was sent with a Hudson's Bay Company party to check out the coast between the Mackenzie and Coppermine Rivers. Richardson was explicitly instructed not to extend his search to the mouth of the Great Fish River.

As this was happening, James Clark Ross prepared two ships – the *Enterprise* and *Investigator* – to find Franklin. The crew of *Enterprise*, under the command of Ross, were largely Irish and Scottish. The *Investigator* was commanded by Captain Bird who, like Ross and Crozier, had been on many of Parry's Arctic expeditions and had also been with Ross on *Erebus* to Antarctica. Their motivation this time was not scientific but humanitarian, and it would be difficult not to admire the enthusiasm, chivalry and romance of their actions.

## Robert LeMesurier McClure

Ross' first lieutenant on *Enterprise* was a Wexfordman, Robert McClure, who had voyaged on *Terror* with George Back to Repulse Bay in 1836–37. McClure was a tough man with an iron nerve; he was well up to his work and had a strict approach to duty. When *Terror* was being commissioned by Back in 1836, Sir Charles Adam, the first sea lord, sent for McClure and exclaimed as he entered the room: 'McClure, you're just the man we want. There is an Arctic expedition fitting out, will you join?' McClure was unsure. He went to the waiting room to think it over. The old porter asked him what was on his mind. McClure told him. 'Well,' said the porter, 'I saw Nelson on that very chair, thinking what he would do, and he took what they offered him.' McClure took the old porter's advice.[1] Ann Savours tells us that

in June 1836, when staying with friends, on his way to visit his recently bereaved

mother and sister in Ireland after an absence of nine years, McClure was introduced to a senior naval officer who might help to advance him in the Service. He learnt that nothing could be done for him in his then post of Chief Mate of a revenue cutter, but that his promotion 'might almost be reckoned a certainty' if he joined the *Terror*, then fitting out for her Arctic voyage. He was only allowed four hours to decide, 'so that in the space of a short time the whole career of my life was altered, my promised visit to my mother and dear sister annulled and in three days I was installed in my new office . . .'[2]

McClure went on to command the first expedition to survive while making the Northwest Passage, crossing from the Pacific to the Atlantic. His Arctic adventures were dashing and daring, but he is often accused of having been ambitious and more concerned to discover and complete the first passage than with the fate of Franklin and his men. Indeed, his harsh treatment of his officers and crew was in stark contrast to the caring culture developed by Parry and his disciples, including Crozier and Bird. In his Arctic exploits, McClure was fortunate to have linked up with two other distinguished Irish naval officers, Captain Henry Kellett of Clonacody, Co. Tipperary and the second lieutenant of the *Enterprise*, Leopold McClintock from Dundalk, Co. Louth. All three were to retire at the end of their long careers knighted and with the rank of admiral (McClintock) or vice admiral (McClure and Kellett).

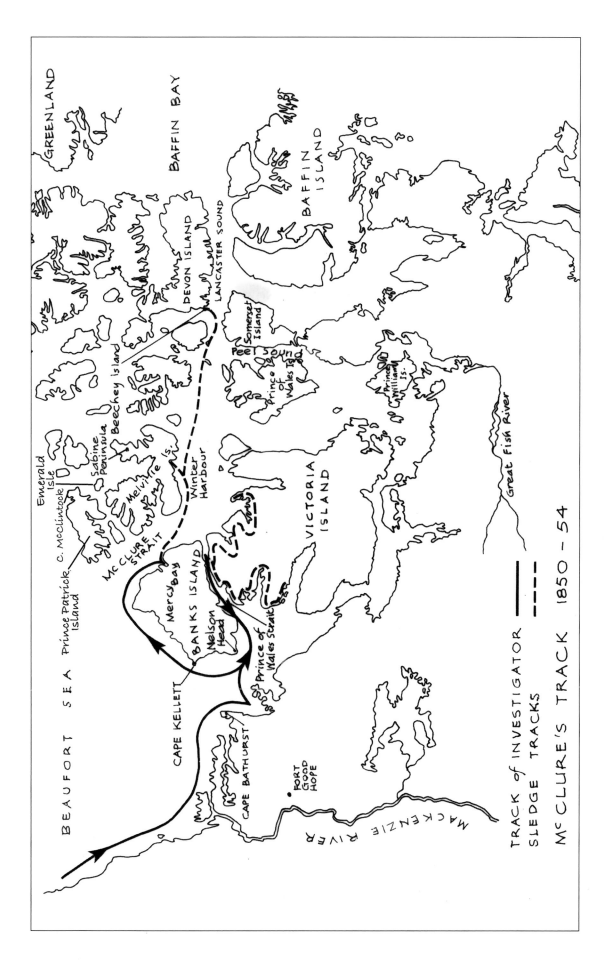

GREENLAND

BAFFIN BAY

BAFFIN ISLAND

DEVON ISLAND

LANCASTER SOUND

Somerset Island

Peel Sound

Prince of Wales Isd

Prince of Wales Isd.

Prince William Is.

Beechey Island

Sabine Peninsula

Emerald Isle

C. McClintock

Melville Is.

Winter Harbour

Prince Patrick Island

BEAUFORT SEA

McCLURE STRAIT

Mercy Bay

BANKS ISLAND

VICTORIA ISLAND

Great Fish River

CAPE KELLETT

Nelson Head

Prince of Wales Strait

CAPE BATHURST

FORT GOOD HOPE

MACKENZIE RIVER

TRACK OF INVESTIGATOR ━━━━━
SLEDGE TRACKS ┅┅┅┅

McCLURE'S TRACK  1850 - 54

Robert McClure was born at the rectory, Main Street, Wexford on 28 January 1807 – five months after his father's death. His father, also Robert – a native of Co. Derry – had been a captain in the 89th Regiment and was mortally wounded at the Battle of Aboukir, in Egypt, under General Abercrombie; his mother, Jane, was the daughter of Archdeacon Elgee, rector of Wexford.[3] They were married at Castlebridge in Co. Wexford on 20 February 1806. Captain – later General – John LeMesurier of Alderney, an old comrade of Robert snr. was the young Robert's godfather and guardian. The Church of Ireland registry of baptisms, marriages and burials for the period[4] also records the second marriage of Jane McClure (widow) to Captain Poole Morphy of the Kilkenny Militia on 20 June 1810. Jane McClure's brother, Charles, was educated at Trinity College, Dublin, and practiced as a solicitor in that city. He married Sarah Kingsbury on 23 December 1809; they had three children, the youngest girl named Jane Francesca. She married the brilliant eye-and-ear surgeon, Dr William Wilde, at St Peter's Church, Westland Row in Dublin on 12 November 1852.[5] During the years of the Famine, Jane, using her *non de plume*, 'Speranza', electrified Ireland with her passionate and patriotic tirades of verse and prose against the English. Her youngest son, Oscar, was the poet and dramatist, Oscar Wilde. Robert LeMesurier McClure was therefore Oscar Wilde's first cousin, once removed.

McClure went to live with his godfather, General John LeMesurier, when aged four, and was educated at Eton and Sandhurst before enlisting in the navy in 1824. He passed his examination in 1830 and, in 1836–37, was mate of the *Terror* under Captain George Back. On the return of *Terror* from Repulse Bay in the Arctic in September 1837, McClure was promoted to the rank of lieutenant. During 1838–39, he was serving on board the *Niagara* – the flagship of Commodore Sandom – on the Canadian lakes during the rebellion. From 1839–42, McClure served aboard the *Pilot* in the West Indies. From 1842–46, in Havana, he had command of the *Romney*, a receiving ship, and in December 1846, he was appointed to the coastguard which he left in 1848 to go as first lieutenant of the *Enterprise* under Captain Bird in the Arctic voyage of Sir James Clark Ross.[6]

*Leopold McClintock*

This first Franklin search-and-rescue expedition also introduced to the Arctic the very talented Leopold McClintock, born and reared in Dundalk, Co. Louth. He was to become one of the greatest Arctic explorers; it was he who was largely responsible for developing a more efficient mode of sledge travel which expanded the capacity of naval expeditions to carry out extensive surveys and explorations, working from ships often beset in ice. His biographer, Sir Clements Markham, said of him:

McClintock was always calm to outward seeming, and inclined to be reticent, but his persistent and untiring efforts during the long course of years proved that the sacred fire burnt with more than passing ardour in his breast.

McClintock's family was of Scottish origin, having descended from Alexander McClintock who settled near Derry at about the time of the Plantation of Ulster early in the seventeenth century. In Co. Louth, John McClintock of Drumcar was a substantial landed proprietor and MP who represented Enniskillen and Belturbet in the Irish House of Commons. In 1766, he married Patience, daughter of William Foster, MP for Co. Louth and first cousin of John Foster, speaker of the House of Commons. The youngest son of this marriage, Henry, joined the 3rd Dragoon Guards as a cornet; on his retirement and through family interest, he was appointed to the office of collector of customs at Dundalk. He married Elizabeth Mellisina, daughter of the Rev Dr Fleury DD, archdeacon of Waterford. She was a pretty woman of remarkable ability and energy. The archdeacon was of an old Huguenot family, from near La Rochelle, and his wife was English.

Francis Leopold was the second son; his elder brother, Louis, died young. There were twelve children in all – five boys and seven girls. His father was a very popular man, a musician, a good horse rider and sportsman. From a very young age, Francis wanted to go to sea, and later recalled three reasons for his having joined the navy: firstly, because his cousin, W. Bunbury McClintock, was a sailor; secondly, because of his attraction to a print of Admiral Berkeley in his splendid uniform which hung in his father's room; and lastly, because he was told that knowledge of Latin was not required to join the navy. His education commenced in a dame school, and when he was eleven years of age, he was sent to Dundalk grammar school. It was during his

second year there that his wish came true.[7]

His entry into the navy came about when Captain Charles H. Paget was commissioning the *Samarang* and had no one in particular to whom he wanted to give the appointment of a first-class volunteer (entitled 'naval cadet' since 1843). He transferred his patronage to his first lieutenant, W. Bunbury McClintock, who at once offered the appointment to his Uncle Henry for his son who wanted to go to sea. The letter was dated 20 June 1831 and the boy was to leave for Portsmouth at once. Young Leopold – who weighed 68 pounds and was 4-foot 6-inches tall – left Dundalk on the mail coach under the charge of Mr Perkins, a tide waiter in the Dundalk custom house. They reached Dublin at 6 a.m. the following morning – 21 June – and embarked on board the steamer for Bristol. A 25-hour voyage was followed by a coach journey of eight to ten hours that brought them to Portsmouth. His appointment was dated 22 June 1831. Mr Perkins' parting words to Leopold were: 'Good bye master Leopold, and never turn your back to the enemy while you have a face to face him with.'[8]

The *Samarang* sailed from Spithead in July 1831 under orders to the South American station, stopping at the Azores, bound for Rio de Janeiro. Leopold quickly found his sea legs and life was pleasant aboard a happy ship. He had a very lucky escape while climbing aloft; he suffered a rope burn in descent and let go, falling 60 feet; fortunately, he landed on a coiled rope. The commission lasted nearly four years, visiting ports on both of the South American seaboards, and this gave Leopold a sound introduction to a career at sea. Training in the navy at that time, Clements

Markham tells us, consisted of seamanship, in all details, acquired through practice and constant study. Captain Paget liked the blue-eyed Leopold; he told him once; 'If he had a sister like him, he would marry her.' Leopold did indeed have a sister, named Caroline, who the smart Captain Paget married in 1840.

When the *Samarang* tied up after three years and eight months, McClintock was fifteen years old and an experienced watchkeeper and sailor. On his next ship, the *Carron*, a steamer, he was the only midshipman aboard; it introduced him to surveying work, conducted round the Isle of Man. While on leave, which was unpaid between commissions, he went shooting and fishing in the River Fane with his father. By nature inquisitive, he climbed the steeple of the church in Dundalk to inspect its beautiful 'green stone', which he was to discover was merely wood covered with copper.

For the next nine years, McClintock served on a range of ships, including HMS *Hercules* in the Channel fleet from 1836–37; then on the corvette, HMS *Crocodile*, in the West Indies from November 1837; having passed his exams for seamanship, he became acting mate. Off Cuba, they chased and captured a slaver named *Mercedita*, on her way to the west coast of Africa to embark slaves. McClintock was chosen as one of the twelve crew members to convey her to Havana where the prize court declared her a lawful capture. McClintock's share was a princely £6 or £7. *Crocodile* sailed to Quebec and Newfoundland where the officers spent some time shooting and fishing.

McClintock came home to pass his exams for lieutenant. He was appointed to *Excellence* and,

at the Royal Naval College, obtained a first-class certificate in steam machinery and practical observations, and a second-class certificate in mathematics. He also received his certificate as gunnery officer from the captain of *Excellence*. At 24 years of age, he combined the practical skills of seaman, gunnery officer, navigator and surveyor with an understanding of the command and management of men.

McClintock was well aware of the revolution regarding steam and the construction of ships, and his next appointment was a very significant one in the history of steam-powered ships in the navy. The *Gorgon*, when it was commissioned, was the navy's twenty-first steamer and, at 1,142 tons, over 400 tons heavier than the next largest navy steamship up to that time. McClintock was appointed one of the two mates; the other, Cooper Key, like McClintock, was also later to become an admiral. This appointment gave him an opportunity to demonstrate his ability and steadiness when the ship ran aground and was buried in 13 feet of sand off Montevideo while they were offering protection to British subjects from General Manual Orbit, who had Montevideo under siege. McClintock proved invaluable to Captain Hotham, a very inventive man who began an amazing salvage operation which, after five months of incessant labour, was successful in refloating the ship. It was estimated that in the course of the work, the men excavated 19,000 tons of sand manually. In a letter to McClintock's mother, Captain Hotham praised her son's contribution to the emergency:

The ship your son is serving in now lies

aground in a situation which renders her removal difficult beyond measure. It is on these occasions that a captain forms his opinion as to the abilities and merits of his several officers; and I can confidently assure you that none stands higher in my estimation than your son. He is without exception one of the steadiest, most zealous and excellent young men ever served with, and is deserving of his promotion or any other favour the Admiralty might confer upon him.[9]

On the recommendation of Captain Hotham, McClintock was commissioned as an acting lieutenant by the commander-in-chief of the Brazilian station, Commodore Purvis. It was the first of three promotions he was to receive for special service in his career.

In February 1843, McClintock's father died at Dundalk from fever; his mother moved to 2 Gardiner Place, Dublin. Three of his sisters were already married, including Caroline to Captain Paget. McClintock had been very fond of his old home at Dundalk and his native Cooley mountains on the nearby Carlingford peninsula. He was a great walker and very fond of shooting and fishing, both of which were plentiful in the neighbourhood of Dundalk. McClintock was a very good shot and a thorough sportsman. He also had an interest in prehistory, antiquities – with which the vicinity abounded – and was fond of exploring the numerous cromlechs, Danish forts and caves that are to be found in the area.

In April 1845, McClintock was appointed as lieutenant aboard the *Frolic*, a sixteen-gun brig in service in the River Plate.[10] After two years at the Brazilian station, McClintock passed some months with his mother in Dublin before going to study on half pay at the naval college in Portsmouth. At that time, Sir James Clark Ross was recruiting a crew for *Enterprise* and *Investigator* to go in search of Franklin and McClintock's countryman, Francis Crozier from Banbridge in neighbouring Co. Down.[11] Through the recommendation of Captain William Smith, his old friend from his first ship, *Samarang*, Leopold McClintock was appointed second lieutenant on *Enterprise*. This was the start of the Arctic career of one of Ireland's – and perhaps one of the navy's – greatest polar explorers; a man who developed and fine-tuned the strategic exploration potential of a ship as a base for sledging in polar regions.

While McClintock was busy fitting out *Enterprise* at Woolwich, he found time to visit Westminster Abbey and, in a letter to his sister, Emma, wrote in fun that among the monuments to the great departed, he had found a place for himself. The *Enterprise* and *Investigator* left the Thames in May 1848. On 7 June, Cape Farewell on the southern tip of Greenland was sighted. Soon after, he saw his first icebergs and was soon among polar ice. On 20 August, the ships reached open water at the northern end of Baffin Bay and, ten days later, were entering Lancaster Sound. In September, they found a safe anchorage at Port Leopold in North Somerset where they overwintered in bleak conditions until the arrival of spring. They then commenced preparations for overland sledge journeys.

McClintock's closest friend on the *Enterprise* was the assistant surgeon, Dr Henry Mathias, a

Dubliner who had studied medicine at the College of Surgeons, Dublin. He was a well-read, agreeable and good-natured fellow, and a favourite on *Enterprise*. On 27 February, an outing was organised to climb up the north-east bluff, a steep ascent of 800 feet which developed into a race to see the returning sun after the long winter. The race was won by one of the officers, Mr Court, who was aided by the use of a coal scraper in each hand. The temperature was -49°F (-45°C). It was a cheering event, but poor Dr Mathias, one of those who climbed the height, was within days spitting blood and gradually losing strength. He died of phthisis – a wasting illness – on 15 June 1849.[12]

The third lieutenant on *Enterprise* was the son of the harbour master at Dublin, Lieutenant W.H.J. 'Willie' Browne; he was four years younger than McClintock. A born artist, he had passed his early youth in the merchant navy. It was at Fiji that his extraordinary talents gained for him an appointment as master's assistant in the *Sulphur*; he afterwards became mate under the notoriously tough Sir Edward Belcher, a position he held for six years. Working so close to Belcher is reputed to have turned his hair grey. But his skills and taste as an artist were undiminished, and he was a great acquisition.[13]

On 15 May, the two sledge parties set out, comprising twelve men each. One party was sent

HMS *Enterprise* and *Investigator* – the first ships to search for Franklin – with the Devil's Thumb in the background. Painted by Lieutenant William Browne, son of the harbour master of Dublin port.
*From* Ten Coloured Views, *W.H. Brown*

to Fury Beach to ascertain if any of Franklin's men had visited there. Ross himself took part in a longer journey with McClintock to the northern and western shores of North Somerset. On the way, a headland between Cape Clarence and Garnier Bay was named Cape McClintock. From Cape Bunny, the party followed the coastline, turned south and reached the furthest point on 6 June; they named it Four River Bay. McClintock walked on some miles and saw land for a distance of 50 miles. He named the most distant headland, Cape Bird, in honour of the captain of *Investigator*. A cairn was built and a record of progress was deposited. They were unaware of how close they were to finding the missing Franklin ships.

The return trip was one of extreme hardship. Constant exposure and insufficient food caused four of the men to break down, and one had to be carried on the sledge. But they had completed the longest sledge journey made up to that time: 500 miles in 39 days. McClintock noted everything and learned a number of lessons from the experience: inadequate meat – the stipulated pound of meat per day in their diet contained too much bone; overly heavy loads on the sledges; inefficient spirit stoves resulting in cold food. He saw the potential of sledge travel and was determined to make improvements.

Meanwhile, two smaller sledge parties had set out on 31 May, one led by Lieutenant Browne who, with four men, crossed Prince Regent Inlet, built a cairn near the northern end of Brodeur Peninsula and returned to the ships on 8 June. Another party, led by Lieutenant Barnard, crossed to Devon Island, returning on 5 June.

With the advent of summer, the lack of fresh meat and vegetables resulted in an outbreak of scurvy. On the *Enterprise*, both Captain Ross and his first lieutenant, Robert McClure, were victims. The management of the ship devolved to McClintock who organised the cutting of a canal through the ice toward open water and made preparation for the summer sailing programme. Most urgently, he mustered shooting parties to provide fresh meat for the sick. It is interesting to note that they were able to shoot 2,300 birds, which yielded 30 pounds of meat per man.

It was late August before they could escape winter quarters and begin a search of Barrow Strait and Melville Island, but the conditions prevented them carrying out their planned itinerary; they got caught in the ice and for three weeks drifted with the flow into Baffin Bay from Lancaster Sound. A change in conditions freed them on 24 September, but the season was gone and Ross decided to set sail for home. The frigate, *North Star*, was sent in spring with stores to supply them for another winter but was unable to get through the ice of Melville Bay in time, and the crews were forced to winter in Wolstenholme Sound on the Greenland coast. They did get through the following summer, landing a depot of provisions at Admiralty Inlet in Lancaster Sound before returning home.

On 5 November 1849, *Enterprise* and *Investigator* reached Scarborough. The crews hoped to find that Franklin had returned safely before them, but there was still no news. They had added a further 250 kilometres of charted coastline to the maps of the region, and carried out an eighteen-month continuous record of meteorological observation together with geological observations. The crews were paid off on 26 November. It also brought to an end the polar careers of Ross and Bird, which had started when both were midshipmen to Parry. In Dublin's Christchurch Cathedral, the officers of the Arctic expedition composed of *Enterprise* and *Investigator* erected a marble memorial to Henry Mathias, assistant surgeon of HMS *Enterprise*, 'who departed this life June 15th 1849 in his 28th year, at Port Leopold lat 74° N.' This finely sculpted memorial to the first volunteer lost in the noble quest for Franklin was erected 'as a just tribute to his varied talents and great moral worth' and can be viewed in the crypt by visitors today.

There was an immediate increase in the public's demand for a new search and the government was forced to put adequate resources into the operation, even now, when it was clear to many it was too late. The *Enterprise* and *Investigator* were re-commissioned to go by way of the Pacific to the Bering Strait under the overall command of Captain Richard Collinson, on *Enterprise*, with Robert McClure – then aged 43 and in his first captaincy – in charge of *Investigator*. In support was the supply ship, HMS *Plover*, under the command of Commander T.E.L. Moore, supported by Captain Henry Kellett aboard HMS *Herald*, which was engaged in surveying work in the Pacific.

The *Herald* left Panama on 9 May 1848, reaching Kotzebue Sound, Alaska on 14 September. Two weeks later, when *Plover* failed to show, Kellett returned south to winter in Hawaii. It had been intended that *Plover*, a depot ship, would be stationed near Cape Barrow to wait with supplies for Franklin. Sailing from Hawaii in August, *Plover* made a long, slow voyage around the western end of the Aleutian Islands to the Bering Strait, not reaching its intended rendezvous point with *Herald* until mid-October – a month after Kellett had left. Moore overwintered at Providence Bay (Bukhta Provideniya) on the coast of Chukotka where he enjoyed 'excellent relations' with the local Chukchi villagers.

There were a number of Irishmen among the crews on both the *Herald* and *Plover*. It seems that crew changes between the ships occurred regularly as part of the support the *Herald* and *Plover* offered to other ships searching for Franklin. Among the men listed in the muster books are many with names associated with Co. Cork and Munster. Many of them are listed as recipients of the Arctic Medal, awarded to all who participated in the search for the Northwest Passage and the search for Franklin (1818–55): Patrick Fitzgerald, *Herald* and *Plover*, 1848–51; John McCarthy, *Plover*, 1848–54, who served as captain of the mast and captain of the foretop, to whom an Arctic Medal was issued; William McCarthy, *Plover*, 1848–54, an ordinary seaman, took part in the boat's expedition to the Mackenzie River from 25 July 1849; he was issued with an Arctic Medal; William McCarthy, an ordinary seaman, *Herald*, 1848–51, had no medal issued; Patrick Sweeney, *Herald*, 1848–51, who served as captain of the maintop and as an AB; Peter Sweeney, *Herald*, 1848–51, possibly related to Patrick Sweeney as they were both from Co. Cork though with thirteen years between them; no medal issued. This may be the same man who served in *Rodney* during the Crimean War and after whom an officially impressed medal exists.[14]

In 1850, a squadron was assembled under the command of Captain Horatio T. Austin to search from the Atlantic. Two barque-rigged vessels, *Resolute* and *Assistance*, sailed with the screw steamers, *Pioneer* and *Intrepid*. Accompanying the expedition were the brigs, *Lady Franklin* and *Sophia*, under the command of an experienced whaling captain named Penny. Captain Austin of *Resolute* was the son of a lieutenant who had served under Nelson; he himself had served as lieutenant on HMS *Fury*, commanded by H.P. Hoppner, during Parry's third Arctic voyage, where Austin gained much experience of ice

work during their long period of besetment. He subsequently developed an expertise in steam with service aboard the battleship, HMS *Blenheim*, and was in charge of the steam reserve at Portsmouth when called for service to search for Franklin. McClintock was promoted to first lieutenant under Captain Erasmus Ommanney on *Assistance*. Lieutenant George Francis Mecham, who was born in Cove, Co. Cork in 1828, was second lieutenant. He had entered the navy as a boy in 1841, serving in the *Ardent* under Captain Russell in whose honour he later named his discovery, Russell Island. A midshipman aboard the *Constance* in the Pacific from 1846–48, he was described by Markham as tall and handsome, a

This picture of a sledge encampment depicts the teamwork inherent in Arctic sledge travelling, as perfected by Leopold McClintock during the Austin search expedition of 1850–51.
*From* Life of Admiral F.L. McClintock, *Sir Clements Markham*

good officer, a thorough seaman, an artist and well informed.[15]

When the *Enterprise* had been paid off, McClintock had gone home to Dublin where he studied sledge travel in detail. In preparing for the multi-vessel expedition, Captain Austin delegated to McClintock the responsibility for victualling and the preparation of all materials for the sledge parties. Leopold took full advantage to arrange everything according to his innovative specifications; this included three years' provisions for the voyage. Captain Austin, who had a reputation for great organisation, personally supervised the adaptation of the ships for winter comfort, including the fixing of a Sylvester stove and warm-air ducts round the living decks. The perfect health of all four crews was due to him.

On 15 April 1850, the little squadron was ready and moved up the Thames to Greenhithe to check their compass swing. Before travelling back to the Arctic, Austin received a letter from Lady Franklin. Dated 30 April 1850, in it she wrote:

> I look to your travelling parties on ice as our main grounds of hope; and I am sure that everything where human ingenuity can devise will be thought of and devised by you. I have entire confidence in you, and I only make it my request that you will all remember that your lives are excessively precious to me, and that even the restoration of him who is most dear to me would be dearly purchased at the expense of those who nobly risk all to save him and his devoted companions.

McClintock carried with him a letter from Mr W. Crozier, addressed to his uncle, Captain Francis Crozier of the *Terror*. McClintock, by letter, assured Mr Crozier that 'success in our present expedition is the summit of all my waking dreams' and 'I shall take that letter when I go travelling in case I should be the fortunate one to find our missing countrymen.'[16]

The Atlantic crossed and Cape Farewell sighted, Whalefish Islands were reached on 15 June; the transfer of supplies took a week to complete. The steam-powered and sharp-bowed vessels, *Pioneer* and *Intrepid*, were engaged with the Melville Bay ice, taking 45 days to break through. The ice was cut with a saw, charged at by the vessels and blasted with gunpowder before Cape York was reached. Clements Markham recorded that aboard *Assistance*, they sang the sea shanty 'Heave Round Rodney' during the 45-day detention in Melville Bay. Here, they also encountered a little schooner, *Prince Albert*, which had been fitted out and financed by Lady Franklin to search Prince Regent Inlet. Having reached that point, the captain returned without probing the place Lady Jane had intuitively selected for a search. In all, twelve ships were searching for Franklin and his men in 1850, including two American vessels from New York, the *Advance* and *Rescue*, both financed by a philanthropist named Grinnell.

Austin's squadron moved into Lancaster Sound and toward Beechey Island, off North Devon. A shore party landed at Cape Riley and found the remains of a camp, suggesting Franklin had wintered thereabouts. McClintock favoured a thorough search, but the sight of open water convinced Captain Ommanney to proceed; the search of Beechey Island was left to *Pioneer*, *Resolute* and the American ships. Search parties from these ships discovered the graves of three sailors at Beechey Island – one from *Terror* and two from *Erebus* – and identified the base of a magnetic-observation station. They also found many empty food tins and other signs of Franklin's winter quarters, but no official records. Still not knowing the cause of the disappearance, they had no clue as to where to target further searches.

When ice prevented further progress, Austin's squadron set up winter quarters at Griffith Island and Cornwallis Island. McClintock's first innovation was to stockpile a supply depot 30 miles from their base. With two sledges, he set out on 2 October, before the onset of winter. On board the squadron's ships, winter was a much more comfortable affair than in the previous year, with an adequate supply of food, organised exercise, lectures, theatre and other entertainments to relieve the boredom of the long Arctic nights. This was in keeping with Austin's view that essential for the preservation of health was good and wholesome food, warm clothing, dry and well-ventilated lodgings, cleanliness and plenty of exercise. No one felt more strongly than McClintock about the need to keep mind and body alert; his view was that the mind reacts on the body and that all tendency to dullness or despondency must be dispelled by continuous amusements, courses of instruction and social intercourse. Each ship produced its own journal, while Willie Browne walked everyday from *Resolute* to *Assistance* to paint the magnificent

proscenium for a theatrical event. It was painted as masonry, with two Doric columns, a vase of flowers on either side and the royal arms above. Dr Ede sculpted two life-sized statues in snow of the Prince of Wales and the Princess Royal.

Austin established a sledge committee but left most of the details to McClintock. His first step was to establish depots for the spring journey. In the construction of sledges, he became the acknowledged expert. They were mainly constructed of Canada elm, with crossbars of ash. The upper and lower pieces were called the bearer and runner. The uprights had tenon joints, a shoeing an eighth of an inch thick, iron 3-inches wide and slightly convex on its under-surface. The length of a sledge depended on how many men were to work it: a 13-foot sledge required ten men, a 9-footer required six (in addition to the officer, who would scout ahead). Each sledge weighed 125 pounds and carried a waterproof tray or boat for ferrying the sledge across water; this weighed 115 pounds. The team of men was equipped with a tent – 8-foot high, 15-foot long and erected with four poles (55 pounds) – seven sleeping bags (42 pounds), groundsheet (12 pounds), a single buffalo-skin robe (40 pounds) and a spirit cooker, kettle and stand (combined weight, 17 pounds). In total, a weight of 406 pounds, to which was added food and fuel. The provisions and fuel for seven men for 40 days weighed 876 pounds which, when combined with the constant 440 pounds, gave a total starting-out weight of 1,316 pounds, or nearly 220 pounds hauling weight per man, reducing by 22 pounds per day.[17] By putting out depots in advance and by adding auxiliary

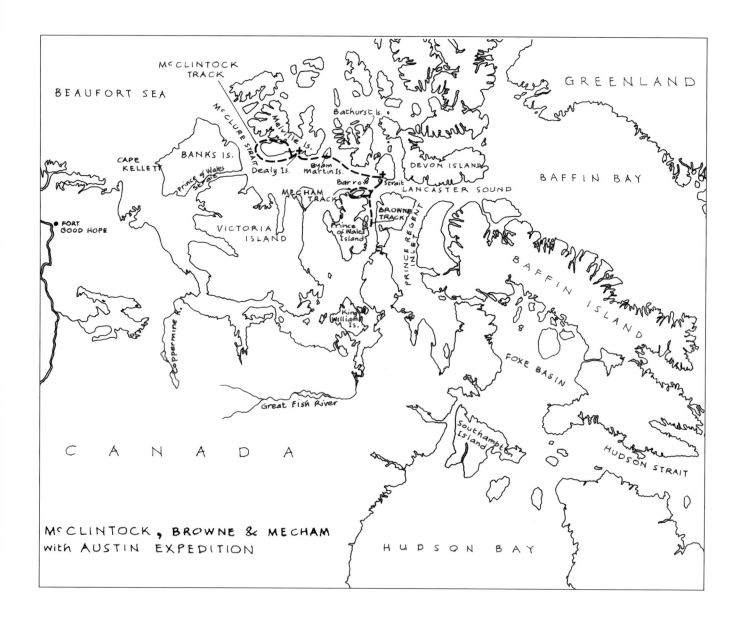

MᶜCLINTOCK, BROWNE & MECHAM
with AUSTIN EXPEDITION

sledges, McClintock could top up supplies, enabling parties to stay out longer and increase their effective range. This plan allowed Austin tremendous scope to search for Franklin and Crozier's men. He had 220 men to select from, when the crews of Captain Penny's ships were added, and each sledge party had a name, motto and flag. McClintock's sledge party's name was 'Perseverance', his motto, 'Perseverance to the end'. Lieutenant Willie Browne's party's name was 'Enterprise', his motto more poetic: 'Gaze where

some distant speck asail implies, with all the thirsting eye of enterprise'.

With the return of the sun, Austin sent out search parties in seven different directions; they covered 7,025 statute miles, including the discovery and charting of 1,225 miles of new territory. Frederick Mecham was away for 28 days and travelled 236 miles, discovering Russell Island. McClintock and his party were away for 80 days and covered 770 miles, dragging the sledge at a daily rate of 10.5 miles. On the return journeys, the summer sledging proved more difficult. The ice crust occasionally collapsed under their weight, sinking them into pools of ice-cold water, or they would be trapped on top of floes surrounded by melt water, which often had to be waded through. They travelled at night and slept during the daytime, breakfasting at 6 p.m. After pitching tents, the floor cloth was installed, the sleeping bags laid out as was the buffalo robe, which would cover them all. Each man took it in turn to cook, supper consisting of pemmican, biscuit and grog. With boots removed, frostbite and snowblindness were treated before the men retired to their sleeping bags. Songs and stories followed until all were asleep.[18] Breakfast consisted of cocoa or tea and biscuit at 6 p.m. Lunch was a short break of hard-frozen pork fat, biscuit and a tot of rum.

Among the many sledge parties searching Prince of Wales Island, Bathurst Island, Cornwallis Island, Melville Island, Byam Martin Island, and the smaller Griffith, Lowther, Garrett and Russell islands, there was only one death from frostbite and three amputations of toes. Despite this, Austin's multi-ship expedition was one of the happiest and healthiest. It was also one of the most successful in eliminating many of the possible search areas. In profiling McClintock's own team's achievement, Markham tells us how their spirit and cheerfulness seemed to prevail above all other qualities. He also notes that John Salmon, a small and wiry man from Carlingford, Co. Louth – a neighbour of McClintock who had been with him on *Enterprise* – was the strongest of his team and that Jim Heels,[19] a 24-year-old marine, sang a good song. The expedition completed extensive coastal surveys and made observations regarding geology, fauna, topography and meteorology. McClintock himself had gained more Arctic experience, as did a new cohort of enthusiastic and accomplished naval officers including Sherard Osborn, Frederick Mecham and Vesey Hamilton, all of them keen on Arctic exploration. However, none of the search parties found any sign or evidence of Franklin's passing. This was in spite of the fact that one of the sledge parties, led by Willie Browne, had searched down the east coast of Prince of Wales Island. He appears to have been in the right place, or to have at least travelled parallel to the direction in which it is now believed the two lost ships sailed.

To access open water in the next navigable season, they had to cut and blast lanes for the ships; this they accomplished on 11 August. They proceeded to search Jones Sound with the *Pioneer* and *Intrepid*, while the *Assistance* checked out Cary Islands in Baffin Bay. *Intrepid* had a severe altercation with a floe and an iceberg, which resulted at one stage in the vessel being lifted 40 feet up the iceberg by ice pressure, only for the pressure to suddenly release and drop the ship and her crew into the water, luckily right-side up. The squadron returned to England on 4 October 1851.

# 8

## McCLURE AND *INVESTIGATOR* SEARCH FROM THE PACIFIC

*To him [Robert McClure] belongs the honour of first navigating the Arctic Sea along the American Coast, and the discovery of Prince of Wales Strait . . . neither of us have succeeded in the grand object which animated our endeavours; but he, being first in the field, has added greatly to our geographical knowledge.*

CAPTAIN RICHARD COLLINSON

While Austin and company were approaching from the eastern Atlantic via Baffin Bay, *Enterprise* and *Investigator*, supported by the *Plover*, had been sent to search for Franklin from the western Pacific via the Bering Strait. The squadron left Plymouth on 20 January 1850.

Both Collinson and McClure were tough, ambitious men; Collinson's motto was 'Discipline is essential for comfort'. McClure's rise to fame and rank had been painfully slow, and now – at 43 years of age – he had for the first time his own ship to command, with orders to find

Franklin via Cape Horn and the Bering Strait, albeit as second-in-command to Captain Collinson. McClure was determined to avail of this opportunity to earn a reputation for himself as a commander. He appears to have had a split personality, something revealed in both his painted portrait and in conflicting accounts of his character. His portrait shows him tall and erect, dressed in his hunting jacket and with a rifle strapped to his back, a telescope underarm. He looks impressive, self-assured and determined, but there is also a noticeable softness communicated through his blue eyes. This is consistent with the narrative of his passage, which was edited – ghostwritten, in fact – by Sherard Osborn. Markham tells us Sir Sherard Osborn was given all of McClure's papers and journals, and the narrative was completed in 1856 on board HMS *Medusa* in the Sea of Azov.[1] McClure is presented as a Victorian upholder of naval discipline and rules, with a 'granite-like view of duty'; a hero who was 'stern, cool, bold in all perils, severe as a disciplinarian, self-reliant and yet modest as becomes an officer'. Others viewed him as a ruthless glory-seeker with an iron nerve, more determined to find the Northwest Passage than to seek out Franklin and Crozier and their men. McClure is also accused of harshly treating his officers and crew; on one occasion, he gave the cook 48 lashes for swearing. We have two other narratives of the historic voyage of the *Investigator* (1850–54): one from the ship's surgeon, Alexander Armstrong, and the other from the ship's Eskimo interpreter, a German named Johann Miertsching, giving us three perspectives on the character of McClure from which to choose.

Ominously, just four days out from England and with a full press of sail, the *Investigator* encountered a squall which carried away the foremost topmast, fore and main-topgallant, and other masts and booms, leaving her a near wreck. *Investigator* sailed via the Magellan Strait, where she was towed through the channel by McClintock's former steamship, the *Gorgon*. They stopped at a place called Fort Famine, in Chilean territory, where the governor was an Irishman – Captain Dunn – and where three of the crew were invalided home by the ship's surgeon; they were sent aboard *Gorgon* for homeward transit.[2]

Johann August Miertsching, a German missionary who had previously spent time with Eskimos in Labrador and who was travelling with the expedition as an interpreter, wrote in his journal about the crew of *Investigator*: 'I feel as if my lot had been cast among half a hundred devils.' He also recorded a storm on 15 May and its aftermath, which explains a lot about McClure

and the quality of his officers and crew:

Last night a terrific squall; everybody, even the captain, feared that the ship was lost. We sailed by some coral reefs, and saw a large fragment of mast floating in the sea. 7am – another squall struck us with an overpowering blast, smashed the three top masts, two yards, flying jib, and the main boom and sail was blown away. This happened while the First Lieutenant, who was an officer of the watch, had quitted the deck for a few minutes; the ship now more than ever, was wallowing amid the waves – the fury of the captain was terrible, positively inhuman. The work which now began with the crippled ship was most difficult; for each man must hold on with one hand and work with the other, with the ship rolling and the waves breaking in cataracts over all.[3]

His report of the following day is in similar vein:

Praise and thanks to the Lord for this disastrous day is over; it has been the most unpleasant that I have yet experienced on board. I kept myself as much as possible to the dampness of my cabin, far from those exasperating folk; for yesterday the devil held high festival on our ship. Now the ship lies helpless, and only on the lower masts are a few sails spread; spare mast there are none; today stout yards are rigged in the place of masts. This morning there was held a solemn inquiry or trial of the

seamen and officers; the outcome was that Lieutenant Haswell was placed under arrest; he is under guard of two armed marines.[4]

It appears First Lieutenant Haswell's performance was impaired by sickness and that the ship had almost capsized a few hours earlier. Four men went overboard, attached to a jib boom; they were recovered by the fast work of their shipmates in getting a lifebuoy to them and getting a boat manned and into the water; tenaciously clinging to the spars, they were brought back to safety.

As a result of the damage wrought by the storm, the performance of *Investigator* was poor; it was not until 29 June that they sighted the snow-capped peak of Mona-Roa, 40 miles distant, on the Island of Owhyhee.[5] They had arrived later than planned at Hawaii, having completed 15,000 miles of a sea voyage. McClure was further shocked to discover that Collinson had already left for the Bering Strait and appeared determined to proceed with the supply vessel, *Plover*, and without *Investigator*, the assigned consort. McClure managed to hastily restock his ship at Honolulu and depart on 4 July with a solitary bullock, a dozen sheep and fresh vegetables sufficient to last only 40 days. He also conducted a sort of court martial, or rather, a court of inquiry, aboard *Investigator*. Miertsching tells us that, after a five-hour debate, the officers promised the captain exact obedience. He also tells us that on the day of departure, the sergeant and his

McClure's ship, HMS *Investigator*, passing through a narrow channel of grounded and pack ice. By Lieutenant S. Gurney Cresswell.
*From A Series of Eight Sketches in Colour, S. Gurney Cresswell*

marines escorted from the city jail a number of men whose release the captain had procured by paying their fines. At muster and roll-call, it was discovered that three sailors had deserted with their belongings; it was reported that five more invalids were transferred to the *Swift*, and nine new sailors were added to the ship's company.

McClure worked hard to improve relations with his crew who were in better humour, despite some of them being on the sick list because, as Miertsching in his journal states, 'they could not refrain from the frightful excesses in Honolulu'. On Sunday 12 July, he notes that it does not seem right to the captain that the men should read Bible tracts, so he ordered the ship's

fiddler to play a tune, and we are told a seaman named John Boyle, a gifted singer and dancer, received from the captain a large glass of wine as a reward for his skill.

McClure noted that the ice was still a full 40 degrees of latitude distant. But with favourable winds, he crossed the Arctic Circle on 29 July, when government-issue warm clothing was supplied to the crew. Armstrong tells us it consisted of one complete suit of blue, double-milled boxcloth, boots, stockings, boot hose, comforters, mitts and caps, all of which he tells us were of excellent quality and well adapted for polar service.[6]

En route to the Bering Strait, McClure took a

Sledging over hummocky ice, April 1853; by Lieutenant S. Gurney Cresswell. The picture illustrates the hardship endured by McClure's men as they hauled through the pack ice a heavy sledge loaded with food, tent and rations.
*From* A Series of Eight Sketches in Colour, *S. Gurney Cresswell*

risky shortcut through the Aleutian Islands in a supreme effort to overtake his commander, Collinson, aboard *Enterprise*; he arrived at the pre-arranged rendezvous off the coast of Alaska two weeks ahead of *Enterprise*. He first met HMS *Plover* on 27 July and spoke to Captain Moore who knew nothing of the whereabouts of *Enterprise*. Miertsching tells us that Moore employed a young Eskimo woman – who dwelt in his cabin – to act as interpreter among the natives. His diary for 30 July also notes that 'the men – and this includes high-ranking officers behave themselves so shamelessly that here one will soon have an Anglo-Eskimo colony.'

The next day, at Cape Lisburne – in the Bering Strait – they met HMS *Herald*. Her captain, Henry Kellett, a wise and experienced commander, was patrolling the waters entering the Bering Strait in company with *Plover*. They were there to give support in the event of *Terror* or *Erebus* coming home that way, and also with orders to support Collinson and McClure in the search for a passage from the west. McClure had difficulty getting Kellett, his fellow countryman – from Co. Tipperary – to agree with him that Collinson had already passed and was gone ahead. Though Kellett freely topped up the provisions of McClure's ship, he signalled McClure as he observed *Investigator* make ready to set sail: 'Had you better not wait 48 hours.' 'Important duty, cannot on my own responsibility', was McClure's reply as he sailed past, satisfied that Kellett could not be sure that *Enterprise* had not passed in the foggy conditions which had prevailed in the region during the previous weeks.

McClure went on ahead, contrary to Admiralty orders: 'We deem it right to caution you against suffering the two vessels placed under your orders to separate, except in the event of accident or unavoidable necessity.' Though now on its own, the crew of *Investigator* supported McClure, as Armstrong expressed in his narrative: 'Hence we could feel but little regret at losing the company of a consort that had hitherto proved so faithless.'[7] In fact, *Enterprise* reached the Bering Strait two weeks after *Investigator*. Following an unsuccessful effort to penetrate the ice to the north, she pulled out and wintered at Hong Kong.

McClure sailed through an open Bering Strait into the Chukchi Sea, but progress was on occasion made only by the men towing *Investigator* – 40 men rowing in five of the ship's boats. In this manner, they passed Barrow Point on 7 August before struggling through loose ice on the edge of the permanent pack ice to reach the mouth of the MacKenzie River. On 14 August, *Investigator* ran aground. McClure tells us:

The boats were got out, all the deck load of provisions embarked in them, some tons of fresh water were started from the tanks in her hold, the anchors lowered into cutters, and then for a fresh attempt, the *Investigator* was got afloat, after being aground for five hours. Unfortunately the ship being obliged to carry canvas to get into deep water, one of the boats laden with provisions capsized whilst in tow, and eleven casks of salt meat were lost – a real calamity to me under such circumstances.[8]

Contact was made with Eskimos and afterwards – in light of his crew's experiences with the Eskimos – McClure reflected in his journal on the veracity of Byron's theory concerning the effect of cold climates on chastity. When Miertsching asked the Eskimo chief why they did not trade with the white men – the Hudson's Bay Company – up the big river, the reply was 'they had given the Indians of water which killed a great many of them and made others foolish, and they [his tribe] did not want to have any.'[9]

McClure observed that the Beaufort Sea was open to Banks Land, which was in the direction of Melville Island. When he reached its southern promontory, he named it Nelson Head after his former commander on *Victory* whom, he felt, 'had not been sufficiently remembered by modern naval discoverers'. He then followed the southern coastline until he reached a narrow passage – he named it Prince of Wales Strait – which he was to discover separated Banks Land from another land mass, Victoria Island. The Northwest Passage was within his grasp; on 9 September 1850, he was within 60 miles of Melville Island to which Parry had sailed 30 years earlier. His ice master from high up the mast could see open water 20 miles away. McClure knew then for sure that a sea route existed and that he had found it; all he was required to do was sail it. Fame and fortune beckoned, and he wrote in his journal: 'Can it be that so humble a creature as I am will be permitted to perform what has baffled the talented, the wild for a hundred years.'[10] However, as the proverb says: 'There is many the slip between the cup and the lip.'

On 24 September, the wind changed to the northwest and, blowing fresh, it became intensely cold. The ship was drifting at the head of a floe, under pressure, heading for a heavy, grounded ice cliff on the western shore of an island. It was so rough at one stage that they were ready to abandon ship. On a collision course with steep cliffs, only at the last moment – when the pressure suddenly and inexplicably stopped – did they avoid catastrophe. *Investigator*, which was listing badly, then righted. Some members of the crew raided the rum barrels and were roaring drunk, as Miertsching relates:

> When every man saw clearly that there was no hope of rescue, that in the very next moment the ship might be crushed like a nutshell . . . some sailors with neither hope nor the fear of God before their eyes, burst open the chamber where the spirits was stored, made themselves and others completely drunk and stupefied their senses, so that in the condition they might escape the agonies of death.[11]

When the wind and the pressure of the drift suddenly abated, they were clamped solid in ice, 30 miles inside Prince of Wales Strait. It was to be their wintering base. When the ship was finally safe, on 30 September, an angry McClure read the articles-of-war to his hungover and shameful crew:

> At 9am the crew was mustered, and after the captain had inspected the ship he read extracts from the articles of war relating to

discipline on board ship, and the punishment by which it is enforced. After the reading he rebuked the men . . . said he was ashamed that such base robbers should walk the deck of an English ship etc. He promised against the offenders the punishment which they deserved and would receive and declared that but for providence they had faced certain death . . . in the afternoon the three ringleaders were punished.

If they could not sail the route, they could sledge and chart it. *Investigator*'s sledge parties mapped the southern coast of Banks Land and the north coast of Victoria Island (McClure called it Prince Albert Island, not realising it was part of Victoria Island). In the first outing with a sledge to the Barrow Strait in the rugged and broken pack, they repeatedly capsized the sledge and eventually fractured it beyond repair. Mr Court, the master, was sent back for another. At the close of the first day, they were each provided with a pint of tepid water into which a little oatmeal was thrown. They retired to their sleeping bags to rest as best they might, with the temperature at -6°F (-21°C).

Despite their lack of preparation for sledge travel, they managed to steer north and find high ground overlooking Point Russell on a small peak they named Mount Observation. From there, all doubt as to the water communication between the two great oceans dissipated when they observed Prince of Wales Strait enter Melville Sound and sighted Melville Island across the pack ice to the north, which Parry had reached 30 years previously.

The *Investigator* had left England little prepared for extensive sledge work and with few, if any, improvements upon the system of sledge travel originally laid down by Sir James Clark Ross. As a consequence, the sledge parties suffered a greater amount of hardship and privation than that experienced by the parties of McClintock and Austin's other officers, all of whom improved upon their predecessor's experience. On the return journey to *Investigator*, when within one day's walking range of the ship, McClure got separated from his crew, who were pulling the sledge behind, and was lost:

> He was benighted and wandered for 20 hours. He came aboard more like a corpse than a living man; his limbs were stiff with cold; he could not speak a word. He was carried to his cabin, where both doctors Armstrong and Piers took charge of him.[12]

On 2 November 1850, McClure gave the crew a good dinner to celebrate their discovery of the Northwest Passage. Also in November, coal fires and one of Mr Sylvester's stoves were lit, providing warmth for the ship. A smaller stove in the sick bay was allocated 7 pounds of coal daily, while a stove located in the officers' mess was permitted 8–12 pounds of fuel daily – depending on the cold – and a stove located in the captain's cabin was allowed to consume 16 pounds daily. The galley fire on the lower deck was used for cooking throughout the day. A school was established for the instruction of the men in reading, writing and arithmetic. Held five evenings a week, it was well attended and proved an agreeable source of occupation for many. Mr Paine, the clerk in charge, was the teacher. Mr Court, the assistant master, also had four students for navigation.

In the spring of 1851, McClure drove himself and his crew with aggressive zeal, leading a number of sledging parties in search of Franklin and, in the process, charting new territory. He expected much from his officers and men, and had little sympathy for those suffering from frostbite, demanding they do their duty despite the terrible privations. There were three sledge parties, each one led by an officer with eight men. Each sledge measured 10 feet in length and was held together with iron. The load consisted of a tent, clothing, bedding, tools, cooking equipment, weapons and provisions – total weight: 1,000 pounds. This entailed each man pulling 125–30 pounds. The officer went in advance of the sledge to find the easiest way through the rough ice, and carried a double-barrelled shotgun, telescope, compass and a notebook for recording the observations made with the instruments.[13]

Lieutenant Wynniatt's party returned to the ship after only nine days out as his chronometer was broken. He was sent back out by an angry McClure on the same day, without a replacement timepiece. Lieutenant Cresswell's party returned after 32 days searching to the north and northwest of Banks Land. Two of his men were suffering from severe frostbite, caused by wearing tight, canvas boots which shrunk when wet, further restricting circulation; one of the men subsequently lost his foot, which was amputated to prevent the spread of infection. As a result of his exploration and surveying, Cresswell was convinced that Banks Land was, in fact, an island.

Back at the ship, Whitfield – a crewman – got lost while out hunting; he collapsed just short of the shore parties' tents and was overcome by the cold. He was found – kneeling, his head back, his open mouth full of snow, frozen stiff and covered in snow. Remarkably, he recovered and survived the expedition. The preserved meats provided to the ship by Messrs Gamble were found decayed to an alarming extent; between 12–18 October, no less than 424 pounds of it were thrown overboard as unfit food.

In July 1851, when the ice thawed, McClure again attempted to enter Barrow Strait. When no progress was experienced by 18 August, he retraced his course in the Prince of Wales Strait and was rounding Nelson Head to the west the next day, having travelled 100 miles in the open channel in one day. He then sailed northwest, following majestic cliffs to Cape Hamilton and a coastline characterised by long, sloping beaches until *Investigator* reached Cape Kellett; here, he placed a message in a cairn on the headland. From here, McClure gradually turned north along the western coast of his great discovery, Banks Island. He got a clear run in a 6-miles wide channel formed between the pack and the shallow shoreline. He faced the 100-foot-high pack to the north, and tried to slip the ship through a channel which was not much wider than the vessel itself but which provided a passage between the rolling pack and the shore. The pack drew 40 or 50 feet of water and rose in rolling hills upon the surface, some of them 100 feet from base to summit. The lane of water between the pack and the coast suddenly narrowed, and the coast became abrupt and precipitous as a wall. In some places, it was so narrow that the sails and ship's boats were near touching the ice on one side and the rocky cliffs on the other.[14] Retreat was now as dangerous as advance; they could not round-to for want of space. Taking their courage in their hands on this frightful coast, each man knew the outcome if the pack closed on the cliff. They got stuck and frozen in for a time before the wind veered south and the ice moved off the coast. The *Investigator* blasted, hacked and warped at the pack ice, trying to get through to open water. Miertsching tells us that on the evening of 20 September, 'We came to a promontory which rises perpendicularly to a height of 300 feet. This headland was named Crozier by the captain. We spent the night beneath the wall of rock.'[15]

McClure was now closer to Melville Island than the year before. On 22 September, he rounded Cape Austin and they were now in the waters of Barrow Strait. The gap was tight again and, on one occasion, the lower sail had to be adjusted to allow passage between the steep cliff and the floes. At the end of September 1851, open water was observed to the east as far as the eye could see but, having just entered the first safe harbour on the north coast of Banks Island – which they had all but circumnavigated – McClure was reluctant to push his luck so late in the season. He named this safe harbour Bay of Mercy (latitude 74° 6' 34" north, longitude 118° 15' west), and though *Investigator* was never to sail from its icy clutches, it was indeed a place

that provided the necessary shelter and game to sustain life. Thankful to be in safe winter quarters, McClure declined the invitation of open sea beyond the pack, particularly given the risk of being crushed in the winter pack, the onset of which was due.

McClure and his crew were to spend the winters of 1851–53 here. He ordered that the officers and men should be placed on two-thirds of normal rations, plus whatever game they could shoot. They were fortunate that the hills in the vicinity abounded with both reindeer and hare, providing fresh meat for the hungry crew; hunting also provided a necessary relief from boredom for the sportsmen. On 6 December 1851, however,

> The captain made it known that as a great amount of provisions must be discarded as spoiled and injurious to health, utmost economy must be practiced, and he had decided gradually to reduce the two thirds daily ration to one half which admittedly small portion would be maintained only for those months when the ship was frozen in, and no work, heavy or light, was demanded of the men, and as soon as the ship was under sail, or any strenuous effort required, the full daily ration of food would be restored.[16]

Candles were also subject to close rationing: three tallow candles were issued to each seaman every fourteen days – in the previous winter, it was three for seven days. Miertsching complained that 'with the light of neither sun nor of days one must exist for 14 days with 18 hours of light.' The hunger pangs were, nonetheless, felt most by the ordinary crew. Each officer had an additional private stock of food and wine, purchased before departure, from which they were permitted to draw. The interpreter/missionary tells us of the happenings of 31 January 1851: 'The daily ration seems to grow smaller and smaller; the men are complaining of hunger. Three sailors have been severely punished for stealing and devouring the dog's food.' The flogging of three half-starved men for taking the portion of Mongo, the ship's mascot, might seem excessive, but McClure dared not show weakness in a crisis, and had to be seen to demonstrate justice and equity in his interpretation of regulations, whatever the circumstances. With a crew of over 60 men, among them some with little personal discipline, it was essential that no breaches were tolerated. The risk of mutiny from a failure to enforce regulations was real. The school, so popular in the previous winter, closed down at the same time; the desire to learn vanishes on an empty stomach.

McClure's achievement was, nonetheless, as significant as it had been bold – arguably reckless. He had established that Banks Land was in fact an island. If only he could cross to Melville Island, to Parry's Winter Harbour, he would achieve a fully charted Northwest Passage. He led a sledge team there the following April (1852), crossing over the rough pack during a seventeen-day journey. There, he found the note deposited by Leopold McClintock of *Assistance* the previous June. The note was concealed in a cairn, built adjacent to the famous sandstone

boulder inscribed by Parry's men 30 years previously. McClure could not believe his misfortune; he realised that, had he sent a sledge team there during the previous summer, he would have met up with the team from the east. He arrived back to his ship and crew on 9 May, his confidence and motivation shattered. Neither ship nor provisions were left; nor had there been a note to say where provisions were stockpiled for his or Collinson's use.

Miertsching felt sorry for McClure; he observed that his sorely tried captain must force himself to wear a cheerful look. McClure now knew they were left on their own and that there was little prospect of any help arriving from the east. Not sending a party to Melville Island in the spring of 1851 had been a serious oversight on his part.

Meanwhile, Collinson – captain of the *Enterprise* – followed McClure through the Bering Strait twelve months after *Investigator* had gone through. Receiving directions from the natives at the Mackenzie River in 1851, he had followed *Investigator* up Prince of Wales Strait – two weeks after McClure had left. Collinson also observed the passage possibilities toward Melville Island but, in the face of ice difficulties, turned back. He followed McClure north to Point Kellett where he was astonished to find, in the shore-erected cairn, his subordinate's note to the effect that *Investigator* was ahead of him. Deciding at this point to pursue a different course, Collinson opted to follow the North American coast by the route charted by Simpson and Dease, wintering at Walker Bay in Prince Albert Land (now Victoria Island). From there, Lieutenant Parks led a sledge party from *Enterprise* to Melville Island,

crossing McClure's sledge tracks and arriving only twenty days after McClure at the Winter Harbour cairn built by Parry's men in 1821. One wonders what would have transpired if the commanders had met, for Collinson, like McClure, had a wicked temper. His junior officer had not only disobeyed orders, but had stolen his thunder by linking Parry's eastern passage with the Bering Strait.

During McClure's trip to Melville Island, the stock of fresh provisions aboard *Investigator* was wonderfully increased by sporting activity. No less than twenty deer were hanging up, and the abundance justified increasing rations to 1.5 pounds of venison on six days in every fortnight, with another six days on preserved meats, and the other two days on salt meat.[17] Sergeant Woon of the Royal Marines, one of the most successful

hunters, had developed a reputation as a marksman and, as such, had become an important resource with regard to health and survival. Others were less successful, and were having the effect of wounding and frightening the game away. Late one evening in early April, Mr Kennedy – the boatswain – went out hunting and wounded a fine buck just as darkness was descending. When he found the buck the next morning, five large wolves were helping themselves to his prize. Shouting and swearing at them, he ended up in a tug-of-war with a large female wolf for the leg of the deer. Mr Miertsching's arrival with others sent the wolves scampering.[18] Such were the deeds of men suffering the pangs of hunger after twelve months on two-thirds of normal rations in the frozen Arctic winter. Despite the extra fresh meat, the

Departure of sledge parties from HMS *Resolute* and *Intrepid* in search of Franklin expedition.
*From* The Eventful Voyage, *G.F. McDougall*

channel was not an option as the distance was too great. Their only hope was a south wind to take the ice from shore; but it did not come, and the temperatures fell again at the end of August. Another winter was their fate, and soon the sorrel could no longer be found. A seaman named Taylor stole a loaf of bread from the oven and received three dozen strokes of the cat. Another young seaman, named Bradbury, was under close watch for three days: he was quite distressed and making terrible noise at night.[20]

As the winter of 1853 commenced, McClure remained positive. He wrote:

It found us ready to combat its rigours as cheerfully as on previous occasions. We were all thinner than we used to be, for we have been twelve months on rations; but we were still in good working condition.

Having reviewed the situation, he spoke to his crew regarding their prospects and options. He told them that if all remained on the ship until the next summer in hope of sailing to the east, and if the water did not raise the ship – enabling them to escape – they would simply all starve. His own sense of duty and pride prevented him from even contemplating leaving the ship entrusted to him. He had decided to send away the following spring all but 30 of the healthiest officers and men. Those travelling would be divided into two parties of fifteen, one retreating by way of North America and the other to Cape Spencer on Beechey Island. Those that stayed with the ship faced the prospect of yet another winter – if the ship did not come free – with the

Parry's sandstone boulder became a notable Irish postbox: it was visited by Dundalk-born Leopold McClintock in June 1851; he left a message which was found by Robert McClure, from Wexford, in April 1852 after having sledged from Banks Island. This message was in turn found by Frederick Mecham, from Cove, Co. Cork, during autumn 1852; Mecham notified Captain Henry Kellett, from Tipperary, who sent a relief party in March 1853 to aid McClure and his men. *From* Life of Admiral Sir Leopold McClintock, *Sir Clements Markham*

total absence of fresh vegetables and the effect on morale at finding that no help was on hand at Melville Island were factors cited in the surgeon's medical report of 1 July, which noted symptoms of debility and incipient scurvy in sixteen men.

The summer did not yield the expected release of the ship. Soft snow and large pools of surface water on top of the ice made hunting difficult, and their stock of game ran out by 7 July. Sergeant Woon came to the rescue again when he shot two musk oxen, yielding 647 pounds of good meat. In slaying them, he had a narrow escape from the rage of the larger of the two, which his last bullet had wounded. As the wounded musk ox approached him, he plunged his ramrod into its body to save himself.[19] Further relief from scurvy came when Miertsching found a quantity of wild sorrel – a salad leaf – which, thereafter, was sought out and picked daily for inclusion in the men's diet, particularly those suffering from the ravages of scurvy.

Though open water was sighted in the strait, the ship was imprisoned in Mercy Bay. Sawing a possibility of retreat in spring 1854. McClure appealed to his men with force and emotion, and told them of his unshakeable conviction that not one of them would be left behind, but felt all would safely reach home. He also told them that, in order to conserve rations, he would further reduce them by a small amount but would share his personal stock on appropriate occasions.

A stocktake of the spirits led to a reduction of the daily issue to half a gill. Hunger was now being felt. The sick sportsmen only managed two deer and nine hares in the month of October to feed the entire ship's company. On 8 October, the crew gathered on the deck in a body to ask for more food. Miertsching tells us:

> Today at midday the entire crew gathered on the upper deck and demanded, through the officers of the watch, a few words with the captain. As he appeared, four sailors approached him, requested his pardon for the unauthorised assembly, and stated that the crew had resolved to present a collective request for a small increase in rations: they could not exist on present allowance; they could not sleep for hunger, etc. The harassed captain listened of necessity to this petition, and after an earnest conference dismissed the men with a promise to grant their request.[21]

But McClure did not increase the rations, though on 26 October, he prepared a meal from his own stock and also provided extra grog to the whole crew, in a further celebration of the discovery of the Northwest Passage:

the officers were invited to dine with the captain; unhappily the poor stricken Wynniatt could not be one of us. A quite unwonted animation prevails on board; everyone is cheery and good humoured.[22]

Mr Wynniatt, the mate, passed each night shouting and raving, and had to be watched day and night lest he do violence to himself or a shipmate. He was the second member of the crew to go insane in the total darkness and trying conditions of the Arctic winter, and in the uncertainty of their situation. McClure was still able to write after Christmas:

> The New Year is about to commence; not one of my original crew has fallen by disease or accident, and all is more promising than I could ever have hoped for. These and other mercies are alone due to that all-beneficial providence, who has so wonderfully upheld us in our many trials and difficulties; relying, therefore on him, I cannot but feel as the wife of Manoah did and repeat her exclamation. If the Lord were pleased to kill us, he would not have shewed us all these mercies.[23]

In contrast to McClure's optimism, we learn from Miertsching that, on 19 January 1853, Mr Wynniatt's condition had been so frantic that he had out of necessity to be kept bound. The ship's baker was also reported to the officer of the watch for thieving meat, flour and dough. When he finally confessed, he received two dozen lashes of the cat on his naked back.

# 9

# THE BELCHER EXPEDITION

*In April 1852, I went to Melville Island, about 150 miles, in hopes of meeting some ship from Captain Austin's expedition, and was sorely disappointed as I had calculated upon it, or else on finding stores. The only notice met with was a few lines left upon a large block of sandstone at Winter Harbour by my friend McClintock of 2, Gardiner Place, Dublin. It is curious that two Irishmen, one coming round the world from the east and the other by the west should leave a notice on the same stone.*

ROBERT MCCLURE[1]

In 1851, the Arctic Council was officially called to advise the Admiralty regarding the search for Franklin. The Admiralty missed the guiding hand of Sir John Barrow who had died, aged 83, on 23 November 1848. The council was made up of all of Barrow's polar stars – Sir Edward Parry, Sir John Richardson, Sir James Clark Ross, Sir George Back, Colonel Edward Sabine, Captain Beechey and Captain Bird – together with three representatives of the Admiralty: Barrow's successor as second secretary, Captain W.A. Bailey Hamilton, Sir Francis Beaufort, the Admiralty's hydrographer, and Barrow's son, John, who was seconded to the Admiralty and who acted as a very effective facilitator. He worked with Beaufort and Hamilton to make the council a more effective and responsive body in the planning and execution of the search for Franklin. The Admiralty's choice of leader for the next expedition, however, could not have been worse. The five-ship expedition to the eastern side was to be led by the notorious Sir Edward Belcher, an officer with limited Arctic experience and who was regarded as the most unpopular man in the navy. Beaufort is likely to have been the primary influence in the subsequently much-regretted decision to appoint Belcher, a long-established surveying captain who would have been well known to Beaufort in his role as hydrographer. This decision may also have prompted Back's unflattering obituary for Beaufort:

*facing page*
Leopold McClintock, regarded as the foremost naval officer with regard to the development of sledge travel for the purposes of polar exploration. Portrait by Stephen Pearce.
*Courtesy of National Portrait Gallery*

And so poor Beaufort is gone! Well peace be with him . . . He lived long enough for his fame – too long for many of his friendships, and probably for his happiness. His judgement was generally clear but he often acted from impulse and was susceptible to flattery.[2]

The commanders and their ships were as follows: Belcher, *Assistance*; Sherard Osborn, *Pioneer*; Henry Kellett, *Resolute*; the newly promoted Captain McClintock, *Intrepid*. The fifth ship in the fleet was the supply vessel, *North Star*, under Commander W.J.S. Pullen. Mecham was first lieutenant to Kellett on *Resolute*. The expedition was divided into two divisions. Belcher was in overall command and also in charge of division one – *Assistance* and *Pioneer* – with orders to search from the Wellington Channel. Kellett was in command of division two – *Resolute* and *Intrepid* – with responsibility for searching from Melville Island. In addition to their orders to search for crews of *Erebus* and *Terror*, they were asked to look out for Collinson and McClure, about whom there was increasing concern.

McClintock went home to Dublin during the winter of 1851. His mother and unmarried sisters lived at 2 Gardiner Place, Dublin. His brother, Alfred, was a rising physician who was afterwards famous in his own right when he became president of the College of Surgeons of Ireland, a position he held until his death in 1881. During these short intervals from the sea, McClintock found a very happy home in Dublin with his family. While there, he made the acquaintance of men of science, forming a

lifelong relationship with Professor Samuel Haughton of Trinity College;[3] these men helped him in his practical research and experiments to compare the relative merits of fuels suitable for cooking in low temperatures.

The Ireland that McClintock had come home to had, in the previous six years, experienced the horrors of famine arising from the partial failure of the potato crop in 1845 and its total failure as a result of blight in 1846. The British government's inability to respond adequately to the disaster is regarded as a watershed in Irish political and social development, leading to demands for improved tenants' rights and also to mass emigration from the scenes of utter desolation. Irish military and naval people who came home at that time must have witnessed many scenes of great hardship and death. They must also have witnessed the hardening of attitudes among the majority Catholic population, particularly the tenant farmers, and they must have been aware of the widespread disgust expressed at the British government for allowing food leave Ireland while so many of its people starved. And so it must have been with mixed emotions that McClintock and his colleagues left home and returned to their naval duties to search for the lost *Erebus* and *Terror* crews, ironically also dying of starvation, albeit in the remote Arctic.

The Belcher expedition sailed up the Thames on 15 April 1852. McClintock, ever growing in skills, handled the *Intrepid* expertly to reach the ice of Melville Bay unscathed. *Resolute* at one stage received a severe nip and was raised 8 feet out of the water and considered in grave danger. The squadron reached Beechey Island on 14

August, where the *North Star* remained as depot ship. On the following day, the two divisions went their separate ways. The *Assistance* and *Pioneer* proceeded up Wellington Channel to winter in a harbour at 77° 52' north, while *Resolute* and *Intrepid* – with their two Irish commanders – went on to Melville Island where they overwintered in a bay off Dealy Island.

Again, there is evidence of Irish names among the seamen. Peter Finnecy (Fenese), who served on both *Resolute* (1850–51) and *North Star* (1852–54), was born in Dublin around 1820 and joined *Russell* as an ordinary seaman in December 1838. He served in *Zebra* as an AB in 1840 and saw action off the Syrian coast. He was captain of the maintop in *Resolute* and served as ice quartermaster on *North Star*. He was known as Finnecy in *Resolute* and as Fenese in *North Star*. Although he evidently did not claim his naval General Service Medal (clasp Syria), his Arctic Medal was signed for as Finnecy, although it is entered in the medal roll as Fenese.[4]

### Captain Sir Henry Kellett

Sir Henry Kellett, commander of HMS *Resolute* on the Belcher expedition, was the son of John Dalton Kellett of Clonacody, Co. Tipperary. Born on 2 November 1806, his home – Clonacody House – is located 3 miles from Fethard on the Clonmel road, and is situated in the heart of the very best of agricultural land; land that has been ploughed and grazed since the Middle Ages. Fethard was established by the Norman William de Braose in 1201, after he was installed by King John as the chief tenant of the substantial terri-

tory which comprised most of modern Co. Tipperary. Many of those who settled in Tipperary were Anglo-Norman planters and appear to have come from de Braose's estates in Wales.[5] Fethard was, from its outset, a planned town systematically laid out with a regular pattern of streets. Its name is derived from the Irish, Clash Alainn, which translates as 'Lovely Stream', and the whole scene is overlooked by the legendary, 700-metre-high Slievenamon (Mountain of the Women). It was here that 2,000 United Irishmen assembled on 23 July 1798, before being dispersed by troops under General Sir George Asgill. Fethard was a garrison town until 1922, when the barracks was closed following the establishment of the Irish Free State. Kellett's family were part of a long, local tradition of service in the military and navy; as the crow flies, the Kellett home was less than 40 miles north of the Cork and Waterford coast and ports. It is fitting that he survived his many naval engagements and exploration exploits to end his days about Fethard, and to be buried in the graveyard within the medieval walls of the town.

He entered the navy in 1822 and, after five years of service at the West Indies station aboard *Ringdove*, was appointed to the *Eden*, under Captain William Fitzwilliam Owen, on a mission to the coast of Africa, thus taking part in the humane effort to extinguish the slave trade. Young as he was, his intrepidity began then to show itself, for twice he was mentioned in dispatches for having gallantly led the boats of his squadron in cutting out 'slavers'. He was involved in the scheme for the colonisation of Fernando Po, and was promoted to lieutenant on

15 September 1828, but continued in the *Eden* during a very trying commission until she was paid off in the summer of 1831.[6]

He was appointed to the *Aetna* surveying vessel with Captain Belcher and, when paid off in 1835, was given command of the *Starling*, a cutter employed in a survey of the west coast of South America. In 1840, he took this little vessel across the Pacific to China where, as a surveyor and pilot, he played a very important part in the operations of the war in the Canton River and in the Yangtse Kiang. Here, he accomplished a deed upon which his reputation for perseverance and fearlessness was established. Having contrived to place buoys along the river with muffled oars, he bravely piloted the fleet up the Yangtse Kiang, with its armed forts on either side – a most perilous action and the pluckiest achievement of the time. Upon his return, the whole fleet paid him the compliment of manning the yards to cheer him and those with him as they passed. On shore, he commanded the naval brigade under Lord Gough, who was also a Tipperary man and a war hero. He was promoted to commander on 6 May 1841, but continued in the *Starling*, which was officially rated as sloop-of-war, in order to give him the necessary sea time for his promotion to post rank on 23 December 1842.[7] He was at the same time nominated a CB (Companion of the Order of the Bath). He returned to England in the summer of 1843 and in February 1845 was appointed to command the *Herald*, a small frigate commissioned as a surveying vessel in the Pacific. Her most important work there was the exact survey of the coast of Colombia, between Guayaguil and Panama,

but this was interrupted by three summer voyages – from 1848–50 – through the Bering Strait to co-operate with the Franklin-search expeditions. He returned home across the Pacific, touching at Hong Kong, Singapore and the Cape of Good Hope, arriving home in the summer of 1851.[8]

In February 1852, Kellett was given command of the *Resolute* in the search for John Franklin under orders from his old captain, now Sir Edward Belcher. He was in command of the second division, with McClintock in command of *Intrepid*. During the winter, Kellett took a couple of hours' walk each forenoon with McClintock, who found him very communicative and pleasant. He was in full sympathy with all McClintock's ideas and plans.[9] On board both vessels, winter passed with the same comforts as in the previous expeditions, thanks to the hard work and planning put into the entertainment, exercise routine and classes for the crews.

McClintock decided to lay out depots in the autumn in advance of the following spring's planned journeys. This time, he went out for 40 days, covering 260 miles. His neighbour – by then Petty Officer John Salmon – was again in McClintock's party. Four other sledge parties laid out depots, Mecham covering 212 miles in 25 days and, in the process, making a very important discovery. He found a record at Winter Harbour, Melville Island, left there by Robert McClure of *Investigator* at Parry's sandstone rock. McClure had left his ship's position and added, chivalrously, that if he was not heard of again, *Investigator* would probably have been carried into the polar pack west of Melville Island, in which case any attempt to rescue him would be useless. However, the achievements of the depot parties was not without cost; a stoker named Coombs, on the return journey to the ship, dropped dead from his exertions. De Bray, the officer in charge of this party, had carried on with depositing the stores to Point Fisher from Point Nias with the corpse aboard the sledge. One of the three young mates on *Resolute* was Richard 'Paddy' Roche, who had been a midshipman on the *Herald* with Kellett from 1852–54; he also led a depot party to Cape Mudge on the Sabine Peninsula. He was later to receive an Arctic Medal and went on to command *Hibernia* at Malta. His presence in the Arctic is commemorated at Roche

Point on the north-west coast of Sabine Peninsula.[10]

The plan for the spring sent McClintock north and west, Mecham to the west and Vesey Hamilton to the north. On 10 March 1853, a sledge party was sent to communicate with the *Investigator* in the Bay of Mercy, a distance of 150 miles. It is a remarkable fact that on the northern polar edges of the then known world, a note left by Dundalk man McClintock under Parry's sandstone boulder at Winter Harbour, Melville Island in 1851 was found by Wexfordman McClure in April 1852, whose note in turn was found by Mecham, that intrepid Cobhman, in the autumn of that same year. On 4 April 1853, the sledging

The Arctic Council (left–right): Sir George Back, Sir William Edward Parry, Captain Edward J. Bird, Sir James Clark Ross, Sir Francis Beaufort, John Barrow, Lieutenant Colonel Edward Sabine, Captain W.A. Baillie-Hamilton, Sir John Richardson, Captain William Beechey. Painting by Stephen Pearce.
*Courtesy of National Portrait Gallery*

programme commenced. McClintock and his party made an amazing journey, lasting 105 days, during which they covered 1,408 statute miles, including 768 miles of newly discovered land. On 14 May 1853, McClintock discovered lands on Prince Patrick Island, which his team explored and charted. He shot three of the eleven deer they sighted, providing his men with a supper of venison and pemmican. It was on this journey that McClintock first made use of what he called a satellite sledge, a smaller sledge branching out from the main sledge. They travelled in deep snow to reach an inlet they named Intrepid Inlet. The main sledge, under George Green, explored the bay, which was named Green Bay, and a point on the northern side, which McClintock called Cape Salmon. He then crossed to Edlinton Island, and travelled to its extreme northern tip at 77° 43' north. On return to Prince Patrick Island, he sent back the main sledge and travelled with the satellite sledge, together with two seamen, Drew and Giddy. On 17 June, they were caught in a gale without a tent and sheltered in the lee of their upturned sledge. On the way back, McClintock shot a Brent goose. On 21 June, an ivory gull was seen on her nest with an egg – the first ever find of an ivory-gull egg. McClintock also observed the geological features of the terrain and recorded that they travelled in places where 'there was needle ice like an aggregation of thermometer stems two to six inches long in vertical columns extremely regular like miniature Giant's Cause-way.'[11]

He sighted land from the north coast of Melville Island. In deep snow, the going was terrible, but he reached it on 27 June and named it Emerald Isle. Having explored and charted the island, McClintock crossed back to Melville Island on 12 July. One of the marines, Hieels, fell ill and was in agony. It took eighteen hours to deal with him, after which McClintock felt 'that all his trials, cares and hopes as a leader of the party during one hundred days seemed as nothing compared to his anxieties as a doctor for eighteen hours.'[12] The ground was now too diffi-cult to traverse with the sledge, forcing them to abandon it and its 550-pound load. Quite worn out and suffering from inflamed feet, chapped heels and rheumatic knees, they went the rest of the way back to the ship on foot, reaching *Intrepid* on 18 July.

Lieutenant Mecham and his party from *Resolute* had also excelled, covering in 91 days 1,173 miles, 785 miles of which was new land. He was travelling 16 miles a day on the outward journey and over 20 miles on the return journey. Vesey Hamilton, the third lieutenant, was away for 54 days, travelling a total of 663 miles. He and his team explored the northern extremity of Melville Island, earlier named Sabine Peninsula by Parry. However, despite their exploration achievements, they had found no trace of Franklin or Crozier.

Some of McClintock's statistics regarding his journeys are worth noting. In a breakdown of his 105 days, he notes 99 marches at an average of 10.5 miles per day, in addition to 62 miles walking around bays and inlets. The number of fixed positions charted was 22, the latitudes cal-culated by meridian and the longitudes by chronometer. He recorded the lowest tempera-ture at -24°F (-31°C) on 16 April, and the highest at 51°F (10.5°C) on 4 July. There were not many rest days in that schedule. He made special mention of George Green for his care of the provisions and for leading the main sledge when the leader was with the satellite. It is no wonder that it took more than a year for his sledge crew to fully recover. Markham tells us that in July 1854, Green and Giddy were still much reduced and shaken, Hieels and Warne were invalids, and Shaw was not what he was; only McClintock, Salmon and Drew were none the worse. Retrospectively, McClintock spoke of the 'Necessity for high physical power and strong mental resolve to endure cheerfully the necessary hardships, in order to triumph over natural obstacles to the achievement of so great an undertaking.'[13]

Meanwhile, McClure and the crew of *Investigator* had survived the winter of 1852–53. He had rationed the fuel for the ship's stoves and reduced the sailors' rations to two-thirds, but not the officers. When he ordered the crew's rations to be reduced to half, the ship's surgeon, Alexander Armstrong, pleaded with him on behalf of a delegation from the crew not to take such severe action. Twenty-one men were out of action with scurvy – one seriously, two had gone insane. Those who suffered amputated toes were in a much-weakened state. McClure still held hopes of completing the passage across what is now called the McClure Strait and planned to do it the following year with the fittest 30 from his crew. He resolved to send from the ship those officers and men who were sick and frostbitten; they would depart in two sledge parties, one to the east – in the remote hope of meeting whaling

ships in Baffin Bay – and the other to the mouth of the Mackenzie River to proceed along the American coast, in the hope of help from one of the Hudson's Bay Company stations. How the sick and infirm would reach safety without the help of the strongest members of his crew is unimaginable. As a strategy, it was callous in the extreme. In preparation for these desperate sledge journeys, McClure allowed the men full rations for a few days. The extra food was too late for poor John Boyle, the singing and dancing sailor, who died from scurvy. It was reported that he had poured together the dregs of various medicines and made himself ill by drinking the mixture.

On 6 April 1853, as the parties prepared to set out on their desperate trip, McClure busied himself searching for a burial site for Boyle on the beach. Suddenly, a stranger approached, calling out: 'I am Lieutenant Pim, late of the *Herald* now of the *Resolute*. Captain Kellett is in her at Dealy Island.' Having been briefed by Pim on the Belcher ships and searches, McClure and Dr Armstrong sledged back with him to the *Resolute*, a distance of 180 miles. McClure was still entertaining thoughts of completing the Northwest Passage and left orders with his officers to continue with the reduced rations.

Aboard *Resolute*, Kellett listened to McClure's assessment of *Investigator*'s situation and gave approval for another winter provided McClure could find twenty volunteers and subject to his own doctor's assessment of the state of McClure's men. While McClure and Dr Armstrong were away, two more members of the crew had died: Kerr and Ames, on 13 and 14 April. Dr Domville of *Resolute* concurred with the *Investigator* surgeon's assessment that all of McClure's crew had traces of scurvy. Nevertheless, McClure insisted on seeking volunteers, his obsession overriding any concern for the health and safety of his crew; he was intent on rescuing the ship and navigating her through the passage he had discovered. When only four men stepped forward to join the five officers, McClure reluctantly prepared to abandon ship and, in an act of sheer spitefulness, needlessly maintained the short rations for his crew. The ship was scrubbed clean before the sad procession of his sick crew struggled the final 180 harrowing and tortuous miles. Miertsching tells us they were glad to be rid of the hunger ship. It took seventeen days before they reached *Resolute* and *Intrepid*, walking for two periods each day and sleeping for two. They were a very sad sight to observe when they finally reached Kellett and McClintock's ships.

The crew of the abandoned *Investigator* was dispersed between the *Resolute* and *Intrepid*. Lieutenant Cresswell and 26 officers and men were sent to the *North Star* at Beechey Island. Escorted by Paddy Roche, it took 22 days of sledging to reach the *North Star*. Roche returned to *Resolute* with an experienced dog handler, a team of five dogs and 120 pounds of bear meat for the dogs; they covered 300 miles in fourteen days at a rate of 21 miles a day over what was considered bad ground. The Admiralty had sent out further supplies with the *Phoenix* and *Breadalbane*; the latter was unfortunately crushed in the ice off Beechey Island and sank. A French officer, Lieutenant Bellot, who had travelled aboard the *Phoenix* to join the search, was presumed to have slipped while trying to cross a drifting floe, as he was never seen again. The human cost of the search for Franklin was steadily rising. Lieutenant Cresswell and his party of sick and deranged sailors went home on the *Phoenix*, which had arrived in May to supply Belcher's squadron.

## Kellett's Storehouse

On Dealy Island – located off the south coast of Melville Island – the men of *Resolute* and *Intrepid*, under the command of Kellett and McClintock, constructed a storehouse to provide for officers and crew of *Enterprise*, in case they should reach Melville Island again. As this was clearly the Admiralty's final search mission for *Erebus* and *Terror*, Kellett's orders were to deposit provisions at a cache for Captain Collinson of the *Enterprise* and others who might – during future expeditions – end up in dire straits. 'Kellett's Storehouse', as it was to become known, was built with 100 tons of sandstone; the double walls were 40-feet long and 14-feet wide, and were filled with sod. The roof, supported by timber posts, was covered with canvas and coal bags. The store, or 'Sailors' Home', was stocked with the complete inventory of supplies typical for mid-nineteenth-century Arctic exploration. Containing sufficient food to sustain, on full rations, 66 men for 210 days, items included 6 tons of flour, over 2 tons each of beef and bacon, a ton of sugar, preserved meats, vegetables, potatoes and 600 pounds of dried apples for desserts. Clothing was also cached, including 108 sets of woollen underwear, 129 pairs of boots and 143 pairs of mitts. A couple of muskets and ammunition were deposited, as were medical supplies and instruments. There was also an inflatable boat and the inevitable Union Jack. Kellett's men built a large cairn on the island's summit, using 42 tons of stone in its construction. Also left on the island were the graves of three crewmen. Kellett placed a plan of the store in the cache and a message for those who needed its contents; it ended with the words: 'Here, Royal sailors and marines are fed, clothed and receive double pay for inhabiting it.'

On 18 July, Commander McClintock returned with his sledge crew in good health. He had explored the coast of Melville Island to the north and northwest during a journey of 105 days, covering 1,200 miles. As with every other search party, he had found no sign of Franklin.

On 18 August, a strong wind became a strong gale, ice moved and broke up, and the ships – together with the ice to which they were anchored – were driven out to sea by high tide. Flung about by the heaving and tumbling ice, they took many hard knocks. The rudder of *Resolute* and two boats belonging to *Intrepid* were smashed to pieces. Toward evening, the storm died away and both ships were beset among the ice mass.[14]

In August 1853 – in a very icy season – the *Resolute* and *Intrepid* broke out of winter quarters, but by 11 November had only managed to move to a new winter position off Bathurst Islands. Miertsching tells us:

On 18 September the two ships sailed from Dealy Island with nine months provisions for 175 men; but as it is now accepted as certain that we shall not reach England this year, Captain Kellett has given orders to reduce the daily rations to two thirds as from today so that nine months will last twelve months.

The plight of the *Investigator* was now linked to Kellett's division, and its crew were resigned to spending another winter in the Arctic, as guests on Kellett's ships. In November, Mr Sainsbury, a lieutenant on *Investigator*, died from consumption on board *Resolute*. He was 26 years of age. On 2 January, Hood of the *Intrepid* died, aged 34 – the fifth member of *Intrepid*'s crew to die during the two years since they were at sea. To the credit of McClure and his surgeon, Armstrong, this was one more death than occurred on *Investigator*.

*Assistance* and *Pioneer* had also moved, but only 52 miles north of Beechey Island. Communication between the two divisions was conducted by use of dog-sledge teams. Lieutenant Hamilton was sent on 4 March with two of the young mates, Roche and Court, and a team of nine dogs to communicate with Belcher. On 7 March, Hamilton returned alone, steaming from perspiration despite the cold temperatures. He had rushed back to report that Paddy Roche had accidentally received a bullet through his thigh from a loaded gun on the sledge. George Nares was sent as a replacement for Roche, and they returned on 10 April with an order to Captain Kellett from Belcher to abandon the ships.[15] A shocked Kellett held a meeting with McClintock, McClure and Captain Richards, who had carried the message. McClintock was sent to meet and reason with Belcher; he would communicate the collective view that their ships were sound and adequately provisioned, and their expectation that they would get clear the following summer. Belcher, who was apparently anxious to return home, responded with an explicit order to abandon ship. Osborn, who commanded the *Pioneer*, was placed under arrest for his disagreement with Belcher and two of Belcher's own officers on the *Assistance* were ordered off his ship and sent to the *North Star*.

During these journeys, McClintock gained much experience in the use of dog sledges. He and a colleague, with twelve dogs, travelled from *Resolute* to the *North Star* in five days, and then on to *Assistance* – a further 52 miles covered in 24 hours. In total, he covered a distance of 460 miles at an average of 31 miles per day. He calculated that two dogs required the same food as one man, and that one dog was able to pull a load a fourth greater than any a man could haul. He established that, if both man and dog were lightly laden, a dog would go twice the distance of a man, but that over a very long period and distance, men are superior to dogs. But he considered dogs to be invaluable in the Arctic for keeping up communications over distances not exceeding 300 miles. He concluded that, to keep a dog at its best, it needs to be well fed and well treated, and should not be overworked.

When *Investigator*'s crew left for the *North Star*, they faced a 200-mile journey on foot. Miertsching said:

The pietistic Investigators had after being mocked and have suffered much unfriendly handling which, with ordinary seamen

would have caused much unpleasantness and demanded retaliation and reprisal.

For the 'revellers' of *Resolute* and *Intrepid* to describe the crew of *Investigator* as 'pietistic' – or pious – indicates the extent to which their conduct had moderated and how their spirits had been crushed as a result of their experiences. Before they left the ships, Captain Kellett assembled the *Investigator* crew on deck and thanked the men for the regular discipline and exceptional good conduct which, to the very last, had characterised the crew of *Investigator*. He handed McClure a letter to the Admiralty in which he gave the crew of *Investigator* a character so good that one would rarely find other ships as worthy. This testimonial letter was to be of great benefit to them when they later arrived home, and when McClure claimed parliament's prize for the discovery and completion of the Northwest Passage.

On 25 April, at Cape Hotham – at the entrance to Wellington Channel – McClure and his crew, en route to *North Star*, met Captain McClintock with his dog sledge on his way back to Kellett with Belcher's order. The chronometers and other valuable instruments were to be brought along, but everything else was to be left behind. The excellent survey work of McClintock's tireless subordinates was to be buried beneath the shame of four abandoned ships by order of their lazy, incompetent commander who was sick and simply wanted to go home. He insisted that the crews of all four ships be crowded aboard the *North Star*. Luckily, Inglefield arrived back with *Phoenix* and another old frigate, the *Talbot*. The subsequent court-martial of Belcher saw him acquitted due to the wide discretion given to him in orders. But the silence as his sword was handed back to him was indicative of his disgrace in the eyes of his navy peers. The promotion of Sherard Osborn – whom Belcher had arrested – and Lieutenant May – whom he had reported to the Admiralty – reflected the Admiralty's scorn for the disgraced 'Tartar' who so easily abandoned Her Majesty's ships. There was no doubt that the ships would have sprung free later in the season.

Belcher's action led to further ignominy for the navy when Kellett's ship, Resolute – unmanned– drifted into the Davis Strait and was boarded and sailed to America by a whaling captain. She was restored and returned to Queen Victoria by the US government – an inglorious end to the Admiralty's official effort to find Franklin and his crew. The expedition had failed to search where Sir John Richardson and Lady Franklin had asked – namely, King William Land (later King William Island). By that stage, the Admiralty was very determined to be finished with the Franklin search and, indeed, with any further Arctic expeditions. The outbreak of the Crimean War confirmed the navy in its desire to avoid further distractions.

On return to England, McClure and his crew were fêted as heroes. He was knighted and promoted to captain, and he and his crew were voted an award of £10,000 by parliament. McClure, however, refused to acknowledge the part played by Resolute in the rescue of Investigator's crew, and declined to share the prize with Kellett and his men. Following a letter to John Barrow from Henry Kellett aboard Resolute – dated 12 April–2 May – suggesting that the Admiralty acknowledge the

contribution of all who participated in Arctic expeditions, the Arctic Medal (1818–55) was awarded to all Arctic-expedition crews of that period. It is interesting to note that Mr Richard Saintfield of Cork proposed the inscription adopted for the medal, which was struck on 1 October 1856. It reads: 'All those of every rank and class engaged in the several Arctic expeditions'.[16]

Among those listed in the Arctic Medal roll were other Irish sailors who served on the Phoenix and Rattlesnake. John McCarthy (AB) was aboard Phoenix, the supply ship to Beechey Island in 1853. Patrick Coleman (AB) served under Henry Trollope on Rattlesnake from 1853–54 in a voyage to deliver supplies to Plover in the Bering Strait via Magellan Strait. Having met Plover on 22 August 1853, Rattlesnake wintered at Port Clarence, Alaska. On 30 July 1854, Rattlesnake again met Plover, and also met Enterprise, under Collinson, the last navy ship to search for Franklin – three years after his absence in the Arctic. Rattlesnake carried home Enterprise's dispatches.[17]

Frederick George Francis Mecham FRGS (Fellow of the Royal Geographical Society) was promoted to commander in 1855, and appointed to Vixen in the Pacific in 1857. He died of bronchitis at the age of 29 in Honolulu on 16 February 1858; thus ended a dynamic but short career, littered with remarkable accomplishments.[18] Cape Mecham – the south point of Prince Patrick Island – and Mecham Island – in the strait between Russell and Prince of Wales Islands – are named in honour of the Corkman.

# 10

## McCLINTOCK'S VOYAGE OF THE *FOX*

*A sad tale was never told in fewer words.*

Leopold McClintock[1]

The earliest evidence of Franklin's fate was discovered by John Rae, a chief factor with the Hudson's Bay Company. In a letter dated 29 July 1854 – from Repulse Bay to the Lord Commissioners of the Admiralty – Rae outlined his findings. While completing a survey of the west shore of Boothia, on King William Land – which Rae had discovered to be an island – he met Eskimos in Pelly Bay who told him of 40 white men dragging a boat on a sledge in the direction of the Great Fish River:

> a party of white men (Kablounans) had perished from want of food some distance to the westward, and not far beyond a large river, containing many falls and rapids . . . in the spring of four winters past (1850).

According to the Eskimos, the men were thin. Later in the same season, the bodies of 30 persons were discovered on the continent and five others on a nearby island. Rae goes on:

> One of those found on the island was supposed to be an officer, as he had a telescope strapped across his shoulders, and his double barrelled gun lay underneath him. From the mutilated state of many of the corpses, and the content of the kettles, it is evident that our wretched countrymen had been driven to the last resource – cannibalism – as a means of prolonging existence.

Could the officer with the telescope have been Crozier? Rae observed in the possession of the Eskimos many personal items that had belonged to the crews, such as watches, silver spoons, forks, compasses, telescopes and guns. Among the items Rae recovered was a bone-handled knife made by Millikin of London and inscribed 'C. Hickey'. This

*facing page*
The opening of a cairn at Point Victory where a signed statement from Captains Crozier and Fitzjames detailed the abandonment of HMS *Erebus* and *Terror*.
*From* The Arctic World

Knife handle engraved with the name of Limerick-born Cornelius Hickey, the 24-year-old caulker's mate of HMS *Terror*. It was found in 1854 in the possession of Innuit hunters by John Rae, a factor with the Hudson's Bay Company.
*From* Illustrated London News

was from the kit of the young caulker's mate born in Limerick. Rae also saw a silver tablespoon made by Josiah Low of Dublin, inscribed with Crozier's crest and initials. One of Sir John Franklin's magnificent medals, presented to him in 1836, was also in the possession of the Eskimos.

Public interest was reawakened with the news, but the government and Admiralty – still fighting the war in Russia and unwilling to shift the focus of their attention – were not in favour of sending another expedition, with its attendant risk to lives and ships. Lady Franklin had always vigorously supported the searching of Boothia toward the Great Fish River, but had been frustrated by the various search missions. Now she decided to purchase and fit out another expedition, and offered Leopold McClintock command. She was outraged at Rae's charges of cannibalism levelled at the men led by her husband, as were many others; Charles Dickens wrote of the injustice of charges against men who, due to their absence, were unable to defend themselves. To the navy establishment and Lady Jane, Rae was *persona non grata* and given little credit for his findings and charted discoveries. Nevertheless, Lady Jane

was anxious to show that if Rae's claim about Franklin's men having reached Back's Great Fish River were true, credit would be due to her husband for having completed the first Northwest Passage to the Canadian coast from Lancaster Sound.

In his narrative of the expedition, McClintock tells us of his own motivation and thinking.[2] On his return from the Belcher expedition at the age of 35, he had been promoted to the rank of post-captain over the heads of 242 seniors – due recognition for his performance while searching and surveying from the platform of a polar sledge. But through a lack of patronage – and despite the Crimean War – he was not given a ship.[3] On being offered command of the *Fox* by Lady Jane, he declared:

How could I do otherwise than devote myself to save at least the record of faithful service, even unto death, of my brother officers and seamen? . . . one of those by whose united effort not only the Franklin search, but the geography of Arctic America, has been brought so nearly to completion, I could not willingly resign to posterity the honour of filling up even the small remaining blanks upon our maps. To leave these discoveries incomplete, more especially in the quarter through which the tidal stream actually demonstrates the existence of a channel – the only remaining hope of a practicable North-west Passage – would indeed be leaving strong inducement for future explorers to reap rich reward of our long continued exertions.[4]

He applied from Dublin to the Admiralty for leave of absence to complete the Franklin search and, on 23 April 1857, received at Dublin a telegraphic message from Lady Franklin: 'your leave is granted; the *Fox* is mine, the refit will commence immediately.'[5]

He had surveyed the *Fox*, a screw yacht of 177 tons, which was immediately sent to Aberdeen for refitting. The velvet hangings and splendid furniture of the yacht were removed, and the vessel was sheeted externally and strengthened with the addition of longitudinal, cross and diagonal beams. Its previous owner, the late Sir Richard Sutton, had only made one trip in her, to Norway. Lady Franklin had purchased the yacht from his executors for £2,000. Eighteen of her crew were polar veterans, including Johann Carl Petersen, the Eskimo interpreter who had been with Captain Penny and the American, Dr Kane, in previous search expeditions. McClintock acknowledged the importance of the electric telegraph for securing Petersen's services. Provisions

The *Fox* exits the rolling pack ice under steam and sail. Drawing by Captain May.
*From* Voyage of the Fox in the Arctic Seas, Leopold *McClintock*

for 28 months were embarked, including 6,682 pounds of pemmican provided by the Admiralty, which also supplied ample Arctic clothing, retained from former expeditions. In order to make sufficient space for food and fuel, McClintock unselfishly modified the captain's quarter to a sparse size, regarded by all as the worst quarter aboard the yacht. On the evening planned for departure – 30 June – Lady Jane and Sophia Cracroft, accompanied by Captain Rochford Maguire RN, came on board to bid them farewell. Seeing how deeply agitated she was on leaving the ship, McClintock endeavoured to repress the enthusiasm of his crew, but to no avail; they gave vent to three rousing cheers.

McClintock had invited instructions from Lady Franklin. Replying by letter, she avoided giving him specific instructions in the knowledge that their views were identical in relation to where to search. She did, however, identify her priorities, expressed in simple terms: 'the rescue of any possible survivor of the *Erebus* and *Terror* would be to me, as it would to you, the noblest result of our effort'. Next in importance she rated the 'recovery of the unspeakably precious documents of the expedition'; lastly, her desire was that 'it may be in your power to confirm, directly or inferentially, the claims of my husband's expedition to the earliest discovery of the passage, which if Dr. Rae's report be true, these martyrs in a noble cause achieved at their last extremity, after five long years of labour and suffering, if not at an earlier period.' Finally, she told McClintock she had no misgivings regarding any possible failure, 'since you may fail in spite of effort, as if you succeed'.

The *Fox* passed through the Pentland Firth on 2 July and was sighted ten days later at Cape Farewell. McClintock dropped off a sick crewman at Frederickshaab (now Paamuit) on 20 July. He wrote regarding the population of Greenland: 7,000 people, a seventh of whom were Danes and who traded mainly in skins, seals and oil. In a social commentary, he reflected on the approach of the Danes to their colonies; a school, a doctor and a Lutheran Church were provided at no cost to the natives. Though not subject to Danish law and having retained their independence, the natives were sincerely attached to the Danes. He contrasted this with the English policy toward its colonies, and particularly toward the Eskimos in Labrador and Hudson Bay.

Having taken on board coal and cod, McClintock continued north. But it was a very bad ice year and the little *Fox* was soon beset in the drifting ice of Baffin Bay, not to be released again for 242 days, during which time it drifted 1,385 miles before finally exiting in the Davis Channel. They had many anxious days and nights during the Arctic winter, culminating the following April in two days of a nerve-wracking exit through drifting blocks of ice in high winds and 13.5-foot waves. To add to his woes, during the drift south – on 2 December – Leading Stoker Robert Scott fell down a hatchway and died of internal injuries. The burial took place two days later when he was 'committed to the deep' through a hole cut in the ice. McClintock described the funeral thus:

What a scene it was! I shall never forget it. The lonely *Fox* almost buried in snow,

completely isolated from the habitable world, her colours half-mast high, and bell mournfully tolling; our little procession slowly marching over the rough surface of the frozen sea, guiding by lanterns and direction posts, amid the dark and dreary depth of Arctic winter; the death like stillness, the intense cold, and threatening aspect of a murky overcast sky; and all this heightened by one of those strange lunar phenomena which are seldom seen even here, a complete halo enriching the moon, through which passed a horizontal band of pale light that encompassed the heavens;

above the moon appeared two segments of two other halos and there were also mock moons or paraselenae to the number of six. The misty atmosphere lent a very ghastly hue due to the singular display, which lasted for rather more than an hour.[6]

He utilised the officers' time in conducting magnetic observations and, with the men, practised building snow huts for use in winter or early spring travel. He considered this knowledge indispensable; by January, he recorded that they could build a snow house in three-quarters of an hour.

When eventually released from the pack in

The funeral of Leading Stoker Robert Scott, drawn by Captain May. Scott is committed to the deep by his comrades; HMS *Fox* and mock moons (paraselenae) are visible in the background. Drawing by Captain May.
*From* Voyage of the Fox in the Arctic Seas, *Leopold McClintock*

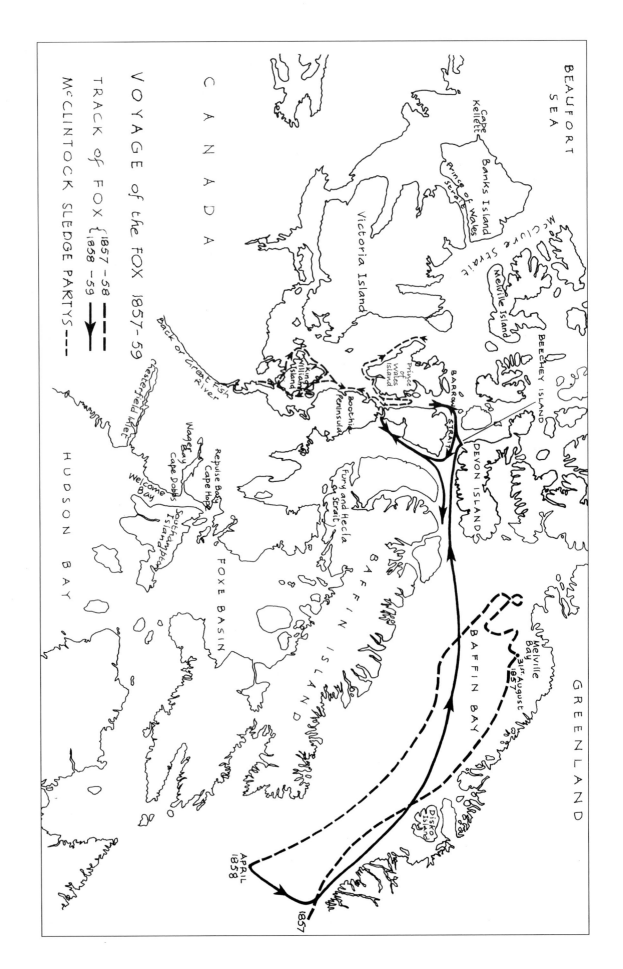

BEAUFORT SEA

CANADA

GREENLAND

HUDSON BAY

FOXE BASIN

BAFFIN ISLAND

BAFFIN BAY

Victoria Island

Banks Island

Cape Kellett

Prince of Wales Strait

McCLURE STRAIT

Melville Island

BEECHEY ISLAND

DEVON ISLAND

BARROW STRAIT

Prince of Wales Island

King William Island

Back or Great Fish River

Boothia Peninsula

Fury and Hecla Strait

Chesterfield Inlet

Wager Bay

Cape Dobbs

Welcome Bay

Southampton Island

Repulse Bay
Cape Hope

Melville Bay
31st August 1857

Disko Island

APRIL 1858

1857

VOYAGE of the FOX 1857-59

TRACK of FOX { 1857-58
1858-59

McCLINTOCK SLEDGE PARTYS - - -

April 1858, McClintock stubbornly steered back north again – to Holsteinsborg – for refitting, to refresh the crew and to hunt reindeer. In the summer season, he crossed Baffin Bay safely and reached Cape Riley on 11 August, where they took on coal mined from the cliffs by the crew. He visited Beechey Island House – a depot left for Franklin or Collinson by the Belcher expedition – and took on board provisions and a sledge boat. Coaling complete, McClintock erected a marble tablet at Beechey Island; it had been carved in New York at the request of Lady Franklin and left at Godhavn, Greenland in 1855 by Captain Harstein, who was searching for the American explorer, Dr Kane. Circumstances prevented the stone being erected at Beechey Island at that time. McClintock left Beechey Island on 16 August and, two days later – in a wild state of excitement – was 25 miles into Peel Strait when he reached unbroken ice; it continued for the next 60 miles. He decided to try Bellot Strait and, if unsuccessful, to go back to Barrow Strait. McClintock expressed his feelings thus: 'we feel that the crisis of our voyage is near at hand. Does Bellot Strait really exist? If so, is it there for me?' While backtracking to Barrow Strait, he stopped at Port Leopold to check the state of provisions left there in 1849, and then entered Prince Regent Strait, passing Fury Strait and Cresswell Bay. On 21 August, he passed between Browne Island and Possession Point, named by Sir John Ross in 1829. Having set up a depot in Depot Bay, he entered Bellot Strait, but was stopped halfway through by 5 or 6 miles of heavy pack. He returned to Depot Bay and unloaded a large stock of provisions. Confident the pack would

Inside McClintock's magnetic observatory. Drawing by Captain May.
*From* Voyage of the Fox in the Arctic Seas, *Leopold McClintock*

clear during the remainder of the season, he intended to advance westward through Bellot Strait to what is now called Franklin Strait. He described the strait as

precisely that of a Greenland fiord, twenty miles long and scarcely a mile wide as its narrowest point and within a quarter mile of its northern shore was 400 foot deep . . . Its granite shores are bold and lofty with a very respectable sprinkling of vegetation. Eastward of Depot Bay is limestone and westward the granite commences and is at once both bold and rugged.[7]

McClintock's quality of observation is impressive, and encompassed geology, astronomy, flora and fauna, hunting and native peoples. On 15 September, he observed a comet beneath the constellation of the Great Bear; 'a series of measurements were commenced for determining its path'. He was also reflective – a ramble in the hills he considered conducive to contemplation, permitting him 'to cogitate undisturbed in a leisurely and philosophic manner'.[8]

McClintock employed a well-developed decision-making process. When the strait was not navigable on a fourth attempt, he decided to winter to the east of Bellot Strait and to sledge from there, over land and frozen seas, in the following spring. The plan was put in place in September. As usual, it was precise and meticulous. There would be three search parties: each would comprise a leader and four men, and would be provided with a dog sledge and driver. The first party would be led by McClintock with whom, Petersen, the interpreter, would travel as sledge driver. They would search the Great Fish River estuary explored by Back and the shores of King William Land. Hobson would lead the second party to the magnetic-Pole area and to the west coast of Boothia in autumn and from Gateshead westward in spring. The third search party was led by Allen Young, a merchant-naval captain who had not only volunteered his services without pay, but had made a contribution of £500 toward the expedition costs. His party would search Prince of Wales Land and the coast between Willie Browne's furthest-searched point and then travel southwestward to Osborn's furthest; both had been reached during the Austin expedition sledge search journeys of 1850–51. Young would then proceed to Four Rivers Point and Cape Bird, previously searched by Ross in 1848–49. The journeys were planned to start on 29 March 1859 and would involve

60–70 days of travelling. In effect, McClintock was at once searching for Franklin while charting the remaining blank spots on the map of Arctic America, utilising his 26 men to the utmost. But first, in autumn, he had to lay out depots and meet the native 'Boothians'. In the process, he would train his teams and dogs in preparation for the spring search programme.

Having constructed a magnetic observatory using ice blocks, from which hourly magnetic observations were carried out, *Fox* was made ready for winter and the stores in casks put out on the shore. At this time, McClintock went for many long walks when he would reflect on the achievements of his team to date. His leadership style was that of an exemplar: he was a role model with an astounding range of practical skills and knowledge. After a long walk, he tells us 'a feeling of tranquillity – of earnest, hearty satisfaction – has come over us. There is no appearance amongst us of anything boastful; we have all experienced too keenly the vicissitudes of Arctic voyaging to admit of such a feeling.' He also had a wry sense of humour. A crackshot himself, he wrote mildly disparagingly of his crew's hunting skills: 'Almost all on board have guns; ammunition is supplied, and a sailor with a musket is very contented and a zealous sportsman, if not always a successful one.'

In November, Mr Brand, the 40-year-old engineer – a steady and serious man – died of apoplexy. It appears he had been gloomy from dwelling on the sudden death of Scott. McClintock was now without an engineer or engine driver and the two stokers knew nothing about the machinery. Though this might have been

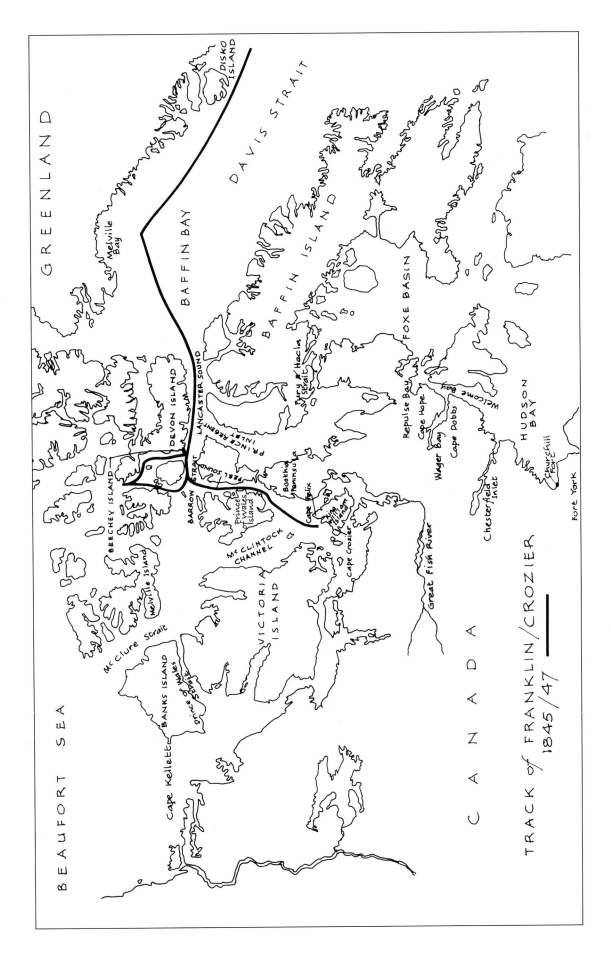

TRACK OF FRANKLIN/CROZIER 1845/47

thought a disaster on some expeditions, McClintock simply took responsibility for the engine himself when the time came to leave. In the meantime, preparations continued for the sledging. The remaining 22 dogs were divided with care into three teams of seven, with the extra dog going to McClintock's team, which had the longest journey ahead of it. Thereafter, each sledge party fed and cared for its own dog team.

On 17 February, Young and McClintock set out. Having travelled 19 miles, they built a snow hut close to Pemmican Rock where, in autumn, they had established a depot. Their equipment included a 'small brown Holland tent, a mackintosh floor-cloth, and felt robes'. Each man also had a double-blanketed sleeping bag and a pair of fur boots for sleeping in. During the day, the men wrapped their feet in strips of blanket, over which they wore moccasins. With the sole exception of these strips, they had no other change of clothes. The sledging day lasted eight to ten hours, without a break save to disentangle the dog traces. The most disagreeable part of the day was the building of the snow edifice to sleep in. Two were employed to cut out blocks and another as the builder. As everybody was tired, they quickly became cold while waiting for the shelter to be built. Then, the dogs had to be fed, ensuring that the weaker ones got a sufficient share in the scramble for frozen supper. Next, the sledge was unloaded and everything needed was carried into the hut, including provisions and the cooking lamp. The door was blocked up, the cooking lamp lighted, footgear changed, diaries written up, watches wound, sleeping bags wriggled into, pipes lighted, and the merits and demerits of the various dogs were discussed until supper was ready and swallowed. Finally, the upper robe was pulled over all and then to sleep. In the morning, after breakfast and the struggle to get into the frozen moccasins, the sledge was packed and made ready for the day's work.

McClintock was looking for the Boothians – the local Innuit who lived south of Bellot Strait in the vicinity of the magnetic North Pole. Ross had made contact with them many years before. On 1 March, they stopped to build their evening hut close to the magnetic Pole, and when they turned around, found behind them four Innuit men, who were out hunting. They had started for their village when darkness descended upon them and were in need of shelter. McClintock traded a sewing needle with each of the Innuit in exchange for an Innuit-built snow hut built there and then. Completed in one hour, both parties slept in it together. McClintock observed that the records of architecture do not include mention of another instance of a house so cheap.

One of the Innuit had a naval button on his dress. Upon inquiry, it was learned that it came from some white people who were starved on an island where there are salmon – this implied a river – and that the iron from which their knives were made came from that place also. One of the men said he had been there for wood and iron, but none of them had seen the white men. Next morning, they travelled 10 miles closer to Cape Victoria; beyond this, McClintock refused to go. Six out of the fifteen dogs were quite useless and the party had depleted rations. The Innuit here built a commodious hut that, despite the gale outside, kept them all warm. McClintock showed

the articles brought for barter – knives, files, sewing needles, scissors and beads, and expressed – through Petersen – their desire to barter for anything the Innuit had picked up which had belonged to the white men. Despite the cold, two of the Innuit took off their outer coats and traded them for a knife.

Next morning, 45 Innuit arrived – the entire population of the village. Silver spoons and forks, a silver medal – property of Mr A. McDonald, the assistant surgeon – part of a gold chain, buttons, knives made of iron and wood from the

wreck – *Erebus* or *Terror* – were produced and successfully traded. Salmon, venison and seal blubber was also purchased. The 'Boothians' remembered Ross and the *Victory*, and when McClintock enquired after a man for whom they had supplied a wooden leg, his daughter was pointed out. Petersen interpreted this to mean that the man had died, as the Innuit did not like to refer directly to the dead. None of the people had seen the white men, though one man said he had seen their bones on the island where they had died, and that only some were buried. With

Captain May's impression of McClintock's sledge party discovering the remains of a cairn at Cape Herschel in May 1859.
*From* Voyage of the Fox in the Arctic Seas, *Leopold McClintock*

this intelligence, McClintock returned to the ship, reaching it on 14 March. The journey of 420 miles completed the discovery of the coast of continental America and added 120 miles to the existing charts.

Young had in the meantime completed his depot-laying task; he had found the ice in Bellot Strait so rough as to be impassable, but had also found an alternative, parallel route via a narrow inland lake. His party lived in tents protected from the wind by snow walls. Not being able to find three cases of sugar in their provisions, Young set off for Fury Beach on 18 March with two men and eighteen dogs. Failing to locate the requisite provisions there, he went to Port Leopold. This episode demonstrated the advantages and usefulness of the dog sledge for communications and for ensuring a supply of provisions to a ship beset.

On 2 April, the main sledge journeys commenced. McClintock and Hobson set out together for Cape Victoria, reaching there on 28 April. From here, Hobson marched directly to Cape Felix, on the northern coast of King William Island, while McClintock headed south. The Dundalk man gave Hobson directions to search the west coast of King William Island in the hope of finding the stranded ship and any records. He was instructed to act on such information as may be derived from the natives and also to complete the search and discovery of the blank spaces between the extremes visited by Captain Collinson and Mr Wynniatt.

McClintock's own party set out for Port Parry on King William Island across rough pack and established a depot for their return. With 30 days' supplies, he followed the coast past Cape Sabine, Wellington Strait and the south-western extremity of Matty Island. He was trying to locate some local Innuit in their winter residences who, he thought, might lead them to the remains of Franklin's crews. He describes the empty huts he found as being 12 feet in diameter, 6–7 feet high and mostly constructed in pairs, with a common entrance passage; a small hut served as a receptacle for articles intended to be kept frozen.

On 7 May, an inhabited snow village was found further south on King William Island. Here, they purchased six pieces of tableware bearing the crests or initials of Franklin, Crozier, Fairholme and McDonald, and also tunic buttons and uniforms. The silver spoons and forks were exchanged for four sewing needles each. The Innuit told them that it was five days' travel to the wreck, that it was accessible and that most of it had already been carried away by the local Innuit. When asked about the condition of the masts, they were told they were down – felled, it seemed, by burning their bases close to the deck. The Innuit said that it was autumn when the ship had been forced ashore and that the last person from their group to visit the wreck did so during the winter of 1857–58. One of these, a woman, said that many of the white men dropped by the way as they went to the Great Fish River. Some were buried and some were not. The Innuit had passed their fallen bodies the following winter.

On 12 May, McClintock's team crossed Point Ogle and reached the Great Fish River where they camped on the ice. Two days of gales forced them to stay put, but on the evening of 14 May, they camped on a small island to the north end of Montreal Island. Ten days later, they marched along the south coast of King William Island to Cape Herschel. Here, using a pickaxe, they took down a cairn and examined the site. Finding nothing, they walked along the shore that the retreating party had passed. Shortly after midnight, on 25 May, McClintock came across a skeleton on a ridge between the beach and the island, lying face down and partly exposed. The tattered remains of the clothing indicated a steward or an officer's servant. A clothes brush and a comb were also found – an indication that the natives had not discovered this corpse. McClintock concluded that this man had selected the bare ridge as affording the easiest walking route, and had fallen upon his face in the position they had found him.

He examined minutely the intervening coastline to Cape Herschel, where he had a particular hope of finding a note in a conspicuous cairn built by Simpson during his exploration of this coastline nine years before. They found the cairn to be only 4-feet high and partly dismantled. McClintock reasoned that, because the cairn was left half dismantled, the natives must have found what they sought. However, his party completely dismantled the cairn and dug beneath it with a pickaxe, finding nothing. His severe disappointment at not finding 'some certain record of those martyrs to their country's fame' was soon to be assuaged. He carried on for about 12 miles from Cape Herschel until he found a small, recently built cairn. It was erected by Hobson's party and contained a note from him reporting to McClintock that he had not seen 'anything of the

wreck or of the natives, but he had found a record – the record so ardently sought to tell the fate of the Franklin expedition.'[9] He had found it at Point Victory on the north-west coast of King William Land. The note was written on a standard printed form of a type usually supplied to discovery ships; they would be enclosed in a bottle and thrown overboard at sea in order to ascertain currents, with blank spaces left for date and position. Any person finding one of these records was asked to forward it to the secretary of the Admiralty, with a note of time and place of recovery. The message read as follows:

28 of May 1847
H.M.S.hips *Erebus* and *Terror* Wintered in the Ice in Lat. 70° 5' N Long. 98° 23' W Having wintered in 1846–7 at Beechey Island in Lat. 74° 43' 28" N. Long. 91° 39' 15" W after having ascended Wellington Channel to Lat 77° and returned by the west side of Cornwallis Island.
Sir John Franklin commanding the expedition.
All well.
Party consisting of 2 officers and 6 Men left the ships on Monday 24th. May 1847
Gm. Gore, Lieut.
Chas. F. Des Voeux, Mate

This brief message meant that Franklin, in the first ice season, had followed orders and had discovered new lands on both sides of the Wellington Channel, whose entry was discovered by Parry in 1819. They went north for 150 miles and reached latitude 77° north, returning by a newly discovered channel between Bathurst and Cornwallis Islands. They had then overwintered at Beechey Island during 1845–46; the statement 'Having wintered in 1846–7 at Beechey Island' conflicts with the dates recorded on the head-stone at Beechey Island and is considered to be a simple error by the writer of the note. In the second season, they had proceeded southwest and eventually reached within 12 miles of the northern extremity of King William Land when their progress was stopped by the onset of the winter of 1846–47. That winter appears to have passed without any serious loss of life and when, in spring, Lieutenant Gore left the ship with a party, all was well and Franklin was still in command. However, a second message, written on the margins of the document, reads as follows:

> 25th April 1848 H.M.Ships *Terror* and *Erebus* were deserted on the 22nd April. 5 leagues NNW of this having been beset since 12th Septr 1846. The officers and crews consisting of 105 souls – under the command of Captain F.R.M. Crozier landed here – in Lat 69° 37' 42" Long 98° 41'.
> This paper was found by Lt. Irving under the cairn supposed to have been built by Sir James Ross in 1831, 4 miles to the Northward – where it had been deposited by the late Commander Gore in June 1847. Sir James Ross' pillar has not however been found, and the paper has been transferred to this position which is that in which Sir J. Ross' pillar was erected – Sir John Franklin died on the 11th June 1847 and the total loss by deaths in the

Expedition has been to this date 9 officers and 15 men.
James Fitzjames, Captain HMS *Erebus*
FRM Crozier Captain and Senior offr.
and start on tomorrow 26th for Backs Fish River[10]

McClintock describes how 'that record is indeed a sad and touching relic of our lost friends'.[11] The first message tells of the success of the expedition in its first navigation season (1845–46) when it navigated and charted Wellington Channel to 77° north, and returned by a newly discovered channel to the west of Cornwallis Island. The second message tells how, in the second season (1846–47), they navigated into Peel Strait and what is now known as the Franklin Strait, where the ships became beset in the pack ice; they drifted and were crushed. In the final statement, the leaders, Crozier and Fitzjames, demonstrate their lofty sense of duty and a calmness having made the decision to struggle for life rather than perish without effort on board their ships; for we know that *Erebus* and *Terror* were only provisioned up to July 1848.

Hobson's note told McClintock that he had found a large quantity of clothing and articles of all kinds lying about the cairn, as if the men were fully aware they were retreating for their lives and had abandoned everything they considered superfluous. Hobson's last observation was that he had experienced bad weather, gales and fog, and feared he might have passed the wreck without seeing her; he hoped to be more successful on the return journey.

McClintock and his team travelled up the west

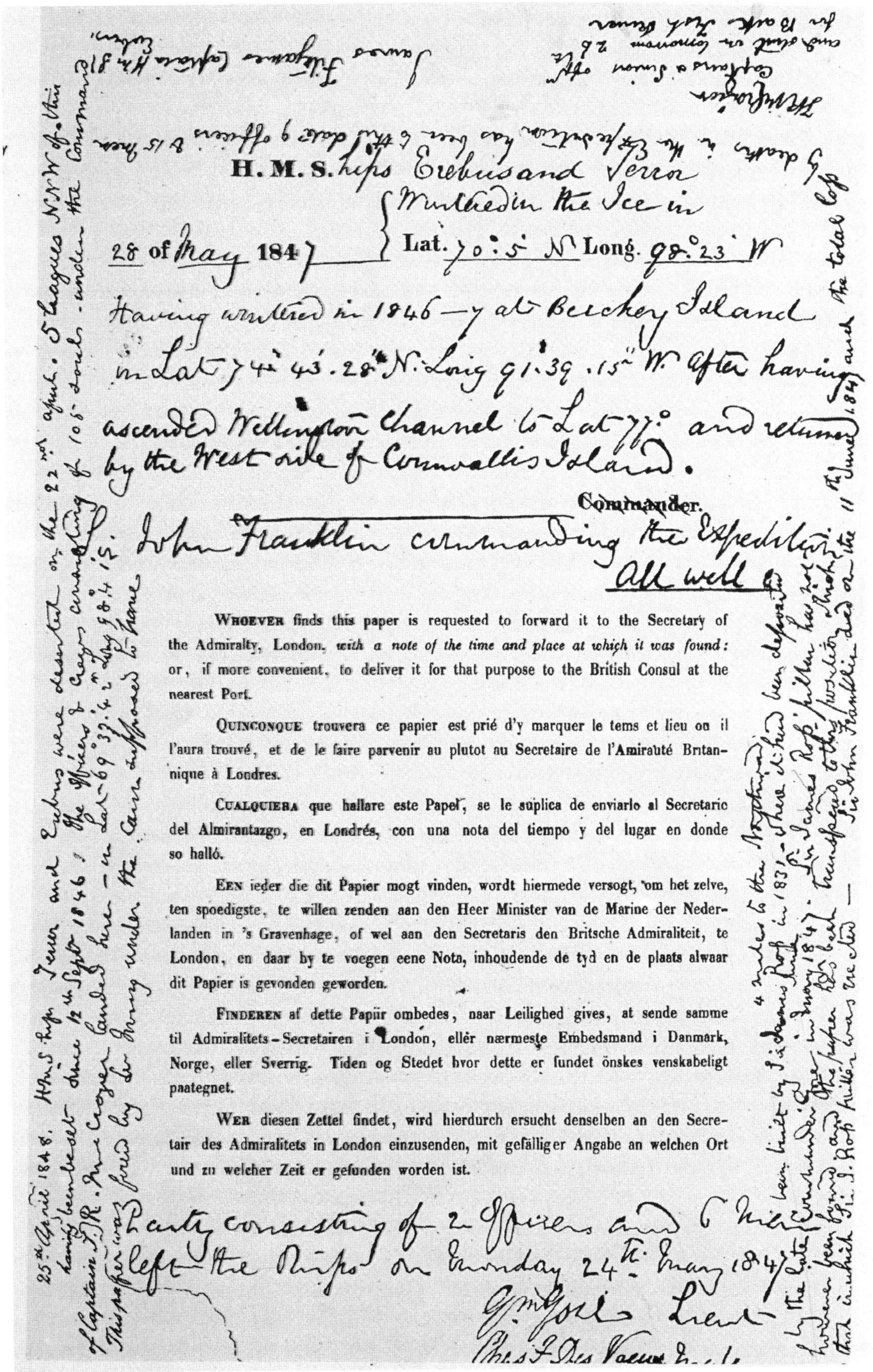

The only written record of the fate of Franklin and Crozier and their men, which was found by Lieutenant Hobson and his party.
*From* Voyage of the Fox in the Arctic Seas, *Leopold McClintock*

H.M.S.hips Erebus and Terror

28 of May 1847 { Wintered in the Ice in Lat. 70° 5' N. Long. 98° 23' W.

Having wintered in 1846—7 at Beechey Island in Lat 74° 43. 28" N. Long 91.39. 15" W. After having ascended Wellington Channel to Lat 77° and returned by the West side of Cornwallis Island.

**Commander.**

Sir John Franklin commanding the Expedition.
All well

WHOEVER finds this paper is requested to forward it to the Secretary of the Admiralty, London, *with a note of the time and place at which it was found:* or, if more convenient, to deliver it for that purpose to the British Consul at the nearest Port.

QUINCONQUE trouvera ce papier est prié d'y marquer le tems et lieu où il l'aura trouvé, et de le faire parvenir au plutot au Secretaire de l'Amirauté Britannique à Londres.

CUALQUIERA que hallare este Papel, se le suplica de enviarlo al Secretario del Almirantazgo, en Londrés, con una nota del tiempo y del lugar en donde so halló.

EEN ieder die dit Papier mogt vinden, wordt hiermede versogt, om het zelve, ten spoedigste, te willen zenden aan den Heer Minister van de Marine der Nederlanden in 's Gravenhage, of wel aan den Secretaris den Britsche Admiraliteit, te London, en daar by te voegen eene Nota, inhoudende de tyd en de plaats alwaar dit Papier is gevonden geworden.

FINDEREN af dette Papür ombedes, naar Leilighed gives, at sende samme til Admiralitets-Secretairen i London, eller nærmeste Embedsmand i Danmark, Norge, eller Sverrig. Tiden og Stedet hvor dette er fundet önskes venskabeligt paategnet.

WER diesen Zettel findet, wird hierdurch ersucht denselben an den Secretair des Admiralitets in London einzusenden, mit gefälliger Angabe an welchen Ort und zu welcher Zeit er gefunden worden ist.

Party consisting of 2 Officers and 6 Men left the Ships on Monday 24th May 1847

Gm Gore Lieut
Chas F Des Voeux Mate

*(margin, left side, written sideways):*
25th April 1848. H.M. Ships Terror and Erebus were deserted on the 22nd April 5 leagues N N W of this having been beset since 12th Sept 1846. The officers & Crews consisting of 105 souls under the command of Captain F R M Crozier landed here—in Lat 69° 37' 42" Long 98° 41' 15". This paper was found by Lt Irving under the cairn supposed to have been built by Sir James Ross in 1831—4 miles to the Northward—where it had been deposited by the late Commander Gore in May 1847. Sir James Ross' pillar has not however been found and the paper has been transferred to this position which is that in which Sir J. Ross' pillar was erected—Sir John Franklin died on the 11th June 1847 and the total loss by deaths in the Expedition has been to this date 9 officers & 15 men.

*(top margin, sideways):*
James Fitzjames Captain H.M.S. Erebus
F R M Crozier Captain & Senior Offr
and start on tomorrow 26th for Backs Fish River

coast of King William Island, 'exerting their utmost vigilance in order that no trace should escape them.' On 29 May, they reached a cape at the western extremity of King William Island, in latitude 69° north, longitude 100° 80' west, which the Louthman named after Francis Crozier, his countryman from the adjoining Co. Down who he described as 'the gallant leader of that forlorn hope of which we have just obtained tidings'. He described the desolate lands, how little game there was or, indeed, few traces of natives in search of game. On 30 May, they camped alongside a large boat – another relic found by Hobson – but again there was no written record. Regarding the vast quantity of tattered clothing, no article bore the name of its owner. On examination, they discovered the boat had been built with a view to lightness and was evidently equipped with utmost care for the ascent of the Great Fish River. Though she had no oars or rudder, paddles were supplied in their place. A remnant of light canvas and a block for reefing, he supposed, were to provide a sail. A sloping canvas roof or rain awning had also formed part of her equipment. The boat's planking had been lightened and changed from carvel to 'clincher fashion' using thin, fir planking. It weighed 700–800 pounds, but the sledge on which she travelled was unusually heavy, being constructed largely of heavy, oak planks – 23-feet long – on which the steel runners were fixed. The combined boat and sledge, McClintock tells us, was about 1,400 pounds, which would require seven healthy men to pull. Given the direction in which the boat was pointed, he surmised that it was on its way back to the ships, which, he cal-culated, were 65 miles to the northeast.[12] Two skeletons were also found in the boat, one of a slight, young person, the other of a large, strongly built middle-aged person. McClintock's opinion was that wolves had probably destroyed much of one of the skeletons; he thought this man might have been an officer. They also found a staggering array of items including two rolls of lead sheeting, nails, saws, files, boots, shoes and silver cutlery, which cumulatively amounted to a considerable dead weight. In the opinion of McClintock, this was a load likely to break down the strength of any sledge crew.

They followed the coast to Point Franklin, which had been named by Sir James Clark Ross in 1830 following his sighting of it from Point Victory. Despite their constant vigilance, they did not spot the stricken ship.[13] They continued trav-elling along the coast until mid-June, when McClintock was forced to abandon the sledge due to ice melt and hardship on his men. He abandoned the sledges and left the foot-sore and tired dogs behind, walking over the remaining hills and valleys until, on 19 June 1859 – after an absence of 78 days – they sighted *Fox*. Hobson, who had arrived a week ahead of him, was still unable to walk from the effects of scurvy; he had been brought back on the sledge. Thomas Blackwell, the ship's steward who had been sick with scurvy on McClintock's departure, was dead on his return, bringing to three the death toll for the expedition. It seems Blackwell disliked pre-served meats and vegetables, and had lived almost exclusively on salted pork for the winter.

Young was not back yet; he had left on 7 April with a sledge party of four men and a dog sledge of six dogs. He searched and surveyed the uncharted southern shore of Prince of Wales Island and, having sent back all but one of his crew, travelled light to complete his work. He attempted to cross what is now called the McClintock Channel, but due to the roughness of its surface, opted to travel down the coast, returning for medical treatment before setting out again to finish the survey, which included both sides of the Franklin Strait. His party found no evidence of Franklin, but they did explore and survey 380 miles of new country.

McClintock was worried about Young; he walked out to recover his own dog team in the hope of meeting him and was very relived to meet him at Pemmican Rock. One can only imagine the party on board *Fox* when all three groups reunited after such effort and long absence. Their achievements were considerable. They had found written records – the only tangible evidence of the Franklin disaster – and the remains of some of his men. McClintock also established that Crozier's party had reached the shores of America, thereby making the first Northwest Passage – ahead of his countryman, McClure – by linking Parry's furthest-west with the known American Arctic coastline discovered by Back, Simpson, Dease and, indeed, Franklin himself. Together, McClintock, Hobson and Young had charted 800 miles of new coastline, filling the remaining blanks in the map of continental America. In the process, McClintock had also discovered the first practical route, by way of the Rae Strait, that would lead eventually to the first water navigation of the Northwest Passage, 45 years later, by the Norwegian, Roald Amund-

sen. This route, and some variations through the Bellot Strait, has been repeated many times since and was successfully navigated in August 2001 by the crew of the 49-foot, Irish sailing boat, *Northabout*; the voyage, from the entry to Lancaster Sound to Point Barrow, took 25 days. The author of this history was a member of that expedition team, which made the first Irish navigation of the route covered by foot and sail by Crozier, McClure and McClintock.

While McClintock waited for the summer thaw to free up the *Fox* for the passage home, he busied himself and the crew in preparing the vessel for sailing. They loaded 12 tons of stone ballast, filled the water tanks, examined all their provisions, re-stowed them and thoroughly cleaned the *Fox*. While Hobson supervised this work, McClintock himself gave attention to the steam engine and boilers with the help of the two stokers. On 1 August, he ran the engine for a short time and was cheered to know that he had steam at his command. He also completed his chart of the west coast of King William Island. Meanwhile, Young was mapping the harbour and making tidal observations, while Hobson wrote a detailed report of his journey, listing the relics and details of where they were recovered. On 9 August, the ice was cleared and McClintock steamed out at 11 a.m. He himself spent the day trying to manage the engines and boiler; at one stage, after the valve in the condenser became free of its seat, the boiler spewed water over the top of the ship's sails. Having resolved the problem, McClintock steamed to Disco Bay and, from there, back to London's Blackwell Docks, arriving on 23 September 1859.

McClintock received a knighthood from Queen Victoria and the freedom of the city of London. Hobson's contribution was acknowledged by his promotion. Parliament – at the instigation of Lord Palmerston and Disraeli – voted £5,000 to the officers and crew. The Admiralty also informed McClintock that, on the instruction of Queen Victoria, he and his crew's period of service on the *Fox* was recognised as 'sea time', thereby entitling all to pay and service seniority. The Royal Geographical Society presented its Patron's Gold Medal to McClintock, and its Founder's Gold Medal to Lady Franklin in recognition of her 'noble and self-sacrificing perseverance'.[14]

In his native Dundalk, on 31 October 1859, McClintock was guest of honour at a dinner at which he received a presentation of silver and an address of welcome. Accepting the address, McClintock said he would 'cherish it always, more than any other honour, as it comes from the town where I spent my youth, from the friends of my boyhood days, from my home.' He also received the freedom of Dublin city while Trinity College awarded him the honorary degree, LLD (Doctor of Laws).[15] The scientific societies of Dublin – the Royal Dublin Society and the Dublin University Zoological and Botanical Society – not only honoured McClintock with an address and presentation, but also had his bust sculptured in marble. The bust – by Kirk – was placed in the society's museum, which he had enriched with Innuit relics and specimens of Arctic geology and natural history. To this day, one can see a polar bear shot by McClintock in the Natural History Museum in Merrion Street, Dublin. Professor Samuel Haughton of Trinity

College produced a paper, 'On fossils brought home from the Arctic regions in 1859, by Capt. Sir F.L. McClintock' for the *Philosophical Transactions of the Royal Society*.[16]

McClintock Channel, which separates Victoria Island from Prince of Wales Island, was named in his honour. It is fitting that it communicates with the Franklin Strait at Larsen Sound. Not far away, Cape Crozier, on the west coast of King William Island, honours the lost Banbridge explorer's Arctic contribution and supreme sacrifice in the quest for polar knowledge.

A committee was established in Ireland to erect a suitable memorial to the memory of Crozier and a fine monument was erected in 1862 at Bridge Street, Banbridge, Co. Down, outside the Georgian house where he was born. W.J. Barre, whose other work includes both the Ulster Hall and the Albert Memorial in Belfast, created the pedestal. The statue of Crozier, with four polar bears looking up at him, is by Kirk, a well-known sculptor who also carved the memorial commissioned by Crozier's family and which is located in Seapatrick Church of Ireland church, which faces his birthplace. The memorial features a profile medallion of Captain Crozier and a representation of *Terror* wrecked among pack ice.

Lady Jane Franklin spent a lot of her remaining life in constant travel, visiting places such as Japan and Nevada, with Sophia Cracroft as her constant companion. Her last work was the completion of a monument to her husband's memory in Westminster Abbey, on which the words of Lord Tennyson were inscribed:

Not here! the white North has thy bones;
  and thou,
Heroic sailor-soul,
Art passing on thine happier voyage now
Toward no earthly pole.

The memorial was unveiled two weeks after her death. Dean Stanley added a postscript to the memorial: 'This monument was erected by Jane his widow, who after long waiting, and sending in search of him, herself departed, to seek and to find him in the realms of light, July 18th 1875 aged 83 years.' She was buried in a vault in Kensal Green cemetery in London. Leopold McClintock was a pallbearer at her funeral. Sophia Cracroft, who never married, followed her to rest there; a marble cross on a plinth marks her nearby grave.

# AFTER THE FRANKLIN SEARCH AND THE NARES NORTH POLE EXPEDITION

*She needed head and heart and hand, combined in one – a
head to judge and decide promptly – a heart to feel as her
own did – and a hand to grapple with every obstacle that
might arise; and she found them all combined in our countryman . . . A man that might be typified in our own
national emblem, the shamrock, a type that blends, three
much-sought friends, head, heart and hand, together.*

DR CORRIGAN ON LEOPOLD MCCLINTOCK[1]

McClintock's findings answered many of the questions regarding the fate of Franklin. But we still know very little of the detail or chronology of events surrounding the expedition's demise; indeed, it is difficult to understand why it happened at all. Franklin and Crozier's contemporaries were baffled by the absence of messages left by the crews of *Erebus* and *Terror*, and had difficulty understanding why no apparent effort was made to establish a food cache to which they could retreat in the event of either or both ships becoming beset. The tactic of sending two ships together was so that each could support the other in the event of one ship having a mishap or becoming beset or sinking; that both ships became beset in the main pack ice in the same place undermined the logic of this tactic.

Crozier's reasons for retreating toward the Great Fish River with the entire complement of both ships is also difficult to understand. It is equally hard to see why he did not at least send one sledge party eastward, where they could have perhaps met with whalers or left messages at Beechey Island or Fury Beach indicating their whereabouts and intentions. The conduct of the expedition is still shrouded in mystery. Why so few written records were found is baffling. Why, for instance, not a single member of crew from either ship survived is still difficult to comprehend, and that not a single page from a journal of one of the officers has been found is simply incredible. There are many theories, but I believe any analysis will conclude that much of the

*facing page*
Sir Henry Kellett from
Clonacody, near
Fethard, Co.
Tipperary. He played a
key role in support of
the search for the
Franklin expedition
and in exact
surveying work on the
coast of South
America. Portrait by
Stephen Pearce.
*National Portrait Gallery*

expedition's planning and organisation was hasty and flawed.

The imperative for the expedition sailing in 1845 appears to have been purely to placate John Barrow's desire that the passage be completed before his retirement as second secretary of the Admiralty. The fitness and suitability of Sir John Franklin as the expedition leader must be critically questioned. His age, health and long absence from active service must have affected his ability as a hands-on commander in a frozen environment where even younger and more active men would be challenged. He vigorously sought the post and, with his wife's aid, had lobbied very effectively the decision makers in order that he might recover his damaged reputation following his sacking and recall as governor of Van Diemen's Land. This was to be his final glory. But Franklin was clearly too old and out of touch with the command of a polar sailing voyage. His exploration reputation was based on his survival during overland expeditions and not as a commander of polar ships. His attitude and behaviour to the leadership of the expedition, prior to departure, seems to indicate considerable overconfidence and complacency.

Crozier's last letter to Ross, from the Whalefish Islands, reveals his misgivings about the conduct of the expedition and is in stark contrast to Franklin's views, as expressed in Lady Jane's diary where she suggests his relationship with his officers and men was superior to that enjoyed by Ross. Jane's assertion that *Terror* seemed less happy than *Erebus* because of Crozier's broken heart also seems less than charitable. These views of Franklin – as recorded by his wife – smack of smugness and egotism, neither of which are hallmarks of one suited to command a polar expedition.

There is no doubt that James Clark Ross and Francis Crozier would have constituted the 'dream team' of the day for this mission, but neither were given sufficient time to rest after spending four-and-a-half years away from home in conditions which appear to have been underestimated by their superiors. It is also very revealing to note that, among the crews of *Erebus* and *Terror*, there were very few of Ross' men or, indeed, other crew with previous polar experience; nor had many of them experience of sledge travel. The crew was selected largely by Fitzjames, aided by John Barrow's son, also John. Franklin gave responsibility for the expedition's magnetic observation to Fitzjames without any prior reference to Crozier, his deputy commander and an acknowledged expert in the field. This reflected his insensitivity toward his second-in-command's status and dignity, and appears also to have been a 'statement' of seniority by Franklin vis-à-vis Crozier. Franklin's overconfidence and arrogance are evidenced by his not leaving dispatches at Beechey Island or in not establishing emergency food depots in the event of becoming beset or being forced to retreat. The absence of such contingencies delayed any directed search-and-rescue efforts, and widened the focus of the search area when it finally got under way. It also reduced the options open to Crozier when both ships became beset and when their abandonment became necessary after the death of Franklin.

Crozier's readiness and motivation for another expedition, so soon after his return from

Antarctica, is also questionable. From a career perspective, he must have found it difficult to turn down the offer of such a prestigious command from the Admiralty. He was clearly very unhappy with the reduced space for food and provisions aboard the *Terror*, caused by the fitting of the steam engines and the necessary coal-storage area. He regarded the state of stowage on both ships as chaotic. We know now that the additional weight arising from fitting the locomotive engines and the necessary space required to stow coal on *Terror* and *Erebus* had the effect of reducing food-storage capacity, and also contributed to deepening the draft of both ships to 19 feet. This would have made it very difficult to complete a passage through the notoriously shallow waters.

In 1987,[2] the anthropologists, Owen Beattie and John Geiger, claimed that lead migrating from soldered cans in which food was stored had been a major factor in the loss of the Franklin expedition. This was subsequently discounted as the result of a study by K.T.H. Ferrar. His paper, published by the *Journal of Archaeological Science* in 1993,[3] concluded that the contribution of canned foods to body levels of lead, or to any incipient ill health in Franklin's crews, was trivial. This counter claim was based on analyses of very old canned foods, which found low levels of migration of lead from solder into the food. Ferrar also asserted that very little lead is absorbed through ingestion – 90 per cent is excreted and, of the remaining ten per cent, virtually all of it passes into teeth and bone. He contends that canned food constituted a low percentage of the overall diet of the men, and that

the background levels of lead evident in British adults during the mid-nineteenth century were very high as a result of environmental factors such as the contamination of cider and beer through the use of lead containers, and by the use of lead piping for drinking water.

It appears that when Crozier abandoned the ships he was not expecting the navy to organise a search, particularly since Franklin had scoffed at an offer made prior to departure by Ross to come looking for them if, after two years, the expedition had not returned. That he was not expecting an eastern rescue party must have influenced Crozier's decision to make for the Great Fish River. Here, he clearly hoped to find good hunting grounds for the fresh meat, seal, caribou and birds which the already sick crew needed to recover and as replacement for the expedition's food, which was clearly the main cause of the scurvy. He headed for a known overland route through Canada, rather than back to Fury Beach, where the food cache was of the same nature as that on board *Erebus* and *Terror*. Sherard Osborn stated that Franklin had been informed before departure that a plan was afoot for whalers to collect the provisions at Fury Beach and sell them at Peterhead.[4] This plan was surely communicated to Crozier; hence, his preference for the Back River. It is also likely that he thought an Admiralty rescue party would come from that direction. That some preparation for this long journey took place is evident, such as the modification of boats to make them suitable for river navigation. However, it is also clear that they overestimated their physical ability, state of health and their strength to pull such heavy sledges, and they also appear to have underestimated the amount of provisions they required to complete the distance. The suitability, readiness and preparedness of the officers and seamen to survive and live off the land, once away from their ships, and the suitability of naval clothing provided to them for such circumstances left a lot to be desired.

Another of the great imponderables regarding the tragedy relates to the early deaths of nine of the expedition's officers from a total of 24 officers and men reported dead when Crozier ordered the abandonment of the ships. It was unusual for officers – usually better nourished than the seamen – to succumb to scurvy before the seamen, not least as it was the custom for officers to supplement the ship's stores with their own private supplies of carefully selected foods and wines. At what point and under what circumstances did the morale and discipline finally break down? What was the sequence of events that led to the total collapse of order? Did murder precede cannibalism? How long did Crozier himself survive in command so as to effect an orderly retreat of his men – seriously debilitated by scurvy and lack of nourishment – in such a hostile environment? Cornelius Hickey's knife was among the relics found by Rae, indicating his presence in that sad and harrowing procession of misery. Perhaps the best guide to their ordeal is to be found in the written accounts of McClure and Nares' men, some of whom died from scurvy. The death of James Hand, from Bray, Co. Wicklow, in 1875–76, is related later in this book. Lieutenant Beaumont, who commanded the sledge journey on which

he died, details the slow and painful death of that seaman from scurvy. One can only imagine the suffering and misery of 105 souls at various stages of the disease, and the efforts of the surgeons and healthier men to care for the sick while at the same time attempting to effect a rescue for all. The shortage of officers must have reduced the opportunities available to Crozier to split his party, some of whom would have to delay to care for those who could no longer march. There is evidence that some men returned to the ship and died there. A second boat was found by later searchers on the coast of King William Island, adjacent to where Hobson had found the first. This boat was hidden from Hobson's view at the time, being covered by drifting snow in a hollow during his search.

Questions are raised about the attitude of the navy toward the development of survival skills in the Arctic. Natives travelled lightly by constructing snow shelters instead of carrying heavy tents, and by hunting en route, they also reduced the weight of provisions to be dragged on the sledges. Eskimos used dogs to pull the sledges and wore clothing made from animal furs and skins, which did not freeze like the wool and flannel the navy issued to its men. The navy insisted on bringing many of the trappings of English life to the barren Arctic environment. That the navy did not learn anything from this disaster is evidenced by Nares' North Pole expedition 30 years later and, indeed, by Shackleton and Scott's South Pole journeys 60 years later. They did not learn, and would not learn until the twentieth century, what the Norwegian, Roald Amundsen, demonstrated to them when winning the race to the South

Pole: the simple good sense of observing and adopting Innuit practices in dress, survival, food and travel.

Regarding the lack of recovered records, some modern experts believe that Crozier – after two years beset in the frozen sea, and on the death of Franklin – had his commander's remains buried on land, along with a cache of the expedition records. In the event of a rescue expedition, or indeed self-rescue, these records would have been recovered. It is unlikely to have occurred to either Crozier or Fitzjames that their entire party would perish without trace before rescuers arrived or some of their number completed the journey upriver to Canada. To this day, there are still people searching for Franklin's grave and for his expedition records. There is other evidence to suggest that records were carried in tin boxes that were eventually discarded and blown open to the elements, to be gathered by native collectors of useful items. It is likely that many marker cairns, such as the one found by Lieutenant Hobson, were erected by Crozier's men as the surviving sailors retreated toward the Great Fish River. It is equally likely that Innuit hunters in search of booty would have dismantled such non-Innuit cairns.

Traces of the expedition suggest that about a third of the men were unable to continue past Terror Bay. There is evidence that they set up two large tents as a hospital; based on Innuit accounts of the number of bodies found there, as many as 30 men perished in the hospital. Because of the slow progress of the march, Crozier split his men into two groups – the sick and their carers, some of whom went back to the ships for more provi-sions and medical supplies – and those able to march. The Innuit spoke of finding a body on a ship that drifted close to shore. Innuit hunters met a party of 40 men – likely, the fittest – marching toward the Great Fish River and traded seal meat with them. The natives vanished overnight, obviously fearing the work involved in hunting and caring for such a big group while also providing for their own families. The Innuit told searchers that the white men had no food and were living on what birds they could shoot. The earlier slow passage and the need to leave food for the sick had obviously made huge inroads into the provisions of the marchers.

We can trace their passage by the trail of graves and bones found by searchers. They reached Simpson's cairn at Cape Herschel, but their progress was hampered by difficult terrain, drifting snow and blizzards. McClintock found the body of Harry Peglar, captain of the foretop on *Terror*, east of Cape Herschel; he was identi-fied by the papers in his pockets. They moved eastward from the Washington Bay area where, it appears, they got lost due to difficult terrain and inaccurate charts. They reached Douglas Bay, where several bodies were found. From here, they made progress to the Piffer River, where evidence of a camp and fishing activity was found. The beneficial effects of the fish was, by then, likely to have been too little, too late to combat scurvy and restore their health. Close to here, a skeleton in an officers' uniform was found. Other remains, found on Todd Island in 1950, indicated the route of the party toward the Adelaide Peninsula on the North American main-land. There, at a place called Starvation Cove, the

Etching of HMS *Terror* by Irish artist, Vincent Sheridan.
*By kind permission of the artist*

majority of those left in that gallant band died; their Promised Land up river was, alas, too far for them in their weakened state. The hoped-for rescue never came; a few of them reached the estuary of the Great Fish River before finally giving in to hunger and cold. Innuit evidence spoke of tin boxes of books discarded there. These were likely the logs and journals of the expedition. The Innuit told of finding the last man who died on King William Island. He was a large man; a telescope lay nearby. Perhaps he was an officer. Is it too fanciful to speculate on this being Francis Crozier?

All that remains of the mortal men of *Terror* and *Erebus*, who sought to complete the details of the geography of North America and to navigate the elusive Northwest Passage, is a trail of graves and bones stretching from Point Victory to the estuary of the Great Fish River. It is folly to speculate as to how long Hickey and Crozier lived or where and under what wretched circumstances they died. It is sufficient to know they volunteered for Arctic service and died in the delivery of their duty. These two Irishmen, along with the other officers and men of *Erebus* and *Terror*, rank among the many other good men who dared for duty and, perhaps, for glory as reward for their hard work, courage and privation in seeking out the secrets of the frozen lands.

Despite the many improvements he had made

to the navy's equipment and techniques in sledge travel, McClintock still favoured man hauling sledges in preference to dogs, particularly over long distances. The Admiralty considered the habits and customs of the Innuit to be primitive and inferior, and failed to adopt Eskimo survival tactics, their clothing, shelter or food sources. This is particularly revealing when one reflects on the fact that, despite the frequent number of expeditions to the Arctic between 1818–45 and the regular engagements with the Innuit, the navy's Arctic officers failed to master the Innuit language. This hindered them finding help when things went wrong. Neither did they employ experienced Canadian furtraders or guides who could communicate with the local people. It is also difficult to believe that they did not seek out and employ experienced Innuit hunters and interpreters to aid hunting and navigation when they found themselves marooned in the barren Arctic environment. The treatment by the establishment and Lady Franklin of the Hudson's Bay Company agent, John Rae, was another error, as well as being quite disgraceful. This great Arctic explorer had found the first evidence of Franklin's fate and had successfully adopted native methods of travel to great effect – one can only imagine what would have been possible if the Admiralty had put Rae to work alongside the inventive McClintock; what they might collectively have achieved in terms of further polar exploration and in improving the navy's polar clothing and sledging skills. As it transpired, they ignored the Orkney Islander and ceased all further polar exploration for another twenty years.

## After the Search for Franklin

In the immediate aftermath of the *Fox* expedition, the Admiralty diverted McClintock, who had developed undoubted Arctic exploration skills, into a new technological venture, the laying of an ocean cable. He was sent to explore and sound a possible route in the North Atlantic in which to lay a telegraph cable from Europe to America. For this project, he was given command, in May 1860, of HMS *Bulldog*. He plotted a course for the cable via the Faroe Islands, through Iceland, Greenland and Labrador. Following this route, he determined that no section of the submarine cable need be longer than 500 miles. On *Bulldog's* return journey, the vessel was forced to put into Killybegs, Co. Donegal in a crippled state. In spring of 1861, Sir Leopold was appointed to HMS *Doris*, then in the Mediterranean, where he served until December 1862. The following year, he was appointed to command a new steam frigate, HMS *Aurora*.

His career following his famous voyage in *Fox* was eventful. In 1868, he was approached by the Conservatives to contest the election for the borough of Drogheda. They hoped his name and reputation might win them a seat in his native Co. Louth; it appears, however, that he had no Catholic support. There was a riot on polling day when some voters arriving by train were attacked by mobs; a number of them were beaten and wounded. The military shot one rioter dead and those who reached the polling station were threatened, among them an 88-year-old Mr Dunlop of Monasterboice House, who was reported to have been severely maltreated. In order to stop further rioting and to save life, McClintock withdrew under police protection after having polled only 150 votes. In the circumstances, he petitioned against the other candidate's victory. He called to ask after Mr Dunlop at Monasterboice and accepted an invitation to stay there during the prosecution of his petition in Drogheda. The trial found the election void and the costs were assigned to the losing side. However, Leopold had already had enough of politics and did not stand in the next election.

During his stay at Monasterboice, he met Miss Annette Elizabeth Dunlop, daughter of Robert Foster Dunlop, who had been invited to entertain the visitors. They were married at Mellifont Church on 12 October 1870, the ceremony performed by the Rev Robert le Poir McClintock, who lived near Drumcar. They went to live in London at 2 Eaton Terrace. In the meantime, McClintock was elected a member of the council of the Royal Geographical Society in 1869 and was promoted to rear admiral on 5 October 1871. He was appointed admiral superintendent of Portsmouth docks on 29 April 1872. On August 5 1877, McClintock – now a vice admiral – was appointed commander-in-chief at the North American and West Indian station. He sailed for Bermuda with his wife and four children; the eldest was born in Dublin, the other three in Portsmouth; a fifth was born in Halifax, Nova Scotia.[5] Leopold was promoted to the rank of full admiral in 1884, just before the age of retirement. His promotion required the voluntary retirement of a senior admiral and is indicative of the esteem in which his peers held him. He died at his home in London on 17 November 1907,

aged 88. His funeral and burial at Kensington cemetery, Hanwell was attended by representatives of the king, the Prince of Wales and the Admiralty; the Norwegian minister, Dr Nansen, was also present. A marble plaque to his honour was later attached to the Franklin memorial in Westminster Abbey; it reads: 'Here also is commemorated Admiral Sir Leopold McClintock 1819–1907 Discoverer of the Fate of Franklin in 1859'.

Robert McClure was appointed to the *Esk* in 1856 for service at the Pacific station; in the following year, he brought her to China to reinforce the squadron there. In December, he commanded a battalion of the naval brigade at the capture of Canton. Later, he was senior officer in the Straits of Malacca and nominated a CB on 20 May 1859. He returned to England in 1861 and, though he had no further service, was promoted to the rank of rear admiral on 20 March 1867. He married Miss Ada Tudor in 1869; they had no children.[6] McClure was promoted to vice admiral, on the retired list, on 29 May 1873. He never returned to Wexford and died in London at Duke Street, St James' on 17 October 1873; he was buried in Kensal Green cemetery, the same cemetery in which Lady Wilde – his cousin – and Lady Franklin were buried. His epitaph reads: 'Thus We Launch into the Formidable Frozen Sea. *Spes Mea in Deo*.' A channel to the north of Banks Island, which communicates with the Beaufort Sea, was named McClure Channel and a cape that faces into it also bears his name.

Henry Kellett, on his return from Arctic service, was appointed commodore in Jamaica from 1855–59. Before he went there, a civic reception was held for him in Clonmel, Co. Tipperary. In the crowded courthouse, the mayor, William Smith, the council and corporation presented to Captain Kellett an address of public congratulations for his splendid services. The *Clonmel Chronicle*[7] tells us that the stories of his daring exploits in China were recounted eloquently and impressively by the Earl of Donoughmore, who had himself participated in that campaign and who spoke from a side gallery to an enthusiastic reception by his countrymen.[8] On 16 June 1862, Kellett was promoted to the rank of rear admiral and, from 1864–67, was superintendent of Malta dockyard. On 8 April 1868, he became vice admiral, was nominated a KCB on 2 June 1869 and was commander-in-chief in China from 1869–71. His obituary records that up to the time of his retirement, he had completed more actual sea service than any previous admiral in the British navy. He was awarded the CB for his services in the first Chinese war and the KCB in June 1869 upon his return from Malta.

Kellett died at home in Clonacody on 1 March 1875[9] and was interred in the family plot in the Church of Ireland graveyard attached to Holy Trinity Church within the medieval walls of Fethard. The gravestone, which now lies flat over the plot, is inscribed with the words: 'Until the day break and the shadows fade away.' The cause of his death was recorded as 'softening of the brain – 3 years duration. Certified'. His brother, Mr Richard Orlando Kellett, contested his last will and testament in the courts of probate; he claimed the will, dated 17 May 1873, was drawn up when the admiral was not of sound mind, memory and understanding, and that he was

unduly influenced by Miss Ruth Pedder – the niece of both the admiral and Richard Kellett – and by others acting with her. The *Clonmel Chronicle* of 26 June 1875 reported that a settlement had been arrived at, and claims of fraud and undue influence on the part of the defendants withdrawn. The bulk of Kellett's estate in Clonacody was left to his brother who apparently resented having to share any of it with his sister's daughters, one of whom, Ruth, wrote regularly to Henry while he was away at sea. Cape Kellett on the south-western tip of Banks Island marks the boundary between the Beaufort Sea and the Amundsen Gulf, and was named in Kellett's honour. In the vicinity of McClure Strait, it links on the Arctic chart three knighted Irishmen.

Francis Beaufort retired from the post of hydrographer in February 1855; in his letter of resignation, he noted that he had been in the naval service for upwards of 67 years, 25 of which were spent in the hydrographer's office. He was invested a knight in 1848, in the Order of Bath, by Queen Victoria. Three hundred donors contributed to his testimonial and the fund of £540 was spent in the commission of a portrait of Beaufort by Stephen Pearce which, when completed, was hung in the Great Hall of Greenwich Observatory. The balance of the fund was used to make an annual award to the officer who received the highest marks for navigation and pilotage in the examination for the rank of lieutenant.[10]

The entries in his daily weather journal continued until 11 December 1857; he died within a week of this final entry. He was buried at Hackney graveyard where his first wife, Alicia, had been interred 23 years before. Honora, his second wife, survived him by only two months. His daughter, Rosalind, with financial help from Charles Dickens and others, built and dedicated to him a small mission hall – St Andrew's Waterside Church at Gravesend, built on a stone pier jutting into the Thames. Its design is representative of an upturned boat. A brass plaque – a memorial to the crews of *Erebus* and *Terror* – was placed in the church by Lady Franklin. She chose to erect the memorial in the church dedicated to a friend, advocate and counsellor who had helped her in her search for her husband and the crews of the lost ships, and whose life-work made the navigation of the oceans safer. During his 25-year tenure as hydrographer, his office produced 1,500 new charts, each of which had to meet his exacting standards.

Edward Sabine had a long and distinguished career due, in no small measure, to his ability to combine his scientific capacity with an attractive personality, grace of manners and renowned cheerfulness. He was elected president of the Royal Society in 1861, holding that prestigious office for ten years until his resignation. He influenced the government of India to undertake the great trigonometrical survey from sea level at Cape Cormorin to the tablelands of the Himalayas; a series of pendulum observations revealed much new information on the earth's crust and local variations of gravity. He repeated the magnetic survey of the British Isles in 1861. He was author of more than 100 papers in *Philosophical Transactions of the Royal Society*, with many more in scientific journals. He received many honours and awards including being made a civil KCB in 1869. He was promoted to the rank of colonel commander of the Royal Artillery in February 1865, lieutenant general in September of the same year and to general in 1870. He was created a DCL (Doctor of Civil Law) at Oxford on 20 June 1865 and LLD (Doctor of Laws) at Cambridge. He was also accepted as a fellow of the Linnean and Royal Astronomical Society. He received the Order of Pour le Mérite of Prussia, SS Maurice and Lazarus of Italy and the Rose of Brazil.

There is a portrait of Sabine in the rooms of the Royal Society and another in the mess of the Royal Artillery in Woolwich by G.F. Watts RA, dated 1876. In that year, he ceased his scientific activity, retiring from the army on full pay on 1 October 1877 at the age of 89. He died at Richmond, Surrey on 26 June 1883 and was buried in the family vault at Tewin, Hertfordshire with the remains of his wife, Elizabeth. They had no children.

*Who Was First to Complete the Northwest Passage?* So, who should be credited with the first completion of the Northwest Passage? It is clear that Crozier's men had reached the estuary of Back's Great Fish River, thereby communicating on foot with the North American mainland from the Atlantic. It is also feasible that a sledging party from *Erebus* and *Terror* had covered the same ground prior to Franklin's death. In 1854, *Investigator's* Robert McClure completed a multi-ship and sledge traverse from west to east with help – some say rescue – from *Resolute* and Henry Kellett's men, and lived to tell the tale. Parliament awarded him and his men its prize in acknowledgement of their efforts and so as to pacify a nation in need of success and heroes. John Rae could also claim that his finding of open water between King William Land and Boothia converted the former to an island on the emerging chart. The later-named Rae Strait was the vital last link in the search for a navigable Northwest Passage. Leopold McClintock, with a few dedicated and hard-working officers and men, completed the charting details to the Bellot Strait and Victory Point following Rae's discoveries. He advised future explorers that the likely route was by Peel Sound and Rae Strait. Richard Collinson's superb achievement in navigating the heavy and deep-drafted *Enterprise* through the Dolphin and Union Strait and the Dease Strait to Cambridge Bay and back proved that the passage west to Point Barrow was navigable.

The passage was finally navigated in 1903–07 by the great Norwegian sailor and explorer, Roald Amundsen. He and a small crew in a 47-ton herring boat named *Gjøa* – with a 9-foot draft and powered by a small petrol engine – sailed from east to west, passing through Lancaster Sound, Peel Sound, Rae Strait and round King William Island. They overwintered at a safe harbour and native settlement, now named Gjoa Haven. There, from a safe base, they unsuccessfully attempted to reach the ever-moving magnetic North Pole by dog sledge. At Gjoa Haven, they made magnetic observations while communing with, and learning polar survival craft from, the native Innuit. The crossing of what is now known as the Queen Maud Gulf – in shallow waters – was tense and nervous until Cambridge Bay was reached, where Amundsen

knew the much deeper HMS *Enterprise* had previously navigated from Point Barrow. He then sailed through Dease Strait and Coronation Gulf to reach the Beaufort Sea and Point Barrow.

Roald Amundsen. The Norwegian explorer successfully adopted the survival skills of the Innuit.
*Universitesbiblioteket, Oslo*

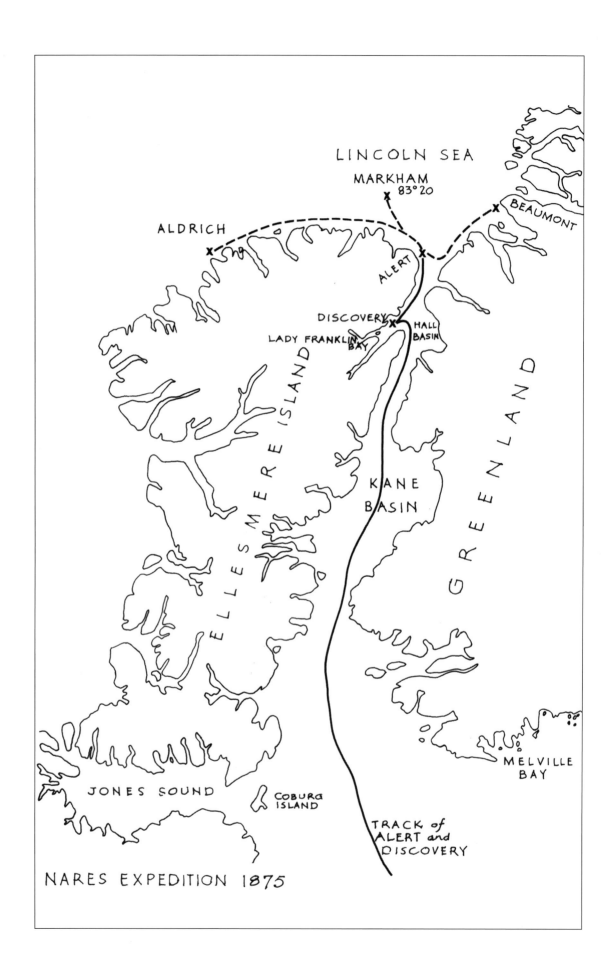

LINCOLN SEA

MARKHAM
83°20

BEAUMONT

ALDRICH

ALERT

DISCOVERY

HALL
BASIN

LADY FRANKLIN
BAY

KANE
BASIN

E L L E S M E R E   I S L A N D

G R E E N L A N D

MELVILLE
BAY

JONES SOUND

COBURG
ISLAND

TRACK of
ALERT and
DISCOVERY

NARES EXPEDITION 1875

Discovery *and* Alert – *The Nares Expedition*

Despite pressure from Sherard Osborn and Sir Clements Markham to renew British polar exploration, it was November 1874 before the prime minister, Lord Beaconsfield, announced that the government would dispatch a new Arctic expedition. The rationale for the expedition was the encouragement of maritime enterprise and for the specific exploration of the region around the North Pole. Captain George Nares, who had served under Henry Kellett on *Resolute* in 1852–54, was chosen to lead the expedition. Under Kellett, he had been in charge of Lieutenant Mecham's depot sledge. Two ships were assigned: the *Discovery* and *Alert*. The expedition was fitted out at Portsmouth dockyard where *Alert*, a 17-gun sloop, was strengthened and prepared for Arctic service. A sealer, named *Bloodhound*, was purchased as the second ship and renamed *Discovery*. She was put under the command of Captain Stephenson, with Lewis Beaumont as first lieutenant.

The fitting out was supervised by Sir Leopold McClintock who was, at that time, the admiral-superintendent at the naval dockyard; he was also responsible for the provision and preparation of the sledge equipment. Sir Clements Markham boasted that the provisions for the ships and sledges were specified largely in line with the Franklin-search expeditions.

There were four Irishmen among the expedition's officers, scientists and men: Henry Chichester Hart, born in Raheny, Co. Dublin was appointed as naturalist to the *Discovery*; Dr Richard William Coppinger, from Dublin, was the fleet surgeon on *Discovery*; Dr Thomas Colan (originally Coughlan), from Cork, was the surgeon on *Alert*; one of the last seamen to sign on to *Discovery*'s muster roll was Able-bodied Seaman James Hand, from Bray, Co. Wicklow.

*Henry Chichester Hart*

Henry Chichester Hart, born on 29 July 1847 at Raheny, a suburb of Dublin, was the third son of Andrew Searle Hart and Frances McDougall. His father was a mathematician and vice-provost of Trinity College, Dublin. Henry's roots were in Co. Donegal, where his family had been settled since Elizabethan times. He was educated at Portora Royal School, Enniskillen and at Trinity College, Dublin. Although principally known as a botanist, he was also an accomplished mountaineer and explorer, with a reputation for physical prowess. In 1889, he walked from Dublin to the summit of Lugnaquilla and back in less than 24 hours. He was also responsible for one of the earliest climbing guides to Ireland when he contributed the Irish section to Haskett Smith's *Climbing in the British Isles*. He had considerable literary abilities, editing in later life the Arden series of plays by Shakespeare. He married Miss Edith Donnelly at Swords, Co. Dublin in 1887; they had two daughters. Following Edith's death in 1901, he married Mary Cheshire, in 1907. Hart came to prominence alongside R.M. Barrington when, under the guidance of A.H. More, he contributed to the 1898 edition of *Cybele Hiberica*. He began studying plants at the age of seventeen in what he regarded as his native county, Donegal, and his published work includes *Flora of Co. Donegal* (1898); Robert

Henry Chichester
Hart.
*From* More People and
Places in Irish Science and
Technology, *C. Mollan et al*

of Joseph William Coppinger, a Dublin solicitor. He received his medical education in Dublin, attaining his MD at Queen's University in 1870. Having entered the medical department of the navy, he was appointed surgeon aboard *Discovery* on 29 May 1875, for the Arctic expedition. He distinguished himself as a naturalist and as a very skilful doctor while in charge of one of the sledge parties. On the return of *Discovery* to England in November 1876, he was promoted to staff surgeon. He later served as naturalist on *Alert* during a four-year exploration cruise off Patagonia, and in Polynesian and Mascarene waters from 1878–82. In 1889, he was appointed instructor in hygiene at the Haslar naval hospital in Gosport. In March 1901, he was appointed inspector general of hospitals and fleets, and was for three years in charge at Haslar. He retired in 1906 and died in Fareham on 2 April 1910.[12]

Lloyd Praeger, an Irish naturalist, botanist and early conservationist, referred almost exclusively to this work for information on the northwest of Ireland in his monumental work, *Irish Topographical Botany* (1901).[11] Hart's botanical work reflected his interest in climate and he maintained meteorological equipment at his Donegal residence. It is not surprising that one with such scientific training and physical attributes would volunteer for an Arctic expedition when the opportunity arose.

### Surgeon Richard William Coppinger

Born on 11 November 1847 in Dublin, Richard William Coppinger was the youngest of six sons

### Surgeon Thomas Colan

When Thomas Colan was born in Cork on 7 November 1830, his surname was recorded as Coghlan. He changed it to Colan in the 1860s. He served as assistant surgeon aboard *Royal George* during the Russian war in the Baltic and later in *Pylades*. He saw service with the advanced squadron in the ice of the Gulf of Finland in 1856 and, in 1860, served aboard *Beagle* during the second China war; he was at the capture of Taku Forts in the Tientsin River, for which he was awarded a medal. In 1863, he was promoted to surgeon. A decade later, he could be found aboard *Rattlesnake* under Commerell, engaged in the Ashanti war for which service he was promoted to staff surgeon in

March 1874. He gained the Gilbert Blane Gold Medal for the medical journal he kept on the west coast of Africa. He was on the drill ship, *Unicorn*, under Brome in 1874 at Dundee. He was the principal medical officer for the Arctic expedition on *Alert*. From October 1877, he spent three years as deputy inspector of hospitals at Port Royal in Jamaica and, in January 1883, was promoted to inspector general of hospitals and fleets, retiring in April of that year. He was a Fellow of the Royal Geographical Society. He died on 18 August 1885, aged 54. He was author of *A Memoir on Parasitic Vegetable Fungi and Diseases Induced By Them*, and also of an article on the west coast of Africa. The following medals were awarded to him: Second Arctic Medal, Baltic War Medal, Second China War Medal (clasp Taku Forts, 1860) and the Ashanti War Medal.[13]

## Able-bodied Seaman James Hand

James Hand was born on 31 August 1847 in Bray, Co. Wicklow – Ireland's 'garden county' on the shores of the Irish Sea. The fifth son of John Hand and Anna Byrne of Bray Strand, he was baptised a Catholic at the Church of the Holy Redeemer on 13 September 1847.[14] He lies buried inside the Arctic Circle at Polaris Bay, on the north-western shores of Greenland, which are washed by the Arctic waters of the Lincoln Sea. Hand joined the navy as a 'boy, second-class' when fifteen years old, going aboard HMS *Ayarr*. He served in that same role on *Bosaivven*, *Revenge* and *Cockatrice* where, on reaching his eighteenth birthday, he was rated ordinary seaman. His naval record, updated during his service aboard

HMS *Immortalité* in October 1872, tells us he was 5-feet 10-inches tall with a fresh complexion, blue eyes and brown hair.[15] Throughout his service, his conduct was rated consistently good or very good. At eighteen, Hand signed on for a further ten years, serving on *Liverpool*, *Royal George* and *Zealous*, where he was promoted to AB. He continued service on *Revenge*, *Excellent* and *Immortalité* before embarking on *Discovery* for his final fateful voyage.

## The Nares Expedition

The expedition's objective was to reach the highest latitude achievable and, if possible, to reach the North Pole. The provisions, we are told, were the same – or meant to be the same – as those used in the Franklin-search expeditions. It transpired, however, that the Admiralty had learned nothing new in the intervening twenty years, particularly regarding scurvy and its prevention. The expedition left Portsmouth on 29 May 1875, calling in at Bantry Bay on 1–2 June, and encountered gales while crossing the Atlantic. It was 6 July when the expedition vessels, including a transport, eventually arrived at Godhavn, on the south coast of Disco Island. There, they took on stores and dogs, a Dane named Neil Petersen and an Eskimo named Frederick. North of Disco, they picked up the resourceful, Greenland-born Hans Hendrik, an accomplished kayaker and hunter who had previously assisted two Americans, Kane and Hayes, on their expeditions up the Smith Channel. The two ships reached Lady Franklin's Bay where Nares decided to leave *Discovery* to overwinter while he took

*Alert* a further 50 miles north, passing 30-foot high floes. He reached the edge of the Polar Sea at 82° 27' north, the furthest north any ship had ever before spent a winter. Despite fresh snow, they laid out depots 40 miles from the ship and faced the winter as cheerfully as they could. Nares' orders were to try to reach the Pole. To communicate with *Discovery*, he sent two young officers – Egerton and Rawson – with the Dane, Petersen, but after two days, the latter collapsed from frostbite and cramp. Egerton and Rawson returned to *Alert* with Petersen on the sledge. Dr Colan amputated his two feet, but he died on 14 May from shock arising from the operation. The two officers set out again and reached *Discovery*.

The main sledge parties set out on 3 April, the Polar Sea party dragging two boats as well as their sledges loaded with provisions; this meant covering the same ground four or five times during each march. Nares sent out three sledge parties: one north over the Lincoln Sea, led by Albert Hastings Markham; the second west along Ellesmere Island's northern coastline, led by Lieutenant Aldrich; the third, from *Discovery*, led by Lieutenant Beaumont and which included Dr Coppinger and AB James Hand. The latter party had first to trek to *Alert*'s position, then north to Cape Union before they crossed the Robeson Channel between Ellesmere Island and Greenland, travelling northeastward along Greenland's north-western coastline.

Unfortunately for Markham's party, the health of most of his men deteriorated quickly. In deep, soft snow – without snowshoes – enormous effort was required to cut lanes in the hummocks through which they could pull the sledge and boats. Scurvy afflicted two of the men in mid-April and, after an heroic effort, they were forced to quit, having reached 83° 20' north on 11 May. It took a supreme effort to get back to the ship, and to speed up their return, they were forced to leave the boats they had pulled so far. When they reached land, one of the party went back to the ship alone for help, there being only three men, including Markham, still healthy enough to pull the sledges. One-third of the party of 21 men and three officers suffered from frostbite; three lost fingers and toes through amputation. One man – a marine – died from scurvy. Lieutenant Parr went lightweight for the rescue; he travelled 40 miles to the ship in 23 hours. By the time the rescuers got the men back to the ship, one was dead and only three were walking. Nares wrote:

On the 9th of July, fifteen days after the return of the last sledge party, 36 of the crew of the ship had been and 24 were under treatment for scurvy. This large number of patients, most of them requiring constant and special attention, necessarily taxed to the utmost the services of Dr. Thomas Colan, fleet Surgeon and his second, Dr. Ed Moss Surgeon. Nothing could exceed their indefatigable patience and care. The deprivation of necessary rest and exercise cheerfully submitted to by Dr. Colan, upon whom the chief responsibility fell, considerably impaired his own health, following as it did so closely on his long anxious watch by the bedside of Neil Petersen.[16]

Meanwhile, Beaumont – when he reached his turning point along the coastline of north-west Greenland – was also aware that his crew was suffering from scurvy, among them James Hand, who was one of the first to succumb to the disease. A full account of James Hand's deterioration and death was recorded in the expedition's medical report by one of the expedition surgeons, Dr Ninnis, who transcribed it from Lieutenant Beaumont's sledge diary. Referring to AB James Hand, Ninnis recounts Beaumont's diary of events thus:

This man was another of the party who belonging to the *Discovery* passed the winter in the *Alert* and thence started sledging. He left the *Alert* and joined the North Greenland Party on 20th April. On the 15th July I heard he had died from scurvy on the 3rd of June when returning to Polaris Bay Depot. As he was not under treatment or seen by medical officers during the period of his illness. The only report of the case is that of the officer in command of the party [Beaumont] from which the following was taken.

May 7th Complains of stiffness of his legs.

9th Rested all day yesterday legs much better but on walking a short distance they were as stiff as ever.

11th Not being able to pull he walks between the drag ropes for support. Legs very stiff. Nausea very thirsty. Continues to eat his pemmican.

12th More cheerful but can only just walk with the aid of a stick.

May 13th Very much done up. There are several black and blue marks on his legs and red rash round calves. He cannot eat biscuit unless soaked as his gums and teeth are very sore. He has a cough which troubles him and makes his breathing very short, the slightest exertion makes him perspire; he cannot walk more than 30 yards over the ice and snow lying down for breath.

14th Somewhat better about the legs but very sick, giddy and short of breath, he can only just crawl along.

15th Very sick, giddy and he has got the 'shivers' vomits his cocoa. It's always worse in the morning and better after the midday halt.

16th Much worse his legs a mass of black and blue spots and marks, very giddy and scarcely able to crawl; has a headache, craves for lime juice.

17th Severe pain through his chest when walking. He talks a great deal of what he will eat when he gets home, constantly talks of vegetables.

18th Cannot walk more than a few feet without lying down, everyday he is less able to eat his pemmican.

19th Very giddy, but his legs are not so stiff. As he can only walk about five yards without lying down. He has been carried on the sledge part of the way.

May 21st From this date he is always carried on the sledge

22nd Is very low, groans a great deal

23rd Face very swollen, hardly eats any

pemmican and no cocoa.

25th Is very peevish poor. His teeth are very loose, two came out today.

31st Breath very short, sometimes gasping constantly shivering although well clothed.

June 1st A little delirious this morning on being put on the sledge

2nd Rested all day appears a little better

3rd Arrived at Polaris Bay Depot at 4.30 pm. Patient appears very bad. Breath very short and quick, clenches his teeth and wanders in his talk. As there is plenty of limejuice in the depot he has as much as he can drink. Likewise fresh preserved meat and vegetables but he only cares for soup.

8.30 pm Appears much worse this evening. He is hot and cold in turns. His breath being very short during the former's.

10.30 pm Wanders constantly in his talk during his fits he breathes forty times in a minute. He complains of cold feet and legs. Two men lie on either side to warm him.

10.45 Dead. About 5 minutes ago his breathing stopped. A little brandy made him gasp but he died almost immediately.

So died a brave Irish sailor who had given all he had. He was buried by his comrades, many of who were also sick and suffering from scurvy in the freezing conditions.

A similar account is included regarding George Bryant, who was barely able to crawl when the party arrived back to Polaris Bay on 3 July. Dr Coppinger arrived there on 7 June and immediately took charge of the sick. He was too late to save Hand, but Bryant was served fresh

seal meat twice a day together with preserved potatoes and limejuice. By 13 July, he had noticeably improved, and was up and about five days later. On 20 July, he was deemed fit for duty. Dr Ninnis also reported that AB Michael O'Regan was suffering from scurvy, which he reported on return to Discovery Bay. He was treated with fresh meat, vegetables, fresh mustard and cress, limejuice and port wine. O'Regan reported back on 23 July.

Beaumont's party was able to take a rest at Polaris Bay and recover with fresh seal meat. Dr Coppinger – who played a full and active part in leading a sledging party – with the help of Rawson and Han Hendrik, the Eskimo hunter, set up a hospital. The last part of the journey was completed by crossing the Robeson Channel in a 15-foot ice boat. Nares noticed how the officers suffered less from scurvy. Realising that the officers' mess was filled with foods they had brought privately – such as eggs, cheese, jams, tongues, rice and vegetables – Nares turned over his supplies to those most ill. He wrote fulsome praise of the Dubliner in his official report:

Great praise is due to Dr Richard Coppinger for his skilful treatment of the disease; living as he and the party did from six to eight weeks in tents on an Arctic shore without extra resources and medicines, except at the last; it is much to his credit that on their arrival on board the *Discovery*, all the patients were able to perform their ship duties.[17]

When all his crew were back, Nares – observing

the extent of the suffering – blasted his way out of the channel and rejoined *Discovery*, where more news of scurvy convinced him his men had suffered enough. Hand was one of four who died on the expedition from scurvy and frostbite.

Though at great cost, Nares' expedition had found out a little more about the Polar Sea and had discovered 300 miles of new coastline facing it. Lieutenant Archer and the remarkable Dr Coppinger made hourly tidal observations for seven months aboard *Discovery*. Hourly data was also observed for two months on *Alert*; both sets of data were reported upon by the Rev Samuel Haughton MD, DCL, FRS of Trinity College, Dublin in the scientific appendices of Nares' expedition narrative. From the observations made, Professor Haughton was able to state that 'The tidal observations made during the recent Arctic Expedition were of great value, and confirm the opinion, formed on other grounds, that Greenland is an Island.'

From the botanical notes – edited by Sir Joseph P. Hooker, who had been south in *Erebus* and *Terror* with Ross and Crozier – it is clear that Henry Hart had also been very busy. We are told that the vicinity of Discovery Bay, as far north as 81° 50', was subject to careful botanical study by Hart, and from that latitude to the eighty-third parallel, the collections were undertaken by H.W.

Feilden. Hooker was astonished by the extent of species obtained, and identified a new species of fungi from Hart's collection (*Urnula Harti*). Hart was not involved in the main sledge journeys but concentrated on his work as the expedition's naturalist. The expedition's scientific observations and collections produced geological, astronomical and botanical data for no less than 40 published reports and articles.

On returning to England, *Alert* and *Discovery* stopped at Haulbowline, in Cork Harbour – on Sunday 27 October 1876 – to replenish their empty coalholds. A public inquiry into the causes of scurvy resulted in Captain Nares being publicly censured for not issuing fresh limejuice to his sledge crews. The inquiry did not inform him how his crews would store or carry the antiscorbutic elixir on their sledges in sub-zero conditions so that the expansion caused by freezing would not crack the containers.

Coppinger Mountains, on the north-west coast of Canada, and Cape Colan, on Ellesmere Island, are geographical reminders of both Irish surgeons' Arctic service. The medal roll for HMS *Discovery*, *Alert* and *Pandora* records that the Arctic Medal was awarded to all the officers and men, including a posthumous award to James Hand which was sent to his father, John, on 19 November 1877.[18]

## 12

# THE PRIVATE ARCTIC EXPEDITIONS OF HENRY GORE-BOOTH

*Deep and widespread feeling prevails in Lissadell and sur-rounding districts owing to the death of Sir Henry Gore-Booth, Bart. In Ballymote, of which town Sir Henry is landlord, great grief was manifested, and the people there speak in high terms of his goodness and consideration as a landlord.*

SLIGO CHAMPION, 20 JANUARY 1900

Henry Gore-Booth, the fifth baronet of Sligo, was one of the largest landowners in the west of Ireland.[1] He was born at Lissadell, Co. Sligo in 1843, in one of the loveliest places on this earth; his wooded estate extended to the shores of Sligo Bay. To the south, across Sligo Bay, atop Knocknarea mountain, can be seen the huge megalithic tomb of the warrior queen, Meabh. The countryside is overlooked from the east by the proud fortress-like mountain of Benbulben whose sheer slopes sweep gracefully to the green landscape adjacent to the sea.

Henry's father, Sir Robert Gore-Booth, the fourth baronet, had represented Sligo in parliament for nearly a quarter of a century. Upon his death in 1876, he left his son almost 32,000 acres. His mother was Caroline Susan Gould. Henry had taken on the management of the estate himself, ten years earlier, when his father's agent died. He managed a good system of accounts and devel-oped a reputation as a popular and benevolent landlord. He was president of the local co-oper-ative creamery and took a great interest in its success.[2] He married Georgina Mary Hill of Tickhill Castle, Yorkshire in 1867. They were parents to two very remarkable daughters: Constance, born in 1868, is better known in Ireland as Countess Markievicz, whose achieve-ments include becoming the first woman elected to the British House of Commons and who was minister for labour in the government of Dáil Éireann from 1919–21. Her sister, Eva, born in 1870 – the third of five children – became involved in suffrage and labour organisations in

*facing page*
**Meeting of the *Isbjørnen* and *Willem Barents* at Matyushin Shar, Novaya Zemlya, 1879.**
*Public Record Office of Northern Ireland*

Manchester; she was the secretary of the Manchester Trades' Council and editor of *Women's Labour News*. She also wrote many pamphlets and published ten volumes of poems, very much in the genre of the Celtic Twilight movement.

The Atlantic Ocean ceaselessly breaks on the beaches of the estate at Lissadell, which is situated on Ireland's north-western coastline, often referred to as Yeats country, in celebration of the poetry of William Butler Yeats who was twice a guest at Lissadell House, in the winter of 1894–95. Yeats, by then in his late twenties, wrote that 'Sir Henry thinks of nothing but the North Pole.' He also thought the girls were beautiful and graceful, and Henry's son, Josslyn, 'theoretically a home ruler, humanitarian and much troubled by his wealth, and was painfully conscientious and not particularly clever.'[3]

Henry's relationship with his tenants was one of friendship. During the famine of 1879–80, he maintained stores of food that were given freely to the needy. He recounted with pride that he always refused police or military protection during troubled times, particularly when land agitation in the west was heightened.[4] He did not need help, for he never exacted high rents, preferring to deal fairly with his tenants. By 1879, he had most of his rents reduced to the Griffith valuation figure, something Michael Davitt and Charles Stewart Parnell had only recently begun to demand from the Land League platforms in the west of Ireland. There is a story told regarding Sir Henry's apparent ideal landlord–tenant relationship, when he reduced the rents in his Ballymote estate by 40 per cent. The local reaction to the announcement saw hundreds of people flock to

town, led by the local temperance band, where a torch-lit procession marched past the residence of a Captain Gethin with whom Sir Henry was staying overnight. Cheers were chanted by the procession for Sir Henry.[5] It is also remembered that when the roof of the Catholic church of Maugherow, near Lissadell, was wrecked, Sir Henry had the damage repaired at his own expense. In 1880, he gave a famous 'harvest home' party to over 300 of his tenants. His wife, Lady Gore-Booth, initiated home industries to help the local women, selling the products of her needlework school in England for the benefit of the makers. Henry devoted himself to his estate and tenants, and to the affairs of Sligo Agricultural Society, of which he was president. He was chairman of the Sligo, Leitrim and Northern Counties Railway, and was in partnership to operate a mine at Gleniff, providing employment to many of his tenants. He was high sheriff of Sligo in 1872, and also served as justice of the peace and deputy lieutenant in his native county.

As Yeats had detected, Henry Gore-Booth was interested in more than just politics; he had a passion for shooting, fishing and yachting. Born within sight and sound of the Atlantic, he learned as a boy to master a half-decked yawl, with a local boy as his 'crew' – Patrick Kilgallon, who was to become a butler at Lissadell.[6] Sir Henry's first voyages to foreign shores followed the completion of his education at Eton, when he spent three summers sailing and fishing with a friend off the coast of Norway. He sailed his own yacht and was proficient enough later in life to hold a master's certificate. He also had few equals with a gun.

Most nineteenth-century polar exploration was conducted by naval and public-funded expeditions due to the cost and scope of such projects, and only a few explorers could afford to mount their own Arctic expeditions. One of these was Henry Gore-Booth. In 1879, Sir Henry and Lars Jorgensen set out on a private expedition with guest naval explorer, Captain A.H. Markham RN. They chartered the little Norwegian cutter, Isbjørnen, and from 18 May–22 September, beginning from Tromsö, made an extensive exploration of the shores of Novaya Zemlya and the Kara Sea. Their objectives included sport hunting and scientific reporting on the state of the ice and other important matters of a similar nature in those waters. They reached Novaya Zemlya, near Mys Severnyy Gusinyy Nos, on 9 June. Ice prevented them from passing through the strait into the Kara Sea until 31 July, when they encountered heavy pack ice. They coasted south for about 60 miles, to a little beyond Zaliv Litke, where they hunted and fished while surveying the coast. They returned to Matochkin Shar where they had earlier hunted seals and collected natural-history specimens. They were in company with the Dutch vessel, Willem Barents, for some days in the Matyushin Strait. They coasted north again, trying to reach Barentsz' winter quarters of 1596–97 in Ledyanaya Gavan. They sailed around the northern tip of Novaya Zemlya in early September, but ice stopped them when within 31 miles of their objective. Returning, they examined the ice edge of the Barents Sea, reaching their highest latitude at 78° 24' north. They continued across the Barents Sea on 15 September to the vicinity of

Hopen, south-east Svalbard, from where they returned to Tromsö.[7] The expedition returned with collections of plants, birds, marine invertebrates, fish, insects and geographical specimens together with information regarding the drift of floes.

The Sligo Independent of 25 October 1884 recounts two further voyages of Arctic adventure by Gore-Booth on his 46-ton yacht, Kara. The first trip came about when he went in search of Mr Leigh Smith, one of his exploring friends who had set out for Franz Josef Land in 1881 on the exploration ship, Eira. It was pre-arranged with Smith that in the event of Eira not returning by mid-autumn, Gore-Booth would lead an expedition to search for him. The Eira had got stuck in the ice and was crushed; mercifully, all of the crew escaped and were rescued by another vessel. Sir Henry had purchased the small sloop for the rescue mission, had it specially reinforced – sheeting the bows with steel plates at Wilkins' Shipyard at Wyvenhoe, Colchester – and renamed it Kara. He sailed in May 1882 with a crew of ten Scottish whalers and his own sailing butler. Heading north, he reached Matochkin Shar in time to meet the rescued Leigh Smith arriving there. His mission over, he sailed further north to reach Berg Island, Novaya Zemlya, where the Kara was driven ashore by the ice and lost one of her boats, an anchor and 75 fathoms of cable. To refloat her, they had to remove all stores – provisions for twelve men for twelve months – and employ a number of empty paraffin barrels. Her strong construction saved her from worse damage from the crushing ice. They sailed home without further incident.

In April 1884, Gore-Booth went north again in *Kara*, this time to hunt whales off the east coast of Greenland; they spotted their first bottlenose whale 100 miles northeast of Iceland. His ship's log gave, in detail, every eventful occurrence of each day. For example, on 27 May at 3 a.m., the first whale was struck. Sir Henry describes the incident:

> The report of the gun awoke me. The noise of the line running out fetched me out of my berth, and the watch yelling out 'a fall! a fall!' caught me with one leg only in my trousers. It appears fish had been some distance off and suddenly rose at the ship's bow, not giving the watch time to call me. They ran forward when one of them got a quick shot from the starboard gun and fastened a fish on the back. I was soon on deck. We lowered mainsail and jib and got out the port boat, while fish slackened after running out two lines [240 fathoms] scoring a deep hole in the [whale's] hollard head as it ran out. Part of the crew began to haul in the line, and the fish rose at last about a quarter of a mile off. She could be detected from the other fish by the harpoon and blood. The boats got up to her, put in a hand-harpoon, and then lanced her, the boat's crew giving three cheers, which was answered for the ship. They brought the fish alongside, and made her fast, with tail forward of the main chains and her head aft, then rigged a wire span from the mizzen to mainmast to which we attached the spec tackles and flinched the fish. Owing to the tremendous weight and strain on mizzen I felt afraid as it whipped very much, but it stood all right. The flinching is a curious process. A chain is passed round one of the fins near the head and hooked on to the after spec tackle. The harpooner makes a cut across the neck and then down the body, taking care to take as little of the flesh – or 'Krang' as the body is called in whaling language – as possible. Two or three hands, heaving on the winch all the while, as directed, heave the fin up till sufficient blubber is cleared off the 'Krang' to cut a hole in it to pass a strop through, when the chain is unhooked and the after spectacle taken to the strop. The two harpooners in the boat loosen the blubber with their spades until enough is loosened to carry a tackle and strop to the fore-end, the hands still heaving on the winch, while the harpooners gradually cut the krang out until the blubber comes off like a blanket. It is then hoisted on board; the tail rope let go and the spec tackle hooked on to a strop through the head. The head is severed from the body and hoisted on board whole, while the krang sinks to the bottom, and we give three cheers for our first fish. We filled several bottles with almost pure oil from the head.[8]

Later, he tells us that the steward scalded his feet with hot coffee and how they were cured in no time by applying the bottlenose whale oil to them. They caught many such whales and, off the north coast of Iceland, also caught some char (trout) before making their way home via the Orkney Islands in September 1884.

For a number of years after this, Sir Henry sailed about Sligo Bay, having many good days with his children on the *Kara*. He made his last whaling expedition to northern waters in 1892, sailing again off Greenland. When his health began to fail, Gore-Booth spent the winter months in more temperate climates, on doctor's advice. He died suddenly, on 13 January 1900, while holidaying at St Moritz, Switzerland; he went down under an attack of influenza. He was buried in Lissadell churchyard and rests there in the hedged-surrounded family plot, just a short distance from the Atlantic shore. The Celtic-cross headstone bears his name and that of his wife, Georgina Mary, who survived him by 27 years. At the base of the cross is inscribed the words, 'He giveth his beloved sleep'.[9]

# 13

# JEROME COLLINS AND JOHN COLE OF CORK

*she was gone . . . her requiem being the melancholy howl of a single dog.*

NEWCOMB (NATURALIST OF THE *JEANNETTE*)

The graveyard at Curraghkippane on the outskirts of Cork city overlooks the River Lee. Here, in March 1884, the remains of Jerome Collins were finally laid to rest having been brought to New York from Siberia and onward across the Atlantic to Queenstown (Cobh) and, finally, to Cork city.

'Jerry' Jerome James Collins was born in Cork in 1840. He lived at South Main Street and his father operated a salt works. He was educated at St Vincent's Seminary by the Presentation Brothers in their school at Lancaster Quay, where he was reputed to have been a keen and fun-loving student. Once, for a prank, he removed the lenses from his teacher's reading glasses. He was over 6 feet tall, powerfully built and very versatile. He

was a good singer and could play the piano. He went to America in 1864 as a civil engineer and found work as a surveyor for the Northern Pacific Railroad. Subsequently, he provided similar services in the New Jersey marshes between Newark and Manhattan. In New York, on 27 June 1867, he was involved in the founding of Clann na Gael, a powerful Irish-American organisation whose aim was to support and unify the Irish Republican Brotherhood (IRB) at home for the purpose of attaining Irish freedom.[1]

In 1870, following an introduction from a mutual friend, the owner of the *New York Herald*, James Gordon Bennett, offered Collins a job as a weather reporter. Collins thus became the first such weather reporter in the world. He learned this new science rapidly, making a particular name for himself in predicting west-to-east movements of weather. Soon, the *Herald* was cabling predictions on European weather to its London and Paris offices, a service eagerly sought after by British and Continental newspapers.

*facing page*
Jerome Collins, born in Cork in 1840. He died on the coast of Siberia during the *Jeannette* expedition. *From Emma De Long (ed.), George Washinton De Long: The Voyage of the Jeannette*

George Washington De Long, commander of the *Jeannette* expedition, whose objective was to reach the North Pole via the Bering Strait.
*From Emma De Long (ed.), George Washinton De Long: The Voyage of the Jeannette*

Collins was sent as a delegate to a meteorological congress in Paris, where the basis of international forecasting was established.

In 1877, when James Gordon Bennett agreed to financially support Captain George Washington De Long in his proposed expedition to the North Pole, Bennett sent Collins as the *Herald*'s man on the expedition. Bennett saw this venture as having the same news potential as his previous support for Henry M. Stanley, who located the missionary Dr Livingstone in Africa. Collins undertook to learn the technology of photography and learned by heart the verses of the musical, *HMS Pinafore*, with which he hoped to while away the long dark hours of the Arctic.[2]

There was another Corkman aboard the *Jeannette* – the boatswain, John Cole. Known as 'Jack' to his shipmates, he was born in Cove in 1830. Jack went to sea to serve his apprenticeship in the merchant service when he was only thirteen years of age, sailing out of his native town. He progressed to become a quartermaster and participated in the Paraguay expedition in 1858 aboard *Harriet Lane* under Captain Faunce. He and the *Jeannette*'s carpenter, Alfred Sweetman, both served on James Gordon Bennett's yachts, with Cole receiving the highest praise from him. 'You will find Jack Cole one of the best sailors you ever had under you. In times of danger he's worth his weight in gold, and his tact with men is wonderful' was Bennett's commendation of the boatswain to De Long. Cole and Collins were among eight non-naval officers and crew shipped as seamen under special shipping articles. The men, on acceptance of the special articles, were enlisted in the US navy. Every man, before acceptance, was subjected to a searching physical examination.[3]

It was Tuesday 8 July 1879 when the *Jeannette* – named by Bennett in honour of his sister[4] – sailed from San Francisco Bay, supported by a chartered tender, *Fanny A. Hyde*, which carried coal and food as far as St Lawrence Bay. There, just south of the Bering Strait, the additional coal and supplies were transferred, and post and dispatches sent back to the navy, the *Herald* and the waiting dependants of *Jeannette*'s officers and crew. On the evening of 4 September, at latitude 70° north, Herald Island was sighted. Henry Kellett had named the island in 1849 after the ship of that name. On 6 September, the *Jeannette* was frozen in and listed 12 degrees to starboard.

As the ship drifted past Herald Island, Collins celebrated his thirty-eighth birthday by inviting the officers to his cabin and carefully rationing a small amount of liquor before leading them in song. On Christmas Eve, the crew of 32 men sang a carol that Collins had composed. On Christmas Day, they held a minstrel show directed by Jerry Collins. Captain De Long wrote in his journal: 'This is the dreariest day I have ever experienced in my life . . . we tried to be jolly but did not make any success of it.' Conditions had deteriorated, living had become difficult and morale was slipping in a party that had never been very cohesive. On New Year's Day, De Long's diary tells us they had a 'capital dinner' followed by a minstrel show where 'Sweetman's songs were very good and Kuehne's violin solo was fine indeed . . . and Mr. Cole gave us a jig with all the gravity of a judge'. One of the features of the evening was the reading of a prologue composed by Jerry Collins in which each one of the crew was made the subject of a rhyme in turn.[5]

As the *Jeannette* continued to drift in the grip of the pack ice, the health and disposition of the crew worsened. Captain De Long ordered daily exercise on the ice so as to maintain the health of the crew. He was not impressed by Collins' tardiness in observing and respecting his orders, and confronted him in this regard. After suspending him from duty and writing a memorandum to the secretary of the navy outlining Collins' insubordination, Collins responded by writing his own formal reply, detailing what he regarded as De Long's disrespect for the non-navy personnel. Even before the expedition departed, De Long had referred to Collins in a newspaper interview as a 'mere scientific accessory'.[6]

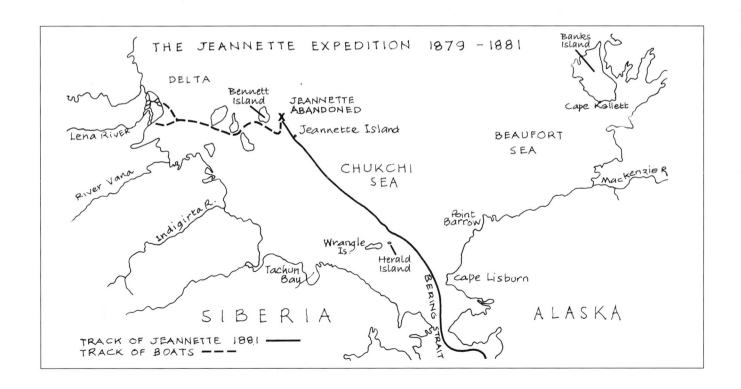

It was in this atmosphere that *Jeannette* drifted toward her doom. En route, they sighted and landed on Henrietta Island, named in honour of Bennett's mother. It was a place of glaciers, gorges and a 1,600-foot mountain that they found to be sheeted in ice. The island was claimed as a territory of the US. It was, as De Long described it, a 'little mass of volcanic rock' that was as pleasing as 'an oasis in the desert'. On Sunday 12 June 1881, the pressure of the pack resulted in continuous snapping and cracking of timbers; the ship tilted and began to take an increasing amount of water. De Long gave the order to abandon the vessel, which had been their home for two years. The boats were lowered and many boxes of provisions and a mass of gear were stacked 500 yards from the *Jeannette*. Dr Ambler, the ship's surgeon, assembled his medical stores and reviewed his sick list. Many had serious ailments, among them the navigator, Lieutenant Danenhower, third in line in the command chain; he had an inflamed eye that was very painful. Prospects for survival were not good. At 4 a.m. on 13 June 1881, *Jeannette* sank. Newcomb, the naturalist, wrote: 'she was gone . . . her requiem being the melancholy howl of a single dog.' Their position was latitude 77° 15' north, longitude 154° 58' 45" east, 750 miles from their goal. The party spent a week sorting itself out before setting out due south toward Siberia. They divided into five groups for camping: each under a commander and each equipped with a tent, a stove and an assortment of single and double sleeping bags.

Thirty-two men and 23 dogs pulled three boats – two cutters and a whaler – and three McClintock sledges weighing 1,600 pounds. In temperatures of 25°F (-3°C), they pulled up their shirtsleeves in the heat, but cold summer rains often drenched them as they struggled south. The direction of the pack drift was working against them, reducing real progress toward their goal to less than a mile on some days. Collins, whose status on the expedition was not officially recognised by De Long, told Bartlett that, in the event of anything happening to him, there were letters on him for James Gordon Bennett and the *Herald*.

On 28 July, they landed on the mountainous Bennett Island and took possession in the name of the president of the United States of America. They left on 7 August and were soon able to use their boats as leads opened up. They were able then to follow currents, and land and sleep on south-headed floes, reaching Thaddeoffshy Island on 30 August. Dunbar, the ice pilot, dropped a seal at great distance with a rifle shot and they had a hearty meal from it, cooked on a fire made from the firewood of their broken sledge. They stayed nine days on the bleak island, but the game that abounded about the place turned out to be rank, rubbery and barely edible, making those who ate it sick. By oar and sail, they made their way toward Kolteny Island, one of the New Siberian Islands. De Long had issued written orders, taking charge of the bigger cutter himself and assigning Lieutenant Charles Chipp in charge of the other; he placed the whaleboat under the command of George Melville, the chief engineer, much to the chagrin of Lieutenant Danenhower, the navigator, who De Long considered to be unfit for command due to his eye inflammation. On 5 September, they

reached Kolteny Island and stayed for 36 hours. This island was also covered in snow and ice. Blistered hands, cold and cramp made progress slow and tempers hot as they moved on to Semonovski Island. On 12 September, they set out for Cape Barkun, a promontory on the east side of the Lena River. Gale-force winds made the seas green, with crests of white waves blowing spindrift that slapped in the faces of the already huddled and cramped sailors. The little boats plunged deep into the troughs and the men, fearing they would be swamped, ran downwind. They trailed a canvas drag and a water cask to act as a sea anchor, weighting the ropes with fire-pots to keep them in the water. In the mist, they became separated. De Long lost his mast and his sea anchor. They fashioned another sea anchor from an oar, with a pickaxe acting as ballast for the rope. Water broke over from all sides as the wind gusted up to 60 knots. A new sail was fash-ioned from a hammock sewn to a sleigh cover.

On Friday 16 September, Melville's whaleboat – with John Cole on board – sailed up the Lena River. The sea journey over, they were at last on the Siberian mainland, though the landscape was devoid of habitation, bleak and icy. De Long's cutter made landfall 120 miles to the northwest, grounded into the congealed mud of the Osotok River. It took them two days to get ashore through the mud. Nindemann directed the men in the construction of a raft, which they used to ferry the crew ashore. Under orders from De Long, the raft was overloaded in its second journey ashore, tipped over and dumped the

13 July 1881: the *Jeannette* sinks. Articles from the ship were found in 1884 on the south-west coast of Greenland. Their discovery led the Norwegian, Fridtjof Nansen, to conclude that the drift across the Polar Sea might be enlisted in the cause of exploration.
*From Emma De Long (ed.),* George Washinton De Long: The Voyage of the Jeannette

miserable crew into the freezing river. Nindemann showed his anger and was told by De Long to consider himself under arrest – an order he quickly withdrew. The raft was repaired and the last to come ashore was De Long, Dr Ambler, a sailor named Ericksen – whose feet were frozen blue – and Snoozer, the last of the dogs, who was by then the expedition pet. De Long insisted on carrying his ice journals, logs and other documentation, which had become a great burden to his then depleted crew of thirteen men. There is no record of what happened to Chipp's party on the second cutter; it is presumed it capsized or was otherwise swamped with all hands lost, including the carpenter, Alfred Sweetman, one of only four men recommended by their commander for medals of honour – his for his gallant work in containing the rate of leakage aboard *Jeannette* before she was abandoned. Meanwhile, Melville's crew – despite having landed in wild and remote Siberia – at least knew they had survived and would live. De Long's band were not so fortunate; they discarded medical supplies, sextant, chronometer and their sleeping bags to reduce weight, but not De Long's journals and logs. They had four days' provisions, arms

28 July 1881; crew from the *Jeannette* land on Bennett Island and take possession in the name of the president of the United States of America.
*From Emma De Long (ed.), George Washinton De Long: The Voyage of the Jeannette*

and ammunition, blankets and tents. Erickson, unable to walk, hobbled with the help of his shipmates and, as a result, progress was very slow.

On Sunday, after prayers, while lying down on the snow, Erickson asked to be left behind. De Long ordered that he be carried a few hundred yards. They made from 3–6 miles a day before they fell down exhausted. Passing signs of habitation, huts, rusting kettles and a fox trap, they hoped a settlement was over the next hill. At night, they lit bonfires from driftwood and branches, warming their bodies and hoping someone would see their signal for help. On Monday, they were compelled to kill and eat Snoozer. On Thursday, during a blizzard, Erickson died. They were too weak to bury him, but made a hole in the ice and slipped him into the river. Having made a wooden cross to mark the spot, and a wooden plaque carved with his name, they divided his clothes between them. On Friday, they moved on again. They had finished the last of the tea. They shot a single ptarmigan – a grouse – with which they made a rancid, undercooked soup, and each man had half an ounce of alcohol with his evening meal.

De Long and the doctor agreed to send the strongest men ahead so as to find help while they were still able. Nindemann and Louis Noros were chosen. De Long instructed them to go south to a place called Ku Mark Surk – shown on the chart as a settlement, where they should find natives – or further south to Ajaket or Bulun. If they found assistance, they were to bring back help as quickly as they could. When Collins offered to go, De Long told him, 'You

would not get five miles away from the camp.' As they struggled after the tracks of Nindemann, the Indian hunter, Alexey, shot ptarmigan from which they again made soup. On 12 October, they were out of glycerine. 'We are in the hands of God and unless he intervenes are lost', wrote De Long in his journal. On Monday 17 October – Collins' fortieth birthday – Alexey and Lee were in trouble. Alexey died at sunset and was placed on the river the next day. They cut up the tent for new footgear. Kaack died on Friday; Lee died a few hours later. Lacking the strength to keep going – and without food or fuel – they lay down in penetrating cold. De Long's diary became a mere litany of deaths:

October 17th Monday 126th day. Alexey dying. Doctor baptised him. Read prayers for sick, Mr. Collins' birthday – forty years old. About sunset Alexey died. Exhaustion from starvation. Covered him with ensign and laid him in the crib.

October 21st Friday 131st day. Kaack was found dead about midnight between doctor and myself. Lee died about noon. Read prayers for sick when we found he was going.

October 22nd, Saturday – 132nd day. Too weak to carry the bodies of Lee and Kaack out on the ice. The Doctor, Collins and I carried them around the corner out of sight. Then my eyes closed up.

Thursday October 27th 137th day. Iveson broken down.

Friday October 28th 138th day Iveson died during early morning .

The separation of the boats in gale-force winds, 12 September 1881.
*From Emma De Long (ed.), George Washinton De Long: The Voyage of the Jeannette*

Saturday Oct 29th 139th day Dressler died during the night.

Sunday October 30th 140th Day Boyd and Gortz died during night Mr. Collins dying.[7]

At that point, De Long's ice journal ends.

On 23 October, Nindemann and Noros met a Siberian who took them westward to a small settlement called Bulun. The two men had survived by finding huts, firewood and game for sustenance, and through their strength and endurance. Bulun was small and isolated, and their inability to communicate the plight of their colleagues to the Siberians meant that rescue would never come for Collins, De Long and the other, last survivors. They died 20 miles from a hunters' hut stocked with food, and a hundred miles from

safe habitation. Retrospectively, it is difficult to understand why De Long spent such a long time on each of the various islands; while they were strong and well provisioned, his delays appear to have affected their physical condition, causing them to arrive exhausted and very weak to the mainland. It is also a mystery as to why, along with rifles, they did not choose to carry shotguns, which are better for hunting game.

More mysterious still is why Melville did not attempt to look for his commander and other shipmates after he had secured his own safety. He and his whaleboat crew spent a month at Geeomovialocke Island recovering before receiving a note from Nindemann and Noros at Bulun calling for assistance. It arrived on 28 October and provoked an immediate response. Melville hired a dog and a sledge team and arrived at Bulun on 2 November. It was clear to Melville that neither of the surviving pair was strong enough at that time to return as guides, so Nindemann and Noros drew diagrams of De Long's journey and the route back to their last camp. Melville set out with a dog team and some natives, but the landmarks he was seeking were hard to find, and were obscured by fresh snows and blizzard conditions. He found De Long's cache in a cairn and recovered the chronometer, navigation books, a Bible and the specimens collected from Bennett Island, along with other objects. Natives stole his dog rations overnight as he slept. He knew he was on the right trail, but bad weather prevented him from continuing. He retired, exhausted, to Bulun where, like the natives, he waited with the remains of his crew for the spring to arrive.

When word got back to the US, James Gordon Bennett sent out another journalist, John P. Jackson, from his Paris office. He had worked with Collins and liked him. 'Find De Long' was the order from Bennett. With an artist named Larsen, of the *Illustrated London News*, they travelled from Berlin to Moscow by train for the first leg of their long journey to Siberia. On 8 January, Melville ordered Lieutenant Danenhower – who still considered himself the superior officer – to accompany home eight of the enlisted men, including John Cole, who Danenhower reported was suffering from mental aberration and in need of a special attendant; Cole was continuously stitching his clothes with a needle and thread. Melville stayed in Siberia with Nindemann and Bartlett – 'the two best men in the party'. With

the assistance of the governor of Siberia and a former Cossack sergeant who knew the territory, they accumulated provisions, horses, reindeer and 100 dogs to transport the men and provisions. On 23 February 1882, the returning *Jeannette* survivors met with newsmen at Irkutsk in south-central Siberia. Danenhower told the full story of the *Jeannette* to Jackson – as he saw it – detailing his perceived injustices to himself and others, including Collins, by De Long and Melville. The story, as told in the *Herald*, was full of jealousies, suspicions and 'might-have-beens'. Danenhower asserted that if Melville had voyaged the one-day journey to Bulun earlier, he would have met Nindemann and Noros, and if they had started north immediately, they might have saved De Long, Collins, Iveson and Dressler. Danenhower admitted to Jackson that he was still feeling very bitter and resentful toward De Long for putting a staff officer – Melville – over him, a line officer. The story became leading news in American and British newspapers – not as an heroic tale, but as the unpleasant saga of the *Jeannette* expedition. The Collins family were aghast. They found it hard to conceive of any reason why their brother would have been under arrest and watched developments with concern for his and the family's good name.

In the meantime, Melville, Nindemann and Bartlett were wading in waist-deep snow through blizzards, looking for De Long with the assistance of hired natives. On 23 March, Melville discovered the bodies of De Long, Dr Ambler and Ah Sam, the cook. De Long's journal was recovered and they read the account of his last days. The following day, the body of Collins was found. His facial expression was very bitter, 'his teeth were clenched, his expression was hard, as if he had died very hard.' When finally all eleven corpses were found, Melville had them moved to Mat Vai, the highest ground in the vicinity – selected so as to preclude flooding – where they were interred in a mausoleum of stone and wood. In May, when Jackson and Larsen reached the site, Jackson dragged out the bodies of De Long, Collins and Ambler so that Larsen might sketch them.

Danenhower arrived in New York on 28 May. Among those waiting to meet him were two of Jerome Collins' brothers, Dr Daniel Collins, surgeon-in-chief of the Mercy Hospital in Minneapolis, and Bernard Collins, of Brooklyn, who was himself employed by Bennett. They wanted to know what their brother had done to be kept under suspension for eighteen months by De Long. Danenhower tried to reassure them: 'He was not guilty of any criminality, but he was suspended for a trivial offence.' This reply failed to satisfy the brothers.

A naval court of inquiry was set up to investigate the circumstances surrounding the loss in the Arctic seas of the steamer, *Jeannette*, and the death of De Long and officers and men under his command. It opened in the old navy building in Washington on 11 October 1882. Most of the officers and seamen found it easier to deny any knowledge of any specific difficulties between the officers and Collins than become embroiled in a dispute; this made their late commander and Melville look unjust and vindictive. The court established a mutual dislike between Collins and both De Long and Melville. Dr Collins came to his own conclusion, pleading that De Long had ambitions to publish a book about the expedition. As this objective was part of Collins' journalistic brief, there arose a jealousy between the two. The court found that the condition of the *Jeannette* was good leaving San Francisco and she was, by necessity, deep-loaded, but 'by arduous labour and skilful devices' she was kept afloat, despite pressure from ice. They had discovered three islands and made a positive contribution to scientific observation. The absence of scurvy was found to be a tribute to sanitary arrangements and great credit to Dr Ambler. Apart from some trivial difficulties, such as occur on board ships under the most favourable conditions, every officer and man had so conducted himself that the court found no occasion to impute censure on any member of the party. Four were singled out for great praise: De Long, Melville, Nindemann and Sweetman. The court also found that everything possible was done to find the two missing groups; those of the captain and of Lieutenant Chipp.

During April and May 1884, the House Committee on Naval Affairs sat to answer petitions from Dr Collins to have De Long's charges against Collins deemed unnecessary and, thereby, insufficient grounds for his suspension. In its deliberations, the committee vindicated neither De Long nor Collins, and decided against a judgement.

The main achievement of the *Jeannette* expedition was the discovery of the westward drift of the Arctic ice-pack. Fridtjof Nansen, the erudite Norwegian explorer, would use this piece of intelligence in his voyage toward the North Pole, from 1893–96, aboard his famous ship, the *Fram*.[8] The dangers that ambition and stubborn egotism can lead to, and the pressures which unscrupulous journalism can bring to expeditions, resounds in this sad, American Polar tale.

Jack Cole, on arrival back to America in June 1882, was committed to a government asylum for the insane near Washington DC. He died there on 28 April 1884, aged 54. He was buried at Holycross Cemetery following requiem Mass at St Peter's Church, Barclay Street, New York, celebrated by Rev Fr O'Riordan.[9] The navy decided to bring back the bodies of his comrades from Siberia to New York, via Moscow and Hamburg. On 22 February 1884, the steamer *Frisia* arrived with the bodies of De Long, Collins and their shipmates.

Following a period of lying in state on Holboken Pier, which was open to the public, a funeral procession led by military bands moved into Manhattan, where thousands lined Broadway to show their respects to the American polar heroes. Collins' body was brought to St Patrick's Cathedral, where a solemn requiem Mass was said. The Rev Fr McKenna delivered the sermon and there followed the playing of 'The Lost Chord' by The Gilmores, a famous Irish band. Fr Lilly, the parish priest at the church of St Vincent Ferrer, was among the throngs of Collins' friends and delegates from the Hibernians who came to pay their last homage to this friendly, witty newspaperman. Later, his remains were sent home to Ireland in the hold of the steamer, *City of Chicago*, completing a journey of 14,000 miles over land and sea, ice and snow, to be buried in

his native Cork soil. Alongside his casket was another, containing the body of his mother – she had died six months after his departure for the Arctic. Jerome Collins and his mother were laid to rest in Curraghkippane graveyard, Co. Cork on 8 March 1884 after requiem Mass in the great cathedral overlooking the town and harbour of Cove.

The grave of Jerome James Collins at Curraghkippane cemetery, on the outskirts of Cork city.
*Author's collection*

# 14

## SCOTT'S *DISCOVERY* EXPEDITION

*In laying down their lives at the call of duty, our countrymen*
*bequeathed to us a rare gift, another of those noble examples*
*not yet rare in our history, and of which we are all so justly*
*proud, one more beacon to guide our sons to deeds of*
*heroism in the future. These examples of unflinching*
*courage, devotion to duty, and endurance of hardship are the*
*lifeblood to naval enterprise.*

LEOPOLD MCCLINTOCK ON THE FIFTIETH ANNIVERSARY OF
THE DEPARTURE OF THE FRANKLIN EXPEDITION, 20 MAY 1895

Toward the close of the nineteenth century, in 1895, the sixth International Geographical Congress was held in London. At its closing session it adopted a resolution:

That this congress record its opinion that the exploration of the Antarctic Regions is the greatest piece of geographical exploration still to be undertaken. That in view of the additions to knowledge, in almost every branch of science, which would result from such scientific exploration, the congress recommends that scientific societies throughout the world, should urge in whatever way seems to them most effective, that this work should be undertaken before the close of the century.[1]

The congress was followed by a succession of expeditions to Antarctica. The first came from Belgium; in 1897–99, the *Belgica*, under Adrien de Gerlache, was first to overwinter south of the Antarctic Circle, off the Antarctic Peninsula. This expedition introduced to Antarctic exploration a Norwegian – Roald Amundsen, first mate of *Belgica*. The expedition's doctor was an American, Dr Frederick Cook, who was later to become infamous for his false claims to have first reached the summit of Mount McKinley in Alaska and later the North Pole. Two German deep-sea expeditions that followed were largely scientific in nature: the *Valdivivia* in 1898–99 and the *Gauss*

*facing page*
Ernest Shackleton, aged sixteen, in the uniform of the White Star Line in whose service his mercantile career started aboard the sailing ship named *Hoghton Tower*.
*From* The Life of Sir Ernest Shackleton, *Hugh R. Mill*

in 1901–03. The first expedition to build huts on Antarctica, in which ten men overwintered in 1898–99, was entitled the British Antarctic Expedition and, interestingly, was led by a Norwegian named Carsten Borchgrevink aboard the *Southern Cross*. A resident of Australia, he received his patronage from Britain. His crew included Norwegian scientists and two Laplanders employed as doghandlers. The expedition reached 78° 83' south on 23 February 1900.

In 1901–03, a Swedish expedition, led by Nils Otto Nordenskjold aboard *Antarctic*, had extraordinary experiences that resulted – in 1903 – with one party of six being dropped off and subsequently marooned on Snow Island, another party of three being forced to overwinter at Hope Bay, and the main party of twenty men and a cat being forced to winter on Paulet Island after *Antarctic* was crushed and sank in the pack ice of Terror and Erebus Gulf. Remarkably, all three parties were rescued by the Argentine naval vessel, *Uruguay*, under the command of Julian Irizar.

It was at this time that the British re-entered the fray of Antarctic exploration. This was to provide opportunities for an Englishman, Robert Falcon Scott, and an Irishman, Ernest Henry Shackleton from Co. Kildare; they would first become colleagues and then rivals. Each separately made bids for polar immortality in the quest to be first to the South Pole and, later, when the Pole had been reached, Shackleton would strive to make the first crossing of Antarctica. Neither was to reach the Pole first, that distinction being claimed by Roald Amundsen. Indeed, Shackleton never achieved many of his specific goals, but both he and Scott did achieve immor-

tality through their heroic efforts, great hardship and suffering. Both their polar careers began with the RGS-organised British National Antarctic Expedition. The *Discovery* voyage of 1901–04 also introduced to polar exploration a below-decks seaman named Tom Crean, from Co. Kerry. As a result of a series of outstanding heroic responses, he has also entered the ranks of the polar immortals.

*Ernest Henry Shackleton 1874–1922*

Ernest Henry Shackleton was born on 15 February 1874 at Kilkea House, in the midst of some of the finest farmland in Co. Kildare. He was the second son of Henry Shackleton and his wife, Henrietta Letitia Sophia; she was the daughter of John Gavan, an inspector general of police in Ceylon and formerly of the Royal Irish Constabulary (RIC).[2] Her family was related to the Fitzmaurices of Co. Kerry. The Shackleton family on his father's side descended from Yorkshire Quaker stock. One of his forebears, Abraham Shackleton, first came to Ireland as private tutor to two local families – the Coopers and Ducketts – and later, in 1726, established a boarding school in Ballitore.[3] Ernest's great-great-aunt, Mary Shackleton – Richard's daughter, born in 1858 – was the first female student at the Ballitore school. She married William Leadbeater, a former pupil who became a teacher at Ballitore. She wrote poetry and kept a diary which were published in 1862, after her death, as *The Annals of Ballitore*.[4]

Ernest's Irish and Quaker ancestry perhaps accounted for his characteristics of strong idealism, reckless courage and, most of all, perseverance. The family motto, 'By endurance we conquer', became his watchword.

In 1880, because of a decline in farming income in Ireland at the time, Ernest's father, Henry, began to study medicine at Trinity College. He moved the family to 35 Marlborough Road, Donnybrook, Dublin. When qualified, he found a practice in Sydenham, South London. In Ireland, Ernest had been educated privately; now he was sent to a prep school in Sydenham and, from there, to Dulwich College as a dayboy in that public school where many of the middle-class attendees were boarders, and where his brogue clearly marked him as Irish in England. One of his schoolmasters at Dulwich, the Rev C.E.C. Lefroy, related that he was sure Shackleton 'found his work in general and myself particularly dull'. This clergyman was in Australia and met Shackleton when he returned there from his South Pole expedition in 1909; to his former pupil, the Rev Lefroy said: 'We never discovered you when you were in Dulwich.' 'No,' said Shackleton, 'but I had not discovered myself.'[5] At school, he was described as 'backward for his age' and was obviously bored and disinterested in schoolwork. He appears to have put the first real effort into his schoolwork when his father – who had wanted Ernest to follow him into medicine – decided to agree to his son's wish to pursue a career at sea.

In 1890, Ernest went to sea as an apprentice – ship's boy – in the mercantile marine, serving in the *Hoghton Tower*, a sailing ship of the White Star Line. Clearly, his father was unwilling to seek a naval commission for him or could not afford to pay the fees of a naval cadetship. In what must have seemed a dream voyage to the imaginative sixteen-year-old, his first trip brought him from Liverpool and round Cape Horn to Valparaíso – rounding the Horn took two months' sailing against the prevailing wind in the middle of the Southern Ocean winter. He made many more similar trips in the steel-hulled and square-rigged sailing ship, learning the ropes and the handling of a sailing ship under full canvas in the twilight years of these vessels; steamship technology was at that time being perfected. In four years, he rounded Cape Horn five times and the Cape of Good Hope once, plying between Liverpool, South America and the East. He qualified as a mate, grew in physical strength and stature, and became an avid reader.

In 1894, he moved on to work on steamers for the Shire Line, where he qualified as first mate in 1896 and as a master in 1898. He applied himself to his nautical training, keeping to himself and resisting the temptations of port, and learning the nature of men at sea. Shackleton then joined the Union Castle Line and, when third officer of *Tintagel Castle*, collaborated with Dr W. McLean to produce a book entitled *O.H.M.S.*, which described experiences when carrying 1,200 troops to war in South Africa. His younger brother, Frank, was by then in the army and served in the Boer War. In 1900, Ernest became a sub-lieutenant in the Royal Marine reserve on the advice of Sir Clements Markham. His selection as a junior officer on the British National Antarctic Expedition was due mainly to his experience of sail.

Sir Clements Markham, president of the Royal

Admiral Sir Leopold
McClintock, c. 1909.
*From Life of Admiral F.L.
McClintock,* Sir Clements
Markham,

When he had painstakingly raised £14,000 from public donations, he was fortunate to receive a single donation of £25,000 from Mr Llewellyn Longstaff, and the keel for the expedition ship, named *Discovery*, was laid at Dundee in March 1900. The committee formed to advise on the design and building of the expedition vessel was chaired by Admiral Sir Leopold McClintock; thus was forged a link between the careers of two of Ireland's greatest polar explorers, Leopold McClintock and Ernest Shackleton.

When *Discovery* sailed on 6 August 1901, she was commanded by Lieutenant Robert Falcon Scott, chosen by Markham as an officer who fitted his ideal of an Antarctic commander. The ideal man should be a naval officer in the regular line and not in the surveying branch; he must be young; he must be a good sailor with some experience of ships under sail, a navigator with a scientific turn of mind; he must have imagination, be capable of enthusiasm, his temperament must be cool, and he must be calm, yet quick and decisive in action, a man of resource with tact and sympathy. How Markham conducted his assessment of these qualities in potential candidates would today interest many human-resource specialists. How well Scott lived up to his sponsor's specification is the stuff of much conjecture; indeed, comparisons of his leadership style with that of his contemporary rivals, Roald Amundsen and Ernest Shackleton, has filled many pages, despite Scott – in death – becoming both martyr and the symbol of British heroic endeavour.

Geographical Society, had initiated a campaign for the renewal of Antarctic exploration in 1893. He first sought support from the general public, confident that once public support had been demonstrated, government support would follow.

There were two Irish officers in the expedition team: Sub-lieutenant Ernest Shackleton and

Hartley T. Ferrar, geologist. Regarding Shackleton, one of the scientists wrote:

> Just as he had been on his former ships, Shackleton was the life and soul of *Discovery*. His mind was alert, his good humour inexhaustible. Besides being in charge of the holds and the stores, he carried out his ordinary duties as an executive officer. He was a fine self-reliant seaman, fearless and dominant, with a stern regard for detail and discipline. He permitted no liberties from those under his command, and could be brutally truculent if such occasions arose. But he was singularly sympathetic and understanding, sentimental to the verge of tears when expressing his own feelings or spouting lines from his favourite poets. In his deep Irish voice he could wheedle and coax; successfully if he required something, which he generally did.[6]

Ferrar, who was born at 3 Grosvenor Place, Dalkey, Co. Dublin on 28 January 1879, was the son of John Edgar Ferrar, a bank clerk, and Mary Holmes Hartley. The family moved to Hollywood, Co. Down and from there to Durban, South Africa, where John Ferrar was appointed a bank manager. A graduate from Cambridge just two months prior to the expedition, Hartley Ferrar was an accomplished rower and is listed as a physicist, palaeontologist and geologist – he had produced a report on the geology of Trinidad.[7] Sir Clements Markham, in his personal narrative of the expedition's origins, provides a potted biography of each of the expedition's officers and scientists. He tells us Ferrar was 22 years of age, single, with an address at Torwood, Windsor Avenue, Belfast.

Shackleton was at that time preoccupied with matters of the heart. He had met Emily Dorman in 1898, the daughter of a wealthy London solicitor and a friend of Shackleton's sister, Kathleen. He and Emily shared a liking for the poetry of Robert Browning and he wrote to her when he was at sea. Before his departure for *Discovery*, she consented to Ernest approaching her father for her hand when his financial future was secured. Shackleton's decision to write to Emily's father instead of meeting him shows his shrewdness and his sense of timing. He wrote to Mr Dorman the day before the royal inspection by Edward VII and Queen Alexandra, just two days before *Discovery* sailed. He benefited fully from the patriotic fervour of the public and press, and it was difficult for Mr Dorman to reject his daughter's hand to one dedicated to such heroic and imperial enterprise. A letter dated 8 August 1901 affirmed his consent to the match 'when you are in the pecuniary position you long for'. Unfortunately, Mr Dorman died suddenly and was buried by the time *Discovery* reached New Zealand.

*Discovery* arrived at Lyttelton Harbour, New Zealand on 29 November. There was a serious leak to fix and coals and stores to load. Shackleton, the experienced merchant seaman, played a key role in this work, receiving high praise from Scott in a report to Sir Clements Markham: 'his interest and enthusiasm, combined with shrewd common-sense and experience in cargo work has proved invaluable.' By the time *Discovery* left New Zealand on Christmas Eve 1901, another Irishman was aboard. Able-bodied Seaman Tom Crean from Co. Kerry was cheered out of Port Chalmers, Dunedin by the crew of his former ship, the *Ringarooma*. Having volunteered to replace one of the two seamen who had deserted the exploration ship, his and Scott's life would be entwined until Scott's death.

Tom Crean was born on 20 July at Gurtuchrane, near the village of Anascaul on the Dingle peninsula in Co. Kerry. The town is close to the magnificent Inch beach and to Mount Brandon, one of Ireland's highest mountains, named in honour of St Brendan, the navigator reputed to have crossed the Atlantic to America in the ninth century in a boat made from the hides of cattle. At the time of Tom's birth, the Dingle peninsula was an Irish-speaking area. One of ten children of Patrick Crean and Catherine Courtney, Tom attended the local primary school. His elder brother, Martin, emigrated to Canada where he worked on the Canadian Pacific Railway; of Tom's other brothers, Michael went to sea and was lost with his ship, Cornelius joined the RIC, while Hugh and Daniel stayed on the family farm at Gurtuchrane, which they divided following their father's death.

On 10 July 1893, when just ten days short of his sixteenth birthday, Tom enlisted in the Royal Navy at Queenstown (Cobh), the deep-sea port of Cork. He was assigned to the training ship HMS *Impregnable* at Plymouth, where he was to learn about life and discipline in Her Majesty's navy as a 'boy second class'. He progressed to boy first class aboard HMS *Devastation*, a coast-guard vessel. His record shows he was promoted to the rank of ordinary seaman on his eighteenth birthday while serving on HMS *Royal Arthur* in the Pacific fleet. He was transferred as an able-bodied seaman to HMS *Swan* while still in Pacific waters. In 1898, he was appointed to the gunnery training ship, HMS *Cambridge*, and later moved to the torpedo school aboard HMS *Defiance*. With these new skills, he was promoted in 1899 to the rank of petty officer (PO) second class while serving on *Vivid*. He was serving on HMS *Northampton*, a training vessel, when he was assigned to HMS *Ringarooma*, a torpedo vessel working in Australian waters. He was by then a tall, impressive and experienced seaman ready for greater challenges and achievement.

His opportunity arose while serving on *Ringarooma* as part of the Australia–New Zealand squadron. When *Discovery* arrived at Lyttelton in November 1901, Admiralty orders for manpower to assist with alterations to the expedition ship's rigging and to trace the leak which caused damage to provisions on the outward journey brought Crean – now aged 24 – into contact with the officers of *Discovery* as a member of one of the work parties. Aware of the vacancies aboard *Discovery*, perhaps he took the opportunity to volunteer or he may have responded to an invitation to join what was clearly a voyage of adventure to the unknown. It was a chance to make a name for himself and perhaps, also, to recover his rank of PO which he seems to have lost while at the Australian station for reasons unknown. The decision to transfer Crean was recorded by Captain Rich in *Ringarooma*'s log: 'Discharged Crean AB to SS *Discovery*'.[8]

Soon, *Discovery* was among the flat-topped icebergs of the Ross Ice Shelf, crossing the Antarctic Circle on 3 January 1902. Lieutenant Albert Armitage, the second-in-command and navigator, described his view from the crow's nest:

Ahead and all around is a vast, illimitable field of ice, which in the farthest distance appears to be absolutely impervious to attack. Somewhat closer are . . . thin black looking streaks of water, and still closer to the ship, the weak places in the line of defence . . . and one is able to guide the ship from one lead to another by the line of least resistance.[9]

It took five days to make the passage through the 270 miles of pack ice by steam and sail, providing an opportunity to observe the bird life of the Ross Sea – southern fulmars, skuas, giant petrels, Antarctic petrels and snow petrels. As they entered open water, Mount Sabine came into view; soon, they were steaming past Coulman Island in sight of the 14,000-foot Mount Erebus, 240 miles away. On 21 January, *Discovery* turned eastward to follow the Great Ice Barrier, rounding the northern corner of Cape Bird and passing inside Beaufort Island. A boat crew was sent ashore at Cape Crozier to take magnetic readings, despite the protests of penguins. The ice shelf was followed for 400 miles until Scott called a halt on 1 February; he turned westward to establish winter quarters. On the return journey, they investigated a bight about 3 miles in length. While the ship lay alongside, two hydrogen balloon ascents were made; Scott

ascended first and was followed later by Shackleton, who reached 650 feet in altitude and took the first aerial photographs of Antarctica. Tom Crean was active among a group of five men, under the command of Armitage and Bernacchi, with orders to examine the surface of the barrier; this team reached 79° 03' south.

*Discovery* returned to McMurdo Sound on 8 February and found it to be free of ice. They set up winter quarters in a little harbour at the head of McMurdo Sound, which came to be known as Winter Harbour. *Discovery* was secured with ice anchors and used as living quarters. A prefabricated hut for indoor scientific work was assembled on a small promontory to the west, and two observation huts were built around a timber skeleton and double sheeted with asbestos. Not long after, Ferrar climbed to the top of Observation Hill where he built a cairn and discovered that they were, in fact, on an island, which is now known as Ross Island.

Shackleton, accompanied by Ferrar and Wilson, was given his first role in command of a sledge, with instructions to make a sledge journey to a nunatak – an isolated rocky peak – which they estimated to be 10 miles away. Choosing not to take dogs or skis, they favoured man hauling their sledge – the hard way, developed by McClintock 40 years before. Markham and the Admiralty old boys – including Admiral McClintock – had advised the expedition in its planning and favoured with a kind of moral fervour this approach which turned sailors and scientists into sledge-hauling beasts of burden. The experiences and practices of previous British explorers, of traders in Canada and of Nansen and the American hardman, Peary, were ignored. This refusal to accept the benefits of high-speed, lightweight travel or to develop skills which would enable explorers to live off the land, dress in fur-skin clothing and build snow shelters when required was what lost the British the edge in polar exploration.

Shackleton and his party went flat out for twelve hours without a break, sweating in their windproof Burberry jackets and wool and cotton clothes. The actual distance proved to be 18 miles, over which they dragged their sledge loaded with a tent, fur sleeping bags, a ground sheet and fourteen days' fuel and rations. They encountered blizzards caused by fine, wind-blown snow crystals and were forced to camp short of their objective. In a state of dehydration and exhaustion, they had their first lesson in how to put up their tent. To make a hot drink of cocoa required familiarity with the Primus stove (invented in 1892 by the Swede, Lindquist). Luckily, Ferrar – who had practised the pre-heating of the burner with methylated spirits aboard *Discovery* – now only had to deal with lighting it in the confines of a tent in sub-zero temperatures. They were frozen all night, the cold seeping up from the ground because of their lack of insulation and wet clothes. The Royal Navy had still not understood the folly of generating perspiration in polar travel – something long known by the Innuit and by inhabitants of the Nordic regions.

On the following day, Shackleton and his men traversed the final miles across the deeply crevassed terrain without the sledge, and reached the nunatak – now called Whites Island. It was mid-night when they climbed to its summit. Though excited by their success in making the first steps on the route toward the South Pole, they were all suffering from varying degrees of frostbite. But the sense of achievement gained by Shackleton from his leadership sustained him through the Antarctic winter of darkness, whose onset was dated 23 April, lasting 121 days into August.

An attempt to reach Cape Crozier before winter resulted in Seaman Vince slipping down an icy slope into the sea and drowning. The rest of the winter passed without incident. Chores included the daily cutting and collecting of ice for drinking water. Daily exercise, occasional lectures – one was given by Ferrar on his scientific work – draughts and cards relieved the monotony. The hut – built in the event of mishap befalling the ship – was known affectionately as the Royal Terror Theatre and was used for plays, concerts and minstrel shows. A monthly paper was published – the *South Polar Times* – featuring articles by the officers and men, and the beautiful illustrations of Dr Wilson. The articles were typed and edited by Shackleton.

In September, Ferrar was once again travelling, this time with Armitage and four men using skis and a sledge. They headed west to find a way through the mountains and onto the mainland. Unbelievably, an outbreak of scurvy caused by insufficient fresh food forced them to return without achieving their objective. Ferrar was one of those to suffer most from this most debilitating condition. The quantity of fresh seal meat was increased in everybody's diet and there was a curtailment in the consumption of tinned food, on which the outbreak of scurvy was blamed.

Shackleton completed a longer, southern reconnaissance with two dog teams and laid a depot at the end of a long peninsula known as The Bluff. From here, the route south beckoned. But would he be in Scott's South Pole party? Wilson – the only person with whom Scott had confided – supported Shackleton's inclusion. Remarkably, he was told of his selection only a week before departure and only then instructed to practice operating a theodolite – an aid to navigation and surveying. Crean was involved in a number of the depot-laying parties which set out on 30 October, led by Lieutenant Michael Barne. Crean's sledge carried his pennant – 'a green flag with a jack in the corner and a gold harp in the centre'.

The three-man polar party – Scott, Wilson and Shackleton – set off on 2 November with nineteen dogs and five sledges in a single train. Sledge pennants fluttered during what would become a daily battle with the dogs while trying to come to terms with overloaded sledges and with skiing. They could not enjoy the pleasure of skiing and sledge travel simply because they had taken no lessons in either. The sledges being too heavy, they were forced to travel the same ground twice with half-loads, covering a mere 4–5 miles a day. McClintock and his companions 50 years before had consistently covered more than 20 miles a day in the Arctic, using dog and ski. One evening, Shackleton managed to upturn the stove, which burned a hole in the groundsheet, and spill the 'hoosh' – pemmican melted with a little water to which was added broken biscuit – the staple diet of British polar expeditions. Scott showed his true feelings toward Shackleton with the tirade that followed. Wilson stemmed the

flow of invective by reminding Scott of his goal.[10]

Progress was painfully slow and disappointment on realising that the Antarctic 'Grail' was slipping from their ambitious grasps was manifesting itself. On 20 November, they calculated they were still only at 81° south despite having

Shackleton, aged 27, in the uniform of a sub-lieutenant of the Royal Naval Reserve.

been out for seven weeks in near-perfect weather. Five of the dogs were dead and a change of strategy was required. A depot was established in which the dog food was deposited; the remaining dogs would be killed – the weakest first – to feed the rest as they struggled south. They had only Wilson's scalpels for this bloody work, which fell to Shackleton and Wilson. It is little wonder that Scott and Shackleton were never keen on dog teams after this ordeal. On 30 December, the game was up; they had reached only 82° 15' south and were simply not covering enough miles per day. The health of all three was under strain and Scott announced they would return.

Scott and Wilson walked on a bit in the afternoon, leaving Shackleton to mind the camp, and managed to record 82° 17' south. Shackleton recorded: 'it's a wonderful place and deserves the trouble . . . it takes to get here'. They named the inlet at their 'furthest south' after Shackleton, before heading back the 270 miles to their second depot and *Discovery*. Shackleton had been coughing badly and was suffering pains and dizzy spells. He wrote:

We eventually found our depot, after which I broke down and haemorrhage started. Then everything we did not need

was thrown away, and all the weight of pulling devolved to my two companions, and it was only owing to their care for me and kindness during this trying period that I was enabled to reach the ship, for I could do no pulling and could only struggle on ahead of the sledges. Captain Scott and Dr. Wilson were at one time pulling 270 lbs. each and they were not in good robust health, having signs of scurvy and being weak from want of food, yet their thoughts and care was always for me, and no man ever had the good fortune to have better, stronger, and more self-denying friends than I had at that time.[11]

Such careful words masked Shackleton's severe disappointment at Scott's decision to invalid him home aboard the relief ship, *Morning*, despite his rapid recovery from scurvy. This must have been soul-destroying to Shackleton, who was counting on polar exploration as a key to his career ambitions. The *Morning* left on 2 March 1903; most of the eight sent home were undesirables or merchant seamen. Scott had considered it a mistake to mix the navy contingent with the merchant contingent on the mess deck.

Those who remained spent another, colder winter in much the same way as the previous one, but with the benefit of experience, particularly in relation to fresh rations. It appears all were fitter when summer again arrived. In mid-September, Crean was again with Barne in a party sent out to lay a depot to the southeast of White Island on the barrier. It was too early and proved unbelievably cold as the temperature dropped to -67°F (-55°C). Joyce suffered severe loss of feeling from the cold and each member of the crew took turns to warm his frozen foot on his chest until life was restored to it. In October, they set out on a longer journey, taking 69 days in awful weather during which they were detained in their tents for nine days. They endured slow progress and had a lot of trouble on broken ground where a glacier from the Britannia Range joined the barrier.

Scott, meanwhile, had undertaken what turned out to be an important journey of discovery to the west over much more pleasing terrain. On the way, he parted with Ferrar and his two-man geological team whose mission was to explore the dry, snow-free valley known as Taylor Valley. Observations determined that the Royal Society Range was composed of rocks comprising thick layers of sandstone which Ferrar named 'beacon sandstone'. He collected specimens, including basalt and granite, and found seams of coal running through the sandstone; he also found a fossil. His discoveries indicated that in previous times, the climate of Antarctica must have been warm enough to support trees and plants. This was a considerable coup for the young geologist.

Scott's party continued west up what is now called the Ferrar Glacier to reach the summit of the ice cap, which Armitage and party had also reached the previous January. Scott completed a round trip of 1,098 miles in 81 days, returning to the ship on 30 November when the ice cap continued to provide no different view other than 'a further expanse of our terrible plateau'. On his return to *Discovery*, he was a happier man than when he had returned from the southern journey the year before; happy, too, at the better performance of his crew of ordinary seamen and at gaining experience in the ways of sledge travel. The immediate task was to set about freeing the frozen-in vessel. Two relief ships arrived, the *Morning* and *Terra Nova*, and it looked like Scott would have to abandon the frozen-in *Discovery*. Fortunately, the floe suddenly opened up and *Discovery* was able to sail.

In one of the few references to Crean by Scott in his diaries, he reported that he had 'fallen in twice yesterday and as he cannot swim had a fairly narrow shave on the last occasion – luckily he kept still in the break until a line could be got to him.' Scott also remarked that Crean was 'very cheerful about it'. In a recommendation for promotion to petty officer first class, effective 9 September 1904, Scott wrote of Crean: 'Specifically recommended for continuous good conduct and meritorious service throughout the period of the Antarctic expedition 1901 to 1904.' Scott also invited Crean to serve as his coxswain.

### The Return of the Invalid

When Shackleton arrived back to England, he wasted no time in visiting Sir Clements Markham. There was a storm about *Discovery* having to spend a second winter at McMurdo Sound, and blame for what was considered professional incompetence was assigned to Markham and the organising committee. Shackleton was commissioned by the *London Illustrated News* to outline – under the guidance of the RGS president – the circumstances causing the expedition to under-

achieve and to explain the value to science of the work to date. The navy had bought a whaler, *Terra Nova*, with which they intended to relieve *Discovery* the following summer. Shackleton was offered a position aboard the ship, but declined.

In order to marry Emily, who had been left an income of £700 a year by her father, Shackleton needed a career that would support a middle-class lifestyle; he wished to acquire status, too, and all this was something he intended to achieve prior to marrying Emily. His attempts at obtaining a permanent commission from the navy failed, not least because of his earlier refusal of a position on the *Terra Nova* relief vessel; neither did the tendering of a personal reference from Sir Clements Markham to the Admiralty help his cause. He tried Fleet Street, securing a position with the *Royal Magazine*, an upmarket monthly. But he tired quickly of this role, especially as it did not pay very well. He lectured widely on his *Discovery* experiences and was capable of keeping his audience enthralled. An opportunity arose when the Royal Scottish Geographical Society (RSGS) needed a secretary, a post which he eventually secured with the help of Hugh Robert Mill, the RSGS librarian who had sailed to Madeira on the outward voyage of *Discovery* to help Scott sort out his expedition papers. Shackleton was appointed in January 1904 on a salary of £200 per annum. With his distinguished new position, he was able to marry Emily; on 9 April 1904, they were wed at Christchurch, Westminster. He had breakfast that morning with Sir Clements Markham who was then aged 74 and who was unable to attend the wedding due to illness.

Shackleton and his bride made their home on the outskirts of Edinburgh. They integrated well and Shackleton even played golf at Dornoch, where they rented a house for summer. He initially brought new energy to the RSGS, but it was not long before he became bored as secretary to the society, his interest shifting toward a career in politics. He was selected in January 1906 as a candidate for the Liberal Unionist Party to run in Dundee. On the hustings, he declared: 'I am an Irishman and I consider myself a true patriot . . . when I say that Ireland should not have Home Rule.' Home Rule was the issue of the day and its support by the Liberals had split the party, with the Liberal Unionists bitterly opposing Home Rule. Conservatives saw it as a signal for the break-up of the British Empire. In Dublin, Arthur Griffith had formed Sinn Féin in 1905 – a republican party whose aim was independence for Ireland. In Belfast, the Ulster Unionist Party was formed to resist Home Rule. In any event, Shackleton was not elected – a Liberal and a Labour candidate were elected in that radical election when Balfour, the Conservative leader, lost his seat and the Labour Party became a new political force in Britain. But Shackleton had enjoyed the rowdy public meetings and commented afterwards: 'I got all the applause and the other fellows got the votes.'[12]

Shackleton, who was by then a father – his son, Raymond Swinford, was born in February 1905 – was again looking for a job. His entry into the political fray had been to the displeasure of many of the RSGS members, who felt his engagement in politics was unbecoming to the dignity and impartiality of the RSGS office. His resignation was accepted in the summer of 1905. He dabbled in business ventures with his brother, Frank, who lived the high life in London and appeared to be doing nicely with residences in London, Dublin and Devon. However, his various business ventures in which Ernest became involved all lost money.

Meanwhile, Ernest sought out sponsors for a private expedition to Antarctica and found support from William Beardmore through his wife with whom it is widely believed he had an affair. Beardmore, an RSGS member with whom Shackleton had stayed when he moved to Scotland, gave him a job as his personal assistant. The steel manufacturer and shipbuilder guaranteed a loan of £7,000 to the expedition. Elizabeth Dawson-Lambton had already given Shackleton £1,000, which he had given to Frank to invest until he needed it. He found a patron in the Marquis of Graham and City backing from a company called Celtic Investment Trust with whom Miss Lambton's £1,000 had likely been invested. Shackleton believed he now had access to £30,000 for the expedition.

Emily gave birth to a daughter, Cecily, just before Christmas 1906. When Shackleton told his wife of his plans, she accepted his restless nature and reconciled herself to a supporting role and to providing him with a home base to which he would return from his expeditions.

# 15

# SHACKLETON'S *NIMROD* EXPEDITION

*A live donkey is better than a dead lion, isn't it?*

SHACKLETON, TO HIS WIFE, EMILY[1]

When Shackleton had his guarantees and his patron secured, his next port of call was the RGS where he told of his plans to lead the British Antarctic Expedition and sought RGS support. Shackleton failed to secure support from either Scott Keltie, the RGS secretary, or Sir George Goldie, the president. It was 11 February 1907 and, coincidentally, he met in the RGS office that same day both Roald Amundsen and Fridtjof Nansen, two very successful Norwegian polar explorers. Amundsen was in London to lecture that evening on his first successful navigation of the Northwest Passage aboard his sailing boat the *Gjøa*. His new focus was the North Pole, for which attempt he sought from Nansen the use of his polar ship, the *Fram*.

Having issued a press statement on 11 Feb-

ruary announcing his plans, Shackleton wrote to Edward Wilson and offered him the post of second-in-command. He was surprised and disappointed when his offer was turned down by Wilson, who claimed he was committed to completing research into a disease that was killing grouse in Scotland. When Shackleton offered the post to George Mulock, the man who replaced him on *Discovery*, Mulock – in turning down the offer – mentioned that he had volunteered to go with Scott. Shackleton deduced that Scott was also planning his own expedition and that the RGS knew of Scott's plans. His deduction was confirmed by a letter from Scott, then at Gibraltar. Having read of Shackleton's plans in *The Times*, Scott revealed that he was also making plans to return to Antarctica and asserted his view that he had a natural right to the *Discovery* quarters at McMurdo Sound and to the Ross Sea region, and that Shackleton should leave that base to him. Shackleton, realising that Scott could and would obstruct his planning and frighten off

*facing page*
Shackleton in 1909, aged 35, looking very much the celebrated public hero. He was invested Commander of the Royal Victorian Order by King Edward VII.
*From* Heart of the Antarctic, *Sir Ernest Shackleton*

his sponsors in an unseemly public squabble, reluctantly agreed not to use McMurdo Sound as a base, choosing instead to adopt a plan previously devised by Armitage – second-in-command on *Discovery* – to establish a base on the Ross Ice Shelf to the east of McMurdo Sound. From this ice shelf, they expected to find an easier and shorter route south, in line with the south-easterly trend of the mountains. At Wilson's insistence, Shackleton signed a note to this effect. It is ironic that this route led Amundsen to the South Pole in 1911. The RGS promised Scott it would take no responsibility for Shackleton's expedition and reminded him that Shackleton's motivation was based on the Irishman's need to prove to all that he was as good as any of those chosen to stay behind on *Discovery*.

Shackleton now had only seven months to prepare. He opened an office in London and invited most of the officers from *Discovery*, all of whom – for one reason or another – declined his offer. Among them was Hartley Ferrar, the Dublin geologist. On his return from Antarctica aboard *Discovery* in 1904, he had married Gladys Anderson of Christchurch, New Zealand. They had two sons and two daughters. He secured a post with the Egyptian government and carried out extensive surveys of the Western Desert. He later worked in the Geological Survey of New Zealand, and served with the New Zealand Rifles in Egypt and Palestine during the First World War. He returned to his surveying post to become assistant director of the Geological Survey of New Zealand. Farrar was later distinguished in his adopted country with the awarding of an honorary doctorate in natural sciences by the University of New Zealand. He died in Wellington in April 1932.[2]

Undeterred by Ferrar and the others not joining him, Shackleton continued to prepare for the forthcoming expedition. He travelled to Christiana – now Oslo – in Norway to purchase polar clothing and equipment, such as sledges made from seasoned ash and hickory, reindeer-fur sleeping bags and finnesko boots from Lapland. In need of a ship, he sought help from the Belgian, Adrien de Gerlache, who found a suitable three-year-old vessel at a cost of £11,000. However, when Shackleton went to Celtic Investment Trust for the promised funds, he discovered there was no money for the expedition, apparently due to his brother's irregular share dealings in the company. The whole expedition was then in real jeopardy. Ever positive and hopeful, Shackleton found in Newfoundland a working sealer named *Nimrod*. Forty-one years old, reeking badly of seal oil, she would need her masts and rigging refitted and her planking re-caulked. *Nimrod* could only manage 6 knots at top speed but, most importantly, cost only £5,000. Rupert England, who had been first mate on the *Morning*, was recruited as commander of *Nimrod*. He, in turn, recommended Dr William Michell, a Canadian, as the ship's surgeon. The application from John King Davis – an Anglo-Irishman – to retain his position as *Nimrod*'s chief officer was approved. Another Irishman, H.J.L. Dunlop, from Ulster, was appointed chief engineer. Alfred Cheetham, the third officer and boatswain, was yet another officer from *Morning* to be appointed by Shackleton.

Having consulted with Nansen, who favoured

dogs and skis, Shackleton nevertheless decided to take Manchurian ponies in preference to dogs, necessitating the need to bring to Antarctica everything the horses would eat, which would then have to be carried onward by sledge toward the Pole. William Beardmore provided the expedition with a motor car from the Arrol-Johnson works in Paisley, which he had recently taken over. It was equipped with special tracked rear wheels for traction on snow and with sledge runners bolted onto the front wheels for ease of steering when in snow. The food was planned on the basis of twelve men for two years. This was later added to when extra men were taken aboard in New Zealand. It was packed into 2,500 special lightweight packing cases made from plywood. A wooden, prefabricated hut was built to accommodate twelve men; measuring 33 feet in length, 10 feet in width and with walls 8 feet to the eves, it was double walled and insulated with cork; its external walls and roof were covered with strong roofing felt. Sledging tents, stoves and a range of wind-proof and warm shirts, underclothes, socks, mitts, sweaters and boots were also ordered.

By July, Shackleton was in urgent need of £8,000 to meet his anxious creditors before the ship could depart. His brother's integrity and reputation was by then under very close scrutiny; he was one of the prime suspects in the case of the theft of the Irish Crown Jewels, whose misappropriation from a safe in Dublin Castle was discovered in July 1907. It took all of Shackleton's great optimism, undoubted charm and immense powers of persuasion to assemble the loan guarantees to cover the amount he required,

in what must have been a very difficult and tense time for him. He sought support from Lord Iveagh – Edward Guinness of the Dublin brewing family – a philanthropist and, like Shackleton, a Freemason; Guinness guaranteed £2,000 provided that Shackleton find the balance from others. Within ten days, he had found other loan guarantors including the Duke of Westminster, Sir Rupert Clarke and Lady Brocklehurst, the mother of Sir Philip Brocklehurst to whom Shackleton had assigned the role of assistant geologist. He managed, without committee or any financial help from the RGS, to put the package together on the undertaking that the guarantees would be redeemed by the proceeds of his lectures and sale of the expedition's narrative on its return. His overtures to King Edward VII for royal patronage resulted in the king agreeing to inspect the ship during Cowes Week. On Sunday 2 August, *Nimrod* hosted the royal party consisting of the king and queen, the Prince of Wales, Princess Victoria, Prince Edward and the Duke of Connaught. The Royal Victorian Order was conferred on Shackleton and he was presented with a Union Jack to carry south on his sledge journey. *Nimrod* was anchored alongside the *Dreadnought*, the home-fleet flagship.

*Nimrod* moved to Torquay and sailed from there on 7 August without Shackleton, who was still trying to raise money. He would join the ship in New Zealand. *Nimrod* stopped at St Vincent, Cape Town en route and arrived at Lyttelton, New Zealand on 23 November. Shackleton did manage to raise £4,000 from his cousin, William Bell, but then found himself seeking a loan of £1,000 from Beardmore to meet Frank's pressing bills. Beardmore obliged with a promise from Ernest that the loan would be repaid within one month. He left on the last day of October from Dover – Emily saw him off from there – but the loan had not been redeemed. In New Zealand, he secured financial help from the Australian government when Bell's contribution was not paid. Through the offices of Thomas W. Edgeworth David – professor of geology at Sydney University – he recruited both David and his protégé, Douglas Mawson – a lecturer in mineralogy and petrology at Adelaide University – into the ranks of the expedition's scientific staff. This gave Australia input into the geology of the Southern Hemisphere and Shackleton the £5,000 he urgently needed to pay staff, to purchase additional stores and to modify and strengthen the ship further. The New Zealand government also contributed a grant, of £1,000, and funded half the cost of towing *Nimrod* to the Antarctic Circle. The Union Steam Ship Company paid the balance, which saved *Nimrod* using valuable coal on the outward journey. Having taken on extra food and provisions for the staff, *Nimrod* left as planned on 1 January 1908. Thirty thousand people cheered her off as the *Koonya* took her in tow. In less than ten months, Shackleton had put together the expedition and was going south again.

The voyage was horrendous; the effect of big seas and gales on an overloaded ship under tow was alarming. *Koonya* towed her 1,500 miles in fifteen days, reaching the Antarctic Circle on 15 January. They immediately engaged with a labyrinth of icebergs through which they steered, sometimes with all hands on deck. On 20 Jan-

uary, they were in the open water of the Ross Sea and, three days later, the Great Ice Barrier came into view. *Nimrod* sailed east to seek out either Barrier Inlet – called Balloon Bight by Scott – or Borchgrevink's Bight.[3] They could not find either and it became clear that they had calved off the barrier and floated out to sea. Captain England, concerned for the overloaded ship, wanted to head for McMurdo Sound immediately. But Shackleton's promise to Scott meant he must try to find an alternative place to land. England was concerned not to waste precious coal trying to comply with what he considered an unreasonable demand. A large bay, where whales were observed spouting, was about all that was left of Barrier Inlet and Borchgrevink's Bight, and it was christened the Bay of Whales. England feared the prospect of becoming frozen in the sheet of solid ice between *Nimrod* and the barrier shore, and preferred the option of waiting until the pack ice broke up naturally and to then land the shore party and equipment. But the thought of the impermanence of the barrier was in the forefront of all their minds. Reasoning that wherever they should land must have a rock-solid foundation for their winter home, they travelled further east, toward King Edward VII Land, until stopped by heavy pack ice. Turning about, they sailed westward, back to McMurdo Sound; it was either there or home. Scott's unreasonable demand created a lose-lose situation for Shackleton. As an officer, honourable explorer but still an establishment outsider, he knew better than most the value placed on the word of a man by the society he was trying to prove himself to. In distress at the time, he later said: 'I had promised and I felt that each mile west was a horror to me.' One wonders what the outcome of the expedition would have been if Shackleton could have landed at the Bay of Whales, 115 miles closer to the Pole than McMurdo Bay.

He was further frustrated when *Nimrod* arrived at McMurdo Sound and found 20 miles of frozen ice protecting the entry to Hut Point on Ross Island. He waited for nature to break it up beneath the shadow of the smouldering volcano, Mount Erebus, with the nervous England getting more and more anxious. Then, on 3 February, Shackleton went ashore at Cape Royds, sounding the depth in a whaleboat, and found a natural ice dock and some black rocks on which to construct the base. They landed the ponies and the prefabricated hut, the outside shell of which they built in ten days. It took another three weeks to complete the sealing, insulation and furnishing to make it a comfortable base for fifteen men to live in during the Antarctic winter. The off-loading of *Nimrod* was full of problems, given the onshore winds and ice. Captain England was very nervous and made heavy weather of getting in close, which led to a row with Shackleton. They eventually got their stores and equipment ashore and *Nimrod* sailed to New Zealand. Dunlop, the engineer, had with him a letter of dismissal for England from Shackleton, to be issued on arrival at New Zealand.

On 5 March 1908, the hut construction complete, Shackleton sent out a team of six to climb Mount Erebus, the active volcano just 15 miles from where they were residing. David, Mawson, Mackay, Marshall, Brocklehurst and Adams were the men chosen to go. Beginning at

sea level, they scrambled straight up the slopes of the great volcano, which they measured with their hypsometer at 13,370 feet. Its height was

Shackleton's men atop Mount Erebus, an active volvano.
*From Heart of the Antarctic, Sir Ernest Shackleton*

The 'furthest
south' camp,
following a
60-hour blizzard.
*From* Heart of the Antarctic,
*Sir Ernest Shackleton*

recently measured at 3,794 metres or 12,447 feet. All except Brocklehurst – who celebrated his twenty-first birthday en route and who suffered from frost-bitten feet – reached the summit after five days. They had camped out on the lower slopes and slept wrapped in the tent cloth on the windy upper slopes in temperatures of -20°F (- 29°C). On the summit, Mawson's angular measurement established the depth of the crater at 900 feet and the greatest width at half a mile:

We stood on the verge of a vast abyss and

at first could see neither to the bottom or across it on account of the huge mass of steam filling the crater and soaring aloft in a column 500 to 1000 feet high.[4]

When a breeze arose, they observed at least three, well-defined openings at the bottom of the cauldron, and established that it was from these the steam explosions emanated. They observed remarkable mounds and cones, and collected specimens of lava, sulphur-coated feldspar crystals and fragments of pumice. Shackleton's scientific team was already successful, climbing a mountain higher than the Matterhorn direct from sea level, with no fuss or specialist mountaineers. On reaching the hut, they celebrated with champagne.

The problem with Cape Royds was that they had no access to the barrier once the pack ice broke up and isolated them from the mainland. This meant sledging could not begin until light returned in August and while McMurdo Sound was frozen over. They overwintered well, eating plenty of fresh and undercooked seal meat to prevent scurvy, and planned two separate journeys – one to the South Pole and one to the magnetic South Pole. Shackleton, Wild, Adams and Dr Marshall were to become the polar party while David, Mawson and Dr Mackay would address the magnetic objective. The journey to Hut Point was used to accustom the polar beginners to polar travel without either dogs or skis; it was just man hauling in the manly British way. Only four ponies had survived the Antarctic winter and they were being saved for the long journey south. No new lessons had been learned in the intervening period regarding techniques of snow travel or the use and management of dogs and skis. They set out for a longer depot-laying journey on 28 September, travelling the first 8 miles by car over hard-packed snow before getting stuck in the first snow bank encountered. Having yoked themselves to the sledge, they made a depot 100 miles toward the Pole at 79° 36' south and returned to Cape Royds on 13 October. David, Mawson and Mackay had left a week before, also intending to man haul every yard of the way.

The polar party set out on 29 October 1908, each member of the party leading out one of the four surviving ponies – Grisi, Socks, Quan and Chinaman – each attached to a sledge. The support party of Joyce, Brocklehurst, Priestly, Armytage and Marston followed Shackleton, man hauling a sledge after progress by car was brought to a halt by a drift. The driver, Day, bade them farewell and rejoined the biologist, Murray, and the cook, Roberts, who would wait for the return of both parties. After nine days, they had covered 54 miles, due to the difficult nature of the terrain and blizzards, one of which kept them in their bags for an entire day. Needing to cover at least 16 miles a day out and back, they were already a hundred miles behind schedule. On 7 November, the support party turned back. Joyce undertook to bring more supplies out to the depot at The Bluff. During the next couple of days, the polar party struggled through an area that was very heavily crevassed, making progress poor. When the terrain suddenly improved, they covered over 12 miles in a single day, raising their spirits in the process.

Elsewhere, the magnetic Pole party was also struggling and having to come to terms with the need to conserve rations. They were covering very bad ground along the edge of the coast, and had travelled barely 120 miles in five weeks. Seals – killed to keep them in fresh food – were cooked on a blubber stove improvised from a biscuit tin; it had been devised by Dr Mackay during the winter. They suffered diarrhoea as a result of this diet but the risk of scurvy was greatly reduced by their scientific reasoning and actions.

On 28 November, Shackleton's party passed

the previous 'furthest south' of the *Discovery* party. That they had covered the ground in 29 days to Scott's 59 gave them great heart; their rate of 13 miles a day would bring them to the Pole around New Year's Day. Despite the better progress, the ponies were hard work and needed a lot of minding, particularly at the end of a long day. Then, a snow wall had to be built to shelter them for the night, they needed to be rubbed down and covered with blankets, and their rations had to be ground down and prepared before the two tents and evening meal could be prepared for the human travellers. The cold, however, was having an adverse effect on the ponies, and Chinaman had already been put down – on 21 November. There were benefits from this: fresh meat to fend off scurvy and a further cache of food for the return journey. Adams had an aching tooth extracted by Marshall without the use of anaesthetic – the first attempt at extraction had ended in a broken tooth. Dr Marshall had been worried about Shackleton from the outset, but he was apparently in good health and showing no signs of sickness, though suffering from snowblindness – a painful ailment that lasts for days and is similar to having grit in one's eyes. They were, however, still 500 miles from the Pole and the other ponies were weakening. Grisi – Marshall's pony – was put down on 28 November, followed by Quan – Shackleton's – on the first day of December. They were stumbling through very difficult diagonal undulations filled with soft snow. The way south being blocked by a range of mountains, it was time for the 'Boss' – as Wild had begun to refer to Shackleton – to find a way. A mountain pass to the south between two

low mountains beckoned; without the sledge or their last remaining pony, a day was spent reaching the summit of a hill they called Mount Hope. From its summit, they observed a steady, long slope in a southerly direction. Wild estimated it was 30 miles wide and 100 miles long to the inland ice. Shackleton wrote: 'From the top we could see the glacier stretching away inland till at last it seemed to merge into inland ice.'

Next day, they started into it, camping alongside the great glacier beneath a pillar of granite, an unmistakable landmark where they made their fourth depot. Shackleton was snowblind again. Progress up the glacier was terrible; Socks vanished into one of the huge, gaping crevasses. Luckily, the straps connecting Socks to Wild and the sledge broke, but Socks and the fresh food he offered were gone. Dr Marshall had factored Socks' food value into the calorie count and now they lacked the food to sustain their physical activity to the Pole and back. Shackleton kept them going, pulling a half-ton between them with 350 miles to go. It was vital to be careful – a lost sledge or man into a crevasse would have serious consequences for all the party. As they set out each day, they hoped that would be the day they would come to the end of their difficulties, arriving, perhaps, at the top of the great ice cap that reached out to the Pole. Ticking off landmarks, they passed a mountain they named Cloudmaker and a nunatak they called Mount Buckley. When they made another depot at the top of the glacier, they had climbed 6,000 feet. On Christmas Day, they were still climbing, dragging and pulling the sledge up the relentless glassy slope. Wild wrote:

May none but my worst enemies spend their Xmas in such a dreary God forsaken spot as this. Here we are . . . farther away from civilisation than any human being has ever been since civilisation was.[5]

At an altitude of 9,500 feet and at 250 miles from the Pole, it was also very cold and windy. Having only four weeks' food, they decided to ration it to make it last six, their margin for error reducing all the time. They pulled on, discarding spare clothing and sledge spares. It got flatter and smoother with no crevasses, but they were starving, dehydrated and getting colder by the day as they walked into a headwind that tore and burned their faces. On 6 January, when at 88° 5' south, it was agreed to get within 100 miles of the Pole. Winds of 80–100 mph and the blizzard that such winds unleash kept them in their bags for the following two days, sustained by their meagre rations. On 9 January, they walked south without sledge or load for five hours, from 4–9 a.m. At the end of their long, uphill walk, Marshall, using dead reckoning, positioned them at 88° 23' south, or 97 miles from the Pole. Having mounted Queen Alexandra's Union Jack on a bamboo pole, they photographed themselves as they formally took possession of the polar plateau and named it King Edward VII Plateau. Turning back, they hoped they would have the strength and good luck to find their first depot after the blizzards of previous days.

It is often claimed by critics that Shackleton failed to achieve his major goals. This is to misunderstand his achievements and their significance, made, as they were, with precious little direct support. In a single push, he had extended the 'furthest south' record by 350 miles. Roland Huntford, in his biography of Shackleton, describes it as 'the greatest single leap forward to either Pole of the earth that anyone had ever achieved.' Having gone so far and with the Pole almost within reach, his turning back 'was arguably one of the bravest acts in the history of exploration . . . especially when it meant publicly admitting defeat and to a despised rival.'

Having gone flat out back to their tent, and with only a drink and an hour's rest, Shackleton and his men set out to find their first depot by following the raised tracks of their sledge which had been profiled by the Antarctic winds. His luck was holding out. For the next ten days, still on half rations, they sailed down the glacier, using the tent groundsheet as a sail. With the wind behind their backs, they made 20 miles a day and were soon meeting familiar landmarks.

On 16 January 1908, David, Mawson and Dr Mackay were also hoisting the Union Jack, at latitude 72° 25' south, longitude 155° 16' east; according to their instruments, this was where the ever-moving magnetic South Pole at that moment resided. The story of their journey was similar to Shackleton's: one of perseverance and misery in constant cold winds and over soft and bad ground. They headed back for the shore-side depot they had left at the Drygalski Ice Tongue and, just as they reached it, heard two gunshots; *Nimrod* was off shore and had spotted them. David afterwards remarked that if they had known of the abundance of seals along the coast, they could have covered the ground in half the time with a team of dogs. Nevertheless, by

The southern party (left–right): Wild, Shackleton, Marshall and Adams aboard *Nimrod* following their return from their 'furthest south'. On 8 January 1909, they reached 88° 23' south, 97 miles short of the Pole. Sir Arthur Conan Doyle later remarked: 'think of that flag flapping down yonder on the snow-field, planted there by an Irishman.'
*From* Heart of the Antarctic, *Sir Ernest Shackleton*

walking and pulling for 1,260 miles in the world's coldest environment – using the most basic resources available to man – they had reached the point where their compass needle was perfectly vertical.

On 20 January, as Shackleton's party reached the Mount Buckley depot, his heels and feet were split; he suffered in silence so as not to slow down the entire party. He became ill the following day and was unable to pull; at times, he sat on the sledge. A couple of bad days followed as the other three put in a mighty effort. By 26 January, with 20 miles to go to the next depot, they were out of food. Sustained only by medication from Marshall, they kept going all day, traversing treacherous, glassy ice crevasses before the familiar rock-pillar landmark of their next depot

came into view. Adams, Wild and Shackleton, having stopped, were cramped and seized up. Marshall, who had taken over effective control, made his way alone to the depot and brought back the necessary sustenance to get the men going again. It had been 40 hours since their last solid food. Next day, they reached the barrier. The daily torture continued; though Shackleton had recovered, Wild now had dysentery. But it was walk or perish for each of them and they carried on their fight for survival.

On 13 February, they reached the depot where Chinaman's carcass was stored. The pony's liver 'tasted splendid'.[6] Though somewhat revived, they were still 108 days out. Sore and blistered, they were finding it harder to get started each morning. Reaching The Bluff depot on 23 February, they feasted on plums, eggs, cakes, plum puddings and mutton. Following the arrival of *Nimrod*, Joyce had recently restocked The Bluff depot and had left a message for Shackleton with details of the ship's arrival. After months of starvation and hunger, they were able to 'eat meals fit for the gods with appetites the gods might have envied'. Marshall, who had been a pillar of strength all through, was by then suffering badly from dysentery. Shackleton and Wild pushed on to Hut Point. On arrival there the next day, Shackleton read a letter informing him that *Nimrod* had picked up the magnetic Pole party and would stand off until 26 February. It was already 28 February. Next morning, the hut was set alight as a signal beacon and soon – as if by magic – *Nimrod* appeared. Shortly afterwards, Shackleton set out again, this time leading a rescue party for Marshall and Adams. Just after midday on 4 March, they were all safely on board *Nimrod*. They had walked 1,700 miles.

Though ultimate success had eluded the Kildareman, his exploits turned him into a national hero. He produced a narrative of the expedition with the help of a New Zealand newspaper reporter, Edward Saunders, who transcribed the text from interviews and working sessions with Shackleton during the voyage home and between subsequent lectures. The book, *The Heart of the Antarctic*, was published by Heinemann within five months of his return from Antarctica. Shackleton commenced a world lecture tour, attended by, among others, the king of England and Kaiser Wilhelm of Germany. He had audiences with the tsar of Russia and President Taft at the White House. Asquith's government authorised a grant of £20,000 and commended the low cost of his Antarctic enterprise. He could now afford to redeem his loan guarantees. Though he had named the great glacier after Beardmore, his most important sponsor did not forgive Shackleton for having left without paying back the £1,000 loan. In Dublin, the public was reminded by the nationalist *Weekly Freeman* of the Irishness of the Shackletons; Ernest himself remarked during a December visit to the then second city of the British Empire that, despite having left as an obscure and unknown boy, Irish he remained. Fellow Irishman, Conan Doyle, asked the people to think of the contribution Ireland had made to the Empire, and to 'think of that flag flapping down yonder on the snowfield, planted there by an Irishman.'

Meanwhile, Scott had organised another expedition, funded to the tune of £20,000 by the Asquith government; it had learned from Shackleton's risk-taking enterprise the extent of public support and interest in a British South Pole triumph. Scott's ship, *Terra Nova*, left in early June with PO, First Class Tom Crean aboard. Though Scott did receive some financial support from the RGS, he had to fund-raise from the public and received donations from expedition members; some even declined wages. Scott could not lose. His rival had whipped up public interest and had mapped the way to within 100 miles of the Pole. It was a very diplomatic Shackleton who called for 'three cheers for Captain Scott' at Waterloo Station as Scott left London on the mail train on 16 June 1910.[7] Shackleton anticipated his 'furthest south' glory was soon to be overtaken.

# 16

## ANTARCTIC EXPEDITION OF *TERRA NOVA*

*To strive, to seek, to find, and not to yield.*

ALFRED, LORD TENNYSON ('ULYSSES')[1]

On return from *Discovery*, Tom Crean was promoted to petty officer first class, dated from September 1904. He served out of the naval bases at Chatham, Kent and at the torpedo-training school at Portsmouth. Upon publication of Scott's book, *The Voyage of the* Discovery, he received a copy from Scott together with a letter requesting he become Scott's coxswain. In a note, Crean accepted the invitation and, in September 1906, joined Scott on board the battleship HMS *Victorious* in the Atlantic Fleet. In early 1907, Scott and Crean moved to HMS *Albemarle* in the same fleet, and Crean later followed Scott to HM Ships *Essex* and *Bulwark* in 1908.

News of Shackleton's 'furthest south' came at about the same time as the claimed conquest of the North Pole by the Americans, Peary and Cook. The last, great geographic quest – the conquest of the South Pole – was now very attractive to Scott. A career navy officer, it gave him the spur he needed to return to the Pole before Shackleton or other, foreign, competitors could get there before him.

At Scott's invitation, Crean joined *Terra Nova* in April 1910 on the Thames, where he re-acquainted himself with his old shipmates from *Discovery* including PO Edgar Evans, Chief Stoker Bill Lashly, PO Thomas Williamson and PO William Heald. At the head of the scientific team was Dr Edward Wilson. Three Cork accents were to be heard aboard *Terra Nova*: PO Patrick Keohane and PO Robert Forde were part of the shore party, and Able-bodied Seaman Mortimer McCarthy was a member of the ship party.

*The McCarthy Brothers of Lower Cove, Kinsale*
Mortimer McCarthy, from Lower Cove, Kinsale, Co. Cork, was one of a family of five children –

Herbert Ponting's photographic study of Patrick Keohane on his return from the barrier in support of Captain Scott's ill-fated polar party.
*Scott Polar Research Institute*

and Shackleton; each was to become associated with one of the great explorers. One of the most familiar native names in the area, the McCarthys descend from the Eóghanacht line, which can be traced back to the third century AD.[3] Kinsale is at the mouth of the River Bandon, where many river bends provide an enchanting setting for its safe and fortified harbours. The Battle of Kinsale in 1601 is recognised as one of the most significant events in Irish history, when a fleet of 26 Spanish ships arrived into the shelter of Kinsale's harbour, landing 3,500 soldiers there. The English army, under Lord Mountjoy, surrounded the town with 6,000 troops. Hugh O'Neill, Earl of Tyrone and Hugh O'Donnell, Earl of Tír Connail – both Irish, Catholic chieftains who had invited the Spaniards to help rid them of the English – brought their armies south, marching in winter and besieging the English. In the ensuing battle, the English won the day and were happy to allow the Spaniards to leave. Thereafter, a British military presence was maintained in Kinsale, right up to Irish independence in 1922.

Every day on their way to school at Summercove, the children of Lower Cove passed Charles Fort, a pentagonal-shaped bastion fort, and the McCarthy children were sure to have played with the children of the soldiers stationed there. A special treat and spectacle for the children must have been Sunday band concerts in summer, and the colour, pomp and ceremony of the marching men at church parades held by the army on special occasions. As the McCarthy children were growing up, there were only half a dozen families living in Lower Cove. Like their neighbours – the Hurleys, Salters, Murrays and O'Donovans – they

three brothers and two girls. The boys were named Timothy, or Tadhg, Mortimer, or 'Murty', and James; the girls were named Anne and Mary.[2] Mortimer and Timothy were both to become participants in the Antarctic legends created by Scott were referred to as the 'crow people' by the people who lived in adjacent townlands. This was a reference to the townland of Preghane where they lived; in the Irish language, *préachán* means 'crow' or, more accurately, the seaside species of the crow family known as the chough, which resided in the area in numbers.[4] The families of Lower Cove were largely dependent on fishing for a livelihood and existed on a healthy diet of fish, potatoes, eggs and vegetables. Working on fishing boats – large and small – was part of the local economy and part of any young boy's education, particularly in summertime when they fished from family-owned drievers (small fishing boats).

At that time, the Royal Navy's chief naval bases were situated along this coast, a coast that could boast a fine maritime tradition among its inhabitants in coastal towns such as Youghal, Queenstown (now Cobh), Ballycotton and Kinsale. The Atlantic Ocean, which washes onto the small, stony beach of Lower Cove, also washes onto the Weddell Sea shores of Antarctica from where Timothy McCarthy was to play a key role in 1916, with Shackleton, in the rescue of his fellow *Endurance* crewmen. In those testing days, he was to demonstrate to great effect the small-boat skills learned in his youth. His brother, Mortimer, or Jack McCarthy as he was later known in New Zealand, went to sea as a boy and, like many others, added a few extra years to his age to qualify for entry. His first recorded voyage was aboard the *Gladys Royle* to the Black Sea. Further trips brought him to Canada, USA and Australia, giving him much experience on a variety of ships. Mortimer joined Scott and the *Terra Nova*

on 25 November 1910 at Lyttelton, the New Zealand port used by many polar expeditions as a base en route to Antarctica.

*PO Patrick Keohane*

Patrick Keohane was born on 25 March 1880 at Coolbawn on the Seven Heads peninsula, near Courtmacsherry, Co. Cork; he later resided at Courtmacsherry. The sea and seafaring was in his family; his father was coxswain of the old Courtmacsherry lifeboat based at Barry Point near Lislee. Keohane's naval record shows he started out as a 'boy third class' on 6 June 1895 aboard HMS *Impregnable*; he was fifteen years old. His height on entry is recorded as 5 feet 1 inch, his hair fair, his eyes blue and his complexion fair. He progressed to boy first class on the same ship, moving to HM Ships *Vivid I* and *Magnificent*, where he became an ordinary seaman. On reaching his eighteenth birthday, he started his first period of continuous service by signing on for twelve years. By that time, his record shows he was 5 feet 3 inches tall and his hair light brown. He spent further periods of service on HM Ships *Nile*, *Vivid I* and *Cleopatra*, in whose service he was promoted to AB in 1899. He had further service on HM Ships *Cambridge*, *Defiance*, *Vivid I* and *Amphion*, achieving his first badge in March 1901. While on further periods of service aboard *Vivid I*, he progressed to petty officer third class in 1904. Periods aboard *Defiance*, *Vivid I*, *Emerald* and *Sapphire II* led to the achievement of his second badge, on 24 March 1906, and to his promotion to petty officer first class in December 1907. He continued to rotate his service between

*Vivid I* and *Defiance* until March 1910. From then until May, Patsy – as he was known in the navy – served under Lieutenant Teddy Evans on HMS *Repulse*. It is interesting to note that his service record lists his height then as 5 feet 7 inches, his hair brown, his eyes grey. When Evans was appointed second-in-command to Scott, he selected Keohane, then aged 30, for *Terra Nova*. Keohane's character during his entire naval career was consistently rated as very good by every captain under whom he served, something that possibly influenced Evans' choice of the Corkman for the Antarctic adventure. His record shows his service was to be borne on the ledger of HMS *President* from 16 April while lent to British Antarctic Expedition 1910.[5]

*PO Robert Forde*

The *Terra Nova* muster list records Robert Forde of 52 Harbour Row, Queenstown (Cobh), Co. Cork as being aged 35 years old when he joined *Terra Nova* on 30 May 1910. The petty officer had transferred from HMS *Ramillies* to join the expedition.[6] He was born on 29 August 1875, at Maviddip, Cork. On entry into the Royal Navy, when sixteen years of age, he was described as being 5 feet 8 inches tall, with hazel eyes, dark-brown hair and a fresh complexion. By eighteen, when he signed on for twelve years' service, he was an inch taller. He joined the service as a 'boy second class' on 7 November 1891 on HMS *Impregnable*, moving to *Lion* – where he was rated as boy first class – and to *Vivid I* where, on reaching his eighteenth birthday, he was rated an ordinary seaman. He progressed to *Warspite* and back to *Vivid I*, where he was promoted to able-bodied seaman on 17 April 1894; he achieved his first badges in August 1896. Periods of service followed on HM Ships *Cambridge*,

*Vivid I*, *Vivid II*, *Nile II* and *Amphion*, on board which he achieved his second badge in August 1901. He was promoted to petty officer second class in February 1902 and, later – on 9 November 1904 – first class. He further served on HM Ships *Cambridge*, *Indus*, *Emerald*, *Talbot* and *Ramillies*,[7] from which he volunteered on 16 April 1910 for the Antarctic expedition of *Terra Nova*. Like all naval officers and ratings on the expedition, his record shows his service was to be borne on the ledger of HMS *President* while lent to British Antarctic Expedition 1910. During his years of service, Forde served with Keohane on a number of occasions: aboard *Amphion* (September 1900–May 1904), *Emerald* (January 1904–July 1906) and *Vivid I* (July–November 1906). Both were petty officers, though Forde, joining earlier, maintained seniority over his fellow Corkonian. His conduct, like Keohane's, was rated consistently as very good throughout his entire career.

*The British Antarctic Expedition 1910–13*

The British Antarctic Expedition 1910–13 left Britain in mid-June 1910, arriving in Melbourne on 12 October. The expedition had both a scientific programme and a clear mission to secure for the British Empire the honour of reaching the South Pole first. Scott set both objectives in order to secure the necessary funds. Like Shackleton, he had resorted to lectures and fund-raising from the British public to raise sufficient funds.[8] A message awaited Scott in Melbourne regarding Roald Amundsen, the man who had completed the first navigation of the Northwest Passage in

1906 and had overwintered in the Southern Ocean with *Belgica* in 1897–99. Now he was sailing to the Antarctic aboard Nansen's polar ship, the *Fram*.

Petty Officer Robert Forde of Harbour Row, Cobh, Co. Cork, photographed by Herbert Ponting.
*Scott Polar Research Institute*

Among *Terra Nova*'s officers was a cavalry officer, Captain Lawrence E.G. Oates of the 6th Inniskilling Dragoons – a man with a distinguished record of service in the Boer War. His first posting to what was regarded as the finest cavalry regiment in the British Army was at the Curragh military camp in Co. Kildare.[9] Also signed to the expedition – aside from the usual complement of scientists, seamen, servicemen and engineers – was Herbert Ponting, a professional photographer and a pioneering film-maker. At Lyttelton, *Terra Nova* took on stores, nineteen Siberian ponies and 34 dogs in addition to the two motorised sledges already aboard. It was here that Mortimer McCarthy joined *Terra Nova*, on 25 November. The passage was rough and the overloaded ship barely survived a force-10 gale. The animals housed on the deck were awash in the crashing waves, and to improve stability, around 10 tons of coal were heaved overboard. When the pumps became blocked, all hands were occupied with buckets to bale her out. There was some consternation among the crew when Captain Oates was observed pouring whiskey down the ponies' throats in order to revive them from the cold wettings they had endured.

On arrival at Cape Crozier in late December, Scott intended to establish a base on shore but, finding it impossible to land, *Terra Nova* returned to McMurdo Sound. Here, at a site 14 miles north of Shackleton's Hut, building of winter quarters commenced. The place had previously been named the Skuary, but Scott chose to rename the site Cape Evans. It took until 17 January before the sledging parties could get under way. One party set out to lay depots on the polar route, while two scientific and geological parties were instructed to explore to the east and west. The depot party of thirteen men – including Crean, Keohane and Forde – took eight ponies, 26 dogs and ten sledges. Not long into the journey, Crean was ordered by Scott to stay at the recently established Safety Camp to look after Atkinson, who had damaged his foot. He was also asked to ferry fodder from the fodder depot to Safety Camp and, in his spare time, to dig a hole into the barrier for scientific observation. Due to the difficulties of travelling in soft snow with ponies, they marched at night when the ground was firmer. Marching 10 miles a day, the first depot – Corner Camp – was established at 35 miles. Heading south, they experienced their first blizzard; lasting three days, it weakened the ponies, two of who were practically useless. Five more days' marching south brought them to Bluff Camp, from where Lieutenant Evans, Keohane and Forde were sent back with the three most exhausted horses: Blossom and Blucher – both of whom collapsed and died on the return journey – and Jimmy Pigg, who survived. The trauma of the voyage, the severity of the work and the cold hastened the deaths of the unfortunate animals.

Scott and party pushed on with the other ponies, though these animals were also deteriorating rapidly. To relieve the suffering of the ponies, One Ton Depot was located at 79° 29' south, 30 miles north of where Scott had originally planned to locate it.[10] This shortfall had fatal consequences later for the polar party. Worse news awaited Scott as he returned to base: a letter from Lieutenant Campbell, commander of the eastern scientific party, introduced a spirit of competition to their endeavours that they had not factored into their wide-ranging programme. Campbell and his party had been ferried eastward along the barrier face by *Terra Nova*, where they planned to land on King Edward VII Land for detailed exploration. They met heavy pack ice along the barrier and decided to seek out Balloon Bight – now Shackleton's Bay of Whales, which they found to be exactly as charted by *Nimrod*. To their absolute amazement, they discovered another ship was anchored to the sea ice at the Bay of Whales, a ship they recognised as Nansen's famous *Fram*. Skiing to what they thought was a hut but was in fact a depot, they met one of Amundsen's men who informed them that Amundsen's winter quarters were about the same distance from the depot as the depot was from the ship. They took a photograph of the *Fram* and *Terra Nova* together. Amundsen, they learned from conversation, had 116 dogs, including ten bitches, some of which were rearing pups. Priestly, the geologist in Campbell's party wrote:

the impression the Norwegians left him with is that of a set of men of distinctive personality, hard and evidently inured to hardship, good goers and pleasant and good humoured. All these qualities combine to make them very dangerous rivals, but even if one did not want to, one cannot help liking them individually in spite of the rivalry.[11]

Despite his anger at the Norwegian challenge, Scott adhered to his original plan. On 24 February, he began to transport more stores to Corner Camp, utilising two sledge teams: the first consisted of himself, Crean and the zoologist, Cherry-Garrard; the second comprised Lieutenant Evans, Dr Atkinson and Forde. Keohane led another sledge drawn by the pony, James Pigg. Scott, Crean and Cherry-Garrard took off ahead of the slower parties, making an impressive 26 miles for the day. During the next day, having discharged their load, they overtook the returning Oates party with the now worn-out ponies; one of his charges, Weary Willie, had fallen down twice in soft snow and had died overnight. Crean and Cherry-Garrard now assisted Lieutenant Henry Bowers to get the five remaining ponies safely back to the hut, knowing the importance of their recovery for the polar journey next summer. They set out across the sea ice that, by then, was in bad condition with many holes and cracks to be avoided. By mid-afternoon, the ponies had tired, so they stopped with a view to travelling at night when conditions were better and the ponies rested and fed. Having constructed a snow wall, the ponies were tethered and sheltered, while the men cooked in the tent. Bowers related the story thus:

we had only the Primus with the missing cap, and it took over $1\frac{1}{2}$ hours to heat up the water; however we had a cup of pemmican. It was very dark, and I mistook a small bag of curry for the cocoa bag, and made cocoa with that, mixed with sugar; Crean drank it right down before discovering anything was wrong. It was 2pm before we were ready to turn in . . . Two and a half-hours later I woke hearing a noise. Both my companions were snoring; I thought – 'My pony is at the oats!' and went out. I cannot describe either the scene or my feelings . . . We were in the middle of a floating pack of broken-up ice . . . It was all broken up heaving up and down with the swell. Long black tongues of water were everywhere. The floe on which we were had split right under our picketing line, and cut poor 'Guts' wall in half. Guts himself was gone, and a dark streak of water alone showed the place where the ice had opened under him . . . Our camp was on a floe not more than thirty yards across.

In an attempt to save the supplies and ponies, Bowers, Crean and Cherry-Garrard worked their way from floe to floe, moving ponies and stores with them. After six hours' hard work, heading south with the wind, they neared a steep ice bank that presented a safe exit. Crean, in the words of Bowers, 'behaved as if he had done this sort of thing often before.' But the floes had become so broken up that it was impossible to move with the equipment or animals. Crean's offer to go for help was accepted by Bowers. Making his way to the ice cliff, 'Crean was hours moving to and fro before I had the satisfaction of

seeing him on the barrier', wrote Bowers later. Crean had climbed up onto the barrier at great risk to himself. Using a ski stick to poke out a toehold on the ice cliff, with one foot on the cliff and one on the moving floe, he dug the ski stick into the top and sprung himself, getting one leg on top and pulling himself up. He made straight for Safety Camp where Oates came out to meet him. After a meal, Crean returned to the scene with Oates and Scott. Bowers and Cherry-Garrard were rescued and the sledges, loaded with stores, were recovered. Despite their best efforts, the four ponies were lost. Scott's transport resources for the push to the Pole had become severely depleted.

The preparation for the spring programme began in September when Lieutenant Evans, Forde and Gran went on a trip to find, re-mark and dig out Corner Camp in advance of Meares and a dog party who would carry fodder in advance of the polar party. From Corner Camp, the route turned south to the Pole. They were out in bad weather, with temperatures at -73°F (-58°C). Not surprisingly, given such temperatures, Robert Forde was very badly frostbitten on the hands, which resulted in his being invalided home in 1912. Scott was very annoyed at this when they returned:

> it argues care; moreover there is a good chance that the tip of one of his fingers will be lost, and if this happens or if the hand is slow in recovery, Forde cannot take part in the Western party. I have no one to replace him.[12]

Later, on 10 October, Scott wrote:

> Forde's fingers improve, but not very rapidly; it is hard to have two sick men after all the care which has been taken. Note: The other sick man Clissold the cook, had fallen while posing for Ponting's film, hurting his back.

On 24 October, two motor sledges were deployed; Day, the mechanic – who had been on *Nimrod* – drove one while PO Lashly took control of the other. Each tractor pulled three sledges loaded with stores, fodder and petrol. They lasted only a week before packing in, having completed about 50 miles from base. Their performance had been erratic: they had overheated, run out of lubricant and suffered mechanical failure; their breakdown left a considerable load to be transported by other means.

The polar party started out on 1 November 1911: ten men and ten ponies left Cape Evans, while Cecil Meares – who entered Kilkenny as his birthplace in *Terra Nova's* muster book – and Dimitri Gerof – a Russian doghandler who Meares recruited for the expedition at Nikolayevsk – followed with the 23-strong dog team. Crean and Keohane each had a pony to lead out: Keohane had James Pigg and Crean coaxed Bones across the sea ice to Safety Camp. As the march progressed and the ponies weakened or gave out, they were shot. Groups of men would head back when their work of hauling the sledges loaded with supplies was done, supplies that would await the final polar party on its return from the Pole. But at that point, no one knew who would be selected for the final push; Scott alone would decide who would return and who would proceed.

The ponies were doing 10 miles a day and the dogs were managing 20 miles per day. By mid-November, they reached One Ton Camp where they decided to give the ponies a day's rest. In an overcast sky, they observed four, very beautiful 'halo rings' round the sun. On 24 November, Jehu was the first pony to be shot. Cecil Meares, when preparing for the expedition, was delegated responsibility for the purchase of the dogs from villages of the lower Amur River in Siberia, and he reported to Scott that Jehu's carcass had made four feeds for the dogs. Next day, Hooper and Day were sent back. At latitude 81° 35' south, they left a depot of one unit at Middle Barrier Depot; a unit was rations and fuel for four men for seven days.

Back on the march south, Keohane was sharing a tent with Scott, Wilson and Cherry-Garrard. Crean was sharing with PO Evans, Bowers and Oates, while the 'man haulers', Lieutenant Evans, Atkinson, Wright and Lashly, shared another. Measuring their progress against Shackleton's march, Scott seemed more concerned about matching that performance than he was about Amundsen. Scott remarked that the walking was tiring on the men, whose feet sunk 2 or 3 inches at each step:

> It was always dismal work walking over the great snow-plain when sky and surfaces merge in one pall of dead whiteness, but it is cheering to be in such good company with everything going on steadily and well.[13]

Meares remarked that the pony prints were 8 inches to a foot deep. The party broke the day into two separate marches, with a lunchbreak of three hours. Chinaman was next to be shot, providing four more feeds for the dogs, allocated for both outward and return. Only four bags of forage remained, which Scott reckoned would last seven more marches. The man haulers started an hour and a half ahead of the ponies, making a trail for the animals to follow. On 1 December, Christopher was shot and a depot deposited so the extra weight did not have to be divided. Scott here makes a remarkable admission:

> Nobby was tried in snow shoes this morning, and came along splendidly on them for about four miles, then the wretched things had to be taken off. There is no doubt that these snowshoes are the thing for the ponies, and had one been able to use them from the beginning they would have been very different in appearance at this moment.[14]

Victor, Bowers' pony, was shot on 2 December because the fodder was in short supply. 'In excellent condition, his carcass made up five dog feeds', Scott tells us. On 3 December, they made 11.5 miles in awful weather; the falling snow was drifting in the strong winds. Next day, Mount Hope was sighted, the gateway to the Beardmore Glacier. 'Looking from the last camp towards the S.S.E where the farthest land can be seen', Scott observed prophetically, 'it seemed more than probable that a very high latitude could be

reached on the Barrier, and that if Amundsen journeying that way has a stroke of luck, he may well find his summit journey reduced to 100 miles or so.'[15]

They were then held up for four days in a storm, when Scott records what he called Keohane's rhyme:

> The snow is melting and everything is afloat,
> If this goes on much longer we shall have to turn the tent upside down – and use it as a boat.[16]

On the third day of the storm, the tents were re-sited; the wet snow had drifted high onto the walls of the tent, making life inside very miserable. On 9 December, they finally got going again, the heavy snowfall making the surface intolerable. The man haulers led the way and marked the trail. Later, Scott tells us:

> the ponies without a leader would not move until PO Evans put the last pair of snowshoes on 'Snatcher'. With the snow-shoes on him [Snatcher] went on without much pressing, the other ponies following and one by one were worn out in the second place.[17]

Marching all day without lunch, it was 8 p.m. before they camped. Here, the remainder of the ponies were shot as the fodder had run out.

When the march resumed, most of the original man haulers were showing signs of tiredness. Lieutenant Evans, Atkinson, Wright and

This picture perfectly illustrates the barren nature of the Antarctic environment. Apart from the invention of the Primus stove, nothing much had changed from McClintock's equipment developed in the 1850s.
*Scott Polar Research Institute*

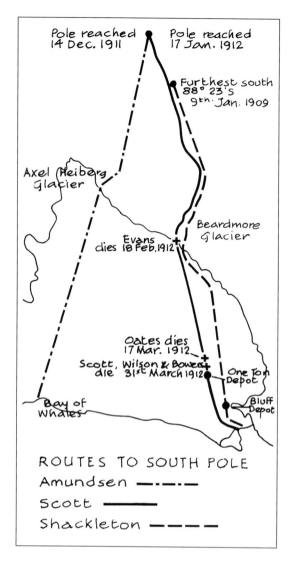

Pole reached
14 Dec. 1911

Pole reached
17 Jan. 1912

Furthest south
88° 23'S
9th Jan. 1909

Axel Heiberg
Glacier

Beardmore
Glacier

Evans
dies 18 Feb. 1912

Oates dies
17 Mar. 1912

Scott, Wilson & Bowers
die 31st March 1912

One Ton
Depot

Bluff
Depot

Bay of
Whales

ROUTES TO SOUTH POLE

Amundsen — · — · — ·

Scott ————

Shackleton — — — —

from snowblindness due to a lack of caution: the sufferers were listed as E. Evans, Bowers, Keohane, Lashly and Oates.

The dog team was sent back on 11 December, their load split between the teams or deposited in the Lower Glacier Depot. Scott remarked

the snow around us to-night is terribly soft, one sinks to the knee at every step; it would be impossible to drag sledges on foot and very difficult for dogs. Ski are the thing, and here are my tiresome fellow-countrymen too prejudiced to have prepared themselves for the event.[18]

On 12 December, when in sight of Cloud-maker, Scott observed that they were about five to five-and-a-half days slower than Shackleton had been. On Wednesday 13 December, after exchanging sledges with Bowers' party, Scott notes: 'Cherry-Garrard and Keohane are the weakest of Bowers' team, though both put their utmost into the traces.' Bowers tells more accurately what sledge pulling in that team was all about:

It was all we could do to keep the sledge moving for short spells of a few hundred yards, the whole concern sinking so deeply into the soft snow as to form a snow-plough. The starting was worse than pulling as it required from ten to fifteen desperate jerks on the harness to move the sledge at all . . . The sledges sank in over twelve inches and all the gear, as well as the thwart-ship pieces, were acting as

Lashly, who had already sledged 300 miles before the pony leaders had taken to the traces, were suffering from hunger, wear and tear. Scott's sledge was performing best. In Bowers' team, Bowers and Cherry-Garrard were up front in the harness while Crean and Keohane pulled together behind. Scott remarked in his journal: 'Keohane is the only weak spot and he only, I think, because blind (temporarily).' He was more concerned about Lieutenant Evans' party who arrived nearly three hours after Scott's. He was also upset about the number of people suffering brakes . . . I have never pulled so hard, or so nearly crushed my inside into my backbone by the everlasting jerking with all my strength on the canvas band round my unfortunate tummy.[19]

On that same day, Amundsen and four Norwegian colleagues were within a day's journey of the Antarctic 'Grail' – 90° south. Amundsen had left Framheim, his hut and winter base, at the Bay of Whales on 8 September 1911 with eight men, six sledges and 86 dogs to restock a depot at 80° south. He had already laid two other depots the previous autumn with 1.5 tons of supplies – one at 81° south and the other at 82° south – within 480 miles of the Pole. Having returned to Framheim to prepare and to await more favourable conditions, they departed on the polar journey on 20 October: five men, four sledges and 52 dogs on a route 65 miles shorter than Scott's. They travelled for five hours every day, covering twenty miles with sledges pulled by dogs and driven by men on skis. At lunch, they would build a snow cairn as an aid to guide their return, and inside each cairn was left a written record of the distance and bearing to the next one. They found a way past a range of mountains leading to the Pole, named Queen Maud Mountains by Amundsen after the queen of Norway. It took them four days to climb the Axel Heiberg Glacier, reaching the top on 1 November. There, they shot 24 of the dogs at a depot they called The Butcher Shop. Progress temporarily being stopped for four days in a bitter storm, they set out again with five men and the remaining eighteen dogs. In appalling conditions of wind,

blizzard and fog, they kept going and passed a dangerous glacier they called The Devil's Ballroom. Shackleton's 'furthest south' of 88° 23' south was overtaken on 8 December. On Friday 14 December 1991, they reached the Pole. Here, they erected a tent, calling it Poleheim (Pole Home), and left a message for Scott and a letter for King Haakon. On 25 January, they arrived safely back to Framheim with five men and eleven dogs, all fit and healthy. Compared to the British team effort, it was a ruthlessly efficient and effective achievement for the secretive Norwegians. In all, it took 99 days there and back.

On the flyleaf of his new notebook, dated 2 December, Scott listed his own name alongside those of Wilson, PO Evans and Oates, together with their ages; he averaged the ages at 36 years. He was already planning his final four to make the historic last leg. Wilson seems to have been his only confidant at this point. All of the crew wanted to be in the party but all knew there could only be four. On 20 December 1911, close to the top of the Beardmore Glacier at latitude 85° 7' south and at an altitude of 8,000 feet, Scott's three man-hauling parties established the Upper Glacier Depot. Scott had told Atkinson, Wright, Cherry-Garrard and Keohane the night before that they would be returning the next day. 'All were disappointed – poor Wright rather bitterly I feel' noted Scott in his journal. At just short of 300 miles to the Pole, Keohane and his new sledge mates had nearly 600 miles to back track to Cape Evans. He wrote sadly and with resignation in his diary: 'sorry to part with old Crean'.[20]

Cherry-Garrard, in his very honest book, *The*

*Worst Journey in the World*, tells us of the second returning party's journey. One day in particular, he tells us, is worth recalling:

> We got into the same big pressure above the Cloudmaker which both the other parties experienced. But where we went west at Wright's suggestion: west was right. The day really lives in my memory because of the troubles of Keohane. He fell into crevasses to the full length of his harness eight times in twenty-five minutes. Little wonder he looked a bit dazed. And Atkinson went down into one chasm head foremost: the worst crevasse fall I have ever seen. But luckily the shoulder strap of his harness stood the strain and we pulled him out little the worse.

Despite their early mishaps, the second returning party reached Hut Point on 26 January 1912.

Subsequent Christmas Days must always have reminded Tom Crean of those last miles up the Beardmore Glacier where they had to be ever vigilant of the deep crevasses that protected the entry to the Polar Plateau. Lashly suddenly vanished into a void 50-feet deep and 8-feet wide, pulling Crean and Evans off their feet backwards. He fell the length of his harness and trace, on this, his forty-fourth birthday; luckily for him, Lieutenant Evans had noticed his rope was rather worn and had replaced it with a new one two days previously. Crean's harness was stuck underneath the sledge, which had miraculously stopped at the edge of the gaping crevasse. Beyond the overhanging walls, Lashly could not

be seen. Bowers and Evans made safe the sledge and freed Crean, and then lowered their alpine rope with a bowline tied at its end, into which Lashly inserted his foot to be dragged out jointly by his own efforts and by the hard pulling of his companions. They were perfecting the skills of crevasse rescue.

They covered 15 miles that day and had a memorable Christmas dinner as only military and naval servicemen can do, wherever they are. Scott records that they had four courses: pemmican with slices of horse meat, flavoured with onion and curry powder and thickened with biscuit; then, arrow root, cocoa and sweetened biscuit hoosh; next, plum pudding and cocoa with raisins; finally, a desert of caramels and ginger. They all slept splendidly. During the next few days, they walked into what Shackleton had called in 1908 the 'pitiless increasing wind'; as it blew into their faces from the south, all looked forward to 'sailing the sledges back before it'. Scott was trying 'to get every inch out of the miles and every ounce out of his companions.' They were achieving 15 miles a day and had caught up on Shackleton's schedule, which was their only barometer of progress. Scott's sledge team was clearly the stronger and fitter of the two teams by that stage. All its members had first started sledge hauling at the foot of the glacier, whereas Lieutenant Evans and Lashly, on the second sledge, had man hauled since the breakdown of the second motor sledge on 1 November. In that time, they had man hauled 400 statute miles more than any of the others.

On 31 December, the first indication of the final team selection came when Scott ordered

The western geological party (left–right): Forde, Gran, Taylor and Debenham. Photograph by Herbert Ponting.
*Scott Polar Research Institute*

Evans' sledge party to depot their skis. During the lunch stop, PO Evans – whom Scott identified 'as the most invaluable asset in his party' – and who was also the largest and most muscular man on the plateau, cut and bruised his hand, which clearly was to affect his performance later. It happened while he was working with Crean to shorten a 12-foot sledge by 2 feet.

On Wednesday 3 January, within 150 miles of the Pole, Scott instructed Teddy Evans, Lashly and Crean to return. Though disappointed, they took it well, he wrote. Bowers was invited into his team tent and they would proceed as a five-man unit. Some time during the previous four days, Scott had decided to take an extra man; five men would now have to share the rations, fuel and tent intended for four. Bowers, alone, would have to manage without skis until the return to the depot.

Scott sent back a note with the returning party: 'Lat. 87° 32'. A last note from a hopeful position. I think it's going all right. We have a fine party going forward and arrangements are all going well.' The parting next day is recorded by Scott:

Teddy Evans is terribly disappointed but has taken it very well and behaved like a man. Poor old Crean wept and even Lashly

Tom Crean after his return from his 'furthest south'. Photograph by Herbert Ponting.
*Scott Polar Research Institute*

The transferring of Bowers to Scott's own sledge without the dropping of one of his existing sledge mates was a grave error, made, perhaps, out of loyalty to Oates or Wilson. Scott ignored the underpinning logic of his own detailed planning. It was also asking a lot of the returning party of three tired men to pull a four-man sledge, particularly if one of the three was to become sick or injured.

The return of the third returning party was to become a struggle for life. Both Lashly and Lieutenant Teddy Evans had pulled 300 miles more than Crean. Through attacks of snowblindness, they veered off course, and to take corrective action decided to glissade on their sledge down a steep ice fall – named the Shackleton Falls – rather than take a three-day detour. It was touch and go as they got up speed, shooting over a gaping crevasse where one of Evans' ski sticks vanished into the void. At the end of the ride, they were bruised and cut. Crean's wind-proof trousers were in shreds and he stood in his woollen drawers and boots. Importantly, they had no broken bones and were on better ground to the Mount Darwin Depot. However, they next ran into an area of huge and dangerous crevasses, one so large that Lashly thought it possible to drop St Paul's Cathedral into its depths. A snow bridge across another chasm was crossed very delicately. First, Lashly gingerly crossed it with an alpine rope tied to him; then the sledge was inched across with Crean and Evans guiding it so it did not fall off the snow bridge. According to Crean, 'We went along the crossbar to the H of Hell.' A great bond developed between the two petty officers and the expedition's second-in-command.

was affected. I was glad to find their sledge nothing to them, and thus no doubt, they will make a quick journey back.[21]

On 30 January, Evans knew he was suffering from scurvy and was not convinced of his prospects of survival. At the start of the march, he fainted. 'Crean and Lashly picked me up', he recalled, and 'Crean thought I was dead. His hot tears fell on my face.' They strapped him to the sledge and pulled him for days until they could make no further progress without help. They were 35 miles from Hut Point. Both were prepared to go for help, but Crean felt Lashly would look after Evans' health better. Cherry-Garrard recorded Crean's recollections of the rescue of Evans:

He started at 10 on Sunday morning and 'the surface was good, very good indeed', and he went about sixteen miles before he stopped. Good clear weather. He had three biscuits and two sticks of chocolate. He stopped about five minutes, sitting on the snow and ate two biscuits and the chocolate, and put one biscuit back in his pocket. He was quite warm and not sleepy. He carried on just the same and passed Safety Camp on his right some five hours later, and thinks it was about 12.30 on Monday morning that he reached the edge of the Barrier, tired, getting cold in the back and the weather coming on thick.[22]

He slipped a lot on the sea ice, falling on his back. Though it started snowing and drifting, Crean kept going. He ate his biscuit with some snow on the side of Observation Hill and then, lacking crampons, had to avoid the ice foot while making his way to the hut beneath it. He walked

in and found Atkinson and Dimitri inside. Crean recalled:

He gave me a tot first and then a feed of porridge – but I couldn't keep it down: that's the first time in my life that ever it happened, and it was the brandy that did it.[23]

He made the hut just before the blizzard that had threatened all day finally struck. After waiting a day and a half for the blizzard to abate, Atkinson and two dog teams came to the rescue. Lashly made it easy for them by improvising a flag from an old coat. The third returning party were safely home. Though the rescue of Evans and Lashly is often attributed to Crean, it is fairer to attribute the rescue to the teamwork and comradeship of Lashly and Crean. Tom Crean received the commendation of his companions; as Ponting said: 'Tom Crean's lone march that day was one of the finest feats in an adventure that is an epic of splendid episodes.'

On 9 January, Scott recorded with elation that they had finally passed Shackleton's 'furthest south' record of 86° 23'. It was not until 15 January that he wrote in his journal about the possibility of meeting a Norwegian flag at the Pole: 'the only possibility the sight of the Norwegian flag forestalling ours'. Twenty miles from the Pole, on the following day, they spotted a black marker flag and, on getting closer, noticed dog and sledge tracks: 'The worst has happened. The Norwegians are first at the Pole . . . All dreams must go.' On 17 January, at the Pole itself, they saw the Norwegian tent; inside it were some odds and ends of clothes and equipment, and a note for Scott which recorded the names of the five Norwegians who had camped there a month before: Roald Amundsen, Olav Olavson Bjaaland, Hilmer Hanssen, Sverre H. Hassel and Oscar Wisting. The note also asked Scott to forward a letter left by Amundsen to King Haakon, the Norwegian king. What should have been joy for the successful party turned to deflation:

> The Pole Yes, but under different circumstances than those expected . . . Great God! This is an awful place and terrible enough for us to have laboured to it without the reward of priority.[24]

Scott and his loyal companions took some forlorn pictures with their Union Jack, paled by the presence of the Norwegian tent. The journey back toward Cape Evans was tragic; all died in a long and bitter struggle to their base. The details of their desperate struggle with cold, weather, scurvy, hunger, depression and the deaths of their comrades are recorded in their diaries. The first to weaken and fail was PO Evans; a strong man, he deteriorated quickly on short rations and was near starvation when they were lost for a couple of days on the Beardmore. Incredibly, suffering in conditions of extreme hardship, they searched out and carried 16 kilos of geological specimens. Evans fell and when they returned for him he was delirious; he died during the night of 17 February. Captain Oates, his feet black with frostbite, was next to die. The gallant Inniskilling Dragoon bade farewell to his colleagues on St Patrick's Day – his birthday – with the immortal

words: 'I am just going outside and may be some time.' By 19 March, the remaining three were within 11 miles of One Ton Camp. But they were forced to lie there in awful weather without fuel, food or drink. Scott, the strongest, was last to die; his final journal entry on 29 March 1912 reads: 'For God's sake look after our people.'[25]

*Terra Nova* had arrived in February with fresh mules and dogs. Campbell's party had been picked up at Cape Adare and landed at Evans Coves. On 3 March, Cherry-Garrard and Gerof had reached One Ton Camp to restock it and to support the returning polar party. Lacking a navigator, they did not venture further south; the two men waited until 10 March before returning to Hut Point. On 26 March, Atkinson and Keohane went out, reaching a point south of Corner Camp, but conditions were so bad they returned; the chances of finding a party except at a depot were slim. This was about the time that Scott made his last journal entry. Cherry-Garrard reported that Keohane did well and was very fit. Unknown to them, they were just a couple of days' march from their dying leader.

*Terra Nova*, with Mortimer McCarthy among its crew, left for New Zealand in late March 1912; among the nine returning due to illness, injury or because they were at the end of their contracts were Lieutenant Evans and PO Forde, whose hand had been slow to heal. There were only two replacements for the second winter. To complicate matters, Campbell's six-man party, which had sailed to Cape Adare on the northern tip of Victoria Land in 1911 and which had over-wintered there in a small hut, surveying and making scientific observations, were collected from there in January 1912 by the returning *Terra Nova* and dropped to Evans Coves in Terra Nova Bay with six weeks' sledge rations. In bad weather, they explored and surveyed the area around Mount Melbourne, during which their tents were badly damaged. At the end of the six weeks, *Terra Nova* was unable to penetrate the 30 miles of ice and therefore unable to pick them up as arranged. They were a worry to Atkinson, who was now in charge since Lieutenant Evans was invalided home.

On 12 November 1912, a party led by Atkinson – which included Keohane and Crean – located Scott's tent and recovered their comrades' diaries and personal effects. The tent poles were removed and the bodies left where they were; a great cairn was then built for these three gallant explorers. A note was left in the cairn, signed by each member of the recovery team. Cherry-Garrard summed up the end with simple poignancy when he wrote: 'And then, eleven miles from plenty, they had nine days of blizzard, and that was the end.' Crean, full of emotion and shedding manly tears, was one of those who entered the tent to retrieve the personal effects and to bid farewell to his comrades and the commander whom he regarded as his good friend. When the story of the Norwegian success

Patrick Keohane, captured by Ponting, applying some final touches to his model of *Terra Nova*.
*Scott Polar Research Institute*

emerged from Atkinson's reading aloud of the diaries, Crean broke the news to Gran, the Norwegian dog-and-ski expert, and offered congratulations for his countrymen's triumph. Such was the respect and civility in the party in that wild and barren place.

The search for the body of Captain Oates commenced the following day, 13 miles further south. His sleeping bag was found hanging on the snow walls at one of the outward campsites built to shelter the ponies; it contained a theodolite, his finnesko boots and socks. The finnesko boots were slit down the front to allow his feet, swollen by frostbite, to squeeze in. Scott's party had obviously brought his bag with them in case they came across him in the open. Failing to find any other evidence of Oates, another cairn was built, on high ground. Lashed to this cairn, they fixed a record:

> Hereabouts died a very gallant gentleman, Captain L.E.G. Oates of the Inniskilling Dragoons. In March 1912, returning from the Pole, he walked willingly to his death in a blizzard to try and save his comrades, beset by hardship. This note left by the relief expedition. 1912.

After their return to camp, it was decided to erect a further memorial. On Observation Hill – first climbed by Ferrar on *Discovery* – a wooden cross was put in place by, among others, Crean and Keohane. On that cross was carved a single line from Tennyson's 'Ulysses': 'To strive, to seek, to find, and not to yield.'

## The Northern Party

Following the discovery of Scott's party, Atkinson decided that getting help to Campbell and the northern party was the next priority. On his return to base – arriving there on 25 November – he was greeted with the best possible news: Campbell's party was well and at Cape Evans.

The story of the northern party is one of unbelievable fortitude and survival, a story overshadowed by the details of Scott's tragic end. When *Terra Nova* failed to get through the 30 miles of pack ice in mid-February 1912 to keep its planned rendezvous with the northern party, the party moved into an ice cave dug in a snowdrift. It was St Patrick's Day – the day Oates died. Beyond the reach of the wind in the bitter cold of winter, the men survived by strict rationing. Their own supplies were supplemented by killing a seal, inside whose stomach they found 36 edible fish. Good discipline and morale enabled them to endure the unending cold and darkness; tiny blubber lamps allowed them to read books aloud to each other – *David Copperfield* was the favourite. Eventually, the men sledged their way back to Hut Point, starting out in September. The trip took 40 days. PO Frank Browning was near to death throughout, but kept alive by the others who sacrificed their single biscuit ration in his favour. His survival was also due, in no small way, to the close attention of Dr Murray Levick. They reached Cape Evans on 7 November 1912, their delight at their own survival short-lived after learning the tragic news of the polar party.

The *Terra Nova* finally left McMurdo Sound on 23 January 1913. News of what has become known as Scott's last expedition was brought to the world when the ship reached New Zealand in February. The words of Scott's final letters were relayed to the public, and the heroic nature of his end stirred the hearts of every Englishman as Europe prepared for war – a war that would change everything.

*Patsy Keohane, Mortimer McCarthy and Robert Forde Postscript*

Following the expedition, Keohane returned to *Vivid I* on 22 September 1913, where he was promoted to chief petty officer on 13 November aboard the ship on which he had served most of his sea time. During the First World War, he served on HMS *Impregnable*, from 1 January 1914 until 20 July 1917. He found time to marry Miss Ivy O'Driscoll, eldest daughter of Michael O'Driscoll, officer in charge of the coastguard station at Courtmacsherry; the wedding was on 21 April 1914 at Barryroe Catholic church. Conducted by Fr O'Sullivan, administrator of the parish on the edge of the ocean, the ceremony was obviously a very naval affair, connecting, as it did, two Cork seafaring families.[26]

Chief Petty Officer Keohane resumed service on HMS *Vivid*, from July to August 1917, and thence to HMS *Cornwall*, from 4 August 1917 until 18 January 1918. He was paid his war gratuity and, it seems, demobilised from HMS *Columbine* before joining the coastguard service. His first posting was at Omeath, Co. Louth, on 1 June 1920. From there, he was transferred to Clogher Head in the same county – on 8 November 1920 – and from there to Dundalk

after the station at Clogher Head had been burned down and was under reconstruction.[27] He was transferred again, in July 1921, to Dundalk, until 20 November 1921, when that station was evacuated. He next moved to Kingstown (Dún Laoghaire) in Co. Dublin, from where he transferred in January 1922 to Cushendall, Co. Antrim, following the approval of the Treaty between the British government and the Irish provisional government by Dáil Éireann – the new Irish parliament. He next transferred to Dungeoness Kent and from there to Looe Cornwall, and later to the Isle of Man, becoming district officer of coastguards until his retirement at the age of 61. Patsy Keohane's coastguard record shows that on 29 August 1921, his wife lived at Dungeoness, Kent and that they had one female child, named Sheila Nova, born on 12 March 1915.[28] During the Second World War, Patsy Keohane – by then in his sixties – re-enlisted in the Royal Navy.[29] He died in 1950 at his home in Birchfield Park, Plymouth. He was then 71 years of age and had been ill for a considerable time. In a tribute written for his burial, Cherry-Garrard described him thus:

> A dependable Irish seaman who took things as they came without worrying overmuch. He was a useful and cheerful man in difficult times and as such was doubly welcomed the third and last year down south. Probably he holds a much to be avoided record by falling to full length of his harness eight times in 25 minutes into crevasses. He wanted to see what was on the other side of the hill. And he saw.[30]

A cake given to him while on the expedition is preserved in a glass case as part of an exhibition on *Discovery* in Dundee's Maritime Institute.

Patsy Keohane's shipmate and countryman, Mortimer McCarthy, was among those presented with the Silver Polar Medal by King George V at a ceremony in Buckingham Palace in 1913, on his return to Cardiff on *Terra Nova*. He signed up for the Arctic Exploration Company as a crewman on the *Willem Barents*, but the expedition was cancelled when the First World War began. He joined the Royal Navy, spending four years in sea warfare, which he survived. He returned to New Zealand in 1921 and married Nellie Coughlan of the Old Head of Kinsale in the Cathedral of the Blessed Sacrament in Christchurch. It appears he had courted her sister, Catherine (Kit) in Ireland, but she was not keen on emigration to New Zealand. Mortimer fell for Nellie when he met her in Christchurch. He is remembered as a tall, good-looking and courteous gentleman, with two fingers missing on one hand due to frostbite. His seaman's Continuous Certificate of Discharge records his eyes as blue, his hair as brown and his height as 5 feet 6.5 inches. Mortimer and his wife set up home in Lyttelton, where they lived with their three sons: John, Brian and Gerard.

His long career at sea had begun in 1901 – mostly in New Zealand waters, though he served in the merchant navy during the Boer War and Second World War. He was best known for his many years on the inter-island express ships, the *Wahine* and *Rangatira*, and finished his days working as a night watchman on ships in Lyttelton Harbour. He returned to Kinsale on a number of occasions and, long after his retirement in 1963, revisited the Antarctic with an American expedition which went to Scott's hut at Cape Evans in February of that year. Then aged 81, he was the oldest man to ever set foot on Antarctica. He died on 4 August 1967 at the age of 89 after a fire at his home. The medal roll shows he received the Silver Polar Medal for *Terra Nova* and, curiously, a medal for the Boer War, but this is listed as returned without reason given. His son, Gerard, and his wife attended the unveiling of a memorial to the McCarthy brothers of Lower Cove in September 2000 by the Kinsale and District Local History Society. Tom Crean's daughter, Mary Crean O'Brien, was also in attendance.

Robert Forde was promoted to chief petty officer on 9 September 1910 and accordingly paid from that date while on service aboard *Terra Nova*. Following the expedition, he resumed service on his old ship, HMS *Vivid I*, from October 1913 to February 1914, and served out the war in *Indus*, *Endymion*, *Vivid I*, *Hilary* and *Resolution*, from which he was demobilised and paid his war gratuity on 17 January 1920. Bob, as he was better known locally, retired to Queenstown (Cobh). He never married or took up employment, living on his naval disability pension with his two sisters at 52 Harbour Row, which overlooks the deep harbour, Spike Island and Haulbowline. His sisters, Susan and Sarah, who preceded him in death, managed a boarding house in that busy port. He spent his last years in Cobh General Hospital. Local historian, John Hennessy, who was also hospitalised there in 1957, remembers CPO Robert Forde. He vividly recalls the old man's frostbitten hand, which he noticed was always bandaged. Bob Forde spoke once to the pupils of the local vocational school about his adventures. Mrs Valerie Tait, a relative of the retired chief petty officer, recalls how, as a young girl, she visited him in Cobh hospital on several occasions with her mother. It appears a family tradition resulted in the burning of all his personal effects after his death. Valerie Tait does, however, retain a piece of *Terra Nova* notepaper and two stamps marked Victoria Land.[31] In the Clonmel (Old Church) cemetery in Cobh, Co. Cork, Robert Forde's gravestone includes a proud reference to his time in the Antarctic: 'With Capt. Scott B.A.Ex 1910/13'[32] Mount Forde, a peak of over 1200 metres at 76° 53' south and 89° 09' west, at the head of the Hunt Glacier, was named in Chief Petty Officer Forde's honour.

# EPIC VOYAGE OF THE *ENDURANCE*

*Leadership is a fine thing but it has its penalties. And the greatest penalty is loneliness.*

ERNEST SHACKLETON[1]

On 17 May 1912, news of Amundsen's South Pole success appeared in the London newspapers. Three weeks later, *Terra Nova* reached New Zealand, bringing with it the news of Scott's last reported position on 5 January 1912. Shackleton cabled Amundsen: 'heartiest congratulations, magnificent achievement'. He acknowledged the Norwegian as perhaps the greatest polar explorer of the time and admired his thoroughness in preparation, the speed of the journey and the fact that Amundsen had made for himself an entirely new route. It is interesting to note that Amundsen was in no doubt that if Shackleton had landed at the Bay of Whales in 1908, the Irishman would have reached the South Pole first.[2] Responding to

Amundsen's first South Pole lecture in Britain, in November 1912, Shackleton drew attention to how Amundsen did not once use the word 'I' but, rather, 'we', a telling comment on the Norwegian's leadership style. The ability to take personal initiative is what the leadership of both Shackleton and Amundsen was all about. Shackleton had learned too late the folly of bringing ponies to the Pole, and the clear advantage of using dogs and skis over man-hauling sledges.

Before the tragic fate of Scott's return journey had become known, Shackleton was already expressing his view that polar exploration was not yet complete, and that the next task was to cross Antarctica from sea to sea. In January 1913, in Philadelphia, he shared the stage with Amundsen and Peary – at that moment, they were billed as the discoverers of both Poles. Shackleton sailed for England as soon as the news from *Terra Nova* reached him. By the time of his arrival, the romantic heroism of his rival had inspired the British public with patriotic

*facing page*
*Endurance* by flashlight. One of Frank Hurley's most memorable photographs, entitled 'Spectre Ship'.
*Royal Geographical Society*

fervour. The establishment and the public alike retrospectively rewarded Scott for his suffering and death sacrifice, thus salving the nation's need for larger-than-life heroes. Arguably, Shackleton's last-gasp decision to turn back in 1908 saved him from similar such idolatry. The 'live donkey' had something new to ponder.

Crean also enjoyed the benefits of the public's goodwill; he was promoted to chief petty officer, the promotion given effect from 9 September 1910. The expedition committee also awarded him and Lashly a bonus of £100 for their whole-hearted efforts. The other surviving members, including Irishmen Mortimer McCarthy, Patsy Keohane and Cecil Meares, were awarded Antarctic Medals by King George at Buckingham Palace. Their dead colleagues' widows and mothers collected their husbands' and sons' medals; Oates' mother, however, asked Lieutenant Evans to collect her son's medal on her behalf. The RGS also awarded each man the King's Medal and the Polar Medal. For saving the life of Lieutenant Evans, Crean and Lashly were awarded the nation's highest award for gallantry, the Albert Medal.

On 29 December 1913, Shackleton announced the formation of the Imperial Trans-Antarctic Expedition. His starting point was a promise from David Lloyd George, chancellor of the exchequer, that if Shackleton could raise the balance, he would provide a government grant of £10,000. Then aged 39 years of age, he knew how to collect money for an expedition; he had the optimism and the promotional abilities to find the financial support he needed. Who could resist an expedition that would attempt the

greatest polar journey ever undertaken, every step of which would be an advance in geographical science? He would start from the Atlantic coast of the Weddell Sea and cross the continent, via the South Pole, to the Ross Sea. In the process, he would re-establish the prestige of Great Britain in polar exploration.

Shackleton's latest plans were made against a background of personal and political turbulence. In January of that year, his brother, Frank, had been arrested overseas and brought to London by Scotland Yard to be charged with fraudulent conversion. In late October, he was found guilty of defrauding Miss Mary Josephine Browne and sentenced to fifteen months' hard labour. The previous year, in Ireland, thousands of unionists signed a covenant to oppose Home Rule and, in 1913, the Ulster Volunteer Force was formed to resist the Liberal government's Home Rule Bill. In August 1913, the Dublin Lockout began as workers fought for trade-union recognition. In November, James Connolly, the socialist trade-union leader, founded the Irish Citizens' Army, arguably the first Red Army. As Irish politics became increasingly more militant and polarised, nationalists founded the Irish Volunteers.

Despite these developments, Shackleton planned his new adventure. He proposed following the tracks of the German, Wilhelm Filchner, who, in 1911–12, discovered and charted the extent of the Antarctic coastline and discovered the southern borders of the Atlantic Ocean, the Luitpold Coast and the Filchner Ice Shelf, named in recognition of his efforts. From his ship, the *Deutschland*, his crew of 33 tried unsuccessfully to establish a station on the ice shelf at a place they named Vahsel Bay. Having just completed the *stationhaus*, the berg upon which it was constructed moved in a massive ice movement and drifted northward toward open water. Spring tides were blamed for the occurrence; one piece of ice, 18 miles long, was also moving alongside and the ship itself was in danger. Before the Germans could establish another base on the continental ice, they became beset. For nine months, they lived through the winter darkness between the ship and the small cabins and tents they had erected on the sea ice. The plan to cross the continent was abandoned and they returned to South Georgia in December 1912.

The unpredictability of conditions in the Weddell Sea raised questions regarding the viability of Shackleton's project. Nevertheless, an unsolicited grant of £1,000 from the RGS got his fund-raising efforts off to a flying start. He opened an office at New Burlington Street, staffed by Wild and Marston, who began sifting through the 5,000 applications to join the expedition. A circular detailing his plans and carrying the endorsement of Nansen was sent to hundreds of wealthy people, eliciting a response from a small number. A donation of £10,000 was received from Mr Dudley Docker of BSA, a Birmingham engineering works; the money went a long way toward purchasing the Norwegian polar vessel, *Polaris*, whose name was changed by Shackleton to *Endurance*, derived from his family motto: 'By endurance we conquer'. Edward Guinness — Lord Iveagh — of the Dublin brewing family, again guaranteed a loan of £5,000 and a banker, Robert Lucas Tooth, guaranteed another £5,000. These loan guarantees were no doubt under-pinned by promises of post-expedition funds anticipated from publication of Shackleton's narrative and the proceeds of his public lectures. The news and pictorial rights were sold to the *Daily Chronicle*. It is not known how much money Miss Janet Stancomb-Wills, of the successful tobacco-company family, donated to Shackleton's cause, but she seems to have been greatly charmed by him and his adventures, and to have supported this particular exploit very generously. As he was later to give her name to one of the three ship's lifeboats in her honour, it must put her donation at least on a par with the contribution made by Dudley Docker. Shackleton managed to purchase for £3,500 a second ship for the expedition, the *Aurora*; owned by Douglas Mawson, it was idle at Hobart.

Shackleton maintained a frenetic pace in his determination to head south. In May, he went to Norway to collect *Endurance* and some specialist equipment, and to practice his skiing. Publicity about this trip seems to have attracted the attention of Dundee millionaire and philanthropist, Sir James Caird, who donated £24,000, free of any conditions. Another fan of the charismatic Kildareman, Queen Alexandra, at her own request visited the *Endurance* at London Docks. Emily was there for the royal visit. She was reconciled by this time to life as wife of the great explorer, which meant less and less contact with him as he lectured, planned and fund-raised for his adventures. Shadows of his brother's dealings still followed Shackleton; he was sued by Miss Mary Josephine Browne who, in response to the publicity concerning Caird's substantial donation, sought legal recourse for the recovery of money that she had entrusted to Frank. The money, through Frank's manipulations, had found its way into *Nimrod*'s account. Ernest settled out of court before he sailed.

As *Endurance* pulled away from the West India Docks on 1 August, a bagpiper played 'The Wearing of the Green' in acknowledgement of the Irishmen on board. At the wheel was Tom Crean, this time in a more senior role: the expedition's second officer. He had been assigned to the expedition by the Admiralty on 23 May, and worked to prepare the ship and stores with the captain of *Endurance*, Frank Worsley, a New Zealander and a polar newcomer. Crean's old *Discovery* mate, Frank Wild, was second-in-command. In the intervening period, Wild had been on *Nimrod* and had also been back to Antarctica with Douglas Mawson's Australasian expedition in 1911–14, making him the most experienced polar explorer in the party. Cheetham, a Liverpudlian, was another veteran of three expeditions, and the Scotsman, Thomas McLeod, had been on *Terra Nova* and *Nimrod*. Among the crew was yet another Corkman, Able-bodied Seaman Timothy McCarthy from Lower Cove, Kinsale, whose older brother, Mortimer, was with Scott on *Terra Nova*. Timothy was a young merchant-navy man, known and liked for his ebullient good humour and gift for repartee. Shackleton described him as the best and most efficient of the sailors, always cheerful in the most trying of circumstances. He is often mentioned as having worked with the ship's carpenter, McNeish, in making repairs and alterations to the ship's boats in preparation for the sea journeys.

The assassination in Sarajevo at the end of June of Archduke Franz Ferdinand, heir to the Austrian throne, had raised the likelihood of war. Austro-Hungary declared war on Serbia; the tsar mobilised the Russian army and, a day later, Kaiser Wilhelm declared war on Russia. On Monday 4 August, following a muster with his captain and crew, Shackleton offered the ship, stores and men to the Admiralty. Within an hour, Winston Churchill replied with a one-word directive: 'Proceed'. Shackleton met King George V for 25 minutes during the day and was presented with a Union Jack to take south.

*Endurance* – minus Shackleton and Wild – left Plymouth on 8 August, visiting Madeira en route to Buenos Aires. At Buenos Aires, Shackleton and Wild came aboard, having taken the mail boat, and immediately addressed some indiscipline and morale problems by dismissing three of the troublemakers and drunks, including the cook. Replacements were taken on board, including Charles Green – who became a dutiful cook – and a seaman, William Bakewell, who had lost his previous ship in Montevideo. An Australian photographer named Frank Hurley, recommended to Shackleton by Mawson, also came aboard at the River Plate port, which Francis Beaufort had surveyed and charted so many years before.

The next port of call was the island of South Georgia off the southern tip of South America – the most southerly place in the British Empire. Discovered by Captain Cook in 1775, he had named it after King George III. Norwegian whalers established their first base there at Grytviken in 1904 and were still in the early

Tom Crean and Sally's pups – Roger, Toby, Nell and Nelson. Photograph by Frank Hurley.
*Royal Geographical Society*

along with the baleen and whale oil. Clarke, the biologist, wrote a report concerning the unpleasant conditions at the whaling stations and the great waste through the abandonment of the carcasses after the blubber was stripped.

While the doghandlers – among them, Crean – took the dogs on practice runs on the frozen Gull Lake on the plateau above Grytviken, Shackleton conferred with the whaling captains, who warned of the severity of the ice conditions. Based on their advice and intelligence, Shackleton decided to steer to the South Sandwich Group, round Ultima Thule, and work as far east as the fifteenth meridian west before pushing south. Extra coal was taken on board along with additional clothing garnered from the various whaling stations on South Georgia. The big question was whether they could find a safe harbour and, if not, would they have to winter the ship in South Georgia? The month spent on the island and the sailing to whaling stations at Leith, Husvik and Stromness and back to Grytviken gave Shackleton's men first-hand knowledge of the layout of the island – knowledge that was to serve them well later.

Within two days of sailing on 5 December 1914, *Endurance* found itself in pack ice and began six weeks of manoeuvring between great areas of floes and gigantic icebergs, as the leads between the floes became narrower. They took to ramming the floes repeatedly until *Endurance* finally forced a crack through the field of white, which slowly widened to allow the ship steam forward again. All the time, the worry was to protect the propeller and rudder, identified as the weakest link in fighting the polar pack. Killer

stages of their bloody oil harvest which plundered the Southern Ocean of its giant mammals, just as British and American sealers had already wiped out most of its seals. Shackleton's men tasted sausages made from South Georgia bacon: pigs fed on whale meat, which was sent back to Europe as a by-product of the processed whales,

whales were observed to smash through the one-metre-thick ice to seize a seal resting on a floe. By 5 January, *Endurance* was moored to a floe. There was time for a game of soccer, during which Worsley fell through thin ice while retrieving the ball and had to be recovered. On 10 January, land was first sighted, with an open lead to the barrier edge. Steering southwest, *Endurance* passed William Bruce's 'furthest south' on *Scotia* in 1902. New coast was charted and named Caird Coast by Shackleton. On 15 January, an excellent landing place was identified – Shackleton christened it Glacier Bay – but he wanted to reach Vahsel Bay, another 100 miles south, to shorten his land journey as much as possible. Worsley noted 'it looked like it would afford an ideal track to the interior'. By 19 January, following a gale from which they had sheltered in the lee of a stranded iceberg, *Endurance* was frozen in. Ice had closed in around the ship and there was no water visible in any direction. 60 miles from Vahsel Bay, *Endurance* was drifting – firmly beset – away from the coast. In the height of the Antarctic summer, temperatures fell to -10°F (-23°C). They were never able to free *Endurance* again.

As the 'might-have-beens' were pondered – had they landed at Glacier Bay – it became apparent that the trans-polar crossing was a quickly receding dream. On 24 February, they ceased to observe ship's routine and *Endurance* became a winter station. A space – 10 feet by 20 feet – was cleared round the rudder and propeller by sawing through the 2-foot-thick pack ice and lifting the blocks with tongs made by McNeish, ship's carpenter. Crean used the blocks

to make an ice house for the dog, Sally, who had added a litter of pups to the strength of the expedition.[3] According to Worsley, they looked on Crean as their mother. One of them, Nelson, brought in by Crean for warmth, howled the ship down whenever Crean went out and stopped immediately on his return. Crean's dogs were wonderfully trained and Worsley describes a typical moment:

> In the midst of a pandemonium of sound Crean places his box of hoosh between his double row of kennels and roars out an order – 'Kennels'. In a second every dog has retired into his abode and nothing but noses and appealing eyes are to be seen. Although the dogs are ravenous – as dogs always are – and food within easy reach, not one attempts to help himself, but waits obediently till Crean capsizes a bowl of hoosh on their floor where it disappears with marvellous rapidity.[4]

For month after month, the ship drifted with the current and wind, but did not appear to be in any real danger. As spring approached, the ice began to move. The first indication of danger came as the floes split with a loud crack like a whip and began to pile up on each other. Great pressure ridges advanced toward *Endurance* like a white wall on the surface of the pack ice. By mid-October, the ship was trapped between two advancing ridges. Powerfully flung over on her side and squeezed, she slowly but surely broke up. Shackleton remarked: 'I cannot describe the impression of relentless destruction. The floes, with the force of millions of tons of moving ice behind them, were simply annihilating the ship.' The crew watched helplessly: 'You could hear the ship being crushed. As the ice ground into her, you felt as if your own ribs were cracking. Suddenly, inside her, a light went on for a moment and then went out. It seemed like the end of the world.'⁵

Shackleton's leadership qualities now shone, as he converted the great respect with which he was held by most of the men to become their beloved leader. The *Endurance* was abandoned on 27 October. There was now only one objective – survival. Shackleton had sleeping bags issued of which only eighteen were made from reindeer skin and the balance made up of woollen blankets. Having drawn lots, it did not go unnoticed by the men that Shackleton, Worsley and Wild – along with most of the other officers – ended up with less-effective woollen bags. Shackleton also allocated places for the six tents, ensuring harmony and socialisation by the careful mixing of the crew, and by putting some of the poor mixers into his own tent. On the first morning – with the skipper and Wild – he heated milk and the three of them distributed it in mugs to the men in their tents.

As much as could be was salvaged from *Endurance* before she disappeared beneath the ice in November. Shackleton issued new winter clothing and a pound of tobacco to all, and each man was to choose from among his personal possessions items to keep, up to a maximum of 2 pounds in weight. Leading by example, Shackleton openly discarded gold sovereigns and his gold watch. After tearing out the flyleaf and some

other pages of the Bible presented to him by Queen Alexandra, he tossed it on a pile of his other discarded possessions. He also disallowed the keeping of pets, which meant the end to McNeish's cat, Mrs Chippy, a decision greatly resented by the outspoken shipwright. One exception was authorised, for Shackleton knew the value of socialisation: Hussey was allowed to keep his banjo – something that would help sustain the men's mental health.

The ship's boats were pulled over the ice, one group hacking and flattening the pack while the others pulled the whalers. But the going was too difficult in soft, wet snow and, after three days, the attempt to reach open water was abandoned. Shackleton, instead, found a solid floe to establish camp – calling it Ocean Camp – where they assembled all their belongings and secured the three boats. Catching seals and penguins became the daily work. Worsley tells us how, one day, an emperor penguin was spotted in a lead:

> Crean goes on all fours and makes a noise like a bit of fish. This brings the Emperor up in a hurry and a quarter of an hour later he is cut up for man meat.⁶

The business of catching seals and penguins could also be hazardous. Worsley tells us:

> On a march, Crean fell into a snow-covered crack and was completely immersed. Emerging soaked in a biting wind, Crean stripped under the lee of a boat . . . and we hastily . . . fitted him out . . . from various members' spares, but he

was almost paralysed before he was reclothed, and was some time before he recovered from the shock.[7]

Shackleton instructed McNeish to build up the sides of the largest lifeboat, which he named the *James Caird*, so as to increase her carrying capacity and improve her seaworthiness. The Dundee man used the timber from *Endurance* to raise the sides 15 inches and added half-decks fore and aft to the 22-foot-6-inch-long, clinker-built boat. Hurley, the photographer – a former metalworker – made a pump from the casing of the ship's compass. Rickinson, the engineer, made a rudder. Marston's oil colours were used to caulk the seams of the *James Caird* and the second cutter, the *Stancomb Wills*. Shackleton was keeping them all busy and positive. On 8 December, the *James Caird* was hauled 250 yards on a sledge to an open lead where it was launched. The men practiced loading and unloading her, completing the task with eleven men and six sledges of stores aboard; she appeared steady when loaded. The exercise was repeated until they were happy with their ability to respond whenever the floes would break up. The dogs were divided into six teams of nine dogs each: Wild, Crean, Macklin, McIlroy, Marston and Hurley each had charge of a team and were fully responsible for the exercising, training and feeding of their own dogs.

Just before Christmas, Shackleton had them hauling again when the floe they were camped on had them drifting eastward. It felt as if they were caught on the edge of an eddy – a place where the current divides – which would take

them away from their desired direction of north-west. The pulling was as bad as the first time, but it did relieve boredom for a week. It was also warm work and leads began to open up. Their progress varied from between 200 yards in five hours to 3 miles a day. But all was not well. McNeish, who regarded the hauling of the boats as a waste of effort, eventually refused to obey Worsley's orders and stopped work. As the ship was lost, he insisted, they were no longer legally under ships' articles and, therefore, not required to obey orders. Shackleton mustered all the crew and read out the articles, which detailed the responsibilities of crew to the master; he warned of the consequences of disobedience to lawful commands and explained that he had signed on at Buenos Aires as master, with Worsley as sailing master. Not only was he the expedition leader but also the legal master and they were still on wages. This revelation won the day and removed any doubts the crew might have had. McNeish was alone in his mutiny and Shackleton threatened to shoot him if he persisted. McNeish resumed his post.

Two days later, after further poor progress in the disintegrating ice, they found another solid floe where they established Patience Camp (10 miles from Ocean Camp) to await the breaking up of the ice. There, in miserable conditions, Shackleton and his 27 men settled down to await their delivery to the edge of the pack by the forces of nature: wind, current and tide. McNeish had made his point. The supply of food dwindled: they ran out of cocoa and, on 29 February, tea was also in short supply. Macklin and Crean led teams back to Ocean Camp to

The kitchen at
Patience Camp where
the staple diet of
hoosh was prepared
by the cook, Green,
who continually varied
the menu of seal
meat; one day fried
with blubber and the
next stewed with
vegetable.
Photograph by Frank
Hurley.
*Royal Geographical Society*

forage for food, bringing back tinned fish, beef cubes and tobacco. Wild, with eighteen men, retrieved the third boat from Ocean Camp as Worsley was worried about the capacity of just two boats to carry the 28 men on the inevitable sea journey. As the seals became scarce and fresh food for man and dog ran out, they were forced to kill most of the dogs, to whom a lot of time had been devoted by Crean and the other dog-team leaders. The dog meat offered some change to the hungry men from the fishy tedium of seal and penguin.

There they waited until early April, sometimes restricted to their tents by heavy snowfall for weeks. All became weaker and, as fuel became scarce, they resorted to melting ice for drinking

water by holding it in tins against their skin. The food was mostly seal meat with a biscuit at midday. Their survival was quite remarkable. Shackleton maintained morale by continually rearranging the menu of seal meat: one day it would be fried in blubber and the next stewed with dried vegetables. Combining it with dried milk, flour, sugar and tea also made a difference. Shackleton knew the value of variation to keep hopes alive and positive. He never claimed any privileges for himself as master and gave the appearance of confidence that they would all survive.

Just when the South Shetland Islands hove into view, the same destructive pack that had crushed and sunk the *Endurance* began to wear thin and to break up into pieces in a heavy swell.

During the night, a sudden crack opened up the floe; Holness, who had been sleeping in the large dome tent, was dumped into the sea. The parting of the floe split the tentsite in two and left the unfortunate fireman floating helplessly in his sleeping bag, down in the depths of the opening chasm between the two halves of the floating floe. Shackleton responded quickest, flinging himself down, grabbing the sodden bag and, with one ferocious heave, pulling the shocked fireman onto the floe just before the gap closed again and the two floes crunched together like the jaws of a vice. He had no intention of losing any of his men. The outcome of this episode was that Shackleton and a number of men were on one half of the floe while the rest of the party and the boats were on the other half. Wild had to launch the *Stancomb Wills* to retrieve Shackleton, who quickly broke camp on the heaving floe.

As the floe became smaller, they observed more and more open water until, on 9 April, just after midday, they took to the boats as a large open lead indicated they were at the edge of the pack. They had drifted around 2,000 miles since *Endurance* had become beset over fifteen months earlier. The men were now physically much weaker than when they had taken to the ice six months previously. The three days that followed were appallingly dangerous as well as miserable, as they rowed and sailed in the *James Caird* and *Dudley Docker*, both of which took turns towing the smaller *Stancomb Wills*.

Shackleton, Wild and McCarthy were among the eleven aboard the *James Caird*, the biggest of the three boats. Worsley was skipper on the *Dudley Docker*, while Crean took over effective command on the *Stancomb Wills* when Hudson, the navigator and senior officer on the little cutter, became unable to cope because of his severely frostbitten hands and his exertions at the tiller during the early stages of the voyage. Around 10 miles were covered the first day before camp was established on a 90-foot-long floe. Realising there was too much weight aboard, it was decided to abandon one-third of the stores. The cook, Green, produced the best and largest meal they had eaten for months. In the morning, they found their floe-berg had shed half its mass. The swell had increased and the pack had closed again. The sight of floes striking icebergs with increasing violence was at once magnificent and beautiful, and equally as terrifying. Their temporary home was being swept away at an alarmingly rapid rate and the prospect of their entering the seething mass of heaving floes was too appalling to contemplate. They went to the highest point to watch out for open water. At 2 p.m., just as their berg rolled and dipped, the men scattered into the boats, slid down a 6-foot cliff and took to the sought-after black band of water. There was no panic when the *James Caird* was grounded on a ledge of ice; her crew smartly pushed her off and saved her from capsizing. It was a narrow escape. Dodging in and out of patches of pack, they sailed 2 miles west into open sea. *Stancomb Wills* could not keep up, so Worsley and the *Dudley Docker* went back to tow her. It was sunset when the three boats were together again.

Finding a floe, they made fast to its lee. Only Green and How landed, equipped with Hurley's patent galley to boil the milk; they were soon handing out mugs of glorious hot milk to the men at rest in the cramped boats, who gratefully washed down their otherwise cold rations. The galley embarked, they were off again as masses of loose ice eddied round the floe, threatening to hole the boats. Keeping together, they avoided patches of ice as best they could, and all hands, wet and shivering, endured the freezing night of first rain and then snow. On the following day, the temperatures rose to just below freezing but persistent sleet and rain ensured everybody remained wet, cold and miserable. On taking sightings with his sextant, Worsley discovered they were being blown the wrong way and were 30 miles further from Elephant Island than he had earlier calculated. A strong head current had poured out of the Bransfield Strait, 90 miles west of them, and its effect had been to carry them back south into the pack.

Next night, each boat crew heated its own milk to go with the cold rations. The *Dudley Docker* took the other two in tow to prevent them from bumping. The temperature fell to -10°F (-23°C), turning beards white with frost. Their jackets cracked when they moved and, later, snow-showers made them feel even more miserable. But the men, in spite of it all, were magnificent, putting their courage and humour up front. They were hardened enough by six months' camping on the pack to be able to cope with this progressive cranking up of the severity of conditions. Grinning and bearing it, no complaints were voiced.

On 13 April, at dawn, it blew from the south-east; with clear weather, it was advantageous for steering to Elephant Island. Stores were divided up in case of separation and they steered north-west. In a fair breeze, their spirits rose; they were making for land. As they sailed, they chopped off the ice that had accumulated on the bows and stern of the boats. Since cooking was an impossibility while sailing, Shackleton gave orders for every man to eat as much biscuit, nut food and sugar as he wanted. Their stomachs were so closed and, without a drink, this was a safe order. In fact, many were too seasick to eat. It was bad enough for the frostbitten men to be cramped and huddled together without seasickness being added to their woes. When areas of loose pack were encountered, they tried to fend off lumps of ice with poles. The *James Caird* was struck by one and was holed, luckily above the waterline, which was quickly stuffed with a piece of sealskin. Coming out into comparatively open water, Shackleton led in the *James Caird*, followed by the *Dudley Docker* and the *Stancomb Wills*. His orders were for each boat to keep within 30 yards of each other. They looked 'like a fleet of exploring or marauding Vikings' as they sailed through large areas of freezing sea characterised by slush and pancakes of snow, into which were frozen countless thousands of dead fish, trapped by the sudden freezing of the sea.[8] The Cape pigeons and petrels were enjoying a rare feast, but the *Endurance* survivors had no time to reap such an unexpected harvest as they pushed through the slushy water. At sunset, they decided to heave-to; the *Dudley Docker* put out a sea anchor of three oars and the other two boats made fast astern of her. Thirst was the main problem now, with all hands suffering. Worsley sardonically observed that the only things dry in the boats were the men's parched mouths. As they sat and dozed, huddled together in the boats beneath the tent cloth, they presented a shivering mass of humanity.

In the morning, the boats were cleared of the accumulated ice on the bows and sterns, which were weighing them down. The oars were found to be encased with ice to the thickness of a man's thigh. In the *Stancomb Wills*, Blackborrow – at twenty, the youngest member of the party – was in bad condition; his feet badly frostbitten, he was tended closely by Dr McIlroy, who occasionally massaged the young stowaway's feet. At daylight, they sighted Clarence Island, tipped with pink against the sunrise, and then – 35 miles away – Elephant Island showed to north-northwest, exactly where Worsley's bearings had made it out to be. Shackleton naturally praised his skipper's accuracy under such difficult conditions. Hunger and thirst were forgotten as they rowed toward their Promised Land. Pulling to aid the sail in the gentle breeze, the exercise warmed those on the oars but also reminded them of their thirst. The *Dudley Docker*, towing the *Stancomb Wills*, went first, with the *James Caird* keeping up close behind. A headwind blew up and rowing ceased to help, so they beat windward and into shelter. The *James Caird*, equipped with a deck cover, could carry more sail so she took in tow the tiny, shallow-draft *Stancomb Wills*. With only 17 inches of freeboard, great skill and care was required to prevent her from being broached or capsized. The two bigger boats, now racing each other in the gale, steered for a large bay on the south-eastern side of Elephant Island. Beginning to ship heavy waves,

it was 'Bale!' and 'Bale like hell!' When the gale moved southwest, going inshore was made easier. In the dark, they tried to stay together as Worsley led the way ashore, but an hour-long snow squall made life very difficult, as winds grew stronger and seas higher. Caught in a riptide, the high seas caused waves to crash over all sides of the boats. But the *craic* and humour prevailed as Greenstreet, on the *Dudley Docker*, shouted, 'Look, the Major's putting out more than we've shipped' – a reference to the Dublin-born Major Orde-Lees' furious efforts to bale while at the same time vomiting overboard. But the seriousness of the situation was not lost on anyone. All prayed that the smallest boat, steered by Crean, was still afloat. When Greenstreet's right foot was found to be frostbitten, the gallant major removed the boot and sock from the sufferer's foot so as to massage it, and then heroically held Greenstreet's bare foot against his stomach under his sweater.

As they tried to run parallel to cliffs and glacier edges, a following sea drove them ashore. Suddenly, as they rounded a point into smoother water, the gale decreased. In the lee of the island, the sky cleared and the sun came out, and they sighted a low, rocky beach that offered a final escape from the cruel sea. Shackleton went aboard the *Stancomb Wills* and ran in with Crean, in the lighter boat, toward an opening in the reef. With a few strokes of the oars, they came in on a swell onto the stony beach. Shackleton gave the honour of being the first person ever to step ashore on Elephant Island to young Blackborrow, not realising how badly frostbitten his feet were. He roughly tried to help him ashore, ending with the poor boy sitting in the surf, numbed and unable to move until Shackleton and his mates pulled him up to a dry place.

They landed at 10 a.m. and quickly gathered around the cook and his galley, consuming hoosh converted from the first unlucky sea elephant they met on terra firma. The men were light-headed as well as light-hearted, revelling in the shingles and running the pebbles through their fingers as reassurance that they were at last on land. All stores and boats were placed above the high-water mark and, in the late evening, they pitched their tents. The men, with red-rimmed eyes from lack of sleep, climbed into their damp or wet sleeping bags on top of stones; they cared not, preferring to sleep on solid land rather than the heaving, precarious ice on which they had spent the previous six months. Young Blackborrow, who was unable to walk on his frostbitten feet, was Shackleton's chief concern, though many of the men were broken, including poor Hudson. Shackleton himself had aged from the responsibility and strain of keeping the boats together and keeping all his men alive.

Next day, Shackleton dispatched Wild and four of the fittest men in the party – including both Crean and McCarthy – with instructions to search westward along the coast for a more comfortable and safer camping place, away from the ravages of the sea and wind; a place where the party could live for weeks or months. The party left just before midday and returned in darkness, the beach being illuminated by a blubber flare which Shackleton had ordered to be lit at the head of the channel. Wild brought back news of a better camping place about 7 miles along the coast, where a snow slope joined a spit and where, Wild judged, the sea would not break over but which would likely be spray blown in a gale from the east or southwest.

On 17 April, the sea was smooth but a line of pack ice could be seen approaching. Three oars were broken so they could be used as rollers for launching the boats. As they set out, a 'willie-waw' wind[9] descended upon them from a gap between a glacier and the cliffs – a forewarning of a southerly gale that duly sprang up an hour later. The *Stancomb Wills* was being rowed with only three oars, and Worsley – in the *Dudley Docker* – having observed the plight of Crean and his men as they fell further astern in the storm and looked at risk of being driven out to sea, dropped back and handed Crean an oar. Later, Worsley related Crean's words of gratitude: 'Skipper darlin, what the hell's the good o' giving me, the longest man, the shortest oar.' Worsley swapped it and those with oars in each boat all rowed with what Worsley called Herculean effort to prevent them being blown out to sea. Because of the squalls and their closeness to cliffs, they dared not put up a sail. Instead, the men took regular turns on the few oars they had and, at 6 p.m., the landing ahead was sighted. The place at which they landed is now known as Cape Wild, named after the man who had found it – a place where he would stay with those who would await rescue. When the boats had been hauled ashore, and the stores and camping gear unloaded, Green cooked up a welcome pot of hoosh, which put fresh life into them all. Camp was made and the men turned in, but before long, the continuing gale ripped the threadbare eight-man tent, which had been roughly treated during the boat passages. While some found new homes in other tents, Worsley and one or two more merely took down the pole and wrapped the tent round the bags to keep out the snow. They slept through the night and awoke covered in a foot of snow.

Next day, in place of the tattered tent, the *Dudley Docker* was upturned, set on rock walls, protected on the weather side by boulders and used as a shelter. Green set up the galley by the rocks close to Shackleton's tent and the blubber stove became the neighbourhood attraction to all. In Shackleton's words, Charles Green earned everyone's gratitude by his unflagging energy in preparing meals that, to them, were both savoury and satisfying. These men needed all the comfort that hot food could give them as well as the consolation that their camp was at last safe.

### The Open Boat Journey

It was clear to Shackleton and Wild that a boat journey in search of relief was both necessary and not to be delayed due to the limited food supply and the health and mental condition of the party. The island of South Georgia was over 800 miles away but lay in the area of the west winds. A boat party might make it and be back with relief in a month. The hazards of the journey across 800 miles of the stormy sub-Antarctic were obvious, but Shackleton calculated that, at worst, the venture would add nothing to the risks of the men left on the island. After having discussed it with Wild and Worsley, he asked for volunteers for the boat journey. Wild, who was

to stay, would be in command on the island and Shackleton had originally agreed to leave Crean as his right-hand man. But Crean begged to come and Shackleton relented. From the volunteers, he chose McNeish, McCarthy and Vincent to join himself, Crean and Captain Worsley, whose navigational skills in difficult circumstances he had come to admire.

In a blizzard, they examined the *James Caird*. McCarthy said that he could contrive some sort

The spit at Cape Wild. The photograph was taken in January 1997 by the author prior to an attempt to repeat the open-boat journey with an Irish crew in the *Tom Crean*, a *James Caird* replica.
*Author's collection*

of covering for the *James Caird* if he could use the lids of cases and the four sledge runners that were lashed inside the boat for use in case of a landing on the Antarctic Peninsula. McNeish proposed to complete the covering with canvas and he set about making plans at once. He cut the mast of the *Stancomb Wills* and fitted it the length of the *James Caird's* keel so as to prevent her buckling in heavy seas. Using the sledge runners and box lids, he provided a base for a canvas cover which was thawed out over the blubber stove, then cut and sewn by Bakewell and Greenstreet to make a cover which was nailed and screwed into position and which gave the boat a more secure appearance. As events proved, the covering served its purpose well, and it is doubtful if they would have survived the voyage without it. McNeish also cut down a mizenmast and sail from the *Stancomb Wills'* mast and sail. The food, tools and stores were appropriated from the already scanty stock of those who would have to stay. Two 10-gallon casks were filled with water, melted from ice on the blubber stove.

Shackleton, anxious to depart before the pack closed completely round the island – something that might delay their departure by weeks or months – decided they would go the next day. Primus stoves and spares, paraffin, sleeping bags and a few extra socks were embarked. For provisions, they took 30 days' sledging rations, nut food, biscuits, dried milk, Bovril cubes, salt and blocks of ice to supplement the water. For instruments, they had a sextant, chronometer, binoculars, compass, sea anchors, charts and a barometer. Ballast was composed of shingle in bags made from blankets and some large, rounded boulders. As a swell arose, the *James Caird* was launched. The *Stancomb Wills* was employed in conveying the provisions and ballast to the *James Caird*, and most of the crew got wet up to their waists; the unfortunate Vincent and McNeish were fully immersed when thrown into the water from the deck by a violent wave. Despite the bad start, the *Stancomb Wills* came alongside to allow the transfer of ballast. On the second run, the *Stancomb Wills* capsized, wetting her crew to the skin. She was turned upside down and emptied before she could bring out the stores and tow the casks of water, one of which was damaged in the process; the damage was not noticed at the time, but the sea water would make the drinking water brackish, something that would have consequences later. As each boatload came alongside, Worsley tells us,

the contents passed over to them with a running fire of jokes, chaff and good wishes from dear pals whom we were leaving behind. Many were solicitous that I might not overeat myself, and that my behaviour on reaching civilisation should be above reproach. As for Crean, they said things that ought to have made him blush; but what would make Crean blush would make a butcher's dog drop his bone.[10]

Some members of the shore party exchanged clothes with McNeish and Vincent before they set out; it is said it took two weeks before the clothes were fully dried. Shackleton bade farewell to Wild and the men. It was a half-hour after noon on 24 April 1916 when this little party cut the painter connecting them to the *Stancomb Wills* and left the pathetic-looking group waving from the shore, who gave three hearty cheers to those they hoped would be their saviours.

It was Easter Monday 1916, the very day Pádraig Pearse was reading the 'Proclamation of the Irish Republic' from the steps of the General Post Office in Dublin. Yeats, the Irish poet, later wrote in reference to the Rising and its aftermath, 'a terrible beauty is born'. Impatience at the lack of progress toward Irish Home Rule was replaced by a new resolve for independence. Among the 800 rebels who fought with Connolly's Citizens' Army in St Stephen's Green and the College of Surgeons was the daughter of Sir Henry Gore-Booth. Constance was court-martialled, like the other leaders, and found guilty of waging war against the Crown. Her death sentence was commuted to penal servitude for life.

An event of equal audacity was unfolding in the Southern Ocean where three more brave Irishmen were engaged in yet another 'glorious thing', namely the rescue of their colleagues from a desolate and frozen place before they would

The launching of *James Caird* on Easter Monday 1916. Irishmen Ernest Shackleton, Tom Crean and Timothy McCarthy were joined in this heroic voyage to the island of South Georgia by Frank Worsley of New Zealand, Harry McNeish from Dundee and John Vincent from Hull. Photograph by Frank Hurley.
*Royal Geographical Society*

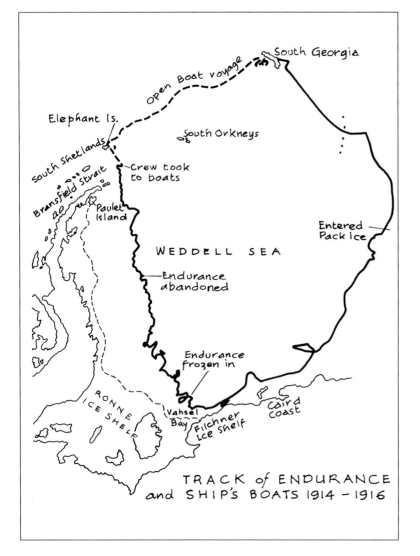

TRACK of ENDURANCE
and SHIP'S BOATS 1914 – 1916

concern was to get free of the pack and avoid any loose blocks of ice that could smash up against and hole the boat:

Cramped in our narrow quarters and continually wet by the spray, we suffered severely from cold throughout the journey. We fought the seas and the winds and at the same time had a daily struggle to keep ourselves alive. At times we were in dire peril. Generally we were upheld by the knowledge that we were making progress toward the land where we would be, but there were days and nights when we lay hove to, drifting across the storm-whitened seas and watching, with eyes interested rather than apprehensive, the uprearing masses of water, flung to and fro by Nature in the pride of her strength. Deep seemed the valleys when we lay between the reeling seas. High were the hills when we perched momentarily on the tops of giant combers. Nearly always there were gales. So small was our boat and so great were the seas that often our sails flapped idly in the calm between the crests of two waves. Then we would climb the next slope and catch the full fury of the gale where the wool-like whiteness of the breaking water surged around us. We had our moments of laughter – rare; it is true, but hearty enough. Even when cracked lips and swollen mouths checked the outward and visible signs of amusement we could see a joke of the primitive kind. Man's sense of humour is always most easily stirred by

succumb to starvation. The tale of sixteen days is one of supreme strife amid heaving waves. The sub-Antarctic lived up to its evil winter reputation.[11] Shackleton divided the crew into two watches of five hours, each crew steering, pumping, bailing and handling sails while three men slept – or tried to sleep – in one of the warm bags vacated by the previous watch. Shackleton described the voyage in his book, *South*, quoted from below and supplemented with extracts from Worsley's equally famous account, *Shackleton's Boat Journey*. On the first day, their main the petty misfortunes of his neighbours, and I will never forget Worsley's efforts on one occasion to place the hot aluminium stand on top of the Primus stove after it had fallen off in an extra heavy roll. With his frostbitten fingers he picked it up, dropped it, picked it up again, and toyed with it gingerly as though it was some fragile article of lady's wear. We laughed or rather gurgled with laughter.[12]

On the fourth day, a severe south-westerly gale forced them to heave-to. Shackleton would have liked to run before the wind but the sea was too high and the *James Caird* was in danger of broaching and being swamped with over-washing waves. They put out a sea anchor to keep the head up, but still the crests of the waves curled over them, causing them to ship a great deal of water. Every wave, they thought, would engulf her, but somehow she survived.

On the sixth day, May Day, they noticed that the *James Caird* was acting more like a log than a boat. So as to lose weight, every superfluous item was discarded, including the spare oars which, by then, were encased in ice and tied onto the deck. Two of the four sleeping bags, wet and frozen and each weighing about 40 pounds, were also lobbed out, and the ice which had accumulated across the bow and stern was chopped away; they did a lot of chopping before the *James Caird* rode the waves proud again.

Crean took charge of the cooking; that is, he boiled the water and stirred in the ration, a chore requiring equal measures of patience and agility. It took three people to steady the Primus stove

Able-bodied Seaman Timothy McCarthy from Lower Cove, Kinsale, Co. Cork. His good humour and skills in a small boat won him great praise and a place in the legendary crew of the *James Caird*.
*Cork Examiner*

and cooker, and to keep the grub and cooking gear free of the omnipresent reindeer hair moulting from the sleeping bags. The greatest trouble was the choking of the Primus stove by dirt and reindeer hair, which took more pricking than required on a sledging journey. The procedure was for Crean to prick and light the Primus – his back against one side of the boat – while Worsley put his against the other, each extending their legs toward each other, jamming the Primus between their feet. Worsley's role was to lift the pot whenever the boat took a leap, so as to save the precious contents from spilling over the flame or into the bilges. At Crean's bidding, McCarthy broke in the lumps of ice. When melted, Crean broke in and stirred the ration – half a pound a man. All eyes, save the helmsman's, were glued to the pot, hoosh pots and spoons at the ready. As soon as it boiled, Crean shouted 'Hoosh!' and blew out the Primus. The pots would shoot out and Crean would rapidly but carefully fill them in turn. They swallowed it boiling hot, having gradually trained their mouths and stomachs to accept the scalding, glorious elixir, which sent heat spreading right through their chilled and numbed bodies. The first to finish immediately jumped outside to relieve the helmsman so that he would have his while still hot. Worsley recounts one session:

> absorbed in watching Crean stirring, I saw him stop and stare into the hoosh. I almost trembled! The next moment a filthy black paw shot out, seized a handful of reindeer hair from the hoosh, squeezed it out, so as to waste nothing, and then threw it away. We didn't mind a little dirt, but we drew the line at reindeer hair.[13]

On the tenth night, Worsley could not straighten his body after a spell on the tiller; he was badly cramped. He had to be massaged before he could unbend sufficiently to get into a sleeping bag. Next day, a hard, north-westerly gale came up in the late afternoon. By midnight, Shackleton was at the tiller and noticed a line of what looked like a clear sky to the southwest. He called to the others that the weather was clearing, but a moment later realised that what he was looking at was not a rift in the clouds but the white crest of an enormous wave. During his 26 years' experience on the ocean – in all its moods – he had not encountered a wave so gigantic:

> It was a mighty upheaval of the Ocean, a thing apart from the white-capped seas that had been our enemies for days. I shouted 'For God's sake hold on!' There came a moment of suspense that seemed drawn out into hours. Then the foam of the breaking sea surged white around us. We felt our boat lifted and flung forward like a cork in the breaking surf. We were in a seething chaos of water; but somehow the boat lived through it, half filled with water, sagging, dead weight and shuddering under the blow. We baled with the energy of men fighting for life flinging water over the sides with every receptacle that came to our hands, and after 10 minutes of uncertainty we felt the boat renew her life beneath us.[14]

It is thought that the massive wave was the product of some great iceberg calving into the sea, or an iceberg at sea breaking up and rolling over in the swell. It took two hours for all hands to bale her out and to readjust the ballast, and a half-hour for Crean to clean and get the Primus going for some hot milk. In the aftermath, Shackleton noted that McNeish was suffering particularly, but showing grit and spirit. He also noted that Vincent had in the past week ceased to be an active member of the crew; Shackleton could not easily account for his collapse.

> Physically, he was one of the strongest men in the boat. He was a young man, he had served in North Sea trawlers, and he should have been able to bear hardships better that McCarthy, who, not so strong, was always happy.[15]

Worsley said of McCarthy:

McCarthy is the most irrepressible optimist I've ever met. When I relieved him at the helm, boat iced over and seas pouring down our necks, one came right over us and I felt like swearing, but just kept it back, and he informed me with a cheerful grin 'It's a foine day sorr.' I had been feeling a bit sore before, but this shamed me. His cheeriness does brighten things up.[16]

Worsley also tells us that Shackleton suffered from sciatica and, at times, was in great pain but never complained; it would clear up in a few days. He was even able to grin at his skipper's Irish joke regarding the malady: 'Pat's query to Mick, who said he'd come home and found his wife in bed with sciatica. Did ya kill the Oitalian divvle.'

The weather improved the next day and Worsley got a sighting which showed they were but 91 miles from the north-west edge of South Georgia. Two more days' sailing they thought. But now, thirst became a problem when the last cask was discovered to be contaminated with sea water. Shackleton forbade any more than a quarter-pint per man per day, knowing from experience the harm it could do.

The fifteenth day – 8 May – was foggy. Knowing they must be near, a close watch was kept. At 7 a.m., Worsley reckoned they were just 12 miles off. Vincent spotted seaweed at 10.30 a.m. – a sign of land nearby. At noon, McCarthy – through the lifting fog – spotted a gloomy cliff and snow about 10 miles dead ahead. It was just fourteen days since they had departed Elephant Island. Their deliverance they owed to Worsley

who had navigated with such precision; in those fourteen days, there were only four clear opportunities to use the sextant. South Georgia could not have looked any more inviting than the desolate Elephant Island and they would still have to cross it; just the same, conversation must have been about fresh water, hot drinks, clean clothes and a comfortable bed. But there was to be a sting in the tail of their voyage.

At 2.30 p.m. they were within 3 miles of land, but observed breaking seas and rollers and sensed a bad change in the weather. Shackleton decided to head back out to sea and wait until morning in the hope of finding a way through the apparent reefs, something they greatly feared. By 11 p.m., they were in a rising gale and, by dawn – after a terrible night – they were being blown toward destruction against the icy cliffs of the island's coast. They fought hard to stay off the shore, parched and starving, for without water they could not heat their food. Vincent and McNeish were by this time very weak and near done in. Later in the evening, the wind and seas subsided and they were able to enter King Haakon Bay, steering through a gap in the reef by tacking five times to enter the comparatively smooth water of the inner bay. At dusk, Shackleton spotted a small cove in a break in the cliff on the south side of the bay; entering, they drifted onto a little beach where a stream of fresh water fell from the glacier to the beach. As they gorged themselves in the simple pleasure of pure, clean water, Shackleton realised in that splendid moment that he had made South Georgia.

When they had unloaded the boat of stores and ballast, they discovered they had not the strength to pull it ashore. Shackleton unselfishly ordered the men to bed; he would take the first one-hour watch holding the painter – a rope – to secure the *James Caird*. Three hours passed before he called Crean to help him in a struggle to hold the boat. A large wave took her out and, on retrieval, they tied her up close to the cave were they slept. Shackleton arranged one-hour watches for the remainder of the night before he finally lay down among the sleeping men, exhausted but surely satisfied. The voyage was a tribute to each man's endurance and seamanship, to Worsley's skill and pinpoint navigation, and to Shackleton's judgement and leadership.

In the morning, they stripped the topside from the boat, took out all the moveable gear and pulled her up past the high-water mark. The rudder was noticed missing, lost during their scramble ashore the night before. Shackleton and Crean climbed the grassy slope behind the beach and reached the top of the headland overlooking the sound. There, they found an albatross and its chick, which they had no hesitation in killing. Thoughtfully conserving what little paraffin they had left for the Primus, which would be needed for crossing the island, Crean made a fire using the deck-covering timbers and made a stew of the bird, which he thickened with a Bovril ration. After the memorable meal, they dried their tobacco in the embers of the fire and smoked contentedly while their clothes dried. The cave was made more comfortable by use of layers of soft grass; the oars and sails provided shelter at the entrance to the cave.

The options open to Shackleton were very clear; either a 150-mile sea voyage around the island to Leith, Husvik or Stromness whaling stations, or a shorter, more direct overland traverse of the mountains and glaciers of South Georgia. This latter option would necessitate a short boat trip to the head of the bay. The condition of his party – especially McNeish and Vincent – eliminated any serious consideration of the sea journey, except as a dire necessity. The boat had been weakened by the voyage and by the stripping away of the top covering. Shackleton favoured crossing the island with a small, strong party, just as soon as they had dried their clothes, had a few days' rest and had plenty of nourishment. His main worry was the absence of fuel. But a couple of seals or penguins would take care of that. He could not but think and worry about the 22 men waiting on Elephant Island for the relief that he alone could bring to them; he knew the plight of Wild's party was very grim compared with his. He must also have wondered about the status of the *Aurora* crew at McMurdo Bay.

In the afternoon, Crean and McCarthy brought down another six young albatrosses, so they were well supplied with fresh food. The smoke from the fire had affected Crean's eyes, and the pain had him twisting and groaning in the night. Sir Ernest attended to him and put some adrenalin into his eyes. It sounded quaint to Worsley to hear Crean demurring like a fractious child and Sir Ernest – like a worried parent – reproving him until he got off to sleep. Later in the night, Shackleton dreamt of the great wave breaking over the *James Caird* and woke the crew, shouting, 'Look out boys, look out! Hold on!'

On Saturday 13 May, the sea brought back

into their little cove the rudder, bobbing in the tide; a lucky omen, they thought. They waited until they could seize it with an outstretched oar. Providence was surely with them – the day was bright and clear, their clothes were drying and their strength returning. Wet blankets were brought up the hill to dry in the breeze and the *James Caird* was prepared for a crossing of King Haakon Bay. Worsley and Shackleton went reconnoitring to get a view; 'stern peaks that dared the stars' peered through the mist, and between them huge glaciers poured down from great ice slopes and mountains that lay behind. They returned to camp with some driftwood for the fire, and a quantity of blubber and sea-elephant liver as a treat for the men.

On 15 May, taking all their belongings, they crossed the bay, landing a mile and a half from the north-eastern corner. The *James Caird* was pulled up above the high-water mark and turned over so as to provide sheltered accommodation. One side was raised on stones to provide an entrance. McCarthy entered into the work with great spirit, Shackleton tells us. That evening, Peggotty Camp – as Shackleton named it – was a place of great contentment and rest. It was stocked with fuel from a pile of driftwood containing the debris of many sunken ships which had foundered while trying to round Cape Horn, and which had been carried by the complex movements of currents and tides to this remote beach. An unending supply of elephant seals was also available on the beach. 'Peggotty House' was covered with tussocks and moss until it looked like an Irish turfed hut, with smoke escaping from a gap they had left near the bows.

To cross South Georgia was the next task. Shackleton chose Worsley and Crean to accompany him, deciding that McNeish and Vincent were in no condition for such a journey. Incapable of managing for themselves, McCarthy was to stay and look after them. Shackleton realised that McCarthy might have a difficult task if his party failed to reach the whaling stations.[17] The weather improved on 18 May and, on the following morning – after a last meal of hoosh – the three-man party set out at 3 a.m., their way illuminated by the bright light of the moon. McCarthy and McNeish walked with them for some of the way. Later, Worsley paid tribute to McCarthy:

> How sad we should have been at parting with simple honest Timothy McCarthy, AB, had we known we should only see him once again for two days. He went down in the war, fighting his gun to the last – three short weeks after landing in England. A big, brave, smiling, golden hearted Merchant Service Jack – we, his shipmates who truly learned his worth in that boat journey, are proud of his memory. I always felt that, no matter where we were or what exalted company we might be in, if Timothy McCarthy passed by he must be welcomed to a place of honour and given the best of everything, as befitted a brave man and one of Nature's gentlemen.[18]

At 4 a.m., they reached the first pass, or saddle – now called Shackleton Gap – and abandoned the little sledge McNeish had cobbled together from driftwood for the journey. Lacking a rucksack, they distributed the gear equally, each carrying three days' food – hoosh, three biscuits and two cakes of nut food – slung in a Burberry sock around the neck. The inventory of equipment amounted to a Primus, an aluminium pot, binoculars, a compass, 90 feet of alpine rope and an adze with a cut-down handle for hacking steps in the ice. Each had a 5-foot long lath of timber from one of the sledges for use as an alpenstock. A fragment of a German blueprint chart of South Georgia – drawn by the Filchner expedition in 1911, showing the coastal outline only – would serve as their map. On their feet, the men wore felt-lined 'Shackleton boots', the soles of which had been fitted by Chippy McNeish with eight 2-inch brass screws, point-down to give good grip on the glacier ice. The woollen underwear they wore had, by that time, seen continuous service for five months. Each man was attired in ordinary trousers, a woollen sweater and a wind-proof Burberry jacket. Clothing was secured at the neck, wrists, waist and ankles, and each man also had a woollen Balaclava helmet and mitts covered by a loose pair of Burberry over-mitts.

Shackleton, Crean and Worsley climbed uphill and eastward until about 7 a.m. – following what is now known as the Murray Snowfield – until

Tom Crean (left), Ernest Shackleton (centre) and Frank Worsley in South Georgia shortly after their heroic journey. The photograph was taken by a Norwegian whaler.
*Scott Polar Research Institute*

reaching another saddle and observing through the mist what looked like a lake. Dropping down to the left toward the lake, they discovered it stretched away to the horizon; it was, in fact, the sea: Captain Cook's Possession Bay. They headed back up a long slope to the right and found themselves above a series of crags and gullies, all of which looked too steep to descend. Having traversed past several of the gullies to the left, they found a slope that offered a more acceptable risk. The first 200 feet were descended by cutting steps with the adze, Shackleton taking the lead. But progress was too slow and, when the angle eased, they took a decision to glissade down the rest of the slope. Each sat on his own section of the coiled rope, all clinging together like a toboggan team with legs wrapped around each other's waists and with their hands on each other's shoulders. Hurtling down the 70-degree slope, they yelled with excitement for what seemed like three minutes, losing height rapidly; as it flattened out, they finished up buried in a bank of soft snow. For Crean, it was something of a rerun of his descent of the Beardmore Glacier with Lashly and Evans in 1912. Shackleton, who had been to the front on this exhilarating shunt, commented: 'It's not good to do that kind of thing too often.' Their clothes were in tatters.

It was 6 p.m. and, following a brew, the party headed up a great glacier for 6 miles – now called Crean Glacier – toward a nunatak they could see in the distance. Passing what they called the Great Nunatak on their left and leaving the three spurs of the Trident on their right, they made for a line of peaks with a gap like a broken tooth. During a short halt, Crean and Worsley

fell asleep; after five minutes, Shackleton shook them awake, telling them they had been asleep for half an hour. They had chosen to travel light, with no sleeping bags or covering – and no time for sleep. They were not yet halfway there. On their left, the outline of Antarctic Bay could be seen, which concurred with their chart. There was a long stretch from the nunatak to what Shackleton called a line of jagged peaks. Having traipsed through steep snow up to the peaks, the men stopped at a wall of crags in the pre-dawn moonlight and had a brew.

Feeling revived, up and over the toothed ridge they went. But they found themselves not above Stromness Bay, as they had hoped and anticipated. Beneath them appeared a glacier that ran down to the sea and they realised from the chart that they were, in fact, above Fortuna Bay. Beyond Fortuna Bay, they knew there was a range of lower hills which, they calculated, was above Stromness or Husvik, their destination. As they brewed up, using the last of their paraffin, Shackleton thought he heard a whistle. It was 6.30 a.m. They listened carefully, watching the chronometer until 7 a.m. when they clearly heard the morning steam-whistle at Stromness calling the men to work. They leapt with excitement, their orientation confirmed. Encouraged, and with something like 10 miles to go, they descended a steep, icy glacier, cutting steps again to their right over precarious ground, icy at first, then contouring over steep tussock grass to bring them to the beach of Fortuna Bay by 10 a.m. Wading first across the soft mud of the mile-wide beach, they then headed up the slope of the final hills which, as they anticipated, stood above the dreamed-of whaling station. Reaching the top of the final slope and crossing a stretch of flat ground, Crean fell through its icy covering and was up to his waist in water; they were crossing a frozen mountain lake. Tom Crean, it seems, never lost his unfortunate habit of falling into water and getting ducked. Cautiously, they made their way off its dangerous surface, spreading their weight as best they could. At 1.30 p.m., they were on the hills overlooking the busy whale-processing factory at the mouth of Stromness Bay and could see two whale catchers steaming in the sea below. Exhausted and impatient to get down the final slopes, they fixed one end of the rope and lowered Crean – the heaviest – down past a waterfall; Shackleton quickly followed him. Worsley, the lightest, came down last, hand over hand. Tiredness and the screws of their boots having worn away caused the three men to fall many times on the icy ground as they headed towards the station.

It was 3 p.m. before they reached the station. Their trek across South Georgia had taken 36 hours. The first two people to see them were a couple of children who scattered at the sight of the three dirty men in their tattered clothes. The station manager, Thoralf Sørlle, who had entertained Shackleton eighteen months before, did not recognise him at first, thinking he was the mate of the *Daisy*. Shackleton's first questions concerned the progress of the war. 'Tell me when the war was over?' he asked. Sørlle informed him that the war was far from being over: 'Millions are being killed. Europe is mad. The world is mad,' said Sørlle.

It was not long before the men had eaten,

taken a hot bath and been issued with clean clothes. Beginning to feel civilised again, they listened to news of the war and to stories of inhumanity being perpetrated in Europe. They also learned about the *Aurora* and the problems of the Ross Sea party, which had been sent to lay depots as support for the *Endurance* party. The ship had visited MacQuarie Island to provision the Commonwealth Meteorological Expedition in December 1914 and continued to the Cape Evans base on Ross Island, where it was intended the vessel would remain for winter. On 6 May 1915, *Aurora* was driven from its moorings by a blizzard, leaving ten men ashore. The stranded men wintered at Cape Evans with minimal supplies and – utilising dogs and a motor sledge – they laid depots southward toward the Beardmore Glacier for Shackleton's proposed trans-Antarctic expedition. *Aurora* became beset and then drifted for ten months in the Ross Sea pack ice, passing Balleny Islands. Freed on 14 March 1916, she sailed for New Zealand.

Shackleton's immediate priority was recovery of McCarthy's party at King Haakon Bay, and the obliging Sørlle dispatched a whale catcher named *Samson* to go and fetch them, accompanied by Worsley. Shackleton next commenced preparations for the rescue of Wild and the Elephant Island men. Shackleton later told Harold Begbie:

> When we got to the whaling station, it was the thought of those comrades which made us so mad with joy that the reaction beats all efforts to describe it. We didn't so much feel we were safe as that they would be saved.[19]

Departing next morning by motor boat to Husvik, he organised the loan of a British steam-whaler named the *Southern Sky*. The number of whalers who volunteered to join the crew of the rescue ship overwhelmed him and Shackleton appointed a Norwegian master named Ingvar Thom as captain for the voyage. It was very fortunate that the ship was laid up for winter at Husvik Harbour, away from any means of communicating with the owner who might not have been quite as understanding.

Worsley arrived back with McCarthy, McNeish and Vincent the following day. They had failed to recognise him aboard the whaler in his shaven and cleaned-up state, thinking him one of the Norwegians. McCarthy was even heard to complain at the absence of any of their colleagues: 'Well, we thought the Skipper would have come back anyway.' Shackleton could now count six of the 28 men safe. The *Samson* crew had also retrieved the *James Caird*. On its arrival at the whaling station, the Norwegian whalers treated the little boat with reverence; as Worsley wrote:

> They would not let us put a hand to her, and every man on the place claimed the honour of helping to haul her up the wharf. I think Shackleton must have felt it was one of his proudest moments. The amazed admiration of these sailor descendants of the Vikings was so spontaneous and hearty that it was quite affecting.[20]

Later that day, in that wild and humble setting, a noble tribute was made by a number of older Norwegian captains, mates and sailors, each with extensive maritime experience about Cape Horn and the Southern Ocean. They expressed their admiration of the wonderful feat of seamanship in bringing the 22-foot open boat from Elephant Island to South Georgia. The crossing of the interior of ice, snow and rocky heights of the sub-Antarctic island was likewise admired. Each asked for the honour of shaking hands with Sir Ernest and his comrades. In a passionate speech, one of the captains ended with a dramatic gesture: 'These are men!' It was a wonderful and proud moment for Ernest Shackleton, Tom Crean and Frank Worsley. It is hard to beat the admiration of one's peers in any walk of life.

The next day, 23 May, Shackleton, having made arrangements for McCarthy, McNeish and Vincent to return to England on the next steamer, went aboard the *Southern Sea* with a view to sailing to Elephant Island and then to the Falklands with, hopefully, the rescued Wild party aboard. Halted 60 miles short by pack ice, snowstorms and a shortage of coal, they made for the Falklands where Shackleton wired the *Daily Chronicle*, Emily, the Admiralty and the king. A second rescue attempt was made on a trawler, the *Instituto de Pesca No 1*, loaned to Shackleton by the Uruguayan government. The vessel reached within 18 miles of the camp on Elephant Island before being stopped by the close pack in a rising swell. Almost out of coal, the trawler returned to Port Stanley.

Shackleton next travelled to Punta Arenas in the Magellan Straits, where the British and Chilean communities very generously subscribed £1,500 to enable the now very anxious Shackleton to charter and fit out the auxiliary schooner,

*Emma.* This time, in the middle of winter and with a motley crew from many nations, they were lucky to escape with their lives as the auxiliary engine broke down and the ship was damaged in heaving ice. When Shackleton arrived back to Port Stanley on 8 August, he learned that *Discovery* was to leave England at once and would be in the Falklands by mid-September. The governor suggested he settle down and take things quietly for a few weeks, but Shackleton and his colleagues were soon fed up walking between what he called the two main attractions in Port Stanley – the graveyard and the slaughterhouse – one at each end of the only street. Besides, Shackleton did not want to risk his men's lives for one day longer at that miserable spit, let alone for six or seven weeks. Neither did he want the navy to rescue his men if he could do it himself.

Employing all of his undoubted charm and emphasising his Irishness, he convinced the Chileans – some say he conspired with them – to reach his men before the arrival of the navy-manned *Discovery*. For the fourth attempt, the Chilean government gave him the necessary assistance and a more suitable ship, the little steel tug-steamer named the *Yelcho*. Providence was with them: they got a good run in better weather and, this time, a southerly gale ensured the ice was open. It was foggy as they approached, but Worsley was navigating with his usual precision and, when the fog lifted, he spotted the campsite under its covering of snow and ice. As Worsley manoeuvred the *Yelcho* between stranded bergs and hidden reefs, Shackleton peered through his binoculars with painful anxiety. He counted the

figures crawling out from under the upturned boat; realising all were present, 'his face lit up and years seemed to fall off his age.'[21] Shackleton, Crean and Worsley solemnly shook hands as if part of some ritual.

Crean and Shackleton went ashore and, as they approached the beach with Chilean sailors pulling on the oars, Shackleton called out to Wild, 'Are you well?' Wild called back, 'We are all well Boss', and then Shackleton heard three cheers. His first act was to throw packets of cigarettes ashore, for he knew how they would have dreamed and talked about them for months. Some of the party were in a bad way, but Wild had held them together and had kept hope in their hearts. Shackleton did not wish to stay a minute longer than was necessary to get every man aboard, concerned as he was with the heavy sea running; he feared a change of wind would bring the ice back at any time. He called them all aboard without disembarking to inspect the camp. The men had prepared well for this day and, within an hour, all were aboard, along with the ship's records and Hurley's photographs. Their patient wait for the return of Shackleton was over; they had survived.

On the journey back to Punta Arenas, Shackleton heard firsthand from Wild and the other men about how they had survived, and was regaled with stories of how their cheerfulness and resourcefulness served them well for four-and-a-half months. They had lived under the two upturned boats, erected side by side 4 feet above the ground, supported by boulders and rocks, and sealed by tent canvas and pieces of blanket. The stove was located between the boats, with a chimney made from a biscuit box. Some lived 'upstairs' in bunks resting on the thwarts, while the remainder slept side by side on the floor. There they survived, often pinned down by week-long blizzards and gales, the winds sometimes exceeding 100 mph. Their eyes were blinded and their faces blackened by smoke and fumes. In June, young Blackborrow had suffered the amputation of the toes of his left foot, an operation conducted by the two doctors, Macklin and McIlroy. When fully acquainted by some of the party regarding the quality of Wild's exemplary leadership, Shackleton must have been very proud. Each morning that the sea was clear, Wild would pick up his kit, roll up his sleeping bag and call out to all hands, 'Roll up your sleeping bags boys, the Boss may come today.' Frank Hurley, in *Argonauts of the South*, described life at Cape Wild:

Those first few days on Elephant Island were hell, and it appeared at first as though many who endured so far, would be unable to survive further persecution and exposure . . . We re-rigged our tent, and all hands turned to in the erection of a wind shelter for the cook's galley . . . Weather conditions being still wretched, we retired daily at five o'clock to saturated sleeping bags, to steam and fug for

The Chilean ship, *Yelcho*, arrives at Elephant Island on 30 August 1916. The beacon fire is lit and bellows out a black smoke signal. Photograph by Frank Hurley.
*Royal Geographical Society*

fourteen hours. The tent walls becoming thickly covered with condensation rime, showering us with every gust.

Of our party, one was a helpless cripple, a dozen were more or less disabled with frostbite, and some were for the moment crazed by their privations . . . Our refuge was like the scrimped courtyard of a prison . . . a narrow strip of beach 200 paces long by 30 yards wide. Before us, the sea, which pounded our shores in a heavy tumult, would at night be frozen into icy silence, only to break up again under tidal influence with a noise like the churning of some monstrous mill. Behind us the island peaks rose 3,000 feet into the air, and down their riven valleys across their creeping glaciers, the wind devils raced and shrieked, lashed us with hail and smothered us with snowdrift. Inhospitable, desolate and hemmed in with glaciers, our refuge was as uninviting as it could be. Still, we were grateful. It was better than the icefloes . . . On August 30th, the one-hundred and thirty-seventh day of our maroonment, Marston and I were scanning the northern horizon, when I drew his attention to a long, curious shaped berg . . . We continued to gaze at it when miracle of miracles, a vessel came in sight from under its lee. We immediately raised a cry . . . which was greeted by derision and mocking shouts . . . When at last we made them realise the truth, they came out crawling through the roof and breaking through the walls. Wild gave the order to

kindle the beacon. It was a worthy occasion on which to expend one of my last three remaining spaces of film and it recorded faithfully that truly historic scene.[22]

In January 1997, the author of this history participated in 'South Arís', the Irish Antarctic Adventure – an attempt to repeat the 'open boat journey' in a *James Caird* replica named *Tom Crean*. The expedition was foiled by a hurricane. While standing in that desolate place, I composed the following words of admiration for Frank Wild and his men stranded on Elephant Island; the verse is entitled, 'Patiently Waiting with Wild':

> There are no crosses or graves at Cape Wild
> Its testimony to your discipline and guile
> And to the six in the boat, the only real
>    hope,
> Of the brave men patiently waiting with
>    Wild.

At Punta Arenas, practically the whole population turned out to welcome them back to civilisation. Shackleton still had one major worry before he could go home. He needed to pick up the *Aurora* and make haste for the base at the Ross Sea to rescue the ten-man shore party. Shackleton travelled with Worsley northward via Panama to San Francisco, the steamship and train companies giving them everything free, and offering the most cordial and generous assistance. From there, at the end of November, they caught a steamer to New Zealand. Shackleton signed on *Aurora* under the command of Captain John K. Davis, who had been a member of his *Nimrod* expedition. The British and the Australian governments, having met the cost of refitting and repairing *Aurora*, as well as provisioning and coaling her for the rescue voyage to Cape Crozier, were adamant that Shackleton would not have command. They considered his arrangements for *Aurora*'s original voyage a disgrace. The men, it was claimed, were under-provided for, and Shackleton was considered neglectful and irresponsible. Reaching his men was more important to him than an argument over command of the voyage on a ship that legally he still owned, so he signed on, acknowledging that there could be only one captain on a ship.

Only seven members of the shore party had survived; they were rescued on 10 January 1917. Mackintosh, who had commanded *Aurora* on the outward voyage, had remained ashore from January 1915 and had laid depots to 83° south for Shackleton's planned Weddell Sea party. He and Hayward had died crossing sea ice on 8 May 1916 while attempting to make their way from Hut Point to Cape Evans. They were overtaken by a blizzard that destabilised the precariously thin pack ice and it is presumed they drowned, having broken through the sea ice. Spencer-Smith died on the return journey from the debilitating effects of the age-old maritime scourge of scurvy. Having managed 1,500 miles and to have laid out depots for Shackleton up to the foot of Beardmore Glacier was a great performance for a party that had only one experienced sledger, in Ernest Joyce, a veteran of the *Discovery* and *Nimrod* expeditions. Frank Wild's brother, also

named Ernest, was another to survive the expedition's hardships and difficulties. The expedition was equipped with wireless telegraphy apparatus and, though contact was made with Cape Evans from *Aurora* and signals received from the MacQuarie Islands, the signal was not powerful enough to reach a coastal station.[23]

Shackleton arrived back to Wellington on 9 February 1917, having seen to all his men. Three had died on the Ross Sea shore party and the rest were home, safe and alive. Five weeks later, on 16 March, Timothy McCarthy of Kinsale lost his life while at his gun post when SS *Narragansett*, an oil tanker on which he was serving in the North Sea, was sunk by a German submarine torpedo. Aged just 29, he had lived quietly and effectively, doing his duty in an heroic age. 'One of nature's gentlemen', was how Worsley was said to have described him. His courage, strength and conduct were a shining example, and a source of great pride to his remarkable maritime family. He was one of those about whom Shackleton's dedication in his narrative of the *Endurance* voyage, *South*, seems most apt.

To My Comrades
Who fell in the White Warfare
of the South and on the Red Fields of
France and Flanders

# SHACKLETON AND CREAN'S FINAL VOYAGES

*Do not let it be said, that Shackleton has failed . . . No man fails who sets an example of high courage, of unbroken resolution, of unshrinking endurance.*

ROALD AMUNDSEN

It was May 1917 before Shackleton returned to Britain. In Wellington, he had sold *Aurora* to repay his New Zealand debts. Visits were made to Melbourne and Sydney, where he addressed an army-recruitment rally, and from there, he travelled to lecture in the US. Edward Saunders, who travelled with him, had already ghost-written much of the expedition narrative, which Shackleton entitled *South*.

Back in England, Shackleton made strenuous efforts to secure a wartime commission or a diplomatic role, so as to redress the charges made against him by some critics for his use of valuable resources during a time of war. He applied for the Polar Medal for his men, though deliberately excluded four of those who had served on the expedition – McNeish, Vincent, Holness and Stephenson – as he regarded the medal as an award for exceptional service rather than a campaign medal. It seems particularly hard on McNeish, whose overall performance and contribution was immense, but his one act of disloyalty and confrontation caused him to be cast aside forever by Shackleton.

In contrast, Shackleton sought a commission for Crean as a warrant lieutenant, the Kerryman benefiting from his patron's written endorsement. He was appointed acting boatswain on 27 December 1916. He was also awarded his third silver Polar Medal. Crean had parted company with Shackleton and Wild at Buenos Aires in October 1916; he sailed back to Britain with the remainder of the party on the liner, *Highland Lassie*. In a letter to Apsley Cherry-Garrard, he expressed his gratitude to Shackleton, while summing up the expedition and his role in a few words:

*facing page*
Sir Ernest Shackleton. In this photograph, he is wearing his sledging harness.
*Royal Geographical Society*

We had a hot time of it the last 12 months when we lost *Endurance*, and I must say the Boss is a splendid gentleman and I done my duty towards him to the last.[1]

Tom Crean, his wife, Nell, and daughters Mary and Eileen.
*Courtesy of Crean Family*

Within six weeks, he was back on duty, operating out of Chatham Barracks before transferring to a patrol ship, HMS *Colleen*, at Queenstown, Co. Cork. He married Eileen (Nell) Herlihy on 5 September 1917. The daughter of a local publican, they had known each other since childhood. They opened a pub in Anascaul, which they named the South Pole Inn. Just as the war ended in November 1918, Crean was sent to HMS *Inflexible*, a battle cruiser. In March 1919, he was transferred to HMS *Fox*. While on service with *Fox*, he sustained a fall, striking his head, arm and legs. He joined HMS *Hecla* at year's end, retiring in March 1920, having been declared medically unfit with defective vision.[2]

Just six weeks after Crean's arrival home, on 21 April, Constable Paddy Foley of the RIC – who had served with the Royal Munster Fusiliers at the front during the war – was kidnapped from Moriarty's Hotel in Anascaul. A native of Anascaul, his brother, Mick, was a member of the Inch Brigade of the IRA (Irish Republican Army). Constable Foley was tried, sentenced and executed by the IRA; his bullet-ridden body was discovered at Deelis, near Castlegregory, two days later.[3] That same weekend at Ballinspittle, Co. Cork, three RIC men – among them, Crean's brother, Sergeant Cornelius Crean – were ambushed while cycling. One constable was shot off his bicycle. In turning to face his attackers, Sergeant Crean was shot fatally in the left lung. He was one of 442 RIC men killed – a further 725 were injured – as a result of political violence from January 1919 until June 1922. The writer, Seán O'Faolain, whose father, Denis Whelan, served with the RIC in Cork city, said of this horrific time: 'Men like my father were dragged out in those years and shot – so be it. Shot to inspire terror – so be it. They were not traitors – they had their loyalties and they stuck to them.'[4] There was much IRA activity and military retaliation in the Tralee and Dingle area in the following months, including the shooting by the Black and Tans of Patrick Kennedy, a brother of the IRA's local intelligence officer. Tom Crean, the now retired and distinguished naval warrant officer, testified on behalf of his neighbour, Daniel Moriarty, who was charged with having taken part in an IRA ambush on a military supply party. Crean gave evidence that, while saving hay, he had heard the shooting and at the same moment observed two people working in Moriarty's meadow. As a result of Crean's testimony, Moriarty – who claimed he was making hay at the time of the ambush – was released, while the other man, Daniel McKenna, who refused to recognise the court, was convicted.

Crean quietly settled down in Anascaul, keeping his exploration achievements to himself and raising his family – two daughters, Mary and Eileen – in republican Co. Kerry in the emerging Irish Free State. He died in Cork at the Bon Secours Hospital on 27 July 1938 at the age of 63, following an emergency operation to remove his appendix.[5] He is buried in a tomb he built himself in the townland of Ballinacourty. Close by, Owenascaul River flows down into the Atlantic whose waters also wash on the shores of Antarctica.[6]

Through the offices of the unionist member of parliament, Edward Carson – the man who many in Ireland accredited with the partitioning

of the country – Shackleton was sent to Buenos Aires to advise the Department of Information regarding wartime propaganda in Argentina. The honorary job – unpaid – ended abruptly when

Bronze statue to the memory of Tom Crean, unveiled in his native Anascaul on 20 July 2003.
*Author's collection*

Carson resigned in January 1918 in opposition to Home Rule for Ireland. Shackleton was then given a new mission, with the support of the establishment, to organise a regional development company in northern Russia, at Spitzbergen, supported by a British military presence. At this time, the Bolsheviks were ruthlessly wiping out their internal opposition. For this project, Shackleton – always the opportunist – was able to enlist some of his *Endurance* crew and saw, perhaps, a future business interest to sustain him into the future. However, the five-month project ended suddenly when the British withdrew from the region. Shackleton and his team were demobilised and sent back to London. When the Bolsheviks overran Murmansk, his scheme faded with the murder of the Russian officials with whom he had been negotiating.

To make a living, Shackleton found himself lecturing at the Philharmonic Hall in London. Here, he would commentate while Hurley's silent film of the crushing and sinking of *Endurance* rolled. From December 1919 until the following May, Shackleton did two shows a day, though the hall was often only half full. *South* was also published – Leonard Hussey had completed Saunders' work – but Shackleton was forced to assign the rights of the book to the executors of one of those who had given him a loan for *Endurance*. And there were other failed business ventures. He spent his time mostly in London, where he had resumed his affair with the actress, Rosalind Chetwynd, returning on occasions to Emily and the family at Eastbourne, where they lived on her small income.

*The Quest Expedition*

Drinking heavily, but aware of his slide, Shackleton began to plan another expedition. After a promise of financial help from the Canadian government for an expedition to the North Pole fell through, an old schoolmate from Dulwich, John Quiller Rowett – who had made his fortune trading rum – came to Shackleton's financial assistance, offering part finance for an expedition. At the outset, Shackleton promised to repay him later from book, lecture and film proceeds, but, as it transpired, Rowett was to meet most of the costs. Due to the lateness of the season, Shackleton soon changed his mind about the Arctic and decided to go south again to Antarctica. The hasty, new plan was to circumnavigate the continent and find and chart the many sub-Antarctic islands. His ship was a wooden sealer named *Foca I* – it was renamed *Quest* at Emily's suggestion. It weighed 125 tons and featured a square-rigged mainmast, but proved to be underpowered and not in the best mechanical shape.

Shackleton rounded up many of his *Endurance* crew, some of whom had not been paid for the previous voyage. But most of them came, for – like him – they wanted just one more time to get away to where their lives had more meaning and purpose. Worsley, Wild, Macklin, McIlroy, Hussey, Kerr and Green sailed again with Shackleton as part of the twenty-strong crew. Among the new men on board was a Canadian geologist named Vibert Douglas and an Australian, George Wilkins. An eighteen-year-old boy scout, James Marr, sailed as a participant in a *Daily Mail* adventure-experience scheme. But this was not

the same Shackleton his loyal men had known; his vitality seemed to have sapped away and he looked ill.

At Madeira, they made repairs, the ship having sailed badly and the engine in trouble. A further halt was called at St Paul Rocks, a scattering of small rocky islets, where they took soundings, and charted and profiled the rocks. At Rio de Janeiro, where they stopped to make further repairs, Shackleton had a heart attack and called in Dr Macklin. It was clear to the doctor how ill he was with heart disease, but since

Shackleton refused an examination, Macklin opted for angina as a diagnosis. Shackleton had experienced a similar attack three years earlier, when in Spitzbergen.

The next port of call was South Georgia, where they arrived on 4 January 1922, passing the familiar sights of Possession Bay and Fortuna Bay. Shackleton and Worsley excitedly pointed out to everybody on board the mountainous terrain they had crossed from King Haakon Bay to Stromness in 1916, recounting their traverse with Tom Crean. They dropped anchor once

Ernest Shackleton and Frank Wild aboard the *Quest*. This is thought to be one of the last photographs of Shackleton.
*Scott Polar Research Institute*

again at Grytviken. He met old friends there, including Fridthjof Jacobsen, the station manager. In the early hours of the morning, Macklin was called to see to Shackleton. He found him suffering another heart attack. A few minutes later, he was dead; it was 5 January. As one of his biographers, Roland Huntford, put it:

The grave of Sir Ernest Shackleton at the Whalers' Graveyard, Grytviken, South Georgia.
*Author's collection*

The last voyage had been an astonishing display of determination. Where most other men would have quietly laid down in bed, he had made himself survive until he had escaped from civilisation.[7]

Emily knew this also. When news arrived of his death and she learned that his remains were on the way back to Britain, accompanied by Hussey, she decided it would be more fitting that her husband be buried in South Georgia. Hussey returned from Montevideo and brought his beloved leader's remains with him. On 5 March, Ernest Shackleton was laid to rest in the Norwegian cemetery adjacent to Grytviken's whaling station, about which he had written his last journal entry on the evening before he died: 'The old smell of dead whale permeates everything: It is a strange and curious place . . . a wonderful evening.' His grave – in the place of burial of long forgotten seamen and whalers, mostly Norwegian – brings a great dignity to a place where the victims of a pelagic oil rush were brought. On the outskirts of this abandoned, rusting, Norwegian whale-processing factory is buried an Irishman who lived and died an inspirational leader-hero of men, a giant during the heroic age of Antarctic exploration. His name and South Georgia are forever conjoined in the history of romantic and heroic exploration. In 1928, a simple granite headstone and kerb were erected. A nine-pointed star, his talisman, surmounts his name. The inscription reads simply: 'Ernest Henry Shackleton, Explorer, Born 15th February 1874, Entered Life Eternal, 5th January 1922'. On the reverse side of the silver granite stone, brought from England, are the words adapted by Shackleton from Robert Browning, the poet he so often quoted: 'I hold that a man should strive to the uttermost for his life's set prize.'

On the northern entrance to King Edward Cove, Grytviken – on a headland called Hope Point – his *Quest* shipmates erected a white cross, planted into a cairn. It points toward the magnetic South Pole, reached during his *Nimrod* expedition. It is ironic that the Royal Geographical Society, which favoured Scott over Shackleton and which gave the Kildare man only token support to his *Nimrod* and *Endurance* expeditions, should in 1932 erect a memorial to him on the outer wall of the society's building in Kensington. Designed by the architect, Sir Edwin Lutyens, the statue by sculptor, Charles Jagger, shows the explorer in his polar anorak and Balaclava, looking down from his niche in the wall on the busy capital city.[8]

How should we judge and compare Shackleton with his rivals, Scott and Amundsen? Sir Raymond Priestly, who served on *Nimrod* in 1907–09, summed him up best:

> For scientific leadership, give me Scott, for swift and efficient travel, Amundsen. But when you are in a hopeless situation, when you are seeing no way out, get down on your knees and pray for Shackleton. Incomparable in adversity, he was the miracle worker who could save your life against all the odds and long after your number was up. The greatest leader that ever came on God's earth, bar none.

19

# THE LEGACY OF THE IRISH POLAR EXPLORERS

*Scarce as the truth is, the supply has always been in excess of the demand.*

GEORGE BERNARD SHAW

How we should regard the collective contribution of Irishmen to the history of polar exploration constitutes the obvious question with which to draw this work to a conclusion. The author's motivation for researching and compiling this history was derived from a personal desire to connect with the various Irishmen engaged in early polar exploration with a view to extracting their personal and unique stories from naval and expedition records and other publications. The hoped-for outcome has uncovered an array of largely forgotten and, consequently, non-honoured and unsung lives, and has answered many questions regarding the contribution made by these men. The time is now right to integrate their life stories and considerable achievements into the wider social, cultural and political histories of Ireland and Britain and, indeed, the histories of continental America and the countries of the Southern Hemisphere.

The Irish identity of many of the heroes of Arctic exploration was not so apparent prior to the partial re-establishment of Irish nationhood, which coincided with the death of Shackleton in January 1922. Post-independence Irish historians have concentrated most of their energies on retelling the history of Anglo-Irish political strife, with less attention being paid to the social and cultural achievements of individual Irishmen within the context of the political union that existed up to 1922. Among the excluded group are the mariners, explorers and scientists who played parts in the military and naval histories of Britain and Ireland, South America, Australia and the USA. Many, in the course of their duty, paid the ultimate price of life, often after having endured much privation, scurvy, disease, insanity and frostbite.

*facing page*
Statue of Commander Francis Crozier in his hometown of Banbridge, Co. Down – a permanent reminder of his heroic status as both sailor and scientist.
There is, perhaps, natural justice in that the only one of the Northwest Passage commanders to have had a significant public monument erected to his memory was the un-knighted Crozier.
*Photo by Kieran Murray*

Frank Hurley's evocative photograph of Tom Crean taken on board *Endurance*; it captures the Irishman's great determination and resolve.
*Royal Geographical Society*

logs and expedition narratives can be difficult. Most of these ordinary seamen were Catholic, often deprived of access to education and usually commissioned from the seaport towns of Co. Cork and adjoining counties. Nevertheless, Tom Crean, Tim and Mortimer McCarthy, John Salmon, Robert Forde and Patrick Keohane deservedly made their mark in the achievements of McClintock, Scott and Shackleton. Their outstanding accomplishments demonstrate how any ordinary but intelligent man could make a considerable contribution to the success of an expedition in the age of sail and ships.

The awarding of knighthoods to many of the Irish officers involved in polar exploration ensured that they, at least, were honoured for their contribution. But just how Irish were the Irish polar knights? They were in the main Protestants, many from Planter forebears. Most had strong family links with Ireland, their families having been domiciled in Ireland for many generations. Their backgrounds, family circumstances and religion influenced their political positions in the maelstrom that was Irish politics in the nineteenth century. The essence of that Christian tradition encouraged the development of individual freedom and responsibility to shape a relationship with God through lived experience. This Irish Protestant tradition is well reflected in the lives and attitudes of Sabine, Beaufort, McClure, Kellett, McClintock, Shackleton and Crozier – who, among that élite band, was the only Irish polar commander not to be knighted, an honour only denied, surely, by his premature death. With the exception of Sabine, an artillery officer who rose to the rank of general, and

The individual, below-decks heroism and dedication to duty of the ordinary seamen and ratings is, regrettably, largely unrecorded in the specific narratives of expedition commanders, and identifying Irishmen from the many ships'

Shackleton, whose maritime experience was gained in the merchant fleet, all were commissioned officers in the Royal Navy. They joined to fight for the Crown in actions and wars against slavery, Spain, France, China, American colonists and Russia from an Ireland governed from London following the savagery of the 1798 Rebellion and its aftermath, and the Act of Union in 1800. Their 'Irishness' may have differed from that of Crean and others like him, but Irish they were. To quote Conor Cruise O'Brien: 'Irishness is not primarily a question of birth or blood or language: it is the condition of being involved in the Irish situation, and usually of being mauled by it. On that definition Swift is more Irish than Goldsmith or Sheridan, although by the usual tests they are Irish and he is pure English.'

Sherard Osborn, in his preface to Robert McClure's *Narrative of the Voyage of HMS Investigator*, declared his main aim for writing was to ensure that

> The work may remain as the history of a great event in naval chronicles, and perhaps awaken in the breasts of future Franklins, Parrys, or McClures, that love of perilous adventure, which must ever form

a most valuable trait in the character of a maritime people.[1]

My own interest was awakened by reading such accounts of heroism, suffering and gallantry, and I have attempted to relate the stories of many Irish lives in the context of international polar history and the accounts of many great exploration events. I have done this without indulging in uncritical praise or by attempting to profile all as heroes, as many fell short of greatness; indeed, some of their polar exploits and expeditions were abject failures.

The exact identity of many other Irish polar seamen is still hidden and more primary research is required before the extent of their polar contributions can be revealed. But each of the Irishmen whose story is related in this volume was motivated by a desire to be useful in endeavours that explored new territories and fields of knowledge. They sought recognition for their skills, fortitude, seamanship, discipline and heroism from both God and man. This they did by daring for duty and glory, and in seeking out the secrets of the frozen lands in the vast polar regions of this earth.

# NOTES & REFERENCES

*Introduction*

1　Quoted in Ann Savours, *The Search for the North West Passage* (London, 1999).

2　Anthony Weir, *Early Ireland – A Field Guide* (Belfast, 1980).

3　John De Courcy Ireland, *Ireland and the Irish in Maritime History* (Dublin, 1986).

4　G.E. Manwaring and Bonamy Dobrée, *The Floating Republic* (London, 1935).

*Chapter 1: Eighteenth-century Exploration*

1　Arthur Dobbs, *An Account of the Countries Adjoining to Hudson's Bay in the North-West Part of America* (New York, 1967).

2　John Barrow, *A Chronological History of Voyages Into the Arctic* (London, 1818).

3　Desmond Clarke, *Arthur Dobbs Esquire, 1689–1765: Surveyor-General of Ireland, Prospector and Governor of North Carolina* (North Carolina, 1957).

4　Ibid. p. 17.

5　Captain Oates, who perished with Captain Scott in 1912, is perhaps the best-known hero of the Irish regiment. His heroic sacrifice was immortalised by his statement to his colleagues as he departed into the polar blizzard: 'I am just going outside and may be some time.'

6　John Barrow, op. cit. pp. 271–86.

7　Desmond Clarke, op. cit.

8　John Barrow, op. cit. p. 285.

9　*Dictionary of Irish Biography* (forthcoming).

10　Ibid.

11　Henry Boylan, *A Dictionary of Irish Biography* (Dublin, 1998).

12　'Antarctica', *Reader's Digest* (1985).

13　M.J. Ross, *Ross in the Antarctic* (Whitby, 1982).

14　Ibid. p. 13.

*Chapter 2: Bransfield Sights the Antarctic Peninsula*

1　James Cook, *Journal of the* Resolution *Voyage in 1772–1775 on Discovery of the Southern Hemisphere* (London, 1775).

2　R.J. Campbell (ed.) *The Discovery of the South Shetland Islands* (London, 2000).

3　John Miers, 'Account of the Discovery of New South Shetland', *Edinburgh Philosophical Transactions*, iii (1820), pp. 367–80.

4　Irishmen were pivotal in the founding and development of many national navies, including the US navy (Commodore John Barry of Wexford), the Argentine navy (Admiral William Brown of Foxford, Co. Mayo) and the Chilean navy (Bernardo O'Higgins, whose father was born in Co. Meath).

5　R.J. Campbell, op. cit. p. 5.

6　*Gravestone Inscriptions in Co. Cork*, Cork Historical and Archaeological Society (Cork, 1990), p. 91.

7　*Journal of Cork Historical and Archaeological Society*, no. 153.

8　*Cork Examiner*, 5 Sept. 1936.

9　A.G.E. Jones, 'Edward Bransfield Master R.N.', *Mariners' Mirror*, 1966, vol. 52.

10　Cove was renamed Queenstown in 1848 when Queen Victoria visited. In 1922, following the establishment of the Irish Free State, it reverted to its original name, though with a phonetic spelling, Cobh – *bh* in Irish is sounded as *v* in English.

11  'The Press Gangs and Ireland', article on the Website www.irishships.com (2002).

12  Henry Boylan, op. cit.

13  ADM 51/1446, Public Record Office, London.

14  Ibid.

15  Colman O'Mahony, 'Press Gangs Off the Cork Coast 1755–1812', *Harbour Lights*, Journal of the Great Island Historical Society (Cork), 1988.

16  Ibid.

17  Ibid.

18  If his recorded date of birth – 1785 – is correct, he was no more than eighteen.

19  ADM 35/1989, Public Record Office, London, treasurer's pay book on *Ville de Paris*, August 1801–January 1804, p. 23.

20  G.E. Manwaring and Bonamy Dobrée, op. cit.

21  John de Courcy Ireland, op. cit.

22  Midshipman Blake became, eventually, Admiral Patrick Blake who was engaged in the first China war and was captain on the *Juno* in the Pacific, 1845–49.

23  John Miers, op. cit. pp. 367–80.

24  'Antarctica', *Reader's Digest* (1985).

25  R.J. Campbell, op. cit. p. 99.

26  Sir Clements Markham, *The Lands of Silence* (Cambridge, 1921).

27  *Literary Gazette*, 3 Nov. 1821.

28  *Journal of the Cork Historical and Archaeological Society*, 1990.

29  *James Caird Society Newsletter*, no. 6, October 2000.

30  D.H. O'Brien, *The Escapes of Captain O'Brien RN 1804–1808* (London, 1932).

31  D.H. O'Brien, *My Adventures During the Late War* (London, 1839), 2 vols.

Chapter 3: Sabine and Crozier Enter the Arctic

1  'Lament for Francis Crozier' by Frank Nugent, written in Peel Sound on 10 August 2001.

2  L. Stephen and S. Lee (eds.), *The Dictionary of National Biography* (Oxford, 1917).

3  Francis J. Woodward, *Portrait of Jane* (London, 1951), p. 98.

4  Frederick Boase, *Modern English Biography* (Truro, 1892), vol. 1.

5  *Transactions of the Linnean Society*, vol. xii.

6  John Ross, *A Voyage of Discovery in H.M. Ships* Isabella *and* Alexander *for the purposes of exploring Baffin Bay and inquiring into the probability of a North-West Passage* (London, 1819).

7  Edward Sabine, 'Esquimaux of the West Coast of Greenland', *Quarterly Journal of Science*, 1819.

8  M.J. Ross, op. cit.

9  The controversy arising from John Ross' erroneous charting of the Croker Mountains caused a rift between him and his young nephew, James Clark Ross. John Ross resented his nephew siding with Parry, one of his adversaries. The rift took many years to heal.

10  Paul Hackney, 'Sir Edward Sabine' in John Wilson Foster (ed.), *Nature in Ireland*, (Dublin, 1997), p. 333.

11  French-Canadian voyageurs were trappers and fur traders employed by two rival furtrading companies, the Hudson's Bay Company and the North West Company.

12  ADM/196/36/495, Public Record Office, London.

13  Ann Savours (1999), op. cit. p. 83.

14  Ibid. p. 124. Jane Griffin is said to have called James Clark Ross, 'The handsomest man in the navy'.

15  May Fluhmann, *Second in Command* (Yellowknife, 1976).

Chapter 4: Sabine, Lloyd and Beaufort Lead the Way

1  L. Stephen and S. Lee, op. cit.

2  Wellington – Arthur Wellesley – was born in Dublin and was then master-general of the ordnance. A Tory, he became British prime minister in January 1828.

3  Daniel O'Connell, a Catholic lawyer, was elected MP for Clare in 1829; however, the law prevented Catholics from becoming MPs, government ministers or judges. After many years of agitation, the government conceded these rights.

4  L. Stephen and S. Lee, op. cit.

5  *Dictionary of Irish Biography* (Dublin, forthcoming).

6  He died there on 17 January 1881.

7  C. Mollan, W. Davis and B. Finnucane, *Some People and Places in Irish Science and Technology* (Dublin, 1985).

8  Paul Hackney, op. cit. p. 334.

9  M.J. Ross, op. cit. p. 16. Beaufort was at the time hydrographer of the navy and a member of the Royal Society's physics and meteorology committee.

10  L. Stephen and S. Lee, op. cit.

11  Alfred Friendly, *Beaufort of the Admiralty* (London, 1973).

12  The Ascendancy in Ireland and the English parliament refused to allow Catholic schools. It was only in 1793 that Catholics were given the right to vote, to go to university and hold certain state positions.

Officially, only Church of Ireland establishments were recognised.

13 R.C. Mollan, W. Davis and B. Finnucane (1985), op. cit. pp. 20–1.

14 Alfred Friendly, op. cit. p. 234.

15 ADM/196/3/77, Public Record Office, London.

16 Alfred Friendly, op. cit. p. 102.

17 Hubert Butler, *The Sub-Prefect Should Have Held His Tongue and Other Essays* (London, 1990).

18 Landlordism and absentee landlords were a focus of Maria's writing; she wrote, 'An Irish landlord must live among the people from whom he draws his sustenance.' Maria's brother, with the help of the Catholic priest and the Protestant rector of Edgeworthstown, founded there a unique interdenominational school that survived for ten years. Maria's novels and children's stories were models of morality based on good neighbourliness, religion and common sense, rather than the fear of God or compliance with the Ten Commandments. When the Famine was at its height and Maria, by then a woman of 80, was launching appeals on behalf of the stricken people of Edgeworthstown, a present arrived for her from America. She was soon able to distribute 150 barrels of wheat and rice from the children of Boston. Hubert Butler remarked that, though Maria Edgeworth is not regarded today as a great novelist, her books and writings are still significant and remarkable for their integrity and campaigning zeal. He maintained that the Edgeworth's greatest achievement was the lives they led, as brilliant personalities who set out not only to observe society, but also to change it. Maria was a propagandist for the common good; Hubert Butler, op. cit.

19 Mr and Mrs S.C. Hall, *Ireland: Its Scenery and Character* (London, 1843).

20 Albert Friendly, op. cit. p. 143.

*Chapter 5: Crozier, Captain of* Terror

1 'Extracts from C.J. Sullivan's narrative on board HMS *Erebus* June 19th 1843', *Polar Record*, vol. x.

2 May Fluhmann, op. cit.

3 There were four civilian scientists aboard *Erebus* and *Terror* whose official title on this expedition was surgeon or surgeon assistant: Robert McCormick and Joseph Dalton Hooker served on *Erebus* in these respective capacities, and John Robinson and David Lyall served on *Terror*.

4 M.J. Ross, op. cit. p. 28.

5 Sir James Clark Ross, *A Voyage of Discovery and Research in the Southern and Antarctic Regions During*

*the Years 1839–43* (London, 1847), vol. 1., p. xxi.

6 Journal of Sergeant William Cunningham, D/869/1, Public Record Office of Northern Ireland, Belfast.

7 Sir James Clark Ross, op. cit.

8 'Antarctica', *Reader's Digest* (1985).

9 Sir James Clark Ross, op. cit. p. 114.

10 Quoted in Ann Savours and Anita McConnell, 'History of Rossbank Observatory', *Tasmania Annals of Science,* 39, 1982, p. 538.

11 Ann Savours and Anita McConnell, 'History of Rossbank Observatory, Tasmania', *Annals of Science*, 39, 1982, pp. 527–64.

12 Francis J. Woodward, op. cit. p. 229.

13 Sir James Clark Ross, op. cit. p. 185.

14 Ibid. p. 183.

15 M.J. Ross, op. cit. p. 89.

16 Sir James Clark Ross, op. cit. p. 217.

17 Ibid. pp. 219–20.

18 M.J. Ross, op. cit. p. 150.

19 Ibid. p. 152.

20 Ibid. p. 155.

21 Ibid. p. 158.

22 J.E. Davis, 'A letter from the Antarctic', *Polar Record*, vol. x.

23 Sir James Clarke Ross, op. cit.

24 J.E. Davis, op. cit. p. 595.

25 Ibid. p. 166.

26 After disputes with Spain over sovereignty, Britain annexed the islands in 1833.

27 M.J. Ross, op. cit. p. 206.

28 Ann Savours and Anita McConnell, op. cit.

29 Sir James Clark Ross, op. cit.

*Chapter 6: The Franklin Expedition*

1 The words of Charles Kingsley, quoted in the introduction to the *Memoir of the Late Captain Francis Rawdon Moira Crozier R.N., F.R.S., F.R.A.S., of H.M.S. Terror* (Dublin, 1859). The memoir was printed for the committee for the Crozier memorial by William Kirkwell, Great Brunswick Street, Dublin in 1859 in honour of Sir John Franklin's second-in-command, Captain Crozier of Banbridge, Co. Down.

2 Richard J. Cyriax, *Sir John Franklin's Last Arctic Expedition* (London, 1939), pp. 17–27.

3 M.J. Ross, op. cit. p. 247.

4 Ibid. p. 248.

5 Alfred Friendly, op. cit. pp. 269–70.

6 Francis J. Woodward, op. cit. p. 251.

7 L.P. Kirwan, op. cit. p. 160.

8 May Fluhmann, op. cit. p. 76.

9 St Mary's, Limerick, parish records.

10  Francis J. Woodward, op. cit. p. 252.

11  M.J. Ross, op. cit. 1982, p. 250.

*Chapter 7: McClure, McClintock and Kellett Search for Franklin*

1  Sir Clements Markham, *Life of Admiral Sir Leopold McClintock* (London, 1909).

2  Ann Savours (1999), op. cit.

3  Interestingly, Jane's father, John Elgee – rector of St Iberius' Church, Wexford – tended to the spiritual needs in the last moments of Bagnell Harvey, Captain Keogh, Cornelius Grogan and Dr John Colclough, leaders of the United Irishmen. These liberal, Protestant Irishmen were hanged on Wexford Bridge for their involvement in the 1798 insurrection in Wexford. That John Elgee was well liked emerges from the dreadful day in 1798 when rebels took the town of Wexford and all Protestants went in fear of their lives. Anyone who expressed strong political opinions was condemned as an Orangeman – the natural enemy of the day to the Catholic population – and tortured and put to death. Throughout that terrifying month, the Elgees remained unmolested in the rectory, which today forms part of White's Hotel.

4  Wexford and Rathaspeck (Church of Ireland) registry of baptism, marriage and burials, 1778–1889, vol. 23.

5  Terence de Vere White, *The Parents of Oscar Wilde – Sir William and Lady Wilde* (London, 1967).

6  ADM/196/1/395, Public Record Office, London.

7  Patrick F. Power in *Tempest Annual* (Dundalk, 1974).

8  Sir Clements Markham (1909), op. cit. p. 8.

9  Ibid.

10  ADM/196/1/450, Public Record Office, London.

11  Seven years later, in 1857, Leopold's youngest sister, Emily, married Mr G. Crozier MA, a nephew of the famous polar commander.

12  Sir Clements Markham (1909), op. cit. pp. 56–7.

13  Ibid. pp. 51–2.

14  Neville W. Poulsom and J.A.L Myres, *British Polar Exploration and Research: A Historical and Medallic Record with Biographies 1818–1999* (London, 2000).

15  Sir Clements Markham (1909), op. cit. p. 74.

16  Ibid. p. 78.

17  Sir Clements Markham (1921), op. cit.

18  Ibid.

19  Referred to as Hieels in Poulsom and Myers (2000).

*Chapter 8: McClure and* Investigator *Search from the Pacific*

1  Sir Clements Markham (1909), op. cit.

2  Alex Armstrong, *Personal Narrative of the Discovery of North West Passage* (London, 1857), p. 27.

3  Johann Miertsching, *The Arctic Diary of Johann Miertsching 1850–1854* (Toronto, 1967), p. 22.

4  Ibid.

5  Alex Armstrong, op. cit. p. 46.

6  Ibid. p. 70.

7  Ibid. p. 78.

8  Robert McClure, *The Discovery of the North West Passage by H.M.S.* Investigator (London, 1856), p. 78.

9  Ibid. p. 87.

10  Ibid. p. 106.

11  Johann Miertsching, op. cit. p. 75.

12  Ibid. p. 88.

13  Ibid. p. 122.

14  Robert McClure (1856), op. cit. p. 204.

15  Johann Miertsching, op. cit. p. 144.

16  Ibid. p. 156.

17  Robert McClure (1856), op. cit. p. 236.

18  Ibid. p. 228.

19  Ibid. p. 239.

20  Johann Miertsching, op. cit. p. 170.

21  Ibid. p. 174.

22  Ibid. p. 174.

23  Robert McClure (1856), op. cit. pp. 249–50.

*Chapter 9: The Belcher Expedition*

1  From a letter written by Robert McClure to his sister, Mrs Thomas E. Wright, of Dublin, from HMS *Investigator*, Bay of Mercy, Polar Sea, dated 10 April 1853. The contents of the letter were communicated to a Dublin newspaper by Dr Wilde, cited in Robert McClure, *The Arctic Dispatches – Containing an Account of the North-West Passage* (London, 1854).

2  Alfred Friendly, op. cit. p. 323.

3  The Carlow-born Professor Samuel Haughton (1821–97) was a polymath whose interests included geology, medicine, mathematics, tides, currents and climate. He is also accredited with the invention of the humane hangman's drop; Henry Boylan (ed.), *A Dictionary of Irish Biography* (Dublin,1998); Sir Clements Markham (1909) op. cit.

4  Neville Poulsom and J.A.L. Myres, op. cit.

5  Dr Tadhg O'Keeffe, *Fethard Co. Tipperary – A Guide to the Medieval Town* (Fethard, 1997).

6  *Clonmel Chronicle*, 3 March 1875.

7  ADM/196/36/743, Public Record Office, London.

8 Berthold Seeman, *Narrative of the Voyage of HMS Herald 1845–51 Under the Command of Captain Henry Kellett, R.N., C.B.* (London, 1853), 2 vols.

9 Sir Clements Markham (1909), op. cit. p. 152.

10 Sir Clements Markham, *The Arctic Navy List 1773–1873* (London, 1875).

11 Ibid. p. 164

12 Ibid. p. 165.

13 Ibid. p. 167.

14 Johann Miertsching, op. cit. p. 203.

15 Sir Clements Markham (1909), op. cit. p. 178.

16 Ann Savours (1999), op. cit. p. 280.

17 Neville Poulsom and J.A.L. Myres, op. cit.

18 Sir Clements Markham (1909), op. cit. pp. 187–8.

*Chapter 10: McClintock's Voyage of the* Fox

1 On reading the record found at Victory Point; Leopold McClintock, *Voyage of the* Fox *in the Arctic Seas* (London, 1859).

2 Ibid.

3 Ann Savours (1999), op. cit.

4 Leopold McClintock, op. cit. pp. 4–5.

5 Ann Savours (1999), op. cit.

6 Leopold McClintock, op. cit. pp. 74–5.

7 Ibid. p. 182.

8 Ibid. p. 187.

9 Ibid. p. 283.

10 National Maritime Museum HSR/2/6 and Scott Polar Research Institute 54/20/1.

11 Leopold McClintock, op. cit. p. 293.

12 Ibid. p. 298.

13 It is believed now that the ship came ashore at O'Reilly Island, west of the Adelaide Peninsula, with some of the returned party aboard.

14 Ann Savours (1999), op. cit. p. 299.

15 From an article in the *Dundalk Democrat* by Garrett McGowan, 5 Aug. 1967.

16 Samuel Haughton, 'On fossils brought home from the Arctic regions in 1859, by Capt. Sir F.L. McClintock', *Philosophical Transactions of the Royal Society*, 1862, vol. 3, pp. 53–8.

*Chapter 11: After the Franklin Search and the Nares North Pole Expedition*

1 Dr Corrigan was speaking at the Mansion House on 27 December 1859; J. Dalton and J.R. Flanagan, *History of Dundalk and Its Environs* (Dundalk, 1864).

2 Owen Beattie and John Geiger, *Frozen in Time* (London, 1987).

3 K.T.H. Ferrar, 'Lead and the Last Franklin Expedition', *Journal of Archaeological Science*, 1993, no. 20, pp. 399–409.

4 Robert McClure (1856), op. cit. p. 380.

5 In 1881, he took a cruise with his brother, Alfred, an eminent physician with a very extensive consultancy practice in Dublin and who was president of the College of Surgeons in Dublin from 1880–81. He lived at 21 Merrion Square, a place where Leopold stayed when he was in Ireland. The cruise, aboard *Northampton*, was intended to improve Alfred's constitution. In October, however, he took ill and died.

6 *Dictionary of Irish Biography* (Dublin, forthcoming).

7 Obituary notice for Admiral Sir Henry Kellett; *Clonmel Chronicle*, 3 Mar. 1875.

8 Ibid.

9 L. Stephen and S. Lee, op. cit.

10 Alfred Friendly, op. cit. p. 331.

11 C. Mollan, W. Davis and B. Finnucane, *More People and Places in Irish Science and Technology* (Dublin, 1990).

12 Neville Poulsom and J.A.L. Myres, op. cit.

13 Ibid.

14 Bray Cualann Historical Society records.

15 ADM/38/8332, Public Record Office, London.

16 George Nares RN, *The Official Report of the Recent Arctic Expedition* (London, 1876), p. 67.

17 Ibid. p. 72

18 ADM 171/38, Public Record Office, London.

*Chapter 12: The Private Arctic Expeditions of Henry Gore-Booth*

1 Kit and Cyril O'Ceírín, *Women of Ireland: A Biographical Dictionary* (Galway, 1996).

2 Obituary from the *Sligo Independent*, Jan. 1900, reprinted in the *Sligo Champion*, 13 Oct. 1937.

3 Gifford Lewis, *Eva Gore-Booth and Esther Rope: A Biography* (London, 1988).

4 Esther Roper, *Prison Letters of Countess Markievicz* (London, 1934).

5 John C. McTernan, 'Here's to Their Memory', *Profiles of Distinguished Sligonians of Bygone Days* (Cork, 1977).

6 John C. McTernan, *A Sligo Miscellany: A Chronology of People, Places and Events of Other Days* (Sligo, 2000).

7 Clive Holland, *Arctic Exploration and Development – An Encyclopaedia* (New York, 1994), p. 315.

8 *Sligo Independent*, 25 Oct. 1884.

9 His will showed his estate was valued at £126,500 on which £32,086 duty was paid. He was succeeded in ownership of Lissadell estate by Jocelyn Augustus Richard, his second-born (1869), who

played an important part in the Irish co-operative agricultural movement, devoting his time and efforts to the building of creameries and cultivating bulbs. He became the first landlord in Ireland to sell his estate to his tenants after the 1903 Land Act, an action motivated by principle.

*Chapter 13: Jerome Collins and John Cole of Cork*

1 James Lyons, 'Corkman in the Arctic', *Cork Examiner*, 3 July 2001.

2 A.A. Hoehling, *The* Jeannette *Expedition* (London, 1967).

3 Emma De Long (ed.), *George Washinton De Long: The Voyage of the* Jeannette (London, 1883), 2 vols.

4 The *Jeannette* was formerly *Pandora*, used by Sir Allen Young who discovered the bones and relics of Franklin's party on Beechey Island.

5 Emma De Long, op. cit. pp. 206–8.

6 In an interview with the *Washington Post* prior to departure, De Long referred to the only non-navy members of the expedition crew, Collins and Raymond Lee Newcomb – the naturalist – as 'two scientific accessories'; this annoyed Collins.

7 Emma De Long, op. cit. pp. 797–800.

8 Dr Fridtjof Nansen, *Furthest North* (London, 1898), vol. 1.

9 *New York Irish American*.

*Chapter 14: Scott's* Discovery *Expedition*

1 *Report of the Sixth Geographical Congress* (London, 1896) p. 780.

2 J.R.H. Weaver (ed.), *Dictionary of National Biography, 1922–1930* (Oxford, 1937).

3 In its first year it enrolled 36 students, and during its existence was to enrol students from France, Norway and Jamaica. It survived until 1836 when the Quaker influence in the area was so dispersed it was unable to sustain itself. Among the 1,000 students who passed through its classrooms to learn classics, history, maths, geography, writing and composition were Edmund Burke, Napper Tandy and Paul Cullen who, as Cardinal Cullen, was to reorganise and transform the Catholic Church in Ireland. Abraham's son, Richard, attended Trinity College before taking over the school in Ballitore, and his son, Abraham, also managed the school. He was more conservative than his father, and he narrowed the curriculum and restricted access to Quakers only. The school closed to boarders in 1802 and was reopened to them in 1806 by James White. However, the tradition of learning, letters and poetry was continued in the family. As Quakers, they were set apart from the establishment and the wider – Catholic and Protestant – community. From this position, they were able to do much good work, which included distributing aid during the Famine years.

4 She married William Leadbeater, became the post-mistress of Ballitore and knew everybody in the area and their business. Her *Annals of Ballitore* is a splendid local history of the time. She also compiled and published her parents' letters, *Memoirs and Letters of Richard and Elizabeth Shackleton* (London, 1822) and knew and collaborated with Maria Edgeworth, Beaufort's sister-in-law, who wrote the introductory notes and a preface to Mary's charming book entitled, *Cottage Dialogues Among the Irish Peasantry*. Published in 1811, it contains literal transcripts of the language of the Irish tenant people, discoursing on subjects such as fidelity, matrimony, courtship and slander. It is, as Maria says, the language 'of the manner of being of the lower Irish'. The book's circulation list, published at the beginning of the book, includes Dr Beaufort, Mrs Croker, Mrs Edgeworth, R. Edgeworth, Miss Edgeworth, William Lefanu (Charlemont Street, Dublin) and Abraham, Sarah and Eliza Shackleton. There is a sense of benevolent superiority laced with levity about the tone of the observations of both Maria and Mary.

5 Harold Begbie, *Shackleton: A Memory* (London, 1922), p. 14.

6 Ann Savours, *The Voyages of* Discovery (London, 1992), p. 30.

7 David Murphy, 'Hartley Travers Ferrar: Antarctic Explorer', *Dún Laoghaire Journal*, no. 10, 2001.

8 Quoted in Michael Smith, *An Unsung Hero* (Cork, 2000), p. 32.

9 Quoted in Ann Savours (1992), op. cit. p. 39.

10 Roland Huntford, *Shackleton* (London, 1985), p. 96.

12 Quoted in Ann Savours (1992), op. cit. p. 64.

13 Quoted in Roland Huntford, op. cit. p. 148.

*Chapter 15: Shackleton's* Nimrod *Expedition*

1 Quoted in Roland Huntford, op. cit. p. 300.

2 *Dictionary of Irish Biography* (Dublin, forthcoming).

3 Borchgrevink, a Norwegian, led a British Expedition in 1898–1900 aboard *Southern Cross*. He landed on the Ross Ice Shelf from which a sledging party using dogs reached a 'furthest south' of 78° 83' 23" in February 1900.

4 Sir Ernest Shackleton, *The Heart of the Antarctic –*

*Being the Story of the British Antarctic Expedition 1907–1909* (London, 1909), p. 184.

5  Quoted in Roland Huntford, op. cit. p. 263.

6  Sir Ernest Shackleton (1909), op. cit. p. 354.

7  Quoted in Roland Huntford, op. cit. p. 329.

*Chapter 16: Antarctic Expedition of* Terra Nova

1  Tennyson's words were carved on the memorial cross erected by the crew of *Terra Nova* on Observation Hill to the memory of Scott's polar party.

2  Terry Connolly, 'Tim McCarthy – Lower Cove', *Kinsale Record*, 1999, no. 9, published by Kinsale and District Local History Society.

3  John Thuillier, *History of Kinsale* (Kinsale, 2001).

4  Terry Connolly, op. cit.

5  ADM/188/309, Public Record Office, London.

6  Agreement and account of *Terra Nova*, MS 12, Scott Polar Research Institute.

7  ADM/188/244, Public Record Office, London.

8  The *Discovery*, which had cost £50,000 to build, had been sold for £10,000 in January 1905 by a joint committee of the RGS and RS to the Hudson's Bay Company, and was thus not available for this expedition.

9  The camp, adjacent to the racecourse on the plains of Kildare where the Irish Derby is run, is a short distance from the birthplace of Shackleton.

10  Apsley Cherry-Garrard, *The Worst Journey in the World* (London, 1948), p. 159.

11  Ibid. p. 168.

12  R.F. Scott, *Scott's Last Expedition: Extracts from the Personal Diary of Capt. R.F. Scott R.N.* (London, 1923).

13  Ibid. 26 Nov. 1911.

14  Ibid. 1 Dec. 1911.

15  Ibid. 4 Dec. 1911.

16  Ibid. 5 Dec. 1911.

17  Ibid. 9 Dec. 1911.

18  Ibid. 11 Dec. 1911.

19  Apsley Cherry-Garrard, op. cit.

20  Patrick Keohane, log of cruise *Terra Nova*, MS 825/2, Scott Polar Research Institute.

21  R.F. Scott, op. cit. 4 Jan. 1912.

22  Cherry-Garrard, op. cit. ch. 10.

23  Ibid. pp. 462–63.

24  R.F. Scott, op. cit. 17 Jan. 1912.

25  Ibid. 29 Mar. 1912.

26  *Cork Examiner*, 5 May 1914.

27  Alongside the military and the police, the coastguard service was considered by the IRA (Irish Republican Army) to be another component of British rule in Ireland. During the last months of hostilities – before the Truce – many buildings were destroyed in west Cork as the IRA believed they were being prepared to house British reinforcements. Among these buildings were the coastguard stations at Howes Strand, the Galley Head and Rosscarbery.

28  Sheila later married Tom Madigan from Limerick; their son, Patrick, now lives in Tavistock, Devon and has continued the family military tradition with service in the Royal Air Force.

29  *Cork Examiner*, 1 Oct. 1985.

30  Michael O'Brien, in an article in the *Cork Holly Bough*, Cork, 1988.

31  From a letter from Valerie Tait to the curator of Kerry County Museum.

32  The graveyard is the burial ground to generations of Cork mariners and hundreds of naval casualties of the First World War, including F.D. Parslow, a Victoria Cross recipient. Two mass graves contain the remains of victims of the *Lusitania*, torpedoed off the Cork coast on 7 May 1916 by a German U-boat. The 'Gorgeous Gael', Jack Doyle, the world heavyweight-boxing contender, was buried there in 1978. Another 'Cobhie' buried in the cemetery is Surgeon James Verling (1787–1858), a Fellow of the Royal Geographical Society who sailed on the *Northumberland* as it carried Napoleon to exile on the island of St Helena. At St Helena, Verling accepted an offer to serve as surgeon to the defeated emperor and stayed there until 1820. He died at Bellavista, Cobh in 1858. A republican plot dating from the Irish War of Independence (1919–21) contains the local dead of a different military campaign. This graveyard poignantly reflects the mixed history and loyalties of maritime Cobh.

*Chapter 17: Epic Voyage of the* Endurance

1  Harold Begbie, op. cit. p. 48.

2  Roland Huntford, op. cit. p. 344.

3  Sir Ernest Shackleton, *South* (London, 1919), p. 36.

4  Judith Lee Hallock, 'Thomas Crean', *Polar Record*, 22 (140), 1985.

5  Sir Ernest Shackleton (1919), op. cit. p. 76.

6  Judith Lee Hallock, op. cit. p. 9.

7  Ibid.

8  F.A. Worsley, *Shackleton's Boat Journey* (London, 1940), p. 33.

9  A type of wind known as katabatic (down-flowing): cold air moving on the surface of the ice cap

flowing towards the coast with warmer airs above.

10 F.A. Worsley, op. cit. p. 75.
11 Sir Ernest Shackleton (1919), op. cit. p. 167.
12 Ibid. pp. 168–9.
13 F.A. Worsley, op. cit.
14 Sir Ernest Shackleton (1919), op. cit. p. 177.
15 Ibid. p. 177.
16 F.A. Worsely, op. cit. p. 104.
17 Ibid. p. 212.
18 Ibid. pp. 156–7.
19 Harold Begbie, op. cit. p. 43.
20 F.A. Worsely, op. cit. p. 185–6.
21 Ibid. pp. 189–90.
22 Frank Hurley, *Argonauts of the South* (London, 1925), pp. 248–76.
23 R.K. Headland, 'Principal Expeditions During the "Heroic Age" of Antarctica' in J. Piggott (ed.), *Shackleton: The Antarctic and Endurance* (London, 2000).

*Chapter 18: Shackleton and Crean's Final Voyages*

1 MS 599/161, Scott Polar Research Institute.
2 Michael Smith, op. cit.
3 T. Ryle Dwyer, *Tans, Terror and Troubles: Kerry's Real Fighting Story 1913–23* (Cork, 2001).
4 Jim Herlihy, *The Royal Irish Constabulary: A Short History and Genealogical Guide* (Dublin, 1997).
5 Judith Lee Hallock, op. cit. pp. 665–78.
6 Tom Crean's contribution to the achievements of both Scott and Shackleton in the heroic age of Antarctic exploration is now better recognised in Ireland as a result of expeditions and TV documentaries, the publication of his biography by Michael Smith in 2000 and by the mounting of an Antarctic exhibition in the Kerry County Museum in Tralee in 2002. A bronze statue to the memory of Tom Crean was unveiled in his native Anascaul on 20 July 2003 in the presence of his daughters, Mary and Eileen, and the son of Lieutenant Teddy Evans.
7 Roland Huntford, op. cit.
8 Shackleton was not the first Irishman to die on South Georgia. A notable zoologist, Gerard E.H. Barrett-Hamilton, BA, FZS, MRIA, also died there. He was conducting an investigation on behalf of the Colonial Office and the British Natural History Museum into the indiscriminate slaughter of whales in the seas round the Falkland Islands and South Georgia. He was struck down with pneumonia and died on 17 January 1914, aged 42. His remains were brought home and laid to rest in the churchyard of Duncannon, Co. Wexford on 2 March 1914. Barrett was born in India of Irish parentage in 1871; when he was three, the family moved home to Ireland at Kilmanock, Co. Wexford. His parents were Captain Samuel Barrett, of Dublin, and Laura Thomson, of York. At Trinity College, Cambridge, Gerard formed a remarkable friendship with Edward Wilson, the illustrator of Barrett-Hamilton's *History of British Mammals*. This was the same Edward Wilson who accompanied Scott and Shackleton in 1902 to their then 'furthest south' and who perished with Captain Scott in January 1912. Barrett-Hamilton was the author of a major work on British mammals, which ran to fifteen volumes; Edward Wilson illustrated the first fourteen parts. *See* obituary article by C.B. Moffat in the *Irish Naturalist*, vol. xxiii, 1914.

*Chapter 19: The Legacy of the Irish Polar Explorers*

1 Robert McClure (1856), op. cit.

# GLOSSARY OF POLAR & NAUTICAL TERMS & CONVERSION TABLES

*Able Bodied Seaman or Rating (AB)*
A seaman able to perform all duties.

*Beset*
The approach of floating ice on all sides, leaving no opening for advance or retreat, leaving the vessel unmanageable.

*Bight*
An inlet, hollow in a bay of ice or ice floe.

*Bore*
To force a vessel through loose or moveable pack.

*Brash*
A small ice fragment from a floe, which has broken up.

*Captain*
A navy officer in command of a warship, below commodore or rear admiral.

*Commander*
A naval officer next in rank below captain.

*Field ice*
A sheet of ice of such extent that its termination is not bounded by the horizon.

*Floe*
A portion of an expanse of floating pack ice, which has become disconnected from the pack.

*Iceberg*
A mass of ice broken off (calving) from discharging glaciers at the edge of the sea by the force of gravity which float and are carried by currents into the sea. Only a seventh of their bulk appears above water.

*Ice blink*
A reflection in the atmosphere over pack ice, seen long before the pack itself can be seen.

*Ice foot*
The low fringe of ice formed on the edge of polar lands by sea spray and the banks of ice which skirt many parts of polar shores.

*Ice Master*
A whaling captain or mate selected for their experience of polar waters and ice. They usually piloted the vessel from the crow's nest or from a plank or platform (ice plank) erected above the deck which allowed the pilot to move from port to starboard while piloting the vessel through the pack.

*Innuit*
A term used to describe the natives of the Arctic regions of what is now modern Greenland, Canada and Siberia, also referred to as Eskimos (raw meat eaters) or earlier as Arctic Highlanders. In the nineteenth century they were nomadic hunters who lived on the Arctic shores on a diet of 100 per cent meat from seal, fish, caribou, musk-oxen and game.

*Lead*

Any open cracks or separation of ice floes offering navigation within an area of pack ice.

*Master*

A seaman or officer certified to be a ship's captain or a captain of a merchant ship.

*Master's Mate or Midshipman*

A naval officer of rank between naval cadet and sub-lieutenant.

*Nip*

When two floes are in motion and approaching each other, the result is a grinding action in passing or until their impetus is expended, which destroys the meeting surfaces and raises long ridges of curled or thrown-up ice. A vessel caught between opposing floes becomes nipped and sometimes overwhelmed or crushed. Vessels preparing for polar service were structurally strengthened in anticipation of such eventualities.

*Old ice*

Ice formed in previous seasons and heavier than young ice, with more density and is often glassy in appearance.

*Ordinary Seaman (OS)*

Lowest rank of seaman, below able-bodied status.

*Pack ice or pack*

A close pack is when broken floes are driven together; pressure is constantly varying due to wind and current and the position of the pack relative to land and open water; it may cover a mile or many miles. It cannot be safely travelled over until cemented together by freezing. An open pack is when the pieces do not touch.

*Petty Officer*

A naval non-commissioned officer.

*Riptide*

A strong surface current running from the shore.

*Scurvy*

Scurvy is the oldest known deficiency disease which first manifests itself as extravascular bleeding. Cumulative hemorrhages break out all over the body in crippling succession, leading to swolen ankles and severe pain at knee joints and hamstrings. Gums become inflamed and teeth loosen while the victim experiences lassitude, shortness of breadth and emotional distress. It is caused by a lack of vitamin C, which was not discovered until early in the twentieth century, although it was known that citrus fruit, fresh vegetables and raw meat prevented and cured the disease.

*Tacking*

The direction in which a ship moves as determined by the position of its sails and regarded in terms of the direction of the wind (port or starboard tack).

*Young ice*

Ice immediately formed on the surface of the sea when the temperature is sufficiently low and when not disturbed by currents and swells or ice of the present season; usually clean white, on surface ice.

---

*Fahrenheit–Celsius Conversion Table*

To convert degrees of fahrenheit to celsius, deduct 32, multiply by 5 and divide by 9. Some examples are given below as a guide.

| Fahrenheit | Celsius |
| --- | --- |
| +32° | 0° |
| 0° | -18° |
| -10° | -23° |
| -20° | -29° |
| -30° | -34.5° |
| -40° | -40° |
| -50° | -45.5° |

*Measurements: Imperial–Metric Conversion Table*

| | |
| --- | --- |
| 1 nautical mile (2026 yards) | 1.85 km |
| 1 statute mile (1760 yards) | 1.6 km |
| 1 yard (3 feet) | 91.4 cm |
| 1 foot (12 inches) | 30.48 cm |

*Weights: Imperial–Metric Conversion Table*

| | |
| --- | --- |
| 1 ton (2240 pounds) | 1016 kg |
| 1 pound (16 ounces) | .453 kg |

*Money: Sterling–Euro Conversion Table (Aug. 2003)*

| | |
| --- | --- |
| 1 guinea (21 shillings) | 1 euro 52 cents |
| 1 pound/£1 (20 shillings) | 1 euro 45 cents |
| 1 crown (5 shillings) | 36 cents |
| 1 shilling (12 pence) | 7 cents |

# BIBLIOGRAPHY

*Books*

Armstrong, Alex, *Personal Narrative of the Discovery of North West Passage* (London, 1857).

Barrow, John, *A Chronological History of Voyages Into the Arctic* (London, 1818).

Barry, Tom, *Guerrilla Days In Ireland* (Cork, 1949).

Baughman, T.H., *Before the Heroes Came: Antartica in the 1890s* (Lincoln, 1994).

Beattie, Owen and Geiger, John, *Frozen in Time* (London, 1987).

Begbie, Harold, *Shackleton: A Memory* (London, 1922).

Belcher, Sir Edward, *The Last of the Arctic Voyages in Search of Sir John Franklin During the Years 1852–53–54*, (London, 1855), 2 vols.

Bennett, Richard, *The Black and Tans* (Kent, 2001).

Berton, Pierre, *The Arctic Grail* (New York, 1988).

Boase, Frederick, *Modern English Biography* (Truro, 1892), vol. 1.

Boylan, Henry (ed.), *A Dictionary of Irish Biography* (Dublin, 1998).

Browne, W.H., *Ten Coloured Views Taken During the Arctic Expedition of Her Majesty's Ships* Enterprise *and* Investigator (London, 1850).

Butler, Hubert, *The Sub–Prefect Should Have Held His Tongue and Other Essays* (London, 1990).

Campbell, R.J. (ed.) *The Discovery of the South Shetland Islands* (London, 2000).

Cherry–Garrard, Apsley, *The Worst Journey in the World* (London, 1948).

Clarke, Aidan, Fanning, Ronan, Johnston-Liik, Edith Mary, Maguire, James, Murphy, Maureen and Quinn, James, *Dictionary of Irish Biography* (Dublin, forthcoming).

Clarke, Desmond, *Arthur Dobbs Esquire, 1689–1765: Surveyor–General of Ireland, Prospector and Governor of North Carolina* (North Carolina, 1957).

Committee for the Crozier Memorial, *Memoir of the late Captain Francis Rawdon Moira Crozier R.N., F.R.S., F.R.A.S., of H.M.S.* Terror (Dublin, 1859).

Confrey, Mick and Jordan, Tim, *Iceman* (London, 1988).

Cook, James, *Journal of the* Resolution *Voyage in 1772–1775 on Discovery of the Southern Hemisphere* (London, 1775).

Cork Historical and Archaeological Society, *Gravestone Inscriptions in County Cork* (Cork, 1990).

Crozier, F.P., *Ireland For Ever* (London, 1932).

Crozier, Francis Rawdon Moira, *Memoir of the Late Captain Francis Rawdon Moira Crozier R.N., F.R.S., F.R.A.S., of H.M.S.* Terror (Dublin, 1859).

Cryriax, Richard J., *Sir John Franklin's Last Arctic Expedition* (London, 1939).

Dalton, J. and Flanagan, J.R., *History of Dundalk and Its Environs* (Dundalk, 1864).

De Long, Emma (ed.), *George Washinton De Long: The Voyage of the* Jeannette (London, 1883), 2 vols.

Delgado, James, *Across the Top of the World – The Quest for the Northwest Passage* (London, 1999).

Dobbs, Arthur, *An Account of the Countries Adjoining to Hudsons Bay in the North-West Part of America* (New York, 1967).

Dwyer, T. Ryle, *Tans, Terror and Troubles: Kerry's Real Fighting Story 1913–23* (Cork, 2001).

Fleming, Fergus, *Barrow's Boys* (London, 1998).

Fluhmann, May, *Second in Command* (Yellowknife, 1976).

Foster, J.W. and Chesney, H.C.G. (eds.), *Nature in Ireland: A Scientific and Cultural History* (Dublin, 1997).

Foster, John Wilson (ed.), *Nature in Ireland* (Dublin, 1997).

Friendly, Alfred, *Beaufort of the Admiralty* (London, 1973).

Glass, I.S., *Victorian Telescope Makers: The Lives and Letters of Thomas and Howard Grubb* (Bristol, 1997).

Hall, Mr and Mrs S.C., *Ireland: Its Scenery and Character* (London, 1843).

Herlihy, Jim, *The Royal Irish Constabulary: A Short History and Genealogical Guide* (Dublin, 1997).

Hickey, D.J. and Doherty, J.E., *A Dictionary of Irish History 1800–1980* (Dublin, 1980).

Hoehling, A.A., *The Jeannette Expedition* (London, 1967).

Holland, Clive, *Arctic Exploration and Development – An Encyclopaedia* (New York and London, 1994).

Huntford, Roland, *Shackleton* (London, 1985, 1996).

Hurley, Frank, *Argonauts of the South* (London, 1925).

Ireland, John De Courcy, *Ireland and the Irish in Maritime History* (Dublin, 1986).

King, Peter, *Scott's Last Journey* (London, 1999).

Kirwan, L.P., *The White Road: A Survey of Polar Exploration* (London, 1959).

Lee, Joseph, *The Modernisation of Irish Society 1848–1915* (Dublin, 1973).

Lewis, Gifford, *Eva Gore-Booth and Esther Roper: A Biography* (London, 1988).

Limb, Sue and Cordingley, Patrick, *Captain Oates – Soldier and Explorer* (London, 1982).

Lloyd, Humphrey Rev, *Observations Made at the Magnetic and Metrological Observatory at Trinity College Dublin* (Dublin, 1942).

Manwaring, G.E. and Dobrée, Bonamy, *The Floating Republic* (London, 1935).

Markham, Sir Clements, *Antarctic Obsession – The British National Antarctic Expedition 1901–4* (Norfolk, 1986).

Markham, Sir Clements, *Life of Admiral Sir Leopold McClintock* (London, 1909).

Markham, Sir Clements, *The Arctic Navy List 1773–1873* (London, 1875).

Markham, Sir Clements, *The Lands of Silence* (Cambridge, 1921).

Maxtone–Graham, John, *Safe Return Doubtful – The Heroic Age of Polar Exploration* (London, 2000).

McClintock, Leopold, *Voyage of the* Fox *in the Arctic Seas* (London, 1859).

McClure, Capt. Robert, *The Arctic Dispatches – Containing an Account of the North West Passage* (London, 1854).

McClure, Robert, *The Discovery of the North West Passage by H.M.S.* Investigator (London, 1856).

McDougall, George F., *The Eventful Voyage of HM Discovery Ship* Resolute *to the Arctic Regions in Search of Sir John Franklin* (London, 1857).

McTernan, John C., *A Sligo Miscellany: A Chronology of People, Places and Events of Other Days* (Sligo, 2000).

McTernan, John C., *Profiles of Distinguished Sligonians of Bygone Days* (Cork, 1977).

Middleton, Christopher, *Vindication of the conduct of Captain Christopher Middleton in a late voyage on board His Majesty's Ship the* Furnace *for the discovering of a North–west Passage to the Western Ocean in answer to certain objections and aspersions of Arthur Dobbs* (Dublin, 1744).

Miertsching, Johann, *The Arctic Diary of Johann Miertsching 1850–1854* (Toronto, 1967).

Mill, Hugh R., *The Life of Sir Ernest Shackleton* (London, 1923).

Mollan, C., Davis, W. and Finnucane, B., *More People and Places in Irish Science and Technology* (Dublin, 1990).

Mollan, C., Davis, W. and Finnucane, B., *Some People and Places in Irish Science and Technology* (Dublin, 1985).

Nansen, Dr Fridjof, *Furthest North* (London, 1898), vol. 1.

Nanton, Paul, *Arctic Breakthrough – Franklin's Expeditions 1819–1847* (London, 1970).

Nares R.N., Capt. George, *Narrative to a Voyage to the Polar Sea 1875–76* (London, 1878).

Nares R.N., Capt. George, *The Official Report of the Recent Arctic Expedition* (London, 1876).

O'Brien, D.H., *My Adventures During the Late War* (London, 1839), 2 vols.

O'Brien, D.H., *My Adventures During the Late War 1804–1814* (London, 1902).

O'Brien, D.H., *The Escapes of Captain O'Brien R.N. 1804–1808* (London, 1932).

O'Ceirín, Kit and Cyril, *Women of Ireland: A Biographical Dictionary* (Galway, 1996).

O'Keeffe, Dr Tadhg, *Fethard Co. Tipperary – A Guide to the Medieval Town* (Fethard, 1997).

Parry, Capt. William Edward, *Journal of a Second Voyage for the Discovery of a North-west Passage from the Atlantic to the Pacific performed in the years 1821–22–23 in His Majesty's Ships* Fury *and* Hecla *under the orders of Captain William Edward Parry, R.N.* (London, 1824).

Parry, Capt. William Edward, *Journal of a Third Voyage for the Discovery of a North-west Passage from the Atlantic to the Pacific performed in the years 1824–25 in His Majesty's Ships* Hecla *and* Fury *under the orders of Captain William Edward Parry, R.N.* (London, 1826).

Parry, William Edward, *Journal of a Voyage for the Discovery of a North-west Passage from the Atlantic to the Pacific performed in the years 1819–20, in His Majesty's*

*Ships* Hecla *and* Griper *under the orders of William Edward Parry, R.N., F.R.S.* (London, 1821)

Piggott, Jan (ed.), *Shackleton – The Antarctic and Endurance* (London, 2001).

Poulsom, Neville W. and Myres, J.A.L., *British Polar Exploration and Research: A Historical and Medallic Record with Biographies 1818–1999* (London, 2000).

*Report of the Sixth Geographical Congress* (London, 1896).

Roper, Esther, *Prison Letters of Countess Markievicz* (London, 1934).

Ross, Capt., Sir. J., *Narrative of the Second Voyage in Search of the North-West Passage and of Residents in the Arctic Regions During the Years 1829–1833* (London, 1835).

Ross, John, *A Voyage of Discovery in H.M. Ships* Isabella *and* Alexander *for the purposes of exploring Baffin Bay and inquiring into the probability of a North-West Passage* (London, 1819).

Ross, M.J., *Ross in the Antarctic* (Whitby, 1982).

Ross, Sir James Clark, *A Voyage of Discovery and Research in the Southern and Antarctic Regions During the Years 1839–43* (London, 1847).

Savours, Ann, *The Search for the North West Passage* (London, 1999).

Savours, Ann, *The Voyages of* Discovery (London, 1992).

Scott, R.F., *Scott's Last Expedition: Extracts from the Personal Diary of Capt. R.F. Scott R.N.* (London, 1923).

Seaver, George, *Edward Wilson of the Antarctic* (London, 1933).

Seeman, Berthold, *Narrative of the Voyage of H.M.S* Herald *1845–51 Under the Command of Captain Henry Kellett, R.N., C.B.* (London, 1853).

Shackleton, Sir Ernest, *South* (London, 1919).

Shackleton, Sir Ernest, *The Heart of the Antarctic – Being the Story of the British Antarctic Expedition 1907–1909* (London, 1909).

Smith, Michael, *An Unsung Hero: Tom Crean – Antarctic Survivor* (Cork, 2000).

Smith, Michael, *I Am Just Going Outside: Captain Oates – Antarctic Tragedy* (Cork, 2002).

Stephen, L. and Lee, S. (eds.), *The Dictionary of National Biography* (Oxford, 1917).

Sutton, Ann and Myron, *Journey Into Ice* (New York, 1965).

Tamiko, Rex (ed.), *South With* Endurance *– The Photographs of Frank Hurley* (London, 2001).

Thomson, John, *Shackleton's Captain – A Biography of Frank Worsley* (Toronto, 1999).

Thuillier, John, *History of Kinsale* (Kinsale, 2001).

Wayman, Patrick A., *Dunsink Observatory 1785–1985 – A Bicentennial History* (Dublin, 1987).

Weaver, J.R.H. (ed.), *Dictionary of National Biography, 1922–1930* (Oxford, 1937).

Weir, Anthony, *Early Ireland – A Field Guide* (Belfast, 1980).

White, Terence de Vere, *The Parents of Oscar Wilde – Sir William and Lady Wilde* (London, 1967).

Woodward, Francis J., *Portrait of Jane* (London, 1951).

Worsley, Commander F.A., *Shackleton's Boat Journey* (London, 1940).

*Newspapers, journals, periodicals and Websites*
*Annals of Science*
*Clonmel Chronicle*
*Cork Examiner*
*Cork Holly Bough*
*Dundalk Democrat*
*Dún Laoghaire Journal*
*Edinburgh Philosophical Transactions*
*Harbour Lights* (Cobh)
*Irish Naturalist*
*James Caird Society Newsletter*
*Journal of Archaeological Science*
*Journal of the Cork Historical and Archaeological Society*
*Philosophical Transactions of the Royal Society*
*Kinsale Record*
*Literary Gazette*
*Mariners' Mirror*
*New York Irish American*
*Polar Record*
*Reader's Digest*
*Sligo Champion*
*Sligo Independent*
*Tasmania Annals of Science*
*Tempest Annual* (Dundalk)
*Transactions of the Linnean Society*
www.irishships.com

*Records*
Bray Cualann Historical Society
Kerry County Museum
National Maritime Museum
Public Record Office of Northern Ireland
Public Record Office, London
Scott Polar Research Institute
St Mary's parish records, Limerick
Wexford and Rathaspeck (Church of Ireland) registry of baptism, marriage and burials

# INDEX